SWAMI DEEKSHANAND SARASWATI:

My Swami Mama Ji

(June 11, 1918-May 15, 2003)

SATISH C. BHATNAGAR

BOOKS BY THE SAME AUTHOR

1. Scattered Matherticles: Mathematical Reflections, Volume I
2. Vectors in History: Main Foci-India and USA, Volume 1
3. Epsilons of Deltas of Life: Everyday Stories, Volume I
4. My Hindu Faith & Periscope, Volume I
5. Via Bhatinda: A Braid of Reflected Memoirs, Volume I

Order this book online at www.trafford.com
or email orders@trafford.com

Most Trafford titles are also available at major online book retailers.

Printed in the United States of America.

ISBN: 978-1-4907-3301-2 (sc)
ISBN: 978-1-4907-3302-9 (e)

Trafford rev. 04/08/2014

Trafford PUBLISHING® www.trafford.com
North America & international
toll-free: 1 888 232 4444 (USA & Canada)
fax: 812 355 4082

SELECTIVE COMMENTS

YOU LOVED HIM A LOT. He was a great soul. Great homage. Well written. Have you thought of writing his biography? **Rahul** (On # 10)

I would be interested in Part II also. I thoroughly enjoyed Part I. It was very nice of you to point out the possible irrelevance of Gurukul education for SURVIVAL in modern times. You seem to have an enormous sense of proportion. I also developed some of it due to my contacts with the WEST. The Vedas have tremendous data. But one must view them as a literature which had relevance in the past and which may have some relevance today. L. Ron Hubbard claims that he studied Vedas and that Scientology is based on basics in Vedas. But you have to know the specific books and specific places where he states it and proves it. I admire your love for Indian Philosophy though you have stayed so long in the West.
Thanks for sending this beauty (Part II). I have just glanced. **Subhash** (On # 16 and 17)

This is wonderful!! It is great to know great people, but it is even greater to acquire their lessons and love. You are very lucky. **Prafulla**

It is a well-written brief commentary on the intellectual traditions of Arya Samaj. A number of reform movements started in the 19th century to reform the religion and society of India. Arya Samaj was the most successful of them all in bringing about a renaissance in Hindu society. The strength of this movement compared with others was also that its source of inspiration was indigenous rather than westward looking. The sheer force of reason and argument and intellect was used by Swami Dayanand and his followers to eradicate many ills to which the society had succumbed. At the same time, he made it clear that he was reviving the old traditions and not giving anything new. **VP Sharma** (On # 21)

This is your best piece ever! Very very well written!!!!-**Vicky** (On #)

I met him along with Swadeep and Archana when they came to Delhi after their marriage. It was at an Ashram like site behind the All India Institute of Medical Sciences. Afterwards, I attended two-three annual functions at New Delhi where his works were released. Occasionally,

I met him at places like New Delhi railway station, etc. I was deeply impressed by his scholarship of Vedic literature and traditions, his simplicity and his lifelong devotion to the cause of Arya Samaj and Vedic literature. He was really a great saint which is rare in these days of materialism. **RS Nigam (on # 19)**

SWAMI DEEKSHANAND SARASWATI:

My Swami Mama Ji

DEDICATED

TO

"DHANYA HO, RISHI!"

SATISH C. BHATNAGAR

DISTRIBUTION OF CONTENTS

A 'BIOGRAPHICAL' PREFACE

I had never thought that it would take me ten months to write and compile this sixth book. It is not the longest interval, though. The gap between my first and second books was fourteen months, as I had to work hard on each reflection in order to establish my identity as an historian too. This book being biographical, I wanted it to stand apart from a pamphlet or a booklet, both in terms of quantity and quality of the contents. There was no question of padding it.

The first time a fleeting thought of writing this biography sprung up in my mind was when I saw a copy of the 2007 biography on Swami Deekshanand Saraswati by Prem Lata Bhatnagar, my first cousin, who lives in India. She had timed it with his upcoming 5th ***Nirvana*** anniversary. At that time, seeing my name on any book seemed to be a far-fetched dream. At age 71, my first book came out in Nov, 2010-having been in production for more than two years.

After publishing five books in five different genres, I turned around to take upon a new writing challenge on a biography. In writing about a legend, one has to be honest-say, when including a specific story associated with the life of that person; its authenticity, full understanding by the biographer, and the interest of the readers have to be ensured. This balancing act is not easy, but I have tried to measure up to it in every piece included in the book.

To the best of my knowledge, Mama Ji never thought of telling a story of his life, though, it is very inspirational especially for those who do not want to follow a cookie cut careers that have been somewhat a rage in India-doctors, engineers and MBAs lately.

The writing of a biography is driven by many factors. Generally, a life examined is either very famous or notorious. In the US, there are professional biographers making their livings by writing on such lives. In the academe, a professor in a discipline of humanities can earn sabbatical leave, merit, tenure. or promotion. In my case, it is a combination of debt to my ancient Indian heritage that Mama Ji symbolized, personal gratitude towards him, and a literary challenge to be a well-rounded non-fiction writer.

There is something more to it. The Hindus, of my generation in particular, were drilled by their elders to play down or even undermine their achievements in the name of misplaced humility. Its one corollary was that they downgraded their leaders too. Inversely, they over lauded the outsiders and their works. This mindset comes from their subjugated Hindu mentality over the centuries. On the contrary, in the US, 'the land of the free', one sees floods of unripe biographies on the lives hardly lived long enough or fully blossomed out.

The book has ended up with four sections, though started with only one section in mind. It has truly evolved while working on it. Section I has 9 introductory types of write-ups on biographies. Section II has my 33 typical reflections and articles written during 2003-2013. Section III has oral and verbal reminiscences from 12 persons associated with Mama Ji. Section IV has 90+ pages of letters exchanged between me and Mama Ji during a span of 40 years; 1962-2002.

A common feature of all my books is that each one of them can be read from anywhere, as all reflections are nearly independent in contents and topics in general. It is good as in today's fast life styles, no one has the time to start a book from its Page Number 1 and then wade it through to the very end. As a consequence, abbreviations are explained again, and certain references repeated as encountered.

Also, I am continuing the practice of dating each reflection so that a reader may have a full perspective of its genesis in terms of time, place and my mindset. As a young reader, I paid no attention to it, but now that I am in my 70s, this is the first thing I look for it. The two dates on a refection means that a revision was done on the second date. Another continuing feature is providing partial and full blank pages for the readers to scribble their comments as they pop out while reading. It comes from my compulsive habit of under-lining and side-lining a significant part of a sentence or paragraph. Such markings become a source of quick reference in future.

This book is delayed by 2-3 months due to various permutations of Section IV material and its technical hiccups. For me, getting the images of the letters in a Word file was such a daunting task that I shuddered at the very thought of it. I spoke about it with UNLV's Reprographic Department. My graduate students, Emi Ikeda and Scott MacDonald, explained it in 1, 2, 3 step manner. But this small sequence of clicks won't register in my mind. Aniruddha, my son-in-law, came over and showed me the steps at my home PC and even watched me inserting 2-3 pages successfully. But I forgot them after 2-3 days!

Finally, it was when Anjali, my granddaughter, who came to Las Vegas during her Spring break that it was all done in a couple of hours! Still, I got stuck for two days on a new set of 13 images in a PDF file which could not be inserted or copied in a Word file. But Avnish, my son, changed the PDF into JPEG on his PC and e-mailed it back to me within a minute. Namit helped in graphics. I am thankful to all of them for enhancing my technical knowledge.

Whenever, I am complimented on my English, I really thank Francis A. Andrew, a Scottish professor of English working in the Sultanate of Oman. We met five years ago in Nizwa, Oman. He has tremendously helped me by providing feedback on each and every reflection-both on the syntax and semantics of the text. Francis is also an established science fiction writer of a dozen books-available on Amazon.

Finally, any errors and omissions are mine. Any feedback and comments would be gratefully acknowledged.

Satish C. Bhatnagar

March 25, 2014

SECTION I

INTRODUCTORY WRITE-UPS

DEEKSHANAND AND ELEPHANT

That is how I start off on my sixth book, a biography of Swami Deekshanand Saraswati. Each of the previous five books is the first volume in five different genres. God willing, at least two volumes will be published eventually in each category. However, the sixth book is going to be a one-volume biography. It provides me a break from a 'volume' series. There are a number of reasons for undertaking a biography of a legend in the world of Arya Samaj.

Swami Deekshanand Saraswati (1918-2003) was a giant of man in terms of physique, intellect and spirit in his times. When pigmies or blinds get closer to an elephant in order to figure it out, then each one of them describes the elephant according to the parts of the elephant that are in front of them. Frankly, I am also one of them when it comes to knowing Deekshanand. Nevertheless, I am fully convinced that there are persons who may have different and deeper assessment of him. At the end of the day, I may be able to put them all together for a composite picture of his persona.

Swami Deekshanand was a family oriented man-though he never married or legally adopted any one. Before taking on to a ***sanyasi*** order in 1975, he frequented his families with firm beliefs of impacting the young ones there. His one niece, Kusum Lata Arya (stopped writing Bhatnagar/1947-97) was his mental offspring (***maaas putri***) in a sense that he chiseled and nurtured her from a little girl of eight to a Vedic scholar of repute.

There were many other family members who were pulled into his magnetic field and were magnetized in proportion to the iron element in them. I have been urging all kith and kin to recall stories of their association-critical and yet objective assessment of Swami Deekshanand. Send it to me in English or Hindi, as soon as possible for verbatim inclusion in a distinct section of the book.

As a leading preacher and Vedic scholar, he gave discourses and performed grand ***yagya/yajana*** in Hindi speaking regions. Also, I recall his regular visits to Hyderabad in Andhra Pradesh, Mumbai and Sholapur in Maharashtra. In the East, he did go to Patna regularly, but I don't think he ever went all the way to Manipur and Nagaland. On overseas assignments, he went to South Africa and Kenya and returned to India after resounding success.

Amongst thousands of persons in his audiences, there must be a few dozen whose life must have been touched or transformed by him. I also exhort them to take time to recall and write before the memories are erased by the mighty Time. In an ultimate analysis, a story of his life will be sum total of tiny slices of our lives too.

This book has to be different both in contents and layouts. Five years ago, my cousin, Premlata Bhatnagar wrote the first book on Swami Deekshanand in commemoration of his 5th anniversary. In contrast to her book, my book shall have no pictures. If you have seen a picture once, then that is enough, except of course, if it is a Mona Lisa caliber! By the way, in all my previous five books there is not even single picture except on the covers.

In conclusion, incredible memory of Deekshanand does connect him literally with an elephant-that is known to forget nothing. Perhaps, for that reason, the two are never seen in hurry in their physical movements. I witnessed this memorable memory sight on Dec 28, 2002-less than five months before he Checked Out from Planet Earth. He was the chief guest at a 3-day annual celebration of a ***gurukul*** in Jaura, a village 50 KM from Nanded (MS). Due to train delays, he arrived one day late-stopped right at the ***pandal*** (makeshift conference hall) in a rented car driven for 8 hours on unpaved rural paths.

The crowd erupted with happiness as he took his seat on a stage without freshening up. Within minutes, he took hold of the mike in his hand-like a baton of a music symphony conductor. For nearly an hour, he enthralled the audience with his sermons studded with Vedic mantras flowing out of his mind in the most effortless manner. His face was glowing and leaving the audience aghast!

It was a feat of memory for me, as I have not memorized anything. Mathematics has trained me to deduce everything. Let us see how we test out in our individual memories about him.

May 20, 2013/July 13, 2013

PS

This ***Reflection*** was sent out to the ***Navrang Times*** for soliciting write-ups from its enlightened readers now spread all over the world.

TURNING AROUND FOR A BOOK

Writing any book was not on my intellectual horizon even as few as ten years ago, when I was already deep into my ***Reflective*** writings. So much so, that I had become reconciled that I would die before seeing my name on a book. As far as mathematics textbook writing was concerned, it is a service to the profession and very laborious. But, I see no creativity at all in permuting the orders of exercises, tinkering with examples and rephrasing the text here and there.

It took me more than two years from the submission of the manuscript of the first book to actual proof-reading, and to seeing it published in Nov, 2010. It turned out to be a transformational moment in my life. I was then almost 71 years old. More than a year went by before the second book came out. Since then, I have sped up the production line, as I am cognizant of the law of averages. In not too distant future, not being able to draw up the creative juices from my well, because of any weakening of my intellectual technology is unimaginable. Is it really possible that I can empty out my well by drawing it all from within? Then, what will happen to my being? It is a very recursive intellectual phenomenon. Whatever is hypothetical, at the moment, I am not going to take off my foot from the gas paddle.

A biography on the life of Swami Deekshanand was not all visualized, though I had written a dozen of ***Reflections*** after his death in 2003. It was a kind period of my wilderness years in book writing. During my sabbatical leave in India-in Fall-2007, I was presented a book on the life of Swami Deekshanand Saraswati, written by Prem Lata Bhatnagar, my first cousin from mother's side. It is a beautiful book. It is written out her absolute and dripping devotion, regards, love, and faith in Mama Ji. Still, I did not jump at the sight of this book, and say that I was going to write one too, or a better one. I read it completely in 2007 and called to compliment her. In fact, I just gave it another reading to make sure that our books stand out altogether on different platforms.

In the summer of 2004, I attended two conferences. One was a biennial conference of the WAVES (World Association of Vedic Studies), held in

Washington DC area, in which I presented a seminal paper***, Intellectual Traditions of Arya Samaj***. The theme of the conference was ***Intellectual Traditions of India in the Global Context***. A few leaders of Arya Samaj were in the audience. At end of my lecture, they persuaded me to give a keynote address at the annual meeting of Arya Pratinidhi Sabha of North America, held in Toronto, Canada. It was during this period that I re-discovered my Arya Samaj roots, new identity and public ties with Mama Ji. I was getting some recognition because of him too! At that time, a seed was planted that I must pay it express this gratitude in some way.

Prior to the 2004 meetings, I was not active in any forum of Arya Samaj in the US. In 2006, I attended another annual Arya Samaj conference in Tampa, Florida. Gradually and subsequently, I kept going deeper into Arya Samaj or more appropriately, call it, returning back to home. One individual and one little magazine played subtle roles too. The person is Girish Khosla, now a ***vanprasthi*** in the Arya Samaj order for the last five years, He and his 35-year old son, Bhuvnesh are totally dedicated to the ideas and ideals of Arya Samaj, and are instrumental in consolidating Arya Samaj centers in North America and Canada.

They also publish the ***Navrang Times***, a small monthly magazine/ newsletter of Arya Pratinidhi Sabha North America. It includes features, stories and tidbits of Arya Samaj. It regularly publishes my ***Reflections*** too. As a matter of fact, his maternal grandfather, Acharya Ram Dev, was a stalwart of Arya Samaj. Above all, Girish and his grandfather knew Mama Ji very closely.

Such is a staggered path of my thoughts revolving around Arya Samaj and Mama Ji while living in the US. Nevertheless, two years ago, I decided to write a unique book on his life. At one time, I wanted this book to coincide with the 10th ***nirvaan*** anniversary of Mama Ji, but the previous book, ***VIA BHATINDA*** took a lot longer. Who knows, my book may inspire someone to write another biography to coincide with his birth centennial to fall in June, 2018!

Oct 16, 2013

A HISTO-PSYCHOLOGY OF AUTOBIOGRAPHIES

I have always enjoyed reading autobiographies, as relatively speaking there is a stronger element of truth and factuality about them. Also, there is a correlation between age and biographies-the younger you are, the greater is the desire to read, be inspired and feel motivated by the lives of great minds. When I look back at my peak of reading period, in the 1950s and 1960s, it seems that I read far more about the lives of the non-Indians than of Indians.

It is now that I can ponder over reasons for this differential. For instance, before independence, Gandhi, perhaps, is the only Indian, who wrote a comprehensive autobiography, and he rightly called it ***My Experiments with Truth***. In late 19th century, blazing Swami Dayanand wrote a very short autobiography, but it has remained relatively unknown and out of print. It needs to be republished for mass circulation. Four months ago, while re-charging my cultural batteries in Bathinda, I read a powerful 80-page autobiography in Hindi of Ram Prasad Bismal, a freedom fighter. He started writing it only 2-3 weeks before he was to be hanged in Dec, 1927 at the age of 27-a year before Bhagat Singh was hanged.

After centuries of political subjugation, even great Hindu minds had never thought of sharing the inspiring stories of their lives for their people. Autobiographies and memoirs are important to individuals, as are official chronicles to the kings and despots. During high school days, we were constantly reminded to follow the footsteps of great men and women. But there were no Indian footsteps! The only footsteps were of the British in politics, literature and public life! No wonder then, even moderately educated Hindus would become not only the admirers of the British way of life, but would suffer from Hindu complex for the rest of their lives.

Swami Mama Ji never talked about writing a story of his life despite the fact that some segments of his life were least known and some were publicly very open. About writing one's memoirs too, there is a mathematical way of looking at it-that one's desire to spend time and energy for the society at large is 'inversely' proportional to the time and energy for one's immediate family. Gandhi is a perfect example. He had relatively little time for his four sons, as he was consumed with the plight of Indian masses and their political freedom.

Mama Ji was never in any active politics-including the organization of Arya Samaj. He simply enjoyed scholarship and spread the wisdom of the Vedas through the power of his public speaking. During mid-1970s through 1990s, he wrote and edited twenty eight excellent tracts on various aspects Hindu life-drawn from the Vedas only. Let me add that the size of a book is not a measure of the value of its contents. Being on the trains most of the time, he just did not have sustained time needed for writing a long track, despite the fact that he traveled with a big box of his reading and writing materials.

However, he too suffered from a Hindu virus of humility, namely, the under-rating of one's work, inordinate praise of others', particularly of the non-Hindus'-in order to show some twisted tolerance or magnanimity. Backing up on Indian autobiographies, Ravindra Nath Tagore, a scion of the British influenced intellectuals, wrote his ***Reminiscences*** in 1912, a year before his getting the 1913 Nobel Prize in Literature. However, Tilak (1856-1920), the greatest nationalist and scholar of his times, and Gandhi's political mentor, did not write his biography.

A few years ago, when I realized this phenomenon, it caused a momentary implosion in me. And so I decided to write my memoirs. It took two years for its form and format to crystallize in my mind. The first volume of ***Via Bhatinda*** (May, 2013) is a story of my life-ongoing, as also seen through the eyes of other persons, and even places and things. That is why it is subtitled as, ***A Braid of Reflected Memoirs***.

At times, I feel amused and irritated whenever a memoir of a US teen hits the stands and media circuit. He/she has attained name and fame as a singer, dancer, athlete etc. It is ok, if the followers want to read it as well. At the same time, it strongly tells me that if there is something readable and memorable in a life that hardly has completed 20 years, then it is time to examine and sift through my life of 70+ years.

If nothing else, a memoire is a solid family record. Let the coming generations judge it the way they want to.

Oct 26, 2013

WHAT IS SO GREAT ABOUT HIS LIFE?

I have to put this question to myself point blank in order to do full justice to this biography of Swami Deekshanand Saraswati, my Swami Mama Ji. Before I left India for the US in 1968, my meetings with him over the years, since boyhood, were mostly incidental. I saw him once or twice a year, when he passed through Bathinda (BTI) during his preaching circuit. Also, during my trips to Delhi and beyond, I would find him in Arya Samaj Dewan Hall, where he lived in the topmost solitary room allotted to him. However, these visits became fixtures when I used to visit India. Then, spending a week or so with him was quite focused.

During my formative years, a family tradition was of joining a government service-be it in any position-from that of a clerk to an IAS (Indian Administrative Service) officer. Now, as an historian too, I can say that the Kayasthas ran the mid-level administration of the British Raj in India. They largely served the departments of education, railways, public works, courts and taxation. The Kayasthas were foremost in mastering English language and adopting English ways of thinking. Most men wore shirts and pants when out on the jobs. The only exceptions in our extended family were my maternal grandfather and Swami Mama Ji, who before initiating into ***sanyasi*** order, was always attired in two white sheets; one around his waist and other around his shoulders. Of course, the ladies, mostly being indoors, wore Indian dresses and learnt Hindi.

Honestly, during the teen years, I was not proud of my grandfather in his khadi attires despite his commanding persona in the community. He was well known for his command over English language and retired in 1935 after working with English supervisors all his life. As freedom movement gathered steam in the 1920s, he turned into a nationalist Arya Samaji. However, all my other maternal uncles wore European.

When I was around 12-14 years of age, Mama Ji, during one of his BTI visits, was talking with kids on the value of aiming high in life. I vividly remember telling him, "What good is an achievement, since we all are destined to die like ants and bugs?" This thought had, perhaps, taken home in my subconscious mind after noticing Hindu religious wall posters depicting futility of human life cycle. Such posters and pictures were very popular and common in homes through the 1950s.

Mama Ji was surprised at my attitude towards life. He told us in very stirring words and conviction that human life is a great gift of God and we should earn all names and fame. Time passed, and this short dialogue kept growing up in my sub-consciousness like a seed planted in a right soil and time. For the last 12 years, uncanny clarity, conviction and courage, noted in the writing of my ***Reflections***, can be traced to that seed planted in that encounter with Mama Ji.

Generally, a life is measured in two ways: one, by person's life-time achievements, which may or may not be understood or appreciated by a whole lot of other people; two, the lives that are inspired by it. Yes, I have also been motivated and touched by the lives of two other uncles-one did a physics PhD in the 1940s-long before India's independence, and the other became an elite IAS officer. For some years, I worked hard to be like them. Now it seems that in my march of life, I have carved out my own path-in some ways, far different and beyond theirs.

Entering into my age years of the 50s, as my sense of history deepened, I started feeling ashamed that most of my forefathers had sided with the British in their struggles with Indians who were awakening to the rule of self-governance. Gandhi's launching of the non-cooperation movement in 1920 was simply meant to exhort the Indians to stop working for the British and boycott British goods. Eventually, this non-violent approach won freedom for India.

In due course of time, Mama Ji's honed up scholarship, charisma and national character rose up higher in my esteem. Intellectually, we did no always agree, but his approaches towards life, at large, were impeccably honest. As ***sanyasi***, he symbolized a great heritage, religion, and lofty way of life. So, writing his biography is also my way of paying off a debt to ancient Indian heritage, my Hindu faith, and family values imbibed from Swami Mama Ji as he lived and preached them.

Biologically speaking, Mama Ji and I do have some common DNAs. At times, I notice his greatness of thoughts is reflected in my writings, in a sense that the origin of some ideas can be connected with my long associations with him. So much so, that I can say it proudly say that my ideas, and my books containing them are peerless and matchless. As I hit mid-70s, it is good to be awakened from a slumber of ignorance-no matter how short the future may be.

Hail thee, Mama Ji for life long memories!

Oct 29, 2013

EXTREMES IN BIOGRAPHICAL CONTENTS

Last year, there was a University Forum (public) lecture on a biography of Katherine Anne Porter (1890-1980), a Pulitzer Prize-winning American journalist, short story writer, novelist, and political activist. The author is Darlene Unrue, who works in a husband and wife duo of English professors at UNLV, and both known to me for over 30 years. Since I was set upon writing a biography on Swami Deekshanand Saraswati, my MamaJi (1918-2003), I went up to attend this evening lecture. The purpose was to possibly get some ideas on writing a biography, and how to present it as a literary buffet to the public at large.

In a brief conversation before the lecture started, I told Darlene about my intentions of writing a biography too. She simply said, "Good Luck". I was a bit surprised at her brief remark. But her lecture revealed the challenges she encountered in collecting some facts, verifying anecdotes, travelling involved, people interviewed, and mounds of material sifted through-from libraries to private collections. It took 2-3 years before the book came out in print.

In scholarship, Swami Deekshanand was not like young academic scholars, who mostly write books for promotion, tenure, and sabbatical and merit awards etc. In contrast, his scholarship became public only at a ripening age while in his 50s. Foremost, he was a renowned public figure and orator in the Arya Samaji evangelism. Yes, I have approached a few of his admirers and close relatives for bits and pieces on his life. But there was no travel or extensive leg work on my part. The most important thing is the uniqueness of my format of his biography. Essentially, people will know him through my eyes and of the others too; hence, readers will get holistic ideas of life around him.

There is another element in writing about a life. From the point of view of the sale of a book, American authors as well as American readers want to write and read juicy stuff in the life of person under microscope. For instance, Porter's literary aspects must have been critiqued by host of other writers and academicians. The pubic, at large, does not care about dry academic critical works, as it feeds on itself. In the complement of academic exercises are human stories of romance, friendships, divorces, remarriages, and children born out of wedlock, etc. During the lecture, I wondered at this summation of Porter's life.

MamaJi never married. He was not cutout for it from the very beginning, though he must have remained the handsomest eligible bachelor in his adult life. Looking at pervasiveness of sexuality in the US and even India today; more so, since the former President, Bill Clinton redefined intercourse; one does wonder how MamaJi lived through his sexually turbulent years.

By the age of 17 and 18 years, the male hormones really burst out violently-so much so, that any time of mental concentration away from sex is short lived. At times, the penile reaction is so strong and long that it seems to smash any object. It reminds me of a warning as part of recent ads on Viagra/Cialis capsules that if erection lasts for more than four hours, then see a doctor. Prolonged erections and successive ejaculations would kill an old man in many ways. In my teen years, I had fun calling night discharges as gods doing blow-up jobs on the penis! There was no other recourse or release of sexual tension except masturbation in puritanical India of the1950s.

Swami Mama Ji may have understood the source of this sexual power and, perhaps, figured it out how to tame and sublimate it. In Hindu scriptures, male erectility is compared with the power of an elephant gone berserk or of cobra fully spread out at the music of its charmer. I don't care about all the tricks and the means of keeping the sexual urges in some control so that a sexually deviant person does not get into trouble socially and legally.

To the best of my observations on MamaJi, he controlled his urges in two different manners. One was that he didn't use any salt in his diet till he turned 30 or so. Even sugar use was minimal. I remember his telling us that no insect bites him and some stubborn mosquitos that bite die way. It seems plausible from the Hindu ways life of doing various penances. They have experimented with many such dos and don'ts, but there is no systematic record on its general viability.

The second approach that Mama Ji used was a psychological weapon to keep his carnal desires in check from his end. He always addressed any woman as his daughter or mother; never a sister. At times, noting women around his age, he still addressed them as ***Mata Ji*** (for mother) or ***Beti*** (for daughter)**.** I know it must be weirdly disarming for a beautiful woman whose mission is to floor down any man to her knees. He probably never hurt the advances of such women. During school and college days in Bathinda, I remember boys calling girl friends as their cousins, but envisioning all kinds of romantic and sexual ties with them. Also, his totally white attire before ***sanyas*** and red orange afterwards must have worked as a shield from the eyes of diehard enchantresses.

Do I have any proof of MamaJi sexual chastity or virginity? No; but who can actually lay such a claim on it? Early on, I never even dreamed of questioning it. Later on, it was clear there was no temptress or seductress in his life-like, Monica or Maneka are rumored. There is a Hindi saying: that ***Ishaq*** (romance) and ***Mushk*** (fragrance) cannot be hidden from public. At the same time, after the mid-70s, the penis that used to curve up towards the sky starts curving down towards the earth. Still, the sexuality is not all dead in the mind. It only dies with death.

Therefore, I have nothing to dig for any romantic stories in his ascetic life, as the Vedic lores remained a passion for him through the entire life. Of course, his sexuality may be left an open question for another biographer to research into. I feel absolutely at peace with whatever has been put together.

Nov 02, 2013

TIME TO CLOSE ON INTRODUCTION

Mama Ji never talked about writing a book on the life of Swami Dayanand, though he daily breathed his name, especially, whenever, he was honored or showered with recognition. He acclaimed Swami Smarpananand, known as Pandit Buddha Dev before ***sanyaas,*** as his Guru, who had a sharp mind, and was also an erudite poet and peerless Vedic scholar of his time. Mama Ji did publish quite a few books of his Guru, but never thought of writing a book on his life either. However, he did name his research institute after his name, known as ***Samarpan Shodh Sansthan***.

Since Swami Samarpananand had died earlier, Swami Satya Prakash initiated Mama Ji into ***sanyaas*** in Dec 1975. He retired as head of the Chemistry Department of Allahabad University. Mama Ji proudly wanted me to meet him during my visits to India. Subsequently, Swami Satya Prakash published a couple of my articles on Vedic Mathematics in a journal that he founded and edited for several years. Again, Mama Ji never wrote any articles on Swami Satya Prakash life too. These are the only persons of higher intellectual stature that Mama Ji admired.

Of course, his not writing on the lives any stalwart of Arya Samaj is understandable. Hindus of his generations were too humble about their achievements in life. Generally, such persons are unable to appreciate the accomplishments of others; rather, feel inwardly jealous. In fairness, I don't think Mama Ji ever thought that someone would write a book on his life while he was alive or afterwards. Yes, he always talked about the debt he owed to ancient Vedic heritage. As a matter of fact, he paid off his debts manifolds to whoever contributed in his intellectual development. On money matters, he could never ask for returning the money that he loaned to so many acquaintances and relatives.

Talking of the loans, he was one of the three persons I asked for money in June/July, 1968 that was needed to meet the cost of my air ticket to the USA and other incidental expenses. Amount of Rs 1000 was expected from him, but he did not have any money at that time! However, he got Rs 800 from a cousin of mine, and gave it to me. This amount of Rs 800 was returned to Mama Ji after a year of my arrival in the USA, as this cousin was just a clerk in a government office. Their gesture touched me and I continued paying it off a thousand fold, as long as Mama Ji was alive. In my life of 70+ years, on my part, there has not been any such investment so far. It is called a hitting a jackpot in Las Vegas culture. Perhaps, that is a magic of a ***sanyasi***!

In 2007, Prem Lata Bhatnagar, my first cousin, wrote a book in Hindi on the life of Swami Deekshanand Saraswati. It is published by ***Samarpan Shodh Sansthan,*** of which her elder brother, Rajindra P. Bhatnagar is a ***mantri***/administrator. The book has essentially three sections. The first section has 23 articles written by Prem Lata-starting from Mama Ji's birth, parents, relatives, to his life as ***brahamchari*** Acharya Krishna, and to his ***sanyasi*** life-all in a chronological order. The second section contains nearly 30 pages of historic pictures capturing landmark events in his life. The third section has fifteen reminiscences and write-ups by her brothers and persons close to her and Mama Ji. At the end, there is a four page list of 87 books-including 28 written by him, all published by the ***sansthan***.

In contrast, my book does not address his life in any chronological manner-except, when it applies to the dates of my ***Reflections***. The book is mostly the end product of my forty ***reflections*** written out over a span of ten years. The other section contains brief and long write-ups by persons in the family and friends. A few persons also responded to my appeals to the public at large through my e-mails and articles in the ***Navrang Times***. However, I did not discriminate between the writers at all when it came to choosing their write-ups. At the end, a composite image of Swami Deekshanand does emerge. That is the purpose of my writing. Of course, the readers will be final judge on its merits.

Nov 06, 2013

ON THE TITLE OF THE BOOK

I ponder and play around a lot over titles, whether of my 'weekly' ***reflections*** or books. It comes from my well-known habit of giving nicknames to the kids, friends, pets, and any object. A caveat is that there has to be something unique about it. For example, people wonder at the word, ***Matherticles***, in the title of my first book. It is not a dictionary word, but cobbled together out of two words, **mathe**matical and pa**rticles**. Likewise, I have coined a new phrase ***'Epsilons and Deltas of Life'*** for the title of my third book. Originality must ooze out in every aspect of life.

The title of this book, ***Swami Deekshanand Saraswati: My Swami Mama Ji*** has gone through several iterations including one during this very write-up. A vacillating point was the word, 'Swami' to be placed or not in the title as ***Swami Deekshanand Saraswati*** or/and in the subtitle, ***My Swami Mama Ji***. Swami is a word of Sanskrit/Hindi origin-meaning, a person who has mastered his senses. Normally, a person is controlled by the senses, causing the experiences of pain and pleasure of life. However, the mind of a Swami remains in a state of equanimity-a result of years of meditation and discipline. Nevertheless, the word, Swami is broadly used for a father figure, owner, master, expert etc. It is now included in English lexicon.

Soon after Mama Ji's entering into a sanyasi order in Dec 1975, he stopped visiting the homes of all near and dear ones. He told everyone to address him as Swami Ji only; not by any shade of 'uncle'. Amongst the Indians, there are half a dozen derivatives of generic uncle in the US. Well, it so happened that I continued to address him as Mama Ji-while face to face with him, and as Swami Mama Ji in letters. That is how the word, Swami is justified into a subtitle.

A question may be asked as to how the possessive noun, '***My***', qualifies ***Swami Mama Ji***. It evolved over years of my association. The clincher came about when I re-read all his letters over a span of 40 years. They are included in the last section of the book. I realized that a special bond had developed. ***My Swami Mama Ji*** alone captures it, and may also be conveyed to the readers.

The name, Deekshanand was given to him at the time of initiation into Sanyaas (renunciation)-generally after all family and social responsibilities are discharged. A Sanyaasi (renunciate) devotes time and energy in the propagation and uplift of social, religious and spiritual awareness. This name was chosen by his initiator, Swami Satya Prakash, a former Professor and Head of Chemistry Department of Allahabad University. I don't remember any reason about the choice of 'Deekshanand'. At the end, 'Saraswati', the name of goddess of knowledge, means here a person of scholarship. Mama Ji was accorded with the highest national honors for his Vedic scholarship.

The Hindi words 'Deeksha' means Vedic knowledge imparted by a guru and 'Anand' means bliss. Hence, 'Deekshanand' means the one who finds bliss in Vedic lores. To complete the story, Mama Ji's birth name was Krishna Sarup Bhatnagar. 'Krishna', the name of God-incarnate, means an all charming person. ***Sarup/Swarup*** means form. Thus, Krishna Sarup means Krishna personified. Well, Mama Ji lived up to his both names-birth and ***sanyaas***! He had a magnetic personality both before and after Sanyaas. I teased him at the 'curses' of many Manekas and Monicas who failed to bring him down to their knees!

March 10, 2014

"DHANYA HO, RISHI!"

Generally, a book is dedicated to an individual(s) living or dead, who has supported and/or inspired its author. In the context of this book, any one, having some knowledge of Hindi, would immediately notice after turning the first six pages, that the book was not dedicated to any individual(s). The '***Dhanya ho, Rishi!***' is not the name of any inspiring person, idyllic place, or an unforgettable thing. Its English translation is: '***Hail thee, Rishi!***'. It is an expression of gratitude coming out naturally in a state of exultation. This now doubles up curiosity about it.

'Rishi' is a word of Sanskrit origin-now included in the English language too. It means a man of universal insights, which are attained through meditation and mastery over the Vedic literature. Rishi, in this exclamatory phrase, is Rishi Dayanand (1824-1883). Whenever, public honors were bestowed upon Mama Ji or he got insights while contemplating over complexities of a Vedic ***sukta*** (a set of ***mantras***), he would softly utter the words, '***Dhanya ho, Rishi!***' In addition, he narrated several stories from his personal life when he felt that all the accolades publicly or privately showered on him were due to the grace of the Rishi.

A curious person may say; how come I am dedicating this book to Rishi Dayanand? How did it happen? It is interesting too. I don't know, nor have I checked out whether Mama Ji had dedicated any one of his two dozen books to Rishi Dayanand. As a matter of fact, dedication of a book to Rishi Dayanand would be trivial when his entire life was dedicated to Rishi's missions. However, it was clearly set in my mind that this book had to be dedicated to someone; however, not all of my previous five books had been dedicated to some person or entity.

On pondering over it for a few weeks, I suddenly realized that by a ***Principle of Transitivity***, I do owe a debt of my thinking to Rishi Dayanand. The ***Principle of Transitivity*** is very simple: if A and B are related with each other and so are B and C, then A and C are related with each other. Mama Ji's life was greatly impacted by Rishi Dayanand. And,

I have been influenced by Mama Ji, though not within the same scope, but certainly in the context of Mama Ji's biography.

Dayanand was an incredible person who was born in 1824 and poisoned to death in 1883. He was 33 years old when in 1857 the British ruthlessly quashed a regional Indian uprising with the support of Indians in its army and the connivance of a few Indian princes. Subsequently, a series of draconian laws and measures broke the backbones of Indians forever. Dayanand saw it all.

Dayanand, born in a family little means, was a rebel at the age of 10 years and run-away from home at 15. Through years of practicing Hath Yoga, studies and contemplations, he developed his physical, mental and spiritual prowesses to unprecedented heights. Thus, he awakened the Hindu masses, intelligentsia, and a few ruling princes. His life mission was social engineering of Hindu society. He staked his life on more than a hundred occasions. He spoke against the extreme practices of idol worship and the evil of untouchability amongst the Hindus. He advocated for the nationalist education and remarriages of Hindu widows. He called for re-conversion of the Muslims and Christians back into the folds of Hinduism. He publicly debated with Hindu diehards, Muslim imams and Christian priests.

His open and public actions infused new courage in Hindu masses, who were reduced to kicking bags for every foreign invader over the previous 1000 years. Incidentally, the Hindus became collectively chivalrous either by becoming the followers of the Sikh Gurus or the followers of Dayanand's Arya Samaj, a reformation movement of Hindu religion. Founded in 1875 in Mumbai, Arya Samaj was the first Hindu organization based on ten simple principles and a monthly subscription four ***Annas***. Only 2-3 years before his murder in 1883, Dayanand had finished ***Satyarth Prakash*** (Light of Truth Expanded), his magnum opus. It is a manual of Hindu life. Within a short period, Arya Samaj spread to over to 60 countries of the world.

Incidentally, Mahatma Gandhi (1869-1948), the leader of India's freedom movement, and who was also murdered, has mentioned Dayanand's name in his autobiography, ***The Story of My Experiments with Truth***, in only one sentence of only one page, and that too in a passing manner. Quite interesting!

Well, that is how this book is indirectly dedicated to Rishi Dayanand, and to his lofty ideals and ideas.

March 11, 2014

FINALLY, THE COVER OF THE BOOK!

Writing on the designing of the front cover of this book is also a tribute within Tribute to Mama Ji. Why? Mama Ji was very particular about every aspect of his books published under his name from the institute-besides, the aspects of writing, editing, and compiling. He was very choosey about the printers and artists consulted for the get-ups of his books.

On the contrary, my books have the same one publisher, ***Trafford***. I have no idea about the printer, as with high-tech publishing technology, the books are printed out within hours of their demands. The outer structure of the book remains the same-paper back with thick-ish cover material and size, 6" x 9". A cover of a book is like facial makeup of a person. A young woman is never out in public without facial make-up-even when she is wearing a full Islamic ***burqa***. On a few occasions, I was really shocked to see the difference in overall looks of women with or without any make-up. In the case of a book, its contents correspond to the content of a person's character. One may fool some people for a short time with outward make-up, but not all the time.

The overall color combination for the cover is of white and orange-both symbols of spirituality radiated by Swami Mama Ji. White color is universally for purity, and it also represents transcendental and other worldly spirituality. The shades of orange color of ***sanyaas*** have stood for spirituality of all eastern religious. In his 1976 letter to me, Mama Ji has touched upon it. The image of a rising sun looking like a symbol of Aum, behind a mountain, is to be set on the top of the cover-capturing the dawn of Vedic knowledge. And, the sun rays falling over Swami Dayanand signifies Dayanand's clarion call to the Hindus-going back to the Vedas. It was the bedrock of his campaign and debates for the Hindu renaissance.

At the center of the cover is Mama Ji's picture taken during his 70s when he had attained a state of poise both in his inner self and outer self. During the 1990s, Mama Ji had also earned reputation as a publisher of high quality Vedic books. His artistic tendencies went far beyond the books. During one of my summer visits to India, I recall his inviting a leading Delhi artist of Arya Samaj leaning for consultations on dozens of murals on the walls of a large hall on the second floor. At that time, it appeared a bit excessive to me. I never dreamed that it had infected me deep.

His artistic side was a bit ignited when as a 16-year old youth, he was sent to learn wood carpentry against his wishes. Subsequently, at the age of 18, he essentially left home and joined the ***Updeshak Vidyalaya*** (preachers training school), Lahore. But carpentry never left him completely. A few pieces of furniture that he had designed gave him joy in later years. A bottom line is that any kind of early education never goes to waste in a long span of life.

As of this writing, there has been no discussion with ***Trafford's*** design staff. It starts off after the file of inside contents has been submitted and proofed. In other words, when the out cover is finalized, I won't be able to make changes in the write-ups, as it would be already finalized. Nevertheless, this semi reflection fits into a larger context of Mama Ji's biography.

March 16, 2014

SECTION II

MY REFLECTIONS & INSPIRATIONS

WHAT IS INSIDE SECTION II?

Broadly, there are two kinds of ***Reflections*** in this section-making a total of 33 of them. Their writings span a period of ten years-from 2003 to 2013. A score of them were written during a year after the passing away of Mama Ji. However, it may be noted that in a few specific years, no Swami ***Reflections*** were written up. The reasons are simple-there was no external stimulus for it at that time. Also, writing a book on his life was not even conceived remotely.

These 33 ***Reflections*** are all wrapped around one particular incident at a time. Each incident is taken to a height of generality where it is unraveled, and is then connected with other aspects of life. The style remains mathematically compact. In other words, each paragraph of 4-6 lines can be easily paraphrased to at least half a page.

The rest of the ***Reflections*** are indirectly **inspired** by Mama Ji, in a sense, that what I imbibed from his presence during the time spent with him in his ***sansthan*** (institute) in Sahibabad; letters exchanged discussions and argumentations on multifarious topics. After all, he and I were composed of different intellectual materials and molds. There is absolutely no comparison in this respect. But deep down, we used to form bridges of dialogues. Also, I enjoyed browsing reading materials from his personal collection of rare books, booklets and pamphlets. Above all, just breathing in the atmosphere of the ***sansthan*** was invigorating intellectually-all this has come out in those ***Reflections*** and articles.

A few of these ***Reflections*** are also included in my book ***My Hindu Faith & Periscope***. This small intersection of material is unavoidable. The very nature of ***Reflective*** writing means my jumping from one node to the other, and at times, connecting two entirely different concepts. Nevertheless, they absolutely fit into material as a whole.

Nov 14, 2013

MY HOMAGE TO SWAMI MAMA JI

He was Swami Deekshanand for the rest of the world, but I always addressed him as Mama Ji. Partly, being overseas for 35 years, I did not know enough of him as ***sanyasi*** in 1975**.** In actuality, 'mama' in him, as a relation, never left him even after his becoming ***sanyasi***! Eventually, while introducing me to his visitors, he would add, "Satish Ji is the only one who calls me Mama." When I got a word on his going into a coma in the hospital, I said, "His time to say Good Bye has come." In fact, he had gone into *mahasamadhi* (kind of deepest meditation) in his Sahibabad *ashram*.

The date, May15, 2003 will be etched in the annals of Arya Samaj for ever. His stature as a great orator, ***pracharak*** (preacher) of Vedic life, publisher of high quality Vedic literature, author of books, and researcher puts him peerlessly at the top of a mountain. He also left a legacy in a reputed *Samarpan Shodh Sansthaan* (Samarpan Research Institute) of Vedic Studies. His towering personality by dint of his achievements was well matched with his physique and countenance.

My memory spans over 5-6 decades. I vividly remember as a 5-6 year old when he ran a small ***gurukul*** (ancient Hindu school) on the outskirts of Bathinda. My most recent memory of him is also associated with a new ***gurukul*** which held its first function on December 27, 2002, in Jarora, a village near Nanded in Maharashtra. On my asking, "How come you did not even give me any names and directions to arrive at this remote place?" he smilingly responded, "Then, you would have never come here from USA!"

For the first and last time, he and I spoke from the same stage. As ***kulpati*** (chancellor) of the ***gurukul***, he extolled ***gurukuls*** as symbols of great Vedic heritage. In my message, I exhorted the ***gurukuls*** to go beyond the study of ***shaastra*** (scriptures) and integrate ***shastra*** (weaponry) and *shatru* (enemy within and without) in the tradition of ***gurukul*** of Raam and Vishvamitra. At the end of my speech sitting on my left, he patted me. It was a great feeling. **The very next day, to my surprise, he suggested**

that henceforth, the *gurukul sanataks* (graduates) would be called *sanskriti yodha* (cultural warriors)!

Mama Ji's every breath was for Rishi Dayanand and Arya Samaj. He was an adherent believer of *guru-shishya parampara* (teacher-disciple tradition of Vedic lore). Many a times while recalling public adulation on him, he would simply say, "***dhanya ho Rishi***! (Hail you Rishi!)" For the last twenty years, I have been spending a few days with him during my India visits. Some times coming straight from Las Vegas to Sahibabad, the physical adjustment would test my limits. But our dialogues would reach a height that he would describe them as the making of an ***upnishada*** What ever he knew he knew it very well. He never doubted his belief systems, and hence never felt a need of any re-examination. It was a combination of clarity and stubbornness of mind

I called his institute, an *ashram,* though it was not nestled in a forest setting, or near a waterway. It was situated in a bustling sector of Sahibabad across a neighborhood park. Nevertheless, it provided an atmosphere for intellectual inquiry, and was open for scholars, his ardent followers and admirers. His day began at 4 AM with ***dhyan*** (meditation) and then ***swadhyae*** (introspective study) for two hours. He was passionate about getting new insights in the Vedas.

Once in a while, I would also remind him, "Your real strength is derived from your being a great ***pracharak*** and you must leave a legacy for it." In a discourse on recognizing one's strength as key to success, he added that in his case it was his ***vanni*** (Speech). In life, he was a perfectionist in whatever he did-say, from designing a jacket of a book, to a piece of furniture, or to art work; he left his signatures on them. Once a devoted couple came to visit him and the lady offered to prepare ***karhi*** (popular Indian dish) for him. Mama Ji first gave an eloquent explanation on the very name ***karhi***, its place in ***Ayurveda*** (ancient medical science of India), and then he went along to the kitchen to give her a complete demonstration!

There was no gap between his public and private dealings. He wrote beautifully and spoke musically. Being generous in praise of others, he got along with every one. He often said that no one has ever put an obstacle in his work. He had no enemies! (***ajatshatru***) Combined with his high moral character and service to Arya Samaj, he eventually became taller than any person or office. Due to a heart surgery in July 2000, at the age of 80, his movements had slowed down, but his mental faculties remained very sharp to the very **END**.

During a conversation on Dec 31, 2002, I asked him straight, "What are your unfinished projects now?" Being used to my direct questioning, he said that **he wanted to write a book on Ved Gita**. He was very satisfied in entrusting his institute to Arya Pratinidhi Sabha. He had full confidence in its President, Captain Dev Ratan Arya.

On early morning of Jan 1, 2001, as I was getting ready to take leave, Mama Ji sat me and Rajindra P. Bhatnagar, my cousin down on the carpet, I too stayed with in Mumbai, and basically instructed, "After I am Gone, you work together for my common cause." I knew it then, that this meeting with him, on the first day of New Year, is going to be the last and a momentous one. Swami Satya Prakash, a renowned scholar, once declared that Deekshanand will be remembered as the only one of his kind for generations of Arya Samajis to come!

May 22, 2003/Aug, 2013

MAMA JI'S DILEMMA WITH LIQUOR

It was April 1965 and the setting was of Dewan Hall Arya Samaj situated in Chandani Chowk, Delhi. For nearly 10 years, Mama Ji lived in a topmost solitary structure allotted to him. I was on a short visit to Delhi. Sanjay, the son of my close cousin, Gyan, was born in Jan of that year. So, one evening, he arranged a small celebratory party over foods and drinks at his place in Timarpur area. Sushil, another cousin, recently transferred to Delhi, was also staying in Dewan Hall with his family. My cousin, Kusum happened to be visiting the place too. Yet, another cousin, Mohan was a permanent fixture in Dewan Hall-putting up with Mama Ji for years till his marriage in 1967.

When Sushil and I returned to Dewan Hall around 11 PM, he straight away went to his bed. All the cots were spread out on the huge roof under the open sky. On noticing Mama Ji still in his study, I went up into his chamber and seated myself on a mat on the floor across his flatbed. He was comfortably inclined. For an hour, we had a very nice conversation on a few philosophical topics. I always looked forward to such opportunities with him. Next day, in the morning, I returned to Kurukshetra University.

After a year or so, when I met Mama Ji again, straight away he asked, "Satish, tell me if you had taken any alcoholic drink on **that night**?" Saying yes first, I added the context of a celebration. He appeared perplexed and was quiet for a few moments. Then it was my turn to ask him, "Now you tell me what made you inquire into it after such a long time?" He could have inquired it by writing a letter instead of 'bottling' it up for a year.

Eventually when the pieces were put together, a story emerged like this. After my departure from Delhi, Kusum told Mama Ji, "Satish Bhai Sahib had some alcoholic drinks last night." But Mama Ji refused to believe it. **He asserted that since Satish had such deep dialogues with him that a drunken person can never engage in**! But Kusum had an ace in her hands. She told that she was 100% sure from her long experience of watching her father coming back home drunk every night. She was very familiar with the alcoholic smell in the breath!

However, as a teenage girl, Kusum could never understand the difference between a drunken person and social drinker like me who takes an hour to finish only one drink. In one case, the brain cells are all messed up, while in the other, they are totally aligned and focused for deeper inquiries and resolution of problems.

That became a point of deliberation for Mama Ji for a long time. He did not like persons close to him taking any kind of alcoholic drinks. But categorizing people on the basis of drinking habits posed a dilemma for him, at least in my case.

Aug 13, 2003/Oct, 2013

MAMA JI'S LOVE FOR SANSKRIT

My earliest memory of Swami Mama Ji is of his running a small gurukul in the 1940's-on the outskirts of Nai Basti, Bathinda. Half of a dozen of students, called ***brahmcharis,*** were members of his extended family, so it was natural to visit the gurukul occasionally. The students were attired in two-piece white wrap overs; one for lower part of the body and the other for the upper one. It appeared their major study was of memorizing ***mantras*** and ***shalokas*** from various Hindu scriptures. For me, memorizing anything has been anathema. I just could never think of being in that mode of learning.

During family visits, Mama Ji encouraged and enticed the young ones to study Sanskrit in schools. He himself had no choice, but to study only Sanskrit in a Lahore gurukul. Even 50 years after independence, Sanskrit is not even an elective subject in the middle schools of Punjab. The British knew it very well that if Hindu majority in India is disconnected from Sanskrit, then they would quickly succeed in revamping the cultural life of India.

The British granted scholarships for the study of Sanskrit, Gurmukhi, Arabic and Persian, but jobs were only available for those studying in the Macaulay system of education enforced in the schools and colleges of British India. It was after Gandhi's taking over the reins of freedom movement that leading nationalist leaders started private schools and colleges for imparting knowledge of Indian culture and Sanskrit. Mama Ji was one of them in a Lahore gurukul.

My younger brother was converted to Sanskrit in his 9th class, but I went on to study science. All throughout college, my distance from Sanskrit kept increasing. Later on, when I studied poorly translated versions of Ramayana and Mahabharata, a real desire to learn Sanskrit was kindled.

In 1983, teaching a short course on Vedic Mathematics at UNLV prompted me to do research into the Vedas. Knowing that I could not learn Sanskrit fast enough to be able to unravel the multilayered meanings in the ***mantras*** of Vedic Sanskrit, I sought Mama Ji's help in connecting me with Vedic scholars who also had some mathematical background. Even today, no college curriculum in India allows the students study math and Sanskrit together. Mama Ji and I had several long sessions conversing on this subject.

I am convinced that the rudimentary and surface presence of mathematics in the Vedas is a tip of iceberg. To the best of my knowledge, no one has been able to identify 18 mathematical ***sutras***, aphorisms as claimed by Shankaracharya Bharat Krishen Teerath, in the Atharva Veda. **It remains an open research question**. I wrote a few papers on the importance of Sanskrit.

After a brief encounter with math and Sanskrit, now, I strongly believe that no matter what a person wants to pursue as a course of study, he/she will reach its greater depth and height with an additional knowledge of Sanskrit. After all, entire Indian heritage is locked up in Sanskrit scriptures. This line thinking used to delight Mama Ji and he would proudly introduce me to his visitors.

Aug 24, 2003/Oct, 2013

A PIONEER OF HINDI MADE EASY

Swami Mama Ji (Swami Deekshanand Saraswati) loved Hindi. His handwriting in Hindi was artistic-a thing of beauty. He spoke Hindi succinctly and slowly. Every syllable was properly enunciated. It seemed that his vocal cords were just made for Hindi and Sanskrit language only. He could truly hypnotize people with his persona and eloquence in Hindi. In public speeches, his command over Hindi would step up a notch, though he generously recited Sanskrit ***mantras***.

It was after his participation in a nationwide agitation for the adoption of Hindi as official language that he wrote a small booklet on ***How to Learn Hindi in Seven Days***. It was a time when Indian government had set up a Hindi department and also charged it with teaching Hindi to non-Hindi speaking employees and develop Hindi glossary for official terms and terminologies. After his release from a short jail term, he put his head and heart to the development of Hindi in the simplest manner. This is where his early genius shined out.

I do not think there was any scholar before him who ever tried to simplify Hindi teaching in a beautiful manner. In fact, he swam in the opposite direction. The trend in the 1950s was to make Hindi sound complex to enhance the image of a few individuals who had mastered it a little bit! Mama Ji bridged a gap between the two classes by demystifying perceived complexities.

An unforgettable cryptic incident from my college days (1955-59) comes to my mind. On getting 'Re-appear' in Hindi exam in 1957, my college friend, Prem, remarked, "***jis bhasha par hamein garva tha, usi bhasha mein hum fail ho gai***!" (It means, that I failed in a language that I was so proud of!)

It was some time in the late 1950s that Mama Ji showed me his booklet on learning Hindi in seven days. On noticing an expression of disbelief on my face, he went on to explain the foundation of his innovative approach. He made Hindi phonetic and symmetrical that any non-Hindi speaking could master all its nuances literally in seven days.

These days at any bookstall in India, one can find booklets on learning different Indian languages. Most of them are in a series; how to learn a language X from Hindi or English. Nevertheless, Mama Ji was a language pioneer in the 1950s. I do not know what happened to the publishing history of that booklet. It may be left in the attics of Dewan Hall, Delhi or Samarpan Shodh Sansthan, Sahibabad.

There must be a bundle of such booklets. At that time, Mama Ji was not in a publishing venture then; he started publishing in the 1980s. Possibly, some Delhi publisher may be aware of it. No matter what, his legacy for Hindi would remain unforgettable.

Sep 28, 2003/Oct, 2013

MAMA JI AND ENGLISH

When I think of English and Mama Ji (Swami Deekshanand Saraswati) then so many incidents flash my mind. Putting them all in one piece is like serving a 21-course meal to a hungry person in a hurry. No one can relish and discriminate between too many good things of life in a short span.

Ever since college days, my growing command over English also enhanced my range of scholarship. Mama Ji told me a few times, "I want to learn English too. Pandit Buddha Dev Ji had promised to teach me, but he did not have time." Pandit Buddha Dev was known as Swami Samarpananand after his initiation into ***sanyaas.*** Mama Ji regarded him as his *GURU.* Pandit Buddha Dev was always on move in his ideas and travels; forget teaching English to Mama Ji! Scholars in any language are not fit for teaching it to the novices.

It was in 1958 when I read Jadunath Sarkar's monograph, ***Aurangzeb*** written in English. It happened to be the only English book in a small library that Mama Ji had in his Dewan Hall abode. Perhaps, it belonged to Pandit Buddha Dev. When I told Mama Ji how Sarkar, a Hindu historian, had elevated Aurangzeb by completely circumventing his tyrannies on the Hindus, and over-rated his Islamic adherence on trivial personal austerities while living in the palaces, Mama Ji just wanted to read the book himself.

As a matter of fact, Mama Ji was just not made for English. Sometimes, I think he did not want 'caught' studying English. After all, learning any language and not being subtly influenced by its culture is not possible. He was steeped into a pristine ancient Indian culture. Only emanation of Sanskrit ***mantras*** and ***shlokas*** from his mouth befitted his persona.

Once I told Mama Ji why don't you get hold of an English primer and start it yourself? He made an effort but he hardly went beyond alphabets. In fact, his enthusiasm turned sour when he noticed bizarre phonetic and structural inconsistencies in English language. His mastery over Hindi became a psychological obstacle in his learning of English! Consequently, he could never write or converse in English.

However, he developed an uncanny skill about English. He claimed that all nouns in English are adaptations of some words in Hindi and Sanskrit**.** That was too much for me to accept it. He would challenge me to throw an English noun, and he would come up with a Hindi word that when transliterated into English would appear like an English word. For example, look at the resemblance between an English word, **character** and the Hindi word, ***chariter*** a close Roman transliteration of Hindi word, ***charitra.*** With my limited vocabulary of English and his profound knowledge of Hindi and Sanskrit, he was always a winner!

Oct 11, 2003/Oct, 2013

HOW I ONCE QUIT EATING MEAT

Mama Ji (Swami Deekshanand Saraswati) was known as Acharya Krishna before initiation into ***sanyaas*** in 1975. Then, he would visit Bathinda (BTI) once a year. After all, BTI was a place where he started his own gurukul and ran it for a few years. His arrival at home was always pleasant and full of conversations with the young ones. In fact, Mama Ji looked forward to be amidst families in order to influence the young ones. It may be called a micro proselytizing!

Non-vegetarian food is a norm in Kayastha families. Hence, meat became Mama Ji's target for stopping it. He used to give all sorts of reasons against meat and benefits of lentils and veggies. One of my younger brothers quit meat at the age of 16. That approach did not work on me, but he did not give up on me either on any occasion. Once, during a Delhi visit after MA Part I exams, he prevailed upon me. Perhaps, I was mentally fatigued by the grueling exams. Nonetheless, I said, "OK. I won't eat meat for one full year. At the end of the year, if the urge for meat disappeared, then consider it quit forever. If not, then I resume it. Do you agree to it?" Almost triumphantly, he said, yes.

Mother was surprised at my vow. As long as I was in BTI, she cooked my favorite vegetarian items and I did not miss meat that much. The real test started when I returned to the hostel life in Chandigarh. There were three days in a week when meat was served at dinner. Earlier, I used to look forward to those days. Now it became different. I recall many a time aroma of meat dishes would get deep into my nostrils and drive me crazy for not being able to eat it.

It was like in the movie, ***Scent of a Woman***! However, girls were off loaded my mind when I would see some one eating meat on the same table right in front of me. In frustration, I went without any meals many a times, as I won't stand for the vegetarian items. Milk and buttered toasts were my saviors. I became a bit testy and angrier person.

Fortunately, my studies of MA Part II remained under control. I once wrote to Mama Ji about my struggle. Like any thing in life, the year was coming to an end. In anticipation, I would get excited with each day passing. It was May 19, 1961, I wrote, **"I tried to refrain from meat, but the desire for it never left me. The year is over."**

He did not write, or say a word when I met him in June. Years went by. He never brought it up again. One day, I heard him saying, "Of all the people who vowed in front of me of not to drink, they drank in hiding; those who vowed not to smoke, they smoked; and those who vowed not to eat meat, they ate. It is only Satish who has been true to his word." This experience welded incredible individuality into my character.

Oct 18, 2003/Oct, 2013

LAST HOURS WITH MAMA JI (PART I)

Sometimes, I get strong premonitions of events to come. One happened last year. Since 1975, with the exception of 5-6 years, I have spent a summer week with Mama Ji (Swami Deekshanand Saraswati) in India. It did not materialize in Y2002 due to my hernia surgery. Feeling a sort of gap, I wrote him about a possible meeting in December somewhere in south in order to stay away from the winter of north. Promptly came his reply informing me of his attending an Arya Samaj program in Nanded (MS).

That really excited me for another reason too. Nanded Sahib was the only holy ***takhat*** (a religious seat of *Sikhism*) that I had not visited! There are five holy ***takhats.*** After Nanded, we agreed to spend some quiet time in Bombay. Before leaving the US, nothing else was cleared up including where to meet him in Nanded. I assumed that the city must be plastered with posters on his upcoming visit.

On arriving in India, I again phoned him in Delhi to know some detail, and he just gave me the name of the train Suchkhund Express he was traveling and the seat number. I was in Indore at that time and the train did not pass through its railway station, so there was no way for us traveling together. My cousin Vinod Behari also wanted to spend some time with Mama Ji. Any way, we directly reached Nanded an hour before his train. But to our dismay, we discovered that he was not there!

It really created a panic that at night where and how to find him. All inquiries were in vain. Luckily, we spotted another cousin, Rakesh who was leading a group of Arya Samajis from Delhi. Incidentally, all three of us are the sons of three real sisters. It may indicate Mama Ji's influence on the families that he regularly visited before his ***sanyaas*** in 1975. Vinod Behari a staunch and active Arya Samaji was also its MP State Secretary. Rakesh, President of Arya Samaj Kalkaji, a Delhi Branch, also runs printing business specializing in printing literature in Vedic Sanskrit.

While in a quandary at the Nanded railway station, Rakesh said, "Mama Ji has no program in Nanded, but he has to attend a function in Jarora, a remote village 50 KM from Nanded!" While giving us the directions to the place that he himself had not visited, he nevertheless cautioned that we won't be able to find it ourselves! I was in no mood to undertake an uncharted course for a couple of hours at night. We decided to check in a nearby hotel and have a good meal to sooth our fazed nerves. But I kept wondering why Mama Ji had played this trick on me!

Next morning, without being sure of Mama Ji's coming to the function, we boarded a rural bus that brought us at a point where we were to trek to Jarora off the main road for an hour. Luckily as soon as we got off, a jeep with flags and welcome signs was ready to take the guests to the function site. It was a great relief. The site turned out to be a new gurukul started a year ago by a second-generation disciple of Mama Ji, who was its ***kulpati*** (Chancellor).

There are only two small buildings and two hutments for a dozen of ***brahamcharis*** (students of a gurukul) in various age groups amidst miles of wilderness around it. It was the opening of a three-day function. In the morning session everyone was wondering as to what happened to Swami Deekshanand Saraswati who was to be the main attraction of the annual function.

It was around 1:00 PM, a white car blowing a small dust storm was noticed in the terrain not motorable even for a four-wheel drive. As it got closer, the entire crowd rose up to their feet when they glimpsed Swami Ji sitting in it! His story of missing the train at some point, and then finding other means of transportation was essentially a story of his determination. **He was 83 in Dec. 2002 and no one could have said that he won't be around after five months**

Within ten minutes of arrival he freshened up, and took control of the dais. He spoke for nearly two hours! "The atmosphere of a gurukul is a symbol of our ***sanskriti*** (culture)." he said. The forest surrounding the gurukul reminded him of the Vedic era. He was just ecstatic to be in this atmosphere. The mantras and quotations were flowing out of his lips effortlessly. I was in a bit of awe at his display of energy. He was at his very best without showing a sign of 40 hours of arduous journey.

I remember a close associate alerting him of the exertion that he was putting on himself. But instead of stopping, he said that was how his mind and body were charged! After the function was over and devotees gone, I asked, "Mama Ji, why did you tell me of Nanded, and not the exact location of this village?" **"Had I told you about this place then you would have never come here from America!" Thus, he made me speechless.**

Now as I rewind this clip of life, I really wonder that Mama Ji was in the best state of mental health. His memory was incredible five months before his ***Samadhi.*** Surely, the body had slowed down, and once he confided that the heart surgery of Y-2000 did extend a quality of his life. His body weight and heart were not compatible. All three days, I used to be with him in the village and return to Nanded at dusk.

The second day shall remain an unforgettable day of my life when for the first and the last time I shared spotlight with him on the same platform. I was already an honored guest for coming from the US, and being related with Swami Ji. However, soon after his address, I was suddenly invited to speak on this occasion. As a toastmaster, I seized the opportunity and composed my thoughts befitting a follow-up to Mama Ji's speech.

The main theme of my speech turned out to be on **shaastra** (Scriptures), **shastra** (weaponry) and **shatru** (Enemy). I opened the speech with a remark that the very culture, as symbolized by the gurukuls, is in danger today. Look, what is happening in Kashmir! It is 99.9% ethnically cleansed of the Hindus, the only votaries of this culture. Hindus are not safe in Jammu; there are Islamic intrusions in Himachal Pradesh, and all along the western border to Gujarat. In northeast 90% of the Hindus are lost to Christianity, and that is the root cause of secessionist insurgency in the east. This is an internationally supported and systematic attack on the Hindu way of life. The Hindu religion-is shrinking within the borders of India!

I also reminded the audience of a golden piece of history connected with Nanded. It was here, 300 years ago, that Guru Gobind Singh came from Punjab to persuade his disciple Madho Das to renounce his asceticism in favour of fight for the protection of the Sikh way of life. His name is immortal Banda Singh Bahadur, who I said, perfectly fits in the mold of ancient gurukul product. I reiterated that the gurukul site is holy for its historic association! I felt the audience charged.

Presently, I said, the only thing common between the gurukul of Vishvamitra of ***Ramayana*** age and this gurukul was the mere word gurukul. At the time of independence there were more than 2000 gurukuls in India, and now the number is less than 200. They are in a very bad shape in every respect. The number of students is hardly 50 in most of them. They do not attract students from every strata of Hindu society, but rather provide a refuge for the children of the down trodden sections.

Then I brought gurukuls in a striking contrast with the religious schools of the Muslims and the Sikhs. Today, the Islamic madarasas are turning out perfect fighting machines in the world. The growth in the number of madarasas in India alone is exponential what to speak of them in Pakistan. They are like the Harvards in Islamic education. From the Sikh religious schools, called ***taksals,*** its youths protect and service the gurdwaras. There is no shortage of employment for the graduates of madarasas and ***taksals*** as both turn out fighters for their religions. However, the graduates of *gurukuls* suffer from inferiority complex, and thus are belittled everywhere.

What is the future of the graduates of a *gurukul*? They are not employable for decent jobs. Their lack of self-esteem is terrible. Above all, the current gurukul curriculum focuses on memorization of scriptures and rules of grammar. It is time that the Arya Samaj takes the lead in the revision of gurukul education.

According to a secret Government report of the 1930s, the 90% of the Hindus freedom fighters were of Araya Samaj leaning. They bravely fought for the independence. Now the fight is for the protection, preservation and perpetuation of Indian heritage. Enemy (Shatru/enemy) is clear within and without. It has to be marked down. The curriculum must include ***shastra*** (weaponry) as the use of weapons builds self-esteem of the highest order.

Gurukuls are perfect religious schools of the Hindus, but the foreign subjugation of a thousand year has completely obliterated their original mission. Lord Rama and his brothers learnt about the ***shaastra*** (scriptures) and every ***shastra*** (weaponry from its psychology to usage) in the gurukuls. Finally, Vishvamitra identified the ***shatru*** (enemies) of the state from within and without in his gurukul. Eventually, Rama eliminated all the enemies, and only then Ramrajaya could be established in India, then called ***Aryavrat.***

My speech took the audience by a new mood. Mama Ji, sitting on my left patted my back, and I felt a new emerging force in me. Later in the day, Acharya (Principal) of the gurukul, Mama Ji and I had a discussion on changing the course of gurukul education; making it three-dimensional from the current one. Most gurukuls, having a lot of land, can undertake armament instruction in its guarded environment. The current rote system of memorizing all the Vedas and Panini's ***Ashtadhiaye*** for everyone is too much. It smothers original thinking and runs against those individuals like me who cannot remember.

In fact, I had told the audience that had I been in any other profession, then I would have been a failure in life. Only in mathematics where the deductive reasoning works, one can excel without rote. When I suggested that the gurukul graduates be called ***sansakriti rakshak*** (protectors of heritage), Mama Ji suggested the name ***sansktriti yodhas*** (warriors of the heritage) I am convinced that without this revision, gurukuls will soon become relics of a past. The introduction of three-part education shall guarantee the survival and protection of the Hindu culture.

Soon the departure day came. This time, Mama Ji and I were set to travel together to Mumbai. Nanded railway station that had dismayed me on the arrival day gave me a big surprise. I was already in the waiting room. Amongst the crowd of passengers jostling all over, entered Swami Mama Ji escorted by 4-5 Acharyas and ***brahamcharis*** (students focused on supreme knowledge). Spotting me, they respectfully bowed and touched my feet. I could see the surprise on the faces of people, as they looked at Mama Ji wearing ***kurta*** and ***dhoti*** in glowing ocher colour, and me wearing denim shirt and jeans. Inwardly, I bowed to the cultural heritage that Mama Ji and I shared with equal passion.

Dec 23, 2003/Oct, 2013

LAST HOURS WITH MAMA JI (PART II)

On December 29, 2002, I traveled free in an air-conditioned class of a train from Nanded to Mumbai as Mama Ji's (Swami Deekshanand Saraswati) personal attendant. He held a privileged railway pass as a freedom fighter; not against the British, but against the Nizam of Hyderabad who had defied his state's accession to India and clamped hardships on his Hindu populace. Any way, that is another story of his life that he only recalled to some of his close associates.

Also, it was also the first time that I had a chance to travel with him! I often travel light, partly, because I prefer to carry my own bags. But it amazed me to see that Mama Ji was having 9-11 pieces of personal luggage. At the age of 83, it is enough, if one can only carry one's brief case. However, there is no shortage of helpers at each end of his journey. People are always in line to see him off at departure time and receive him over on arrival.

Once we were settled in our berths, I jokingly inquired about the contents of each bag. Besides bags of his clothes and bedding for all seasons, he carried one suitcase of his manuscripts and files. He writes and reads a lot during his travels too. Depending upon the number of people coming to attend the function he presides, he carries one or two boxes of publications of his ***sansthan*** (Institute). During the event, they are put on display for sales. With the help of an artist he created some very illustrative and educational posters on varied aspects of Vedic life, and thus he carries rolls of posters for exhibition and sales.

Talking of luggage pieces, a funny thing was a box containing two tiffins of meals and snacks! Mama Ji loved to eat good food cooked in ***desi ghee*** (clarified butter); loved to cook delicious food; and no less loved to serve it too! In fact, those who have ever watched him peeling and dicing vegetables would testify his dexterity and pleasure at doing small culinary things.

My concern was for the safety of his numerous bags from the train thieves while we would be sound asleep. I have heard of very creative stories of thieveries in the air-conditioned compartments of running trains, in particular. However, Mama Ji never had any such anxiety! I vividly remember an incident though it happened 50 years ago at Bathinda railway station; family members were there to see him off. I suggested him take a seat in a rear end compartment for safety reasons in the event of a train accident. Promptly, he said, **"The train in which I travel can never meet an accident!"** His life certainly has proved him right since he remained on the road or rail for 7-8 months in a year. Any way, after a hearty meal, we both had a good sleep. Next morning, I thanked my luck in finding all pieces intact.

Our conversations in the train were mundane. He is relatively an early sleeper, but I am a late one. Besides, his seat was on a lower berth and mine was an upper one and perpendicularly across. During all my stays with him, I have noticed that Mama Ji gets one of the best sleeps whether during day or night time. He would be asleep in a few minutes once he pulls a cover over his head. In homes, he was not at all disturbed by people around his bed talking or watching TV. I believe a quality of life can be measured by the quality of one's sleep. It not only tells about the general health of a person, but also about the ideals of life one lives for.

In the morning, he was already up and mediating when I woke up. Soon after the day break, the train stopped at our destination. There were two parties at the railway station to receive Mama Ji. One was the son of Captain Dev Ratan, President of Arya Pratinidhi Sabha, and the other, a son of my cousin. Both insisted on taking him to their respective places. I just watched and reflected at the magnetic nature of Mama Ji's life to pull people towards him. In contrast, the US life is so cut and dry when it comes to home hospitality. Its most irksome feature is that a guest has to have host's approval to visit before knocking at the door. Otherwise, it is unimaginable to be a house guest or have one.

I stayed for two days with him in Mumbai. My cousin, Rajindra is very close to Mama Ji. Our mothers are real sisters. After settling down in the house, I took out a beautiful leather document case that I had brought for Mama Ji. However, on noticing that he already had a similar one, I said, "Mama Ji, I did bring this briefcase for you, but if you permit, then I can present it to Rajindra Bhai Sahib." It was a delicate situation essentially caused by our plan of stay. While Mama Ji was holding and fondly looking at the brief case, my cousin sensed the situation and said, "It is OK. Let it be for Swami Ji." That is how he always addressed his Mama Ji. He did not say a word. I have known Mama Ji admiring all good things of life, except one; woman, the God's best creation for Man!

During one afternoon, we had a session on our favorite intellectual pursuit of Sanskrit (ancient Indian language) and ***sanskriti*** (ancient Indian culture). The incredible similarity between the two words with so different meanings suggest that in order to understand Indian heritage, one must understand Sanskrit language in which all great epics and literature are written. In my latest understanding, Sanskrit is the most suitable language for its compactness and power for codification in an unambiguous and lasting manner.

With years of labor and study, Mama Ji had discovered amazing relationships between vowels and consonants of ***devnagari*** (name of Hindi/Sanskrit script). For example, he identified only five vowels (transliterated in English as *a, e, uh, rhi, lrhi*) and derived the remaining vowels and some consonants from them.

Gradually, he takes the principles of language to a new height, when he connects them with profound principles of Hindu Philosophy. Sanskrit and ***sanskriti*** are the reduced to the two sides of a coin. This time, I placed my note book in front of him to write it on. Thus I have a page of his last hand writing as of December 30, 2002 afternoon! His hand writing was very steady; shapes of letters were so perfect that they belie any sign of his imminent Departure.

There is one topic on which I used to tease Mama Ji that he was stuck in his thought process. He and I had the same beginning on the understanding of the universe with a theoretical frame work of ***traitwad,*** (principle of **three-ness**), which consists of ***jeevatma*** (individual soul), ***parmatma*** (Supreme God) and ***prakriti*** (Nature). This is what he learnt at the age of 16 in a gurukul, and he never challenged and wavered from it for the rest of his life.

My story of life on this philosophical and scientific topic is that I moved on from ***traitwad*** to ***dwaitawad*** (principle of **two-ness**), and finally, it is resting on the ***advaitwad*** (principle of **one-ness**), as my understanding of the universe kept expanding with my study of science, mathematics, and philosophical contemplations.

However, for this **Last time** I silently listened to his beliefs on ***traitwad*** without saying a word. For me, it was like a glorification of Euclidean Geometry that I greatly enjoyed at the age of 15. But as I studied higher mathematics, Non-Euclidean Geometry and other geometries, it has extended my scope understanding far beyond the early one.

Next day, I specifically asked him a question, "Mama Ji, what is left to be finished in your life now?" He pondered for a minute and said of **three** things. But what stands out in my memory is only one of ***Ved Gita*** (ways of leading active life based on the Vedas). Whenever I ask such a direct question from a person, it compels me to figure an answer in my own life too.

With my cousin, lives his married son too. Everyone including their friends and relatives want a piece of Mama Ji time, ***darshan*** and blessings whenever he is on a visit. It was mid-morning of Jan 01, 2003, greeting Mama Ji for the New Year, I said, "Mama Ji, this meeting of ours is unique since I have seen you both in Y-2002 and Y-2003!" In my heart of heart I knew that this was my last meeting. He also sensed it.

Summoning up my cousin and me closer, Mama Ji said. "I have handed over the charge of the ***sansthan*** (institute) to Arya Pratinidhi Sabha to be managed by a Trust. Looking toward me, he added that," From the family side, Rajen and Jaidev Ji are its members. I want you both to work together in enhancing the mission of the ***sansthan***." I told my cousin-see how Mama Ji had bonded us in a common cause; otherwise, we had hardly maintained any communication. **Late in the morning, Mama Ji and I knew that we were taking Final Leave of each other**!

Dec 27, 2003/Oct, 2013

SANSKRIT, MARRIAGE & DEEKSHANAND

It has been exactly one month since my younger daughter, Annie (Anubha) was married. People still ask me-how did it all go? The one thing that stands out is her entire Hindu marriage ceremony. Annie and I were on the same page on it, though 41 years apart! It was Jan 1963, when my marriage preparations were going on in Bathinda. Swami Deekshanand Saraswati, then known as Acharya Krishna, enthusiastically agreed to perform the wedding ceremony.

However, for the reason of intelligibility of the ceremony for the wedding gathering, I insisted that it be performed in Hindi, rather than in Sanskrit. I don't remember how he convinced me to stay with Sanskrit. But he did spend a couple of hours, a day before marriage, in explaining me the meanings of all the Sanskrit ***mantras***. Without knowing Sanskrit, one cannot have emotional and intellectual association with the marriage rituals.

Sanskrit being never a language of the masses, failed to promote national unity amongst the Hindus in the last millennium when the waves of foreign attacks started on India. To the best of my researches, Sanskrit with its most perfect grammar in the world to date was a language of the scholars and code keepers of Vedic literature.

Moreover, at the time of Annie's marriage, we both wanted that the ceremony be completed in 45 minutes with English translation of the Sanskrit ***mantras***. My sister Madhu assisted by Anal, her husband, did an outstanding job of performing the marriage ceremony. They laboriously scanned the entire ***Vedic vivah sanskar*** (Vedic Marriage Manual), chose the right ***mantras***, and translated them as close to the vernacular English as possible. A week before marriage, both of them went through a full rehearsal of their marriage ceremony with both Annie and Alex-in our presence.

For the last twenty some years, I have been struck at the contrast of marriage ceremonies in Hindu religion with that of other religions. The Sikh marriage ceremony, being in Punjabi, is understood by all. The

Muslim wedding is relatively brief and done in a local language mixed with understandable Arabic words. Christian marriages are not in ancient Greek or Roman, but in national languages of their respective countries.

How does Sanskrit help a marriage has been beyond me? It may be a vestige of a Brahamanical caste hold on the Hindu society. In Punjab, there is phrase-***eh kere mantar parne hain. eh kam tan bara asaan hai*** (means: it is the recitation of the Sanskrit ***mantras*** that is difficult-the chore at hand is very easy). Paradoxically, recitation of Sanskrit mantras had become a benchmark of a challenging task! An oral phrase captures the heart of a social custom. The more I ponder, the deeper I understand the abysmal state Hindu society for centuries due to blind belief systems. Hindus just nod and blindly do the rituals without any question or appreciation during a religious ceremony.

Madhu and Anal have a computer file of the entire Hindu marriage ceremony in English. They are willing to share it with any interested party. A marriage ceremony is a social occasion that also brings a unity in a community through a common and meaningful practice.

May 10, 2004/Sep, 2013

COMMENTS

1. In principle, I agree with your thoughts that wedding vows should be translated to the language of those being married. Rest of your conclusions is very much debatable. **Rahul**
2. Madhu and Anal have done a great job indeed. Entire Ceremony should be published in Hindi also. I would love to download it for someone's use. Brahmanism is the GREATEST CURSE. It might be next only to the CURSE of MYTHOLOGY inflicted upon the masses of this ancient land . . . .
3. Read your reflections; very difficult for me to comment. I feel our ancestral beliefs and rituals should not be given up in the name of 'liberal Hinduism'. To me, Hinduism and rituals associated with it are not rigid and are the best example of 'secularism'. There is no rigidity in its teaching by whosoever it is done and through whatever rituals and language they are performed on various occasions in one's life. One may have faith and practice in whatever manner one wants; there is high degree of flexibility to suit every one and every environment. Individual rights of observing some basic morals and daily routine connected with one's circumstances, likings, resources, etc. are adequately reflected in Hinduism. **RS Nigam**
4. . . . Vedic Mantras are potent with potency, efficacy and effectiveness. Their Correct pronunciation, comprehension of the correct meaning and their recitation with full faith will indeed charge the chanter and listeners with bubbling vibrations . . . Do ***sadhana***, examine, practice and then pass your verdict. Do not claim authority over a subject which is unknown to you. Thanks, **A Commentator**

A HOME THAT OWNED A SWAMI

It has been a while since I wrote on Swami Mama Ji (Swami Deekshanand Saraswati) despite his first Departure Anniversary looming in the back of my mind. Today, I heard that there was a great memorial function to be held on May 14-15 at his ***sansthan*** (institute) in Sahibabad. I have requested a cousin to provide some detail on it.

Yes, Mama Ji had a deep attachment with his ***sansthan***-like, any mother who has it with her baby. He would long to return to it after his short and long preaching circuits. However, hardly his batteries were charged without any special care that after a month or two, he would set out again. The way construction at the ***sansthan*** went on in mid 1990s, he also needed to raise cash for it.

Since his turning 70 years, his numerous admirers and followers beseeched him to come and live in their homes. He would give them a pleasure to serve him for a month or two, and then would return to Sahibabad. Inwardly and outwardly, he always attributed the love and affection bestowed upon him by public to the great work and genius of the Rishi (Swami Dayanand).

At the ***sansthan***, he had no regular assistants in kitchen to take care of him. It appears whether in his room upstairs or down, he was fully at peace with its environment. During the last few years Mama Ji read a little, wrote more, but spoke and contemplated a whole lot more. Often, he said, **"What I am speaking out if not recorded, it would not be found for a long time!"**

During my summer visits to Sahibabad in July/August, I recall some days of terrible heat, no power, and no help in the kitchen. Forget Mama Ji ever eating or getting food brought from a restaurant, he won't even let me eat out, or a guest either. I know he did wonder at my coming to Sahibabad leaving behind the comforts of US life. I too wondered at his choices. But our dialogues made our days. It was the magic of the ***sansthan*** that brought our creativity out.

Around 1978, Mama Ji was convinced of the merits of buying a plot for his ***sansthan*** near Delhi. But, he had a dilemma about owning a property since he had accepted a ***sanyas*** order in 1975. After some consultation, he agreed to buy a plot in the name of Kusum, his niece, who was inspired by the ideals of Mama Ji and Vedic scholarship. The land deed was thus signed and completed. While Mama Ji technically was not the total owner, yet his investment and attachment with ***sansthan*** kept increasing with years.

For years, Mama Ji had operated out from Arya Samaj Dewan Hall in Chandani Chowk, Delhi. Gradually, due to construction supervision, he moved to Sahibabad with his library. He literally put his signatures everywhere in the dynamic architecture and construction of the ***sansthan***. His huge library of rare Vedic studies was essentially his whole household. The rest, perhaps, could be put in four suitcases. It is a befitting tribute to his memory to hold the first anniversary function in the ***sansthan.***

May 23, 2004

BASKING IN REFLECTED GLORY

It is natural to take pride in the achievements and high statuses of close relatives, friends, or one's children, as, on balance, we are no less shamed by their embarrassing actions. Association with a person, place or idea is a two-edge sword. However, some thing that happened to me last week is a bit off these mundane experiences.

During the Fifth Biennial Conference of the **WAVES** (World Association of Vedic Studies) in July 9-11, 2004, I presented a paper on the ***Intellectual Traditions in Arya Samaj***. Its summary being already published in a program, quite a few people had come out to listen to my talk. I opened my lecture with a dedication to the memory of Swami Deekshanand Saraswati. He Departed on May 15, 2003.

I told the audience that Swami Ji let me address him as Mama Ji even after his initiation into ***sanyas*** in 1975. He was two years younger than my mother. The moment I spoke these words quite a few people in the audience were taken in by some awe and surprise.

The paper was deeply pondered and researched. I had dug out an intellectual tradition of Arya Samaj that was never understood before. Consequently, there was a dual effect of my lecture and my lineage with Swami Deekshanand. As soon as the session was over, I was surrounded by the admirers of Swami Deekshanand and followers of Arya Samaj. Their pride and joy overwhelmed me. I was pressed to attend the annual function of the North American Arya Samaj in Toronto, Canada next month, and a function in Vedic Center, Atlanta in April, 2005.

Mama Ji's exultation, ***DHANYA HO RISHI*!** (Hail thee Rishi/ Dayanand**!**), suddenly flashed my mind. He used to utter this salutation to Maharishi Dayanand whenever he was publicly showered with adulation. But I simply said, "Thanks, Mama Ji!"

July 14, 2004

INTELLECTUAL TRADITIONS IN ARYA SAMAJ

(Dedicated to the 1st Memorial Anniversary of
Swami Deekshanand Saraswati)

The year 1857 is a watershed mark in the history of modern India. The British scholars chronicle 1857 as the year of Indian Mutiny, but the nationalist historians characterize it as India's First War of Independence from the British yoke. Irrespective of this debate whether it was well planned or not, the fact remains that it set off a period of 25 years (1858-1883) when a section of Indians masses was led by a few thinkers! **It gave birth to the first militant intellectual tradition in an impoverished country ridden with strifes and superstitions.** For the first time, the waves of chivalry swept over the nation.

By and large, the ***Bhakti*** (devotional) trends are not intellectual traditions. The *Bhakti* suspends the collective intellect of the people. They are Bury-the-Head-in-Sand cults, or Hide-Under-Cover till the danger passes away. The ***Bhakti*** life style made the Hindus, over the last millennium, very docile and obedience. For centuries, they did not even challenge their foreign subjugation. Dayanand used ***HAVAN*** and related rituals to bring the Hindu masses publicly together at one place. He only opposed the extremes in idol worship.

Dayanand (1824-1883) was 33 when the 1857 Mutiny was set off. At that time he was very much near the hot fighting spots of Kanpur and Meerut. Surprisingly, no record is known of his participation in the Mutiny. I have raised this question several times with Arya Samaj scholars including Swami Deekshanand. After seeing how Indians in the British police and army were beating up and shooting at Indian mutineers, the young Dayanand must have gone deeper for reconstruction of the Hindu society. That is why the year 1858 is the beginning of the renaissance of modern Hindu India.

It is difficult to separate the life of Dayanand from his intellectual legacy. His genius was in the realization that social re-construction of Hindu Society and new intellectual traditions must go hand in hand. **Intellectual**

traditions are often nurtured in prosperous societies. In this regard, in the 19th century impoverished India, Dayanand's emphasis on the total development of body, mind and spirit was an historic anomaly. Coming from an insolvent state of Gujarat, but through the practice of ***HATH YOGA*** and dedicated scholarship, he transformed himself into a fearless champion of a new tradition. There are well known legends of his physical prowess and intellectual convictions.

Swami Dayanand used ***shastratha*** (public debates based on scriptures) on social issues and ills to his greatest advantage. They were no different from modern TV debates used in molding public opinions. Being an accomplished ***HATHA YOGI***, erudite scholar, and topped with magnetic physique, he psychologically overwhelmed his adversaries. Consequently, for the next 100 years, most Hindu orators and freedom fighters came from Arya Samaj. Besides histrionic skills and intellectual convictions, an orator must have physical courage which comes from the support from Hindus united under the banner of Arya Samaj for the first time.

Shortly after his intellectual victory tours, several princes of Rajasthan became his devotees. The masses always follow their kings. If there was one place where he was quickly idolized, it was Lahore, the capital of united Punjab, and a nerve center of India during freedom movement. Lala Lajpat Rai (1865-1928), the great freedom fighter and scholar, popularly known as the Lion of Punjab, met Swami Dayanand while he was a student. Young Lajpat Rai was active in a new Social Reform Movement in Punjab. This indicates that Swami Dayanand reached out the youth and intelligentsia of the states he visited. Also, Lala Hardayal (1884-1939), the founder of the Hindustan Gadar Party, was deeply influenced by the rationalism of Arya Samaj movement.

Swami Dayanand's approach of awakening the Hindu masses was a call of **Back to the Vedas**-declaring Vedas as the source of all knowledge and practices. He boldly opened the closed gates of the Vedas to every section of Hindu society and exhorted them to study the Vedas and listen to Vedic discourses. It was his highest stroke of social engineering. For centuries, large sections of Hindus were forbidden from Vedic knowledge which gradually led to their total fragmentation and weakening of Hindu society.

The Sanskrit word, Veda itself means knowledge. Dayanand realized that the Hindus too must have **one Book of Knowledge** for unity. **It was an act of great moral courage on his part to tell the masses to seek the Vedas over scores of other Hindu scriptures**. He was convinced that in order to bring unity, as he observed amongst the Muslims and Christians, one Hindu scripture must be singled out. The holy Gita carries the practical essence of the Vedas. Moreover, it is portable.

Because of the size of the Vedas, obscurity of Sanskrit language, and the lack of resources, the Vedas are still not publicly seen-like the Bible and Quran are. Swami Dayanand undertook the first authentic translation of the Rigveda. To the best of my knowledge, he was the one who said: ***WOH HINDU KAA GHAR NAHIN JIS GHAR MEIN VED NAHIN*** **(**It is not the home of a Hindu, if a Veda is not there**)**. I was around 20, when I actually saw a copy of a Veda for the first time in a Dewan Hall library of Swami Mama Ji. In 1975, I bought the centennial edition of all the four Vedas with Hindi translation.

In order to foster unity amongst the Hindus, Dayanand stressed the worship of formless God in public. He was different from the Muslims, who not only smashed the idols of Hindu gods and goddesses, but also demolished millions of Hindu temples in history. Swami Dayanand observed that the Hindus had stopped at the idols, whereas, the search of the Supreme was beyond the idols.

Unfortunately, even his ardent followers did not grasp the purpose of national unity behind his opposition to idol worship. Dayanand knew of terrible battles between the Hindu kingdoms of the southern states of India-one worshipping Vishnu and the other, Shiva! That weakened every fabric of political India. It is a kind of sign of progress amongst the Hindus in the USA, where a new temple tradition has been started by installing the idols of all major deities in one sanctorum.

During discourses and debates, Dayanand always referred to the Vedas to validate his arguments, calls and appeals for the eradication of social ills. He advocated universal education for the women and remarriage of the widows. His advocacy for equal status to the Hindu women in the society was far ahead of time. In the UK, the women got **limited voting** rights in 1918, and in the **US in 1920 after the 19th Amendment to the Constitution**. India was not free, but Dayanand was a free thinker. It is because of his groundwork that women in free India got equal voting privileges on the same day.

To unify the Hindus in public life, his biggest and boldest attack was on the eradication of untouchability and caste system based on birth. Arya Samaj continues to lead in this direction even to the present. Again and again, his mastery of the Vedas brought resounding victories while advocating such combustible issues. Think of it for a moment that even in today's Tamilnad, Hindu untouchables in the villages are treated the way it was 100 years ago all over India!

Swami Dayanand is the first champion of the so-called, Dalits, the exploited sections of Hindu society. Dr Bhimrao Ambedkar (1891-1956) came upon the scene much later during the freedom movement. I vividly remember in late 1940s, Swami Deekshanand, then known as Acharya Krishna, used to visit the colonies of the schedule castes and untouchables in Bathinda (BTI). He eventually won their hearts to have their children come to his newly started ***Gurukul*** on the outskirts of the town. Arya Samaj remained in the forefront of caste eradication till the 1960s, when the Dalits adopted a militant stance which has completely polarized their issues.

Swami Dayanand's emphasis on the Vedas was never to stop at the Vedas! Unfortunately, his overzealous followers have taken it literally. Most Hindus erroneously believe that the Vedas contain the recipes of all ills, solutions of all problems, and even the principles and formulas of all sciences and mathematics. **The Vedas only provide a template of a great mind rather than of unknown knowledge.**

On close examination, one discerns that Swami Dayanand sowed the seeds of several intellectual traditions both at the individual and institutional levels. Dayanand Anglo Vedic (DAV) institutions have set the highest standards in all aspects of education in the entire country. However, the ***gurukuls*** have taken a nosedive. Dayanand's model of ***gurukul*** was an amalgamation of ***shaastra*** (The knowledge of Hindu heritage), ***shastra*** (Weapon training to spread and defend Hindu beliefs and values) and ***shatru*** (Identification and elimination of the enemy within and without).

Presently, the Gurukul curriculum has been reduced to the rote-study of ***shaastra*** only. The ***gurukul*** graduates lack self-confidence, modern skills and are generally misfits in life. Dayanand had envisioned a revival of ***gurukul* of *Ramayana*** era, where Ram and his brothers went out to learn ***shaastra, shastra and shatru in the gurukul of Rishi (*Seer*) Vishwamitra.***

In Dec 2002, at the first anniversary celebrations of a new ***gurukul*** near Jarora village, 50 KM from Nanded in Maharashtra, I reminded and exhorted the audience on this historic mission of the ***Gurukuls***. Swami Deekshanand being its Chancellor was elated to hear my message. Later on, he told me that from now on the graduates of ***gurukuls*** will be called ***SANSKRTI YODHA*** [cultural warriors].

The Chapter Three of the ***Satyarthaprakash*** (means ***Light of Truth's Meaning***); a magnum opus of Swami Dayanand, delineates a plan and time taken to finish Vedic studies. To become a qualified scholar of Hindu religion, one would take about 15-20 years. That was a kind of Dayanand's model of an educational institution/gurukul, where open researches on religion, arts and science would take place.

Swami Dayanand was a prolific writer. His productivity is amazing when one finds him moving from one place to the other all the time. It was an era when India had no rail roads or public transportation. He is the author of ten books-including his greatest, the ***Satyarthaprakash***. He dictated this book to a disciple in three months! He was a rare combination of great intellect, social architect and nation builder.

His interaction with Europeans was very suave and political. Being fully aware of German support for the Indian nationalistic causes, he took full advantage of it. He was in communication with a German principal of a technical school to provide training to Indians in watch making. It was nearly 125 years ago, when he thought of transfer of technology. That correspondence is available in the archives of Arya Samaj. It clearly proves that Dayanand would have never restricted the present *Gurukul* curriculum to the memorization of the ***Shaastra*** only.

Dayanand's greatest intellectual coup was in using the word Arya in reference to India in his speeches and in the naming of Arya Samaj, a rejuvenation movement of the Hindus. Arya Samaj founded in 1875 in Bombay, is neither a card membership party, nor another creed or sect of the Hindus. For over 125 years, it has affected the lives of the Hindus of every stratum. It is a living tribute to the organizational acumen of Swami Dayanand.

The mid-19th century was a period when the colonization of Africa and Asia was at its zenith. The European scholars were hijacking the native cultures by denigrating and denouncing them. On realizing the wealth of knowledge in ancient Indian heritage, **the British intellectual conspiracy was to prove that the Aryans were not the natives of Aryavrat (India that Dayanand called), but were of European stock in central Asia etc**. Dayanand single handedly outclassed them and popularized the word Arya in every social and political arena.

On a personal note, I vividly remember all the kids of 'untouchables' attending BTI ***Gurukul*** being given the last names Arya after their first names. My first cousin, Kusum Lata **Arya** (1947-1997), an acclaimed female Vedic scholar of her times (from Jaipur), preferred Arya over Bhatnagar. Interestingly enough, Arya is gender neutral, and applies to males and females equally.

It is not out of place to add an example of Dayanand's organizational acumen when he essentially refused to merge the Arya Samaj movement with the Theosophical Society, also started in 1875. There is an extensive correspondence between Swami Dayanand and Madam Blavatsky and Leadbeater, the two founders of Theosophical Society. The Theosophical society was more into occult, and **Swami Dayanand knew that the Hindus were already steeped into social evils worse than occult.** Without offending them, he kept Arya Samaj focused on the Hindus, and their societal regeneration.

Swami Dayanand was a multidimensional intellectual who rose from the ashes of the failed 1857 Mutiny like a phoenix. Quickly he shot into the sky. As a meteor, he blazed many intellectual trails in the firmament that shall continue to inspire generations of Hindus.

Aug 06, 2004/Aug, 2013

PS: Excerpts of this article were presented at the 5th biennial conference (July 9-11, 2004) of the World Association of Vedic Studies (WAVES), held in Washington DC. The theme of the conference was **India's Intellectual Traditions in Global Context**.

COMMENTS

In many ways we are very similar, with two differences. What your Mamaji did was done by my mother. Second difference is Scientology, which in my view is ultimate knowledge on this planet, which claims Vedas as its ancestors. The condition of India, the poisoning of the psyche by idol worship, total disloyalty of Indians towards their fellow men (beating by Hindus in British Police), lack of logic in the lives of Indians, all these problems are my favorite. Sincerely, **Subhash Sood** (MD)

2. Dayanand took active part in Mutiny. Read his AUTOBIOGRAPHY, which he instructed to publish after his death. It was published. It contains all the details of his participation and British Suppression. **Subhash Sood**

I wrote: Thank for your two part comments! I did read the autobiography years ago, but obviously I missed and forgot it. Certainly, I shall check it up. Let me ask you how different, as person, I would have been had I read the book on dianetics 20 years ago?

Subhash: . . . . Dianetics is a tool and not indoctrination. It is based upon scientific observation and experiments. Important thing is to change oneself if one has a desire to change or if one has a goal. You may not have a goal to change. In that case you will not change. Dianetics does not hypnotize, it is enemy of hypnotism. Important thing is not to learn flute or Sitar. Important thing is to know about flute or Sitar. Book of Dianetics has sold over 20 million copies in 52 languages. This is no mean achievement. I feel you should at least have an idea what it is. I am engaged in translating this monumental book into EASY HINDI. If Dianetics is ushered in India, people will start thinking for themselves and stop being indoctrinated by parents and Gurus. You are a rather FREE BEING, you do not need Dianetics desperately, no doubt. But you can understand why Indians are the way they are.

Excellent article. It contains not only message of Arya Samaj to Hindus and provide them food for thought in shedding the socio-cultural evils and lethargy, has given a picture of this movement for reformation of Hindu social structure and firm linkage with the political realities of colonialism and independence movement and sacrifices of the open minded intellectuals. Cult culture to which the theosophical society was also wedded has been discarded all together, and perhaps its deep seededness could not make Arya Samaj a true movement beyond Punjab, Haryana and Western U.P. where idol worship in almost all formats is still dominant way of religious rituals. **Nigam**

Satish; Excellent article, I love history and India is emerging as such and economic and intellectual power that it is great to learn the background to it. Thx. **Steve** (Pastor)

Thanks, Satish. Very interesting. It took me back to my school days in Ajmer. After taking various exams for three years I got the diplomas of Siddhant Saroj, Siddhant Ratna & Siddhant Bhaskar. Didn't go for Siddhant Shastri. I wasn't aware of Dayanand's reference with 1857 . . . . Your mama was a privileged one. **Hemendra** (MD/Maine)

Thank you Bhatnagar Ji. Namaste. I have also read your article and I will use it in my next newsletter of Arya Prathinidi Sabha America published by me every month. **Kewal Ahluwalia** (NA Arya Samaj)

FLOW OF LIFE

Life is like a river. At times, even the calmest river flows over its banks sometimes. My professional life has been relatively in a steady state for the last 40 years. There have been a few bumps and periods of highs and lows. But the question of leaving the academic life has never arisen, though I have worked in seven different institutions. Lately, with expanding intellectual horizons, some new possibilities seem to be emerging.

On reading an announcement of a conference on ***The Intellectual Traditions of India in Global Context***, I put my head together. I hate going to the hoary Vedas for everything to be identified as glorious in India. Little is known of any national resurgence before or during the Mughal control of north India. The Muslims were ruthless in the decimation of the Hindu heritage. The Bhakti sects are not intellectual milestones, as they mortgage individual thinking process. Here, only one person thinks, and the rest blindly follow. It was Swami Dayanand (1824-1883) and his Arya Samaj movement that jolted the brain cells of the Hindus at large. Last month, I presented a paper on ***The Intellectual Traditions in Arya Samaj*** in the **WAVES** conference held in Washington DC area.

In the audience were the leaders of the ***Arya Pratinidhi Sabha***, America (the apex body of Arya Samaj in the US and Canada). They pressed me to attend its 14th annual convention in Toronto, Canada. I never attended one before, nor have been active in any organizational forum of Arya Samaj. Later on, they asked me to give a keynote address, ***Arya Samaj in North America***! As a toastmaster, I couldn't let this opportunity pass by me. Also, having been raised around Arya Samaj, I felt it obligatory. As a challenge of giving a direction, I accepted it.

For six days, I immersed myself into this topic. I essentially followed a recently imbibed ***mantra* of Care, Dare and Prepare** in Public Speaking. Yes, I care for Arya Samaj for its ideals of one formless God, one Book **(Gita/Veda),** and no birth-based castes. Dare is my hallmark. I can make insightful points that drive home into the hearts and minds. As a professor, going over-prepared for lectures has been my nature. For the three-day duration (Aug 20-22) of the conference, the compliments on my speech did not stop. One person told me how for the next two hours, he could not stop thinking!

That is where I stand. We all go for a second serving of a good dish. I tell my students, "If you have enjoyed my course, then you owe yourself one more course in the same area irrespective whether it is in your major or not." When I shared this experience with my younger daughter, she said, "Dad, don't become a Rajneesh!" Later on, I said, "Who wouldn't like to be Rajneesh's daughter?"

Do I feel like a re-born Arya Samaji? Well, during the flight back to Las Vegas, I read an autobiography of Swami Dayanand that was purchased from a gift-cum-exhibition corner at the convention. I had read it 25 years ago-so it was like a fresh reading. The flight time of five hours hardly hanged on me.

Aug 24, 2004/Oct, 2011

COMMENTS

I do not think you know much about Bhakti Movement. A person with limited historical background will call that movement a "movement without thinking process". As for Arya Samaj I think after it lost its giants it has also become an association of people who cannot think outside the box. Yes they have become ritualistic, as have other religions. Had this movement been as jolting as you claim to be then whole of Hindus or at least a majority would have joined it as they joined the freedom movement? Did not happen. The bottom line is that good and gifted leaders keep the movements vibrant and once that movement loses good leaders it becomes adyanamic and stops thinking. Can you name a current living famous Arya Samaji leader who is known very well in India for his intellect? I too studied in DAV College and was exposed to Arya Samaj in Punjab. **Rahul**

What a wonderful experience! Keep me posted . . . **Renee** Riendeau,

ARYA SAMAJ-CHAMPION OF WIDOWS

A question is raised how Arya Samaj has championed the cause of Hindu widows? Since the history of Arya Samaj, founded in 1875, is very short, one can back go to its source, the founder, Swami Dayanand Saraswati (1824-1883) He was absolutely a meteor, a visionary 100 years ahead of his time, and yet fully anchored in the social, political issues and events of his time.

Dayanand fully understood the British onslaught on Hindu heritage, customs, education, and beliefs. They did not want any repeat of the 1857 Rebellion that was ruthlessly quelled. Some punitive bills were subsequently introduced. I must admit not all social legislation-like abolition of ***sati*** (widow burning herself at the pyre of her dead husband) and ***thuggery*** (wayside robberies), were bad. Though the number of ***sati*** instances was insignificant, but its evil side had taken over the Hindus of Bengal in particular.

Calcutta was then the capital of British India, and Bengal was the first state to come under the British hegemony. Swami Dayanand witnessed socio-political conditions of the Hindus and particularly the plight of Hindu widows during his visit to Bengal at the invitation of Keshav Chandra, the leader of Brahmo Samaj, a Hindu reformation movement in Bengal.

Even after 100 years, the condition of Bengali Hindu widows is pitiable. Most are thrown out on the streets to beg, or pushed into the temples of Mathura to sing ***Bhajans*** (devotional songs) for Re 1.25 @ day, or forced into the ***sona gachii*** (land of gold), the brothel district of Calcutta. A celibate ***(balbrahamchari)*** Dayanand alone could be moved by such sights. Many Hindu intellectuals had turned to Christianity after Raja Ram Mohan Roy's leaning towards it. Incidentally, Raja was his Muslim title and it has no connection with any Hindu royalty.

The greatness of Swami Dayanand lies in his five star genius and scholarship. In reviving the Hindu intelligentsia, he led them to their very source, the Vedas. Not only for equal rights for men and women that he preached, but also when it came to remarriage, he unequivocally advocated equal rights to widows as were for the widowers. He knew of undeniable glorification of ***sati*** as mentioned and sanctioned in Hindu folklore. One has to read Chapter Four of his magnum opus, ***Satyarthaprakash*** (Light of the meaning of truth) for his stand that Arya Samaj took upon in later years. In support of remarriages of the widows, he has given copious references to the ***Vedas***, ***Manusmriti*** and other scriptures.

The other reason for his widow cause was that he noticed that in Islam the problem of widows is over-solved when Islam sanctions a man to have up to four wives. Amongst the Christians, widow problem is non-existent. It must have baffled Dayanand on seeing its scourge on the Hindu society that was bound to limp on one leg and weakening for centuries. A question that I pose today is that how far has the present Hindu society come to grip with this problem?

Oct 28, 2004/Sep, 2013

ARYA SAMAJ VIA NORTH AMERICA

BACKGROUND

This article essentially forms the keynote address that I delivered at the 14th annual convention of the Arya ***Pratinidhi Sabha*** (the apex body of Arya Samaj) of North America held in Toronto, Canada (August 20-22, 2004). It turned out to be a sequel to the paper, ***The Intellectual Traditions in Arya Samaj*** that was presented at the 5th biennial conference of the World Association of Vedic Studies (WAVES), an interdisciplinary organization-held on July 9-11, 2004 in Washington DC area. It was prompted by the conference theme, ***India's Intellectual Traditions In Contemporary Global Context.***

In the choice of the title, there seems to be a divine hand. It was amazing to realize that this is what I often asked from the late Swami Deekshanand Saraswati during my annual visits to India: **What is the relevance of Arya Samaj today?** Anal Madhu, my brother-in-law and a social thinker, often told him: "Arya Samaj has no mission in the present time, and should wind up its shop". Swami Mama Ji smilingly avoided arguing over it. All his life, he breathed the message of the Vedas, spread the work of Arya Samaj, and hailed the greatness of Swami Dayanand. Nevertheless, a good question eventually penetrates the consciousness at such a depth that the questioner alone has to find a satisfying answer from within.

I started off my speech by putting the following two questions to the audience and thematically came to them during the speech.

1. What was the mission of Arya Samaj when started in 1875?
2. What is **you**r identity? (***aapaki pehchan kya hai?)***

It was stressed upon the delegates to make a mental note of thoughts or whatever pops up in the minds.

Knowing one's identity is self-realization, and establishing one's identity in a society is to raise its global consciousness. That defines a great life style. Elaborating it, there is an individual component of identity-for example, at home; as a son, mother and grandfather etc. Also, individual identity is determined in an office, factory; or by a profession, and so on. However, all these individual identities pale into insignificance when one digs deep into the psyche to search for what drives one's moral conduct and ethical behavior. There is a definite identity that is capsulated by beliefs in God, divinity and associated public rituals.

I reminded that today that the Hindus are nearly at the crossroads at which Swami Dayanand found them in 1857. They were absolutely divided, emaciated and beaten up socially and politically. By joining with the British in police and army, the Hindus were beating up and killing their own brethren. The world knows 9/11, now called **The Attack on America**. But how many know of the 12/11 tragedy in the same year 2001, when the Indian Parliament was attacked. Its members escaped a massacre from the hands of Islamic terrorists? It was followed by Hindu tragedies of untold proportions at Godhara railway station and Akshardham Hindu Temple in Gandhi Nagar-both in the state of Gujarat. To make it real worse, there is little reporting in India on such events affecting the Hindus! In one case, Christian majority in the US won't let the world forget it, but in the other case, Hindu majority in India is powerless for lack of unity.

The 9/11 has united the Muslims more than ever before. The Christians are already organized. A couple of hate crimes against the Sikhs have forged a unity amongst them. But why the question of unity amongst the Hindus does not even arise? **The group identity is a function of individual identities in public and conversely**. It seems because of infinite diversity at the individual level the sum total of collective Hindu identity is ZERO! Does it amount to saying that there is no crystal clear identity of Hinduism? Paradoxically enough, the Christians, Muslims and Jews all know it well, who the Hindus are! I don't quibble about the terms-whether, it be called Hindu Dharma, Hindu religion, or Hinduism.

I shared a couple of common place incidents when the Hindus shirk in identifying themselves as Hindus. They often hide behind the national origin, Indians. No wonder a campaign was started to remind them: say proudly that you are a Hindu (***garve se kaho hum Hindu hain***). The question of individual identity is tied with the identity of Hindu religion. They are like two sides of the same coin.

The mission of Arya Samaj was and is the unification of the Hindus. It is paramount today. The Hindus today are no less divided. They have no political and social identity in India-their own country, or in their adopted countries! The call of the hour is to define it-first and foremost. In the ultimate analysis, the unity of the Hindus brings out an identity of the individuals and of Hindu religion. Thus the two questions raised are reduced to one!

ARYA SAMAJ IN NORTH AMERICA

The one formless God, one Book (***Gita/VEDA***), and no birth-based castes are **three great pillars** of Arya Samaj. They are the beacons of the present times. Every organization goes through a cycle of ups and downs. For a continual growth, an organization must have a nursery for replenishment and an infusion of new blood. Above all, it must have leaders and thinkers who can navigate the course of organization with the changing time and culture.

From the presence of only three children in the audience, it was obvious that the present activities of Arya Samaj are not in tune with the youth in North America. On the following Sunday, I watched a couple of hundred Sikh teenagers resting in front of Toronto City Hall after finishing a 125-mile relay race from Niagara Falls to Toronto. At least a thousand kids must have participated under the guidance of many adults. In the process, they raised $ 50,000 for the welfare of the overseas Sikh youth.

It is a big myth that the Hindus are the only ones who are born in Hindu families-a corollary of caste by birth-by vocation. Arya Samaj led in the re-conversion of the Hindus (Hindus to Muslims/Christians, and back to Hindu folds). But in the open society of North America, the non-Hindus should be invited and welcomed to the services and functions in Hindu places of worship. **Proselytization is a free market of life styles and beliefs.** It also works on the principle of the survival of the fittest. Hindus have encountered it internally since the advent of Buddhism and Jainism in India 2500 years ago.

The main objective of the formless worship of the Supreme is/was to loosen the iron grip of the idol worship from the minds. Inertia of body and mind had set in amongst the Hindus since the 10th century. Arya Samajis have never gone on a rampage of smashing the idols. However, some Arya Samajists have taken an extreme stance on it. I narrated a Delhi incident in the 1950s in which a renowned Arya Samaj scholar, when challenged by another scholar, publicly kicked a portrait of Swami Dayanand, and claiming to imply no insult to Dayanand!

The women folks and young ones by nature are inclined to idol worship at initial stages. It is time to open dialogue with every group of Hindus. Arya Samaj can take a role of religious leadership in a federation of different Hindu creeds and sects The Hindu youth in schools and colleges are not openly proud of their faith-particularly, when it comes to explaining and defending that every Hindu is free to worship his/her own god.

I shared with audience of my struggle in getting Hindu students form a Hindu Students Association on the university campus. The US universities encourage student associations based on national origins as well as on religions. The students can publicly discuss formless god on scientific grounds, and I boldly added that my god is mathematics!

The one great advantage that the Arya Samaj in North America has is of a common English language for communication. Swami Dayanand, being from Gujarat, struggled to learn Hindi. But, he advocated for Hindi to unify the Hindus. The story is different overseas. During the convention, it would remain an unforgettable sight to see the Hindus from Fiji, Guyana, Holland, Kenya, and Surinam enthusiastic about Arya Samaj. Without English, they would be left out while they form majority in the audience!

I also narrated the marriage of my younger daughter three months ago. The site chosen was a multi deity Hindu temple. It was performed in 45 minutes by my sister and her husband. Both are well-versed in the Vedic marriage through scholarship rather than by birth. Recitation of the ***Mantras*** in Sanskrit was followed by English translation.

CONCLUSION

I said that neither we have assembled here to speak out our bits and pieces and leave, nor to out-speak the others. Also, neither we are here to listen out any one, nor listen in everything. The purpose is to support and agree on a plan of action-be it minimal. That will be a measure of its success, when the convention meets next year.

In 1986, while visiting a library of rare manuscripts in Tanjore/India, I read the following observation in the preface of a diary of a British officer who lived in India while serving the East India Company in early 18th century: **The Muslims think and then act; Sikhs act and then think; Hindus think and think**.

Aug 27, 2004/Sep, 2013

COMMENTS

1. Dear Dr. Bhatnagar: Thanks. I think you articulated the ideas well. **BhuDev Sharma**

My dear Satish Ji, ***saprem namaste***. I am really thankful to you for coming to Toronto. It was a nice experience to meet you personally. My old days with Swami Ji are assets to me. I remember in 2001 February, after his recent bypass, he was taking rest at Santosh Raheja's house in Greater Kailash. In spite of doctor's orders, he took me to Sahibabad. He was very affectionate. Several times he asked me to be the trustee of ***sansthaan***, but I did not accept. I was telling every time may be next year. Now you are fully associated with Arya pratinidhi sabha. We need your guidance to run this organization. Regards, **GIRISH**

Dear Satish; Here is my reply to your current article; very important. I shall also reply to your previous articles in future. 1. Arya Samaj has no role today. I respect your Brother-in-law Anal in this matter 2.

Arya Samaj can have a role, if it improves the survival of individuals in clear-cut terms. 3. Arya Samaj had a role because 1. There was threat to Hindus. 2. There was the personality and spiritual power of Dayanand behind it. There is no clear-cut threat today, and there is no spiritual personality behind it. 4. Arya Samaj is no more than a vestige (spelling may be wrong) or ***kesh*** of a Sikh in USA. 5. Arya Samaj was created mainly on the basis of opposition to idol worship and Superstition. Its members are openly attending idol worship (most of them). Purpose is gone. 6. Arya Samaj had a hidden purpose to drive the British out of India. British are not in India now. 7. Arya Samaj has no purpose left. **Subhash Sood**

Sh. Satish ji Namaste. Hope you are fine there. Received your articles. They are really very nice. It's very nice to know that you are so devoted towards Arya Samaj. I am really sorry I am replying late. I will read your articles thoroughly and write you again. Thanks. **DK Shastri**.

SWAMI JI ON THE ANVIL

There is a big difference between theory and practice in sciences; a significant difference between one's beliefs and actions in social sciences, and world of a difference between preaching and practice in everyday life. Also, in every society, leaders are measured on a different yard stick than the commoners. That is what I thought of Swami Deekshanand Saraswati today, whom I have always addressed as Swami Mama Ji. It has been more than a year since he took ***Samadhi*** (giving up life in a self-control manner), but the memories of my association with him shall last forever. Off and on, I have been writing ***Reflections*** drawn from my associations with him and buried reminiscences.

All his life, Mama Ji breathed Vedic ***mantras***, tirelessly worked for the tenets of Arya Samaj, and hailed the glory of Swami Dayanand. He was over and above the infested politics of Arya Samaj. One of his social pastimes was to forge matrimonial alliances, though he himself never married (***bal-brhamchari***). In fact, I too enjoy this match making hobby, or call it a free social service. He found matches for his nieces, nephews, and kids of his admirers. Being on preaching circuits most of the time and all over the country, he met a lots of nice families. They trusted his judgment.

A couple of weeks ago, I received an invitation card from Uma, my first cousin, on the wedding of her only son. Uma was widowed nearly 20 years ago when her son, the only child, was hardly 4-5 years old. It must be pointed out that Uma and all her seven brothers and sisters have been extremely close to Swami Mama Ji since their childhood days. Being out of India for 36 years, my direct contact with Uma used to be only when she too would be in Sahibabad during my annual visits to Swami Mama Ji. After 50, the strength of a tie between people depends upon common ideas and ideals.

While looking at the invitation card, a thought surged out my mind: how come Swami Mama Ji neither encouraged Uma to get re-married nor found a match for her? He knew it that the cause of widow's remarriage was one of the great social uplift works that Swami Dayanand did for the

Hindu renaissance in the 19th century. The more I pondered, the more this treatment of Uma gnawed at me. Besides, none of her seven brothers and sisters, all very active in the affairs of Arya Samaj, ever pushed this idea of Uma's re-marriage into action. All this is true to the best of my knowledge.

How strong are certain social customs, or how hypocritical, the leaders are sometimes! Every Hindu will support re-marriage of widows, but few will apply this principle to their widowed sisters or mothers. Neither I am pointing to the evil of widow torture, nor assuming that every widow wants to re-marry. The focus is on intellectual weakness of Hindu leaders when it comes to upholding general social norms in their personal lives.

Oct 27, 2004

TEMPLE VERSUS TEMPLE!

Some events do not fade away even in their intensity. Of course, they are unforgettable. This one happened five weeks ago during our brief stay in Houston, Texas. It was Sunday morning and we decided to visit a newly opened (BAPS) Swaminarayan Temple nearby. BAPS standing for ***Bochasanwasi Shri Akshar Purushottam Swaminarayan Sanstha***, is a ***Bhakti*** (devotional) organization that has made international headlines by constructing scores of beautiful Hindu temples all over the world. I was taken in awe the moment I saw the Houston Temple from a distance. Its exterior is made of pure white Turkish limestone and the interior of pure white Italian marble.

Above all, it is made with pure white love of the devotees. It is a monument of BAPS' dedication to the Hindu heritage and its lineage of gurus. When I guessed its cost at $27 million, a manager said it was only $7 million! Labor being voluntary, its cost is not included. On reading its literature, I learnt that the organization traces itself back to1800. It was a time when every brand of European Christian mission was landing the west coast of India. The present Shri Pramukh Swami is the fifth Guru in succession. The temple sits along the bank of an aqueduct on a 20-acre lot. Besides the best India gift shop that I have seen, the temple complex has a large community center and a small ***gurukul*** (ancient Indian school).

The architecture of the temple simply takes the breath away. The carving on over 130 pillars and 70 sections of the ceiling is stunningly unique! Not even a square inch of pillar surface is left uncarved with a motif. There are high-tech illumination at night and other media projections.

Living in the post 9/11 period, I cautiously asked a volunteer, "Are there enough security measures to protect this temple from defacing, vandalism and acts of terrorism?" Any beautiful object attracts extreme social elements. One adores the beauty as divine, and some abhor it out of sheer jealousy. I said it was time that the Hindu temples start spreading total awareness and knowledge of ***Shastra*** (weaponry), ***Shaastra*** (scriptures) and ***Shatru*** (enemy) in their philosophy of thoughts and actions. If you cannot protect and fight for your beliefs, honor and treasures, then you simply do not deserve to hold them.

After a couple of hours, we set out to visit the Houston Arya Samaj Mandir (temple) about 10 miles away. I was briefly acquainted with its founder and the resident priest. It was not easy to locate the Mandir, though it was off a major street. Since I was still in the mental frame of Swaminarayan Temple, a comparison between the two was natural. The time being about 1 PM, the weekly Sunday ***HAVAN*** was over, but its organic fragrance was still in the air. The Mandir has a big hall for Sunday gatherings. It seems the building is minimally used during a week. In contrast with crowds in Swaminarayan Temple, we were the only visitors in the Mandir.

The Mandir also has a place for outdoor ***HAVAN*** congregation and a Montessori school for kids. Besides a few pictures of the early leaders of Arya Samaj, there was nothing touristy about the Mandir. To a large extent, the internal austerity of Arya Samaj mandirs is not very different from the interior of Muslin mosques. There are no idols in the mandirs either, as Arya Samaj shifted the tilt away from idol worship. However, in size and exteriors, the opulence of national mosques would outdo grandeur of any Hindu temple. The Houston Mandir is located on a 5-acre parcel. It is the result of one Mahajan family's generosity and devotion to the ideals of Arya Samaj which was founded in 1875 to rejuvenate the Hindu society.

A question arises; where does Arya Samaj stand in its mission of cleansing the Hindu religion? Today, the Arya Samajis are only exemplified by the ones who perform ***Havan*** every day and recite ***Sandhya*** (a collection of Vedic Mantras) twice a day. At one time, Arya Samaj spearheaded against social evils like dowry and Hindu caste system. No identifiable agenda is seen today. Arya Samaj lays out ten cardinal principles on personal beliefs and social conducts. They are as solid as the Ten Commandments in Christianity. But even great ideas need propagators.

However, my thoughts were buffeted between these two temples. The BAPS Temple is a Shiva dance in architecture. I share its heritage and its creation filled me with pride. The Arya Samaj Mandir is an integral part of my total being, as I grew up around Arya Samaj. Nonetheless, I don't feel upbeat about the future of Arya Samaj. No organization can sustain, flourish and expand without a clear mission consistent with the changing time. Most importantly, it needs periodic infusion of new members; men and women, young and old from other belief systems.

Such are my thoughts that seem to be clamoring for an outlet for this long. The websites www.baps.org and www.aryasamaj.com have more information on these temples.

Nov 09, 2004/Sep, 2013

COMMENTS

Dear Bhatnagar Sahib: I am in receipt of your latest "Reflections" on the Hindu religion. Incidentally, I have 105 of your 120 reflections as I have made a separate folder for them in my e-mail at the University.

I do not agree with you (as also on many other of your reflections) on the future of Hinduism which you say needs to be "protected" against terrorists and vandals, etc. since ". . . (If) you cannot protect and fight for your beliefs, honor and treasures, then you simply do not deserve to hold them." You also compare the ostentatious temple of the BAPS group and the abstentious Arya Samaj temples.-One of the secrets of the survival of Hinduism these last 5000+ years is its tolerance of the diversity of the way people are at liberty to practice this religion.

While the BAPS sect goes in for such grandiose and flamboyant displays of its devotion, it is these very practices that the Arya Samaj sect primarily was born against. And yet they are both as much a part of Hinduism as are the Ram Bhagats, the Shiv Bhagats, the Durga Bhagats, the Nagas, and the uncountable other sects that live and practice this religion in India and elsewhere. A religion that has survived the ravages of time and innumerable attempts to eradicate its very existence since times immemorial, I am sure, will survive into the future also. Sincerely, **Anand Bhatia**

Dear Bhai Sahib Ji! Namaskar (BUENOS DIAS) I am reading your e-mails. They really contain interesting topics. That way you are really a versatile writer with marvelous writing skills.

Your affectionate brother, **Sushil**

FACTORING PARENTAGE

The unusual birth conditions of human life are no different from those of plants that are seen to sprout from the tiny cracks of walls and rooftops of the old homes and public buildings. No one can deliberately plant them in such inaccessible places. And, yet they are known to survive and thrive.

The childhood period of Swami Mama Ji, known as Swami Deekshanand Saraswati (1918-2003), is relatively less known. He seldom talked about his boyhood. Any thing, not brought on the forefront of a mental ledge, is eventually erased. **However, a paradox is that if one consciously tries to forget it, then it makes deeper grooves in human memory disc**! Mama Ji remained silent on this segment of his life, and no one ever inquired it either.

Six months ago, it stuck me to uncover it. Generally, one assumes, for simplistic reasons, that greatness of an individual is directly related with parental genes or being born with silver spoons, etc. I wrote to another Mama (KS Bhatnagar), mother's first cousin, if he could recall some tidbits about Swami Mama Ji's early days. Actually, being the sons of two real brothers, they are first cousins too. As a sidebar note, KS Mama joined IAS and retired as secretary of Government of India. Today came his reply, and its reading moistened my eyes.

Swami Mama Ji's mother died when he was hardly a couple of years old. He had no other sibling. The father was a police inspector in Hissar, one of the largest districts in the united Punjab before India's partition in 1947. Having to deal with largely rough and tough criminals on a daily basis, his life style was not normal either. Particularly, when it came to the pleasures of the palate, he indulged in foods and drinks. The father too suddenly died in 1936. Mama Ji was then around 18 years of age.

Sometimes, a particular meeting with a person, listening to a sermon, song, or talk can change the entire course of life. Though KS Mama never saw Swami Mama Ji's parents, he had heard of his mother's gracious nature. May be, Swami Mama Ji inherited his tranquil composure from his mother. Genetically speaking too, its probability is higher when it comes from mother to son.

It is still not clear how he was raised from infancy to 8 years of age. His father being not short of resources may have hired a person to take care of the household and the infant son. No relative is known to have shared this responsibility. However, after the death of his father, father's older brother (my mother's father) took charge of him.

Still, he may have been shuttled back and forth from one place to the other. That, perhaps, built his self-confidence in travels, and it became a trademark for the rest of his life. During the last six months of life, he showed an incredible stamina for traveling hundreds of miles across several states by cars on unpaved roads and trains!

Swami Mama Ji was both street wise and book wise-a rare characteristic. He learnt as much from the people who came into his contact, as from the vast library of books he built in his Vedic Research Institute in Sahibabad. On the top of being very observant, he had a contemplative mind to ingest the facts. I often joked about his tunnel vision. But he could penetrate very far with it.

I really missed my annual meetings with him during the last three trips to India!

Jan 26, 2006/Oct, 2013

THE FIRST GURUKUL OF MAMA JI

One never forgets one's first love in any walk of life-be that first romance, first job, first vehicle, first home, first child, and so on. The gurukuls remained integral in the life of Mama Ji (Swami Deekshanand Saraswati) to the very End. The three day (Dec 27-29, 2002) annual celebration of a new gurukul near Jarora village in Nanded District (MS) was his last major gurukul function before Checking Out from the Planet Earth on May 15, 2003.

One of the early gurukuls in Punjab was founded in Bathinda (BTI) by Mahatma Hans Raj (MHR), one of the great stalwarts of the Arya Samaj movement in the united Punjab. Later on, an MHR Arya high school was started in his name in BTI. At one time, both institutions were at different outskirts of the city. The urban growth of BTI has devoured the MHR high school from all sides. However, the Gurukul still remains sufficiently away from the center of the population.

Since we all six brothers studied in MHR H/S, a short visit to this school is a must. I stop by the Gurukul only during a morning walk to the North end of the city. When Mama Ji decided to run a gurukul after his triumphant return from the Hyderabad ***satyagrah***, he was very keen about running this Gurukul. For some reasons, he could not get its control. He loved it for its location-being only 200 yards away from Sirhind canal. Mama Ji always envisioned a gurukul near the bank of a river. A few acres of land around it could be used for agriculture and to inculcate dignity of labor amongst its students, called ***brahamcharis***.

For years, a huge 30 ft. high gate was Gurukul's landmark entrance. It was only out of my instinctive measures of familiar distances that I recognized the site without its high gate, which was gone with its age. That was during my last Dec visit to BTI. In a small newer building, an elementary school was running. The old structure of the Gurukul was in a dilapidated condition with rooms set in a quadrangle with open space in the middle.

On watching me taking inspection of the old building, a woman walked over to greet me. I thought she was a lady Acharya of the Gurukul, like the first lady Principal of MHR H/S I had met earlier during this visit. It turned out that she and her husband only managed the place. I told her about my association with it and a little history of the place. She had no clue. I gave her some money for having a plaque plastered in a wall saying that the Gurukul was founded 100 years ago, in 1905 by MHR.

The land around had residential plots cut out indicating that a chunk of Gurukul land has been sold to the developers. It is equally possible that some land has been illegally encroached. I know this Gurukul would have been a showpiece, if Mama Ji had run it. Instead, he started his own gurukul in Ganesha Basti, BTI. He was eventfully pulled away to the Prabhat Ashram/Gurukul situated right on the bank of a canal near Modi Nagar, Meerut.

Just like most people these days go to the beaches for fun and voyeurism, Mama Ji always went to one the several gurukuls he patronized during his lifetime. There, he used to feel as if he was teleported to the ancient Vedic period of India!

Feb. 02, 2006/Oct, 2013

COMMENTS

Dear Shri Satish Ji Bhatnagar, Saprem Namaste! As we grow old, the nature of our memory take centre stage in our life and each episode moves like a movie film in our memory, unwinding one after the other incident, which may appear trivial to others but very important & dear to us; repetition-repeated reconstruction of the memory-strengthens it. It is this mastery of the ordinary moments that makes the fantastic stories of your memoirs.

I admire your reconstructing of the Gurukul & atmosphere around as was established by respected Mahatma Hansraj or your Swami MamaJi, your nostalgic visits to Gurukul, its 30 feet high entrance gate, a land mark, as well as of its present woman Administrator, Financial crunch & its present encroachments from all sides and above all, the thunderous welcome your MamaJi, our Swami Deekshanand Ji had received on his triumphant return from Hyderabad Satyagrah against that Worst Cruel Rule of Nizam of Hyderabad against Hindus only; amongst millions of suffering Hindus, Arya Samaj alone had the courage to fight & launch peaceful Satyagrah against all the atrocities of NIZAM.

As a staunch dedicated & selfless Arya Samaji, I draw a great pleasure to know the wonderful dedication of our earlier selfless people as your late respected MamaJi, Swami Deekshanandjee Saraswati was with his wonderful selfless deeds, like establishing Gurukuls, seats of Learning's, everywhere. Whatever he did was within the teachings of Arya Samaj & for Arya Samaj, which in real terms, were for entire humanity at large. In earlier days, people like your MamaJi, Swami Deekshanandjee Saraswati Maharaj used to give everything to Samaj, never expecting anything in return, neither name, nor money nor anything else.

Recently in our International Arya Mahasammelan at Gandhidham, I was amazed to observe the wonderfully simple & quiet looking Shri A K Kundra (of Florida, USA) proposing a few valuable remedies in smooth running of Arya Samajs in a professional manner and his ability to remember & sing the true patriotic GEET (song) of ". . . Rang de Besant Chula . . . Oye rang de Basanti Chola . . . ." before the entire gathering of students of Dayanand Hindi School at Mumbai, infusing in them the old Nationalist spirits. **SC Gupta**

I wrote: Thanks for your heartfelt outpouring! The holes and mismanagement are all due to lack of leadership in every Hindu organization! Furthermore, this lack of leadership is due to our Hindu faith putting premium on individual freedom! Consequently, we have been collectively failing and falling forever. It is time to shift our focus on working together, rather on the failings.

I appreciate your quick brief response and I fully endorse your views that it is time to shift our focus & work together. **S C Gupta**

LOSS OF THE FIFTH VEDA!

It was dusky and quiet in the backyard when I came out for bench press, my physical and meditative routine. While doing it, my eyes close by themselves. A question surfaced up about the Vedas, the ancient scriptures of India. How did this holy stream of Vedas stop at four? Chronologically speaking, out of the four Vedas, Rig Veda is the oldest and Atharva Veda, the youngest!

The essence of the Vedas lies in their meaning itself-that means knowledge. Thus the Vedas are akin with knowledge, but knowledge is not akin with the Vedas! Consequently, the Vedas are not fixed and bounded! Knowledge is expanding with universe. Therefore, the Vedas were never supposed to stop at four. Along the way, it is the Hindu intellect that stopped in its tracks.

The pertinent question is: how and when did it happen? That is one of the saddest chapters in Hindu history! It was eventually followed by a 1000-year subjugation of the most enlightened people in human history. When the very survival loses its zest, then who cares about the heritage?

Present Sanskrit scholars believe that it is nearly impossible to conceive and construct a ***mantra*** like the ones are there in the Vedas. Vinoba Bhave (1895-1982), a great ***rishi*** (a person who is both spiritual and intellectual) of the 20th century composed a couple of ***mantras*** that are considered of the Vedic caliber. The bottom line is that new knowledge only flourishes in a free and affluent society.

Fifteen years ago, a friend launched a Hindi magazine in the US, and its mission statement said that any material against the lofty traditions of Hindu culture won't be published. In a light and yet deeper vein, I wrote, "If persons like you and I can judge the lofty traditions of our heritage, then Hindus would not have suffered this terrible fate for a thousand years. Also, it is appalling, if there are no persons left to re-kindle the torch!"

While India is heralded as software giant, the Hindus are becoming more superstitious. They consult priests for any thing. Never in my memory, was astrology that much embedded in public life. My nephew in the US chose the time and date for his wife's C-delivery after consulting a priest. He never thanked the modern neonatal technology that saved his first child. A friend credits the recovery his wife's illness to his 40 consecutive visits to a temple rather than to the best medical treatment she received in a hospital. Increasingly, the Hindus are seen wearing a faded red-yellow thread (***kalava***) tied around their wrists for 24/7 divine protection!

Swami Dayanand (1824-83), the founder of Arya Samaj, stressed upon the study and understanding of the Vedas, but never worshipping them. Knowledge in the Vedas is in distilled form. During the dark period, intellect being less discriminating, the Hindus erroneously started believing that all past, present and future knowledge is locked up in the Vedas! Any time a great scientific theory or principle is reported in the media, it is unabashedly linked with the Vedas using a convoluted logic.

The Vedas only provide the templates of developed mind! Fortunately, some Hindus are waking up out of this long slumber. If the Nobel laureate Ravindra Nath Tagore (1861-1941) Tagore comes back to life today, then he would re-title his famous poem as ***Let My Hindu Brethren Awake***!

Sep 08, 2006/Sep, 2013

COMMENTS

Dear Shri Satish Ji, Saprem Namaste! GREAT! Exceedingly well thought of! Wonderful thinking of a Great Thinker like you only. Innovation is the mother of all progress: with your such extra-ordinary, revolutionary explicit views even on our Vedas, we have to think afresh, do a lot of perpetual research & bring out some new things of our own, instead of confining ourselves to Just FOUR. Our four Vedas as you very rightly said, these could be templates for our guidance only; tremendous work has yet to be done on them, or on the basis of our guidelines: Vedas, which are certainly NOT for worshipping but for imparting knowledge to us.

Yes, you are RIGHT that the superstitions have spread in every walks of our HINDU Life. I agree that perhaps it is getting worse than what it was in Maharishi Dayanand's days. All such people suffer immensely owing to their superstitions, still they do not learn any lessons. I believe, MEDIA is to blame for its spread and the so called Babas, Gurus & 100's of self-Styled Bhagwaans, Pirs, Fakirs who squeeze & cheat ordinary people, I mean people with No Commonsense. Media & Politicians are playing their dirtiest game in this respect.

It is our luck that we are born in Arya Samaji Families, but others are NOT so lucky & hence they continue to believe what their parents, relatives believe or what they see in their own community. As an Arya Samaji, every day is a lucky & Good day, whether for a child birth or for marriage or anything, even the day of death is equally lucky as on that day the soul, leaves this old & diseased body & travels to meet the Supreme Eternal Body. Lastly, I would love to be favoured with your learned thoughts & views through such mails again. Sincerely yours, **Satish/Mumbai**.

Have you heard the ***subhashita: Bharat panchamo Veda*** . . . . ***jamata dashamo graha***?

There Mahabharata contains history of India and its Chandravanshi rulers, and also ***shrimad bhagavt*** Gita is considered 5th Veda. Incidentally, Mahabharata was written by the same person who wrote other 4 Vedas, namely Bhagavan Vedavyasa. **Bhanu Joshi**

ARYA *SAMAJANI,* USHA SHARMA

The US is the biggest magnet in the world for a person with any vision, dream, and entrepreneurial spirit. It is safe to say that even if you have not succeeded anywhere else, you can still succeed in USA. Also, if you cannot succeed in USA, then you cannot succeed anywhere! That is why USA is called a land of opportunities. More importantly, the US provides a level field for any enterprise one wants to engage in.

Two days ago, I spoke with Usha Sharma after many years. I have 'known' her for 40 years, but our paths never crossed more than a couple of times. It was a sequel of coincidences that I came to know of her visiting USA. Recently, Harish Chandra, a Hindu preacher of its own kind was introduced to me. During his 2-month USA-Canada visit, we had several communications. It was during our last exchange that he mentioned Mauritius and Arya Samaj. Usha Sharma was a natural corollary, as she is pretty well known in Mauritius for her Arya Samaj work in the community.

Usha Sharma's husband Jaidev Shastri is the first disciple of Swami Deekshanand Saraswati. I met Jaidev each time I was with Swami MamaJi during my India visits. Both husband and wife have served the Hindu communities in Greater Delhi for years. Usha comes from a family of dedicated Hindu leaders. After PhD in Sanskrit from Delhi University, she taught in Delhi, and later on, in Mauritius. During her stay in Mauritius and Kenya for 6-7 years, she also authored a number of books and booklets. Incidentally, both husband and wife have been leading a ***Vanprastha*** (dedicated to public service) life.

The strength of a community lies in its unity, and the unifying force of any community is generally in the hands of its religious leaders. They alone have the ability of bringing the masses and intelligentsia of all rank and files together at one place. Honoring them is our cultural obligation. While giving her an idea of **Post 9/11 USA**, I apprised her that whereas, the Christians and Muslims are far more than united, but the US Hindus remain marginalized. It is a challenge for any Hindu preacher to first bring the Hindus out collectively, and then convince them to drink water from the same fountain.

Arya Samaj, Oakland is first to host Usha Sharma. Besides Hindi and Sanskrit, she is fluent in several other Indian languages, and well versed in performing Vedic ***Sanskars*** (religious ceremonies). This being her first visit to USA, she is here through the end of March. Female preachers are very rare even in India. But they are not unexpected in the realm of Arya Samaj, as its founder, Swami Dayanand Saraswati (1824-1883) advocated for women's emancipation and education far more than any other social reformer of India.

Jan 02, 2007

THE FLYING DNAs OF DEEKSHANAND

Ideas fly off the mind by their nature. Yet, it is amazing to observe them landing on. The flying seeds of certain plants and trees are well understood. In a backyard or front yard, particularly during spring time, some natural growth cracks out of the ground. However, one wonders at the established plants 'visiting' out homes, though never seeded or planted. In our backyard, a corner protects an oleander found nowhere in the neighborhood, as it is banned due to its pollen allergies. I won't pull it out, and a few more like it are around. I enjoy watching them. It is like providing shelter to the abandoned pets!

The sprouts of the flying ideas belong to a different dimension. Basically it means that someone was touched by your life, and you are not even aware of this chemistry. Of course, the lives of Buddha, Jesus, Socrates and Alexander inspire people all the time. These thoughts recently coalesced around Swami Deekshanand Saraswati (1918-2003) who was a towering figure of Arya Samaj due to his large physique and dedicated work. He was a lifelong celibate and an ordained ***SANYASI***. He greatly influenced people who were close to him by blood or closeness of ideas.

He truly 'lived' in Vedic era of his imagination and only spread its word. With the sharpness of his mind and power of oratory, he was the most sought out speaker of Arya Samaj. Towards the end, he got into publishing of the classic books, and also guided a few scholars in their researches. But his heart always longed to travel and preach. For charging his batteries, he had a few favorite places: the ashrams in Dina Nagar and Dehradoon, and Gautam Nagar gurukul in Delhi. Once his research Institute was established in Sahibabad, he camped there most of the time. I often teased him for not grooming even a single preacher of a caliber!

In life, individual influence seeps mysteriously into society, as water permeates the ground differently. During the last few months in the US, I got to know three persons off the main stream of Deekshanand. One is Usha Sharma whose husband was his first disciple. At the time of her marriage, she had not even passed high school. The irony of her life is that Deekshanand did not encourage her to study! But the magnetic field around him was so powerful that she followed her dreams all the way to earn a doctorate and became a leading female preacher of Arya Samaj.

The second person is Harish Chandra. His professional story is unbelievable. After studying engineering at IIT Kanpur and doing PhD from Princeton, he switched gears of his life to become a fulltime Hindu preacher. He immersed into the study of Sanskrit, religion and philosophy, and during this course, he came in contact with Deekshanand.

The third one is Anand Suman Singh, converted from Islam at the age of 20. For the last 25 years, he has been spreading Hinduism amongst the Muslims converted to Islam-one or two generations ago. He met Deekshanand in Dehradoon. Deekshanand was never active in the conversion of the Muslins, though he brought many outcaste Hindus into the main stream of Hinduism. In fact, he started this work of social integration in Bathinda when he opened his own gurukul in 1945. In ultimate overview, there is no one blue print of leaving legacy.

May 19, 2007/Sep, 2013

COMMENTS

Namaste: This was very timely when his "***punya-tithi***" is around. He was a tower figure-both in size and content. I vividly remember hearing his speech (indeed, 2 speeches) in April 2000 at Dinanagar on the occasion of Swami Sarvanandaji's centenary. Actually, we would have expected that Swami Deekshanand will also have his centenary, but both passed away almost close to each other.

While in Las Vegas, I would probably like to integrate his words in one of my talks. He was an expert in symbolism like Swami Samarpananandji. His contributions were enormous, including the books he published. His passing away looked as if the "***jnana-varsha***" (in the form of the books that he was bringing out) had suddenly stopped. You and members of the extended family should be proud of him; every Aryan should be.

The other day, somebody in the Arya Samaj online group enquired about Swamiji's book collection. When the extended family meets next then under your guidance a suitable action may be taken about his personal book collection. There is a momentum among a youth group in Delhi that may be able to buy it out and then make it reachable on internet for everybody. Warm regards, = **Harish Chandra**

TIME TO EMBRACE THE CONVERTS

I was visiting India when the married Hindu Deputy Chief Minister of Haryana state and divorced (?) Hindu Assistant General of Haryana both converted to Islam in order to legalize their adulterous relationship. Because of their high profiles, romance, jealousies and politics, it was reported even in the English dailies of Oman. Some thirty years ago, famous actor Dharmendra was the first married celebrity to convert to Islam for marrying with actress Hema Malini.

The masses follow what their leaders do. Such high-profiled conversion stories give credibility to Islam at the cost of a few weak tenets in Hinduism and adverse laws against it. It is unimaginable that the Hindu Marriage Act (essentially one woman for one man and vice versa) passed in Indian Parliament in 1951 without much discussion, just because Prime Minister Nehru pushed it. If one spouse has no objection in the other spouse marrying again, then Hindu Marriage Act needs to be amended accordingly.

Well, my focus is on something else. A colleague told me, while teaching in Yemen, he was offered the most beautiful girl of the village, if converted to Islam. When he told the community elder, that he was over 55 and was happily married, the village elder responded, "What age has to do with it, you can have the pleasures of a young wife too." Incentives to convert to Islam have been known for ages. There are specials funds for it. Apart from material benefits, the entire Muslim community protects a new convert. That is why it is dangerous to reject Islam and embrace other religion, particularly, Hinduism, a religion not of the west.

This reminds me of Anand Suman Singh of Dehradoon (DDN) who faced scores of attacks on his life after he walked out of Islam. He was then in his 20's, college graduate, politically active, and came from a very wealthy family. He approached Swami Deekshanand Saraswati for 'conversion' to Hinduism. Gradually, not overnight, he was initiated into Vedic heritage. Deekshanand got him married with the daughter of an Arya Samaj preacher, and financially assisted him in buying a house.

It has been more than 25 years, but the Hindus in his neighborhood still have not embraced him in their folds. My acquaintance with Anand is based upon our common ideas that crossed in e-mails. During my 2007 visit to DDN, it was amazing to find out that he lived hardly 300 yards away from my sister-in-law's house, where I had stayed. Their boys have known each other since childhood!

There is a contrast of the Hindus towards a Hindu, converted from Islam. Soon after my DDN visit, a family celebration was to take place at my sister-in-law's house. I suggested her to invite Anand & family. No guessing, as to what happened. It reflects a failure of present state of Hinduism. Neither, the Hindus are willing to change the Hindu Marriage Act, nor embrace a few brave Muslims who put their lives at stake for Hinduism. The least Hindus can do is to socialize with them. Hinduism is projected by our attitudes and behaviors towards the followers of other creeds. Religions are open markets of ideas and ideologies too, and Hindus must not lose their share of it. Buy out the others with love or/and money.

Feb 16, 2009 (Oman)

BHARAT *DARSHAN* IN LAS VEGAS

This is perhaps the first time in life (of nearly 70 years!) that I have visited a Hindu temple twice within a week. Neither of my parents regularly went to temples, nor did they urge their kids. This was partly because my hometown, Bathinda, didn't have even a single Hindu temple of stature before independence. Also, the Hindus were historically forced to satisfy this collective identity by setting up makeshift temple-ttes in the closets of their homes.

Today, I really felt pulled by the spiritual gravity of the devotees in the Hindu Temple of Las Vegas. According to the Indian calendar, this lunar month is the beginning of major Hindus festivals. Last Sunday was the first day of Lord Ganesh's Birthday celebrations that goes on for 7-10 days. Ganesh is the only recognizable Hindu god all over the world. Amongst the non-Hindus, He is known as the elephant god for the obvious reason.

While sitting on the carpet, great panorama of Indian culture started flashing through my mind. Having lived in Las Vegas since 1974, I have come to know lots of people by names or faces. In the sanctorum, I recognized the Hindus from the states of Maharashtra, Gujarat, Bengal, Bihar, Karnataka, Tamilnad, Kerala, Rajasthan, Andhra, MP, UP and Punjab. Since the Temple's opening in 2001, the first priest hired has been from AP. However, he is now adept in performing the associated rituals of any regional festival or prayer. The scant numbers of Hindus from other states reflect smaller sizes of those communities. Also, Las Vegas is a true 24-hour town-one has no idea of its pace unless one lives here.

The Hindu temple life in India is either non-existent, or has no semblance to the one witnessed in Las Vegas. Even in most major temples of India visited so far, the devotees seem homogeneously drawn from only 2-3 neighboring states. There is a general touch of Hindu parochialism in India versus symbolic 'nationalism' in Las Vegas. Let me add, at the outset, that so far, Las Vegas has only one major Hindu temple. In major US cities where there are a couple of temples, one is often identified as south Indian, the other, north Indian etc. After all, the Hindus cannot simply break away from their mental conditioning of centuries-be that religious, political, or educational. Nevertheless, the overpowering influence of US life styles is of unifying the Hindus living here.

The ceremonies lasted for two solid hours, followed by the ***shradha bhoj***, sanctified luncheon sponsored by the ***Marathi Mandal***. It is not easy to sit through the ceremonies at one spot. The purpose of my temple visits is also to develop and nurture acquaintances. I have long 'graduated' from the weekend ***khanas*** (dinners and drinks) popular amongst Indians. Temple atmosphere is meant to mix spirituality with sociability. It is an ideal place for small talk-of course, outside the deity hall. At times, one of the randomly tossed-out seeds of brief encounters sprout roots into good relationships.

I really admire the vision and philanthropy of a few Hindu leaders that one of the most beautiful temples became a reality in Las Vegas. It took six years, and is the only public place in Las Vegas where the Hindus are collectively seen. "I have been in Las Vegas for eight years," On hearing such a remark during run-ins, I respond by telling of my being in LV for 20-35 years. This dialog has taken place numerous times in stores and malls.

One may observe that a Christian is a member of a new community the day he/she arrives there, as through the old church, advance information is conveyed to a church in a new place. A Muslim or Sikh remains stranger for a week at most, as by going to the Friday Namaz in a mosque. or to a Sunday ***sangat*** in a gurdwara, the person no longer remains a stranger. The Jews and the Mormons are far more tightly organized in their faiths.

In every Hindu temple, all the rituals are performed in Vedic Sanskrit, different from the one taught in schools and colleges. Thus, Sanskrit is the unifying language of the Hindus. However, this is paradoxical since few western educated Hindus understand it, including even most temple priests. With eighteen official languages of India, ceremonies performed in any one of them may offend others. No one objects to the usage of Sanskrit in the temples, since it is the bedrock of ancient Indian heritage.

Moreover, the ***rishis***, great sages of ancient India, used Sanskrit for 'locking up' the Vedas, Upanishads, Ramayana and Mahabharata, and other scriptures from the ravages of time and adulteration by lesser men in course of time. They had perfected a science of sounds and meanings of Sanskrit words for material manifestations. Material changes are supposedly triggered by vibrations through perfect enunciation of special mantras. **It is a science of *lifetrons*, the subtlest 'particles' of nascent thoughts**. This science is lost, but it lives incognito in the faith of the Hindus, in the power of the Vedic Mantras. Despite 1000 years of subjugation of the Hindus and their forced conversions to Islam and Christianity, Sanskrit remains a divine language for the Hindus.

Ganesh ***Chaturthi*** buffeted my thoughts on the long history of Hindu religious festivals. Adi Shankaracharya (788-820 AD) established four ***muths*** (seats of Hindu religion) in four corners of India. The traditions dictate that the Hindus, say of from South India, must go for their pilgrimages to the other three ***muths*** for bonding with people from the rest of India.

In modern times, a similar religio-political approach was taken by freedom fighters Bal Gangadhar Tilak (1856-1920), the author of magnum opus, ***The Secrets of the Gita*** (written in prison) and Bipin Chandra Pal (1858-1932), founder of the ***Bande Matram***. They infused life into the dying embers of Hindu psyche. During the 1890s, Hindu leaders, like Tilak in Western India and Pal in the Eastern India, exhorted the Hindus to come out publicly and celebrate Ganesh ***Chaturthi*** and ***Dussehra*/** ***Durga Pooja*** for 7-10 days.

The idea of public processions was to awaken courage and bring unity amongst the Hindus for political freedom. The Hindus then were worst off of all the religious believers, in their own homeland! How better off they are in present India is a matter of debate too. In the current political system of India, the religious minorities are more dominant in India, the land of Hindu majority. In the world, it is an unprecedented state of affairs for 80 % ethnic majority.

At Ganesh ***visarjan***, the concluding ceremony of the celebration, an esteemed reader of my ***Reflections*** remarked, "You must write on what is going on." "You have rightly read my mind, as it is already working on it!" I said. It was a time well spent and invested.

Aug 29, 2009

COMMENTS

You have excelled in the form of self-depreciation by twisting facts. **Rahul (**MBBS)

Satish Ji**,** I have enjoyed reading your observations as an Arya Samaji visiting the Hindu temple in Las Vegas. The truth of the matter is that no Arya Samaj temple can compete with the hustle and bustle of the traditional Hindu temples. There is always a gaiety in those temples with ringing of bells and puja and aartis. It offers a free flowing country fair scene with an aura of spirituality. And of course these temples are the best places of socializing no different than the churches, gurdwaras or mosques even if a little more boisterous!

But anyway, it is interesting to read your observations from Las Vegas. Next time when we visit LV, I will love to visit the temple. How far is it from the center of the LV? Normally when we go to the LV, we rent a car to go on a trip to Zion Canyon or Grand Canyon. We do not enjoy or participate in gambling dens but instead may attend some shows and visit the sites. In future, we may add the Hindu Temple to our visit. With best wishes and regards, Vijay **Kapoor**

3. Satish, Great work. Thanks. **Gopal** (MD)

4. Hi Satish: Greetings! This is a good 'reflection.' You have provided a historical dimension as also the need for unification of the divergent Hindu stratifications. Sometimes I wonder at the sense of religiosity we experience here in the U.S.; I believe the other religious believers

have their institutionalized principles unlike Hindus who in India didn't experience such oneness as we do in the U.S. **Moorty**

5. Dear Sir; . . . . The article on temple visit was very fascinating for me too. This was the only time we did not visit the Vegas temple . . . In our child hood, 'GOOD Christians do not go for movies and do not become artists, etc.' Those who did were looked down upon. The famous play back singer YESUDAS of GORI THREA GAON MERA PYRA was sneered upon by the VEDIC EXPONENETS OF CLASSICAL music when he enrolled in the music college. He has confessed later that the comment from one of his teachers "FROM WHERE SANGEETAM WILL COME TO A CHRISTIAN hurt him and enthused him to take it as challenge to show that music will come to a Christian. To sum up even as a child, the temples fascinated me.

Now coming to one point in your reflections. Scholars in their zest to keep the sanctity of VEDAS and Scriptures have LOCKED UP Sanskrit and thus they have KILLED THE LANGUAGE. There can never be sanctity by locking up and they undid the language. The slokas and hymns recited at the marriage ceremonies (Hindu marriages) of both sons not a word anybody around the yonder understood. But the boys having been brought up outside Kerala, the Christian ceremonies were done not even in Malayalam but in English. This kind of flexibility and adaptability help the church to grow and shield fragmentation to a great extent in Christianity.

My eldest grandson Akash when he came to India was 3. He is used to temple in Vegas and as they came from Ahmadabad must have visited some temples there with his maternal grandparents. While in Kerala he was shown churches and he was asked to pray. He knows his share of Jesus too. He stood at the portals of the church, folded his hands, closed his eyes and PRAYED. His prayer was "Jesus, give me Prasad "What a blend of secularism! Or was it me the small girl in me craving for Prasad in a church after 55 years or so. **Valsa Abraham**.

SEEING NONE OR MANY?!

"Satish Ji, I have enjoyed reading your observations as an Arya Samaji visiting the Hindu temple in Las Vegas. The truth of the matter is that no Arya Samaj temple can compete with the hustle and bustle of the traditional Hindu temples. There is always a gaiety in those temples with ringing of bells and puja and aartis. It offers a free flowing country fair scene with an aura of spirituality. And, of course these temples are the best places of socializing no different than the churches, gurdwaras or mosques even if a little more boisterous! But anyway, it is interesting to read your observations from Las Vegas. Next time when we visit LV, I will love to visit the temple. How far is it from the center of the LV? . . . In future, we may add the Hindu Temple to our visit . . ."

It has been a week since I read this quote in an e-mail from Vijay Kapur, a college Professor. Sometimes, a ***Reflection*** gets going after its core has jelled in my mind. There seems to be two messages. One: how come, as an Arya Samaji, I visited a Hindu Temple, where various gods and goddesses are worshipped? Two: if I, as an Arya Samaji, go to such temples, then the other Arya Samajis may have no qualms either. The debate on idol worship, amongst the Hindus, has been intense since Swami Dayanand Saraswati founded Arya Samaj in 1875. Many leaders have been sucked into it. **The debate has only divided the divided Hindus-thus has been weakening the Hindu society**. As a kid, studying in Arya High School, Bathinda, I used to think that either Arya Samajis are not Hindus, or the ***Sanatanis*** are not!

Personally, the conflict of formlessness and formfullness of the Supreme Power is resolved in my mind. In ultimate analysis, **Supreme is the Limit of one's experiential projections**. In life, you get what you put in, whether it is a set of beliefs or/and actions. Call it the ***Law of Karma*** of materialism/spirituality, or a version of ***Newton' Third Law of Motion*** or ***Advaitya***, the ***Principle of Non-duality*** of Adi Shankaracharya, or ***Unified Field Theory*** of modern physics.

However, any one's realization can never take others to their destinations of realization. Truth is a pathless path, according to J. Krishnamurti, and Gandhi realized-Truth is God. Formlessness (***Nirguna***) is a distillation of formfullness (***Saguna***), and formfullness is temporal manifestations of formlessness. These rarified spiritual thoughts have provided me both fulfillment and escape at individual levels. But for centuries, neither they have collectively turned the Hindus into rulers of their own lands, nor helped them live in dignity and honor with Hindu identity. That is where Arya Samaj provided glue to the disintegrated Hindu society in the 20th century.

It is befitting here to share some Arya Samaji links of my family going back to 125 years. My maternal grandfather was one of the very firsts converted to Arya Samaj, when Swami Dayanand, like a meteor, extensively toured pre-independence Punjab in late 1870s. Naturally, all the four maternal uncles including Swami Deekshanand Saraswati (1918-2003) were steeped into Arya Samaj of freedom fighters' era. Om/Aum is the Vedic name of the formless God, according to Arya Samaj. **Note, Om/Aum has a form!**

Since my maternal grandmother died before my mother was married, I have no knowledge of her religious disposition. However, my mother and her three younger sisters continued to believe in various Hindu deities in their households. Every year, on ***Janamashtami***, the birthday of Lord Krishna, we, as kids, enthusiastically helped mother in transforming a room into Bal (Baby) Krishna Temple that the outsiders used to envy. My maternal grandfather and an uncle, living in the same 'mansion', known as ***Bal Niwas***, never ever stopped mother from performing and celebrating these rites.

Generally, the females, and men of malleable tendencies gravitate towards concrete forms for support in their lives. This debate has a parallel culture in mathematics-the source of my bread and butter for nearly 50 years! Mathematics is popularly 'divided' into pure and applied mathematics like physics-theoretical and experimental. It took me 40 years to realize that sooner or later all topics of pure mathematics, known for their dizzying abstractions, find applications in real life problems. Thus they become a part of applied mathematics. Cursorily, the reason women do not pursue higher mathematics has nothing to do with intelligence. It is their innate inclination towards materialistic and sensory points of views on life. If this were not the case, the babies won't be born out of love, and then raised tenderly from infancy into adulthood.

Well, if the Arya Samjis, for the sake of, say, family peace, can tolerate forms of idol worships in their homes, then why not in Hindu community at large-if, for example, a Hindu colleagues, neighbor, relative, or friend goes to a temple? Let me emphasize that the **Ten Principles of Arya Samaj** are highly commendable, and comparable with the **Ten Commandments of the Bible** from perspective on social cohesion.

Incidentally, Vijay Kapur and I have common roots in Kurukshetra region, which is historically famous for the site of Lord Krishna's ***Gita,*** the discourses He gave to Arjun on the battles of life before the epic Mahabharata war. Even most armchair historians do not know that all the three Battles, of so called, Panipat (1526, 1556 and 1761) were fought in the same geographical region, known Kurukshetra in the BC era.

Also, the communal riots of 1947, after the partition of India, turned Kurukshetra into the largest transition refugee camp in the world. Arya Samaj brought in all the resources for helping out the displaced persons. That is why most post-independence Indian leaders in politics and education came out of these displaced Arya Samajis. Thank you Vijay, for stirring up these memories! You will be more than welcomed in Las Vegas next time.

Sep 04, 2009

COMMENTS

Hinduism is a league of religious beliefs under one big umbrella. One belief might meet need of one but not the other. Then one can always graduate to next level of belief and still remains a Hindu. So it for the onlooker to decide if he is seeing one or seeing too many. **Rahul**

. . . . For me '***nirgun***' meditation is as valid as is '***sagun***'. Everyone has their own mental, intellectual and spiritual limitations. My analogy goes with the usage of computer. A majority needs icons to operate a computer and then there may be computer wizards who grasp the computer language and codes who work with key board without the need for icon shapes and forms. Just as computer potency is not wrapped up in the icons but is in the hard disk and circuits within the box, but nevertheless icons play a vital role in facilitating to access the 'hidden' power imbedded in a computer. The role of icons as the facilitators and the computing power within the chips embedded in a computer must not be confused.

In fact, I consider forms and shapes as fundamental to communication. The civilization as we know it would have never advanced without forms and shapes. After all thoughts, numbers and languages are abstract. Had we not given shapes to numbers 1-2-3 etc. we would not have advanced the knowledge of math. The same applies to languages. We give shaped to sounds. Inherently sounds do not dictate what form should be given to an alphabet. For sake of mass communication the alphabet forms have evolved in different languages. Thoughts within a brain are all abstract. However, we need to give those thoughts linguistic forms to communicate . . . . In fact, the monotheistic religions, Judaism, Christianity and Islam have rendered a great disservice by demonizing the 'idols'.

So getting back to Arya Samaj's '***nirgun***' and '***sagun***' debate, I see enlightenment in the Bhagvad Gita's message that both methods are valid so long the worshippers understand 'what' and 'why' of the modalities.

I personably do not think that any number of Hindus confuse Ganesh or Shiva or Durga with God or Goddess. The frequently used word for idols or '***murti***' is '***nimit***'. In fact the ritual of ***'pran-pratishth***a' is like a child selecting a doll from a toy store and adapting that 'particular' doll as her own as if giving 'pran-pratishtha' to that specific doll. From that point on a child develops an emotional relationship with that 'specific' doll in contrast to all others. For that child all 'other dolls' are just dolls (toys) to be looked at without emotional bearings.

The very process of ***'pran-pratishtha'*** signifies that the worshipper is infusing value in that particular form for his/her own comfort, convenience and devotion. That inherently an 'idol' is simply a clay form until it is infused with value by a devotee. A devotee is empowered to choose a tool of devotion. (For more than last ten years, I have been volunteering to teach "Hinduism, Buddhism and Monotheism" to the classes of seniors (over 50 years old) organized under the tutelage of the Burlington County College. Above is an illustration of how I approach the inevitable subject of Hindu Gods and Goddesses vs. the Biblical condemnation of the 'idol worships'.) **Vijay Kapoor**

CHIVALERY IN ARYA SAMAJ

The September issue of the ***Navrang Times***, a bilingual monthly publication from Detroit, Michigan, has two readable articles. One is on a very close connection between ***Shaheed*** (martyr) Bhagat Singh (1907-31) and the main historic branch of Arya Samaj in Kolkata. The other lists great Arya Samajis who laid their lives for Hinduism and India's freedom.

It raises two important questions of historic significance. **Number One**: How did Bhagat Singh, an ardent Sikh, got involved with Arya Samaj, a 19th century reformist movement of Hinduism? **Number Two**: What and where does lie the magic of Arya Samaj which transformed such a great number of Hindus into eminent scholars, orators, public servants, and fierce freedom fighters in a short span of its founding since 1875? They are important questions for the new generations of Hindus to be aware of, so that the missions of Arya Samaj are rightly served in the 21st century.

These questions first stirred my mind six years ago, while researching in the Gadar Memorial Center, San Francisco. The Gadar Movement was a brainchild of a few Indian revolutionaries in the US-including an activist intellectual, Lala Hardayal Mathur (1884-1939), who, in his youth, was influenced by Arya Samaj. The Gadar Movement was headquartered in San Francisco, with a sole mission of armed liberation of India.

In the 1930s, a British CID (Central Investigation Department) report clearly established that nearly 100% of the Hindu freedom fighters were influenced by Arya Samaj. It puzzled them as to how the Arya Samaj teachings were instilling courage and unity amongst the Hindus, known for centuries, by and large, as most divided and most timid people in India. The British knew the Sikhs as a martial race, so the Sikh militancy never surprised them. In fact, the Sikhs wanted to regain the Sikh Empire, stretching beyond present Pakistan, that the British had illegally and forcefully annexed ten years after the death of Maharaja Ranjit Singh in 1839. A lesson of history is that the masses, at large, are quickly transformed by voluntary adoption of a new religion, ideology, or an inspiring leadership.

For finding answers to these questions, I went back to the basics. While teaching a mathematical topic, I often tell my students, 'that whenever you have absolutely no ideas about solving a problem, then go to the definitions involved in that problem'. On my part, I studied the **Ten Principles of Arya Samaj** (Just Google/Yahoo Arya Samaj) carefully and early crusades of its founder, Swami Dayanand Saraswati (1824-1883). At times, I felt like writing a ***Reflection*** on each principle both from their historical context and present relevance.

The first five principles of Arya Samaj are focused upon the **individual development**, but the last five are on the **collective development** of the community. That is a fundamental departure from the self-centric practice of Hinduism of the last millennium. Arya Samaj temples are designated places for Sunday morning prayers. There are regular dues for the members, like in a club. The funds are used for new Arya Samaj temples and community welfare.

Swami Dayanand saw that the Muslims worshipped together every Friday, and Sikhs and Christians on Sundays. **Collective prayers alone bring unity at the deepest levels**. No research is known to have been undertaken into any organized aspect of Hindu religion before 1000 AD, but certainly, it had been completely absent till the advent of Swami Dayanand. That explains why the Hindus of Arya Samaj leanings became courageous and patriotic. **Furthermore, chivalry attracts chivalrous people**.

Giving a personal touch to this scenario, Lahore, now in Pakistan, was one of the strongholds of the freedom fighters in North India, as Kolkata was in the East. My father-in-law (1912-1990) grew up in the narrows alleys of Guru Dutt or Bhatti ***mohallah*** (neighborhood), one of Lahore's many ***mohallahs*** perfect for organizing, conspiring, and for hiding when chased by police. Once I probed him, as to how come he did not join a gang of rebels that he personally knew since his boyhood. He could not answer. But I knew in his heart of heart, he had missed an historic moment in his life. Partly, because, he never came into contact with Lahore Arya Samaj. That association would have unlocked his individual courage into greater collective courage and national pride. I told my wife that she missed being known as the daughter of a freedom fighter!

Though, the Hindu community was relatively poor and most divided of all other communities, yet even the modest buildings of Arya Samaj-temples, schools and colleges-played crucial roles in supporting the freedom fighters in all respects, besides providing the nationalistic education. With India's independence as their only purpose in life, the freedom fighters did not care for caste or religion. That is how and why Bhagat Singh was twice secretly sheltered and supported by Arya Samaj in Kolkata-once before and once after the assassination of the British officer, Sanders, in 1928. Incidentally, the most popular picture of clean shaven Bhagat Singh wearing an English felt hat was taken during his brief stay in Kolkata.

With emphasis on the formlessness of The Supreme, there are no idols for worship in Arya Samaj temples. However, the Sunday prayer gatherings in the temples are usually followed by broad updates on community affairs. It keeps the community into the mainstream of life and helps in the development of histrionic and leadership skills. Again, Swami Dayanand seems to have borrowed this practice from the Christians, Muslims, and the Sikhs. Historically, Arya Samaj is characterized by public debates in the backdrop of the Vedas (***Shastrartha***) for settling and sorting out any differences-religious, political, or social.

The unity of minds comes only when people assemble at one place on a regular basis. It never takes place by only wishing for it, or working alone. However, willingness to sacrifice a bit of personal interest for the larger welfare of the community, sits at the heart of Hindu unity today. It is clearly enshrined in one of the ten principles of Arya Samaj.

Sep 24, 2009

COMMENTS

Namaste Satish, Thank you very much. Bhai Parmanand, a colleague of Bhagat Singh and another Sikh, started Arya Samaj in Guyana around 1910. I prepared a History of Arya Samaj in Guyana. My father did all the research and I prepared on my computer. It will be printed shortly in Canada. Kind Regards**, Vijay**

Hi, Uncle! The magic of Arya Samaj in this day and age is the celebration of the feeling without too much ritual, keeping the meaning intact. The weddings are explained in detail in a language of your choice and when one commits to a vow, they know what they are getting into.

The ceremony following a death truly celebrates the person's life-they sing the departed person's favorite songs and give the gathering the time and space to grieve the person without the pressure of the rituals. Some death related rituals I have seen (non-Arya Samaj) are pretty brutal and insensitive to the family left behind.

If I had seen an Arya Samaj wedding before, I would have chosen it over any other any day-truly spiritual and Hindu without ritualistic religion. Now that I know what the death ceremony can be like, have made my wishes known on this one! :-Do keep writing. Warm regards, **Sangitha**

Bhatnagar Sahib: You have a good exposition of the second question. Regarding the first question: what is the evidence that Bhagat Singh was close to Arya Samaj, and what is the explanation? By the way, the more I learn about real Sikh teachings, the more I feel Arya Samaj is closer to Sikhism than to the ritual laden "Hinduism" both past and present. **Ved P. Sharma**

Hi Satish: Greetings! Yes, this 'reflection' is both informative and enlightening laced with historical connections. A good piece for everybody. **Moorty**

THE EVE OF ENERGY IMPLOSION

Maha Shivratri (MS) means the Great Night of (Lord) ***Shiv/Shiva***. It is one of the few holy days of the Hindus that are observed in every state of India, and equally amongst the Hindu Diaspora. Moreover, any variation in celebration is only in form, but not in substance. For me, the 2010 MS became a bit more memorable. Last year, I was in Oman during MS. Oman is an Islamic Sultanate, where any private or public Hindu religious functions, except inside one or two government approved Hindu temples, are essentially prohibited. It seems that this year, I made it up by attending the MS festivities in two different places.

From 7-8:30 PM, I was in the grand Hindu Temple of Las Vegas. Nearly 300 people peaked during the rounds of ***Abhishek*** ceremony. ***Abhishek*** is a ritual of bathing ***Shiv Lingam*** with ***panchamrit*** that consists of five ingredients-milk, yogurt, honey, brown sugar and ghee (clarified butter) in specific proportions. The devotees takes turns, one at a time, by holding ***panchamrit*** in a conch shell and then let it flow out in a fine stream at the topmost point of the ***Shiv Lingam***. This action is synchronized with the priest reciting the appropriate Vedic ***mantras***, the 'charged' syllables. Of course, the devotee must have his/her inner state of mind aligned with the act.

The temple visit provides an opportunity to meet and greet friends and make new ones. I am not one of the temple worshippers who rush into a temple, do the obeisance and prostrations, and then run out of the temple within 20-30 minutes. The present-day Hindus, for many reasons, are not used to the culture of visiting their temples, as the Sikhs, Christians and Muslims are to their respective places of worship.

It is particularly true of the Hindus living in or coming from north-west India. For instance, my hometown, Bathinda, did not have even a single Hindu Temple of any stature before independence, though 150+ year old gurdwara, church and masjid are still standing there. Though the Hindus are living in a freest and most open US society, yet regular temple visits are not integral to their lives. There is no collective identity of the US

Hindus, though they number nearly 2 million. Consequently, they are totally marginalized in the US public life.

I don't recall anything from my childhood that we as kids specifically looked forward to on MS. Of course, mother had another excuse to observe a fast-that generally meant eating a little bit of uncommon foods not taken routinely. I first 'heard' of spiritual powers of MS, when I met an ancient history research scholar in Kurukshetra University during 1966-67. Apart from strict fasting, he meditated, like a 'Hath Yogi' for hours to supposedly effect material changes in the environment around him. I never witnessed anything tangible, but during our conversations, his faith and conviction in MS used to make him look unworldly. On my part, I continued to lay all my experiences at the altar steps of mathematics and sciences.

From 9 PM to 1 AM, I was at the ***Amritam***, as named the house of my sister, Madhu. It is also an official address of the American Hindu Association. Madhu and my brother-in-law, Anal, known as Baba, meticulously organized the MS function, as a 24-hour ***Shiva*** prayer with ***Abhishek*** every three hours. At the Temple, the ceremonies lasted for four hours. After the ***charnamrit*** runs over ***Shiva Lingam***, it is generally collected and distributed as ***prasad***, ***Shiva*** offering, amongst the devotees. I am told that at the Temple nearly 100 gallons of ***charnamirt*** was simply plugged into a sewer drain. However, at the ***Amritam***, every single drop of delicious ***charnamrit*** was devotedly taken away for consumption.

I also noticed a marked difference in the atmosphere at these places. In the Temple, a pall of fear and some anticipation was spread over the devotees, who were all Hindus from nearly every state of India. Not even a single non-Hindu was noticed in the congregation. However, at the ***Amritam***, nearly 50% were white/Caucasian Americans. After the Bhinderwala militant movement in Punjab, started in the 1970s, even the clean shaven Sikhs have stopped joining in worships at the Hindu temples. Organized religions and politics always go like hands in gloves.

The ***Shiva Lingam*** is a metaphor of 'spiritual' energy-to be released, whether symbolically in an orgasmic coitus or in a nuclear fission. The outburst of any uncontrolled energy can spell total destruction. It has to be channeled. The repetition of ***abhishek*** ritual is a symbolic exercise in cooling and channeling the energy. The all-night observance reminds the individuals to harness all explosive energies including sexual and spiritual for the benefit of the community at large.

At the ***Amritam***, some white ***Shiva*** devotees sang variations of ***Om Namah Shivaye mantra***. It set in a meditative mood. Lord ***Shiva***, also as known as ***Natraj***, is the primordial source of all dances-which are seen as manifestations in the entire universe. Thus, the devotees danced in a group on a ***Shiva*** song-taken from International Peace Dances. Some played flute and drums. Dance and music being spontaneous, it engendered an exalting mood at midnight hours.

Having been raised and schooled in the Arya Samaj culture, the MS celebrations reminded me of a young boy Mool Shankar of 10 to13 years in age. He was struck by a bolt of inner realization on MS. Later on, he came to be known as Swami Dayanand Saraswati (1824-1883). He singlehandedly galvanized the doormat Hindu society of the 19th century and in 1875 founded Arya Samaj, a reformist movement of Hinduism.

The beauty of human life is that no one can get his/her enlightenment by following forever in the footsteps of any particular enlightened soul. "Truth is a pathless path", as J. Krishnamurti (1895-1986) famously put it. With such thoughts fermenting my mind, I got up and drove back home, as the ***Shivratri*** was closing in at the break of the dawn.

Feb 14, 2010

COMMENTS

Dear Bhai Shri Satishji, Saprem Namaste! I must congratulate you for writing such a wonderful account of the celebrations of Maha Shivratri at the Hindu temple of Las Vegas. You write so well in a free flowing lively manner that it entrails its readers as if he/ she himself / herself is present & watching all the live celebrations by one's own eyes. I have no hesitation to accept that I have become your fan, though we have had a very brief introduction at Tampa, Florida in 2004 during Arya Pratinidhi Sabha of America's Maha Sammelan by Shri Girish Ji.
Sincerely Yours, **Satish Chandra Gupta** (Mumbai industrialist)

This Shivratri is a unique holy-day! As per Raam Navami or Janamashtami which are birth day celebrations of Lord Raam and Krishna, Shivratri is not a birthday of any avataar. Shiva is considered as ***ajanma*** which is never born, so no birthday. Shiva is ***mahadev***-means the bigger god. When we say god, we look up and ***deva*** which has its own light are the stars or suns. Our earth is biggest for us but Jupiter is 1000 times bigger than earth and called Guru. Sun is 1000 times bigger than Jupiter and is the owner of entire solar system, the ***deva***, then more than a million times bigger than sun is ***mahadeva***, the black hole of our Milky Way galaxy. Imagine Shiva (the black hole that no one can see) and surrounded by Ganga (***AAkash Ganga*** or Milky Way. This is the end of everything or death or ***kaal*** which eats everything. All big stars rush into it, an ultimate end. And on his head a moon (Chandra mauli!)-now compare this picture with our devotee drinking bhang as prasad on Shivratri, **Joshi** (PhD Chemist)

Hi Satish: Reading your reflection made me vicariously experience the Maha Shivratri. Occasionally as a child I used to participate in 'fasting' and 'jagaranam', i.e. not sleeping all night by playing games, reading, and reciting the mantras. Thank you for opening my eyes. **Moorty** (Retd English Professor)

5. Dear Sir, I have read your wonderful reflection on Maha Shivratri (MS). It's very impressive. Go on Posting. With my best regards. **Ashit Chakrovarty** (Statistics Professor)

MOORATI POOJA AND *MOORAT POOJA*

"Today, in the 125-year history of Arya Samaj, and after Swami Dayanand, no other person, besides Swami Shradhanand, is there who fully dedicated himself to the service of his religion, society and nation." This quote is translated from an article in Hindi, on Swami Shradhanand (1856-1926), by Bhavanilal Bharatiya, a well-known Hindu scholar. Written ten years ago, it is re-published in the Dec 2010 issue of the ***Navanrang Times*** (Year 18, Vol 09)-sponsored by the Arya Pratinidhi Sabha America. Its reading jolted my train of thoughts, and triggered dormant memories of my conversations with Swami Deekshanand Saraswati (1918-2003). During annual visits to India, our discourses on various topics included downward spiraling of Hindu leadership in every facet of life-going on for a millennium.

However, at age 70+, a solid reason of Hindu leadership crisis bolted in my mind. It is mainly the result of ***Moorat Pooja*** (leader worship). If people are polled on a couple of popular traits of Arya Samajis, then regular ***havan*** and opposition to ***Moorti Pooja*** (idol worship) would stand out. I have heard read stories of numerous Arya Samaj leaders falling into the trap of ***Moorti Pooja*** in practice. They never took into consideration the social and political conditions leading up to the 19th century India, when Swami Dayanand crusaded against ***Moorti Pooja***. Dayanand historically understood-how the Hindus when attacked, instead of picking up arms and fight varied foreign invaders, gathered in front of their deities in homes and temples, and prayed for protection, as if their gods would break out of the idols and fight for them. Consequently, Hindus were butchered like sheep, and subjugated in their own homeland for centuries.

This mindset has hardly changed in the last ten centuries. During natural disasters and severe illnesses, the Hindus are seen to start prayer-thons, rather investing money, time and energy in finding cures. The Hindi movies thrive in perpetuating these scenarios. However, it reminds me of wounded Lakshman in Ramayana. Raam did not use his divine powers to heal Lakshman. Instead, he dispatched Hanuman to bring over the best physician and medicines/***Sanjivani***. Dayanand only wanted the Hindus to get away from their suicidal faith in ***Moorti Pooja***. He did not break any idols, nor ever advocated it.

In their frenzied opposition to ***Moorti Pooja***, the Arya Samajis shifted the focus on their leaders to the extent that adoration has reached a level of ***Moorat Pooja***-from sycophancy to genuine praise. There is a remarkable connection between ***Moorti*** and ***Moorat***. With emotions, people can breathe 'their own life' into anything-including pets, rocks and idols. It is perfectly OK to focus on higher mental states through any medium. It is no different, say, from an alcoholic drink taken by most poets, painters, writers, thinkers, mendicants for mental concentration.

There is some justification of ***Moorti***, **provided it is eventually transcended**. While staring a ***Moorti*** is OK, but staring a person, for too long, is offensive. For a moment, stare turns a living into non-living. ***Moorat*** turns into ***Moorti***, and vice-versa-what an insight! This has been going on for the last 1000 years. By excessive adoration and adulation, the Hindus reduce their leaders puerile, and eventually they do it to themselves. It is incestuous-emotionally, intellectually and spiritually.

A personal touch is in order here. Swami Deekshanand was my maternal uncle, and known as Acharya Krishna before initiating into ***Sanyas*** in 1975. Because of this association, I personally knew all the Arya Samaj leaders of the 1950-70 era-namely, Ram Gopal Shalwale, Prakash Veer Shastri, Pandit Buddha Dev, Shiv Kumar Shastri, Om Prakash Tyagi, Acharya Bhagwan Dev-to name a few. Arya Samaj Dewan Hall was the center of activities, and I often stayed with Mama Ji in a solitary ***vihar*** on the topmost floor. Yes, I alone addressed him as Mama Ji all through his life. Towards the end, he also introduced me to his visitors likewise. Naturally, I saw too much of foot-touching obeisance, open patronizing and condescending behaviors coming down from the seniors and going down to juniors. In the present US society, these attitudes are anathema to mutually enriching relationships.

It is worth noting that Dayanand and Gandhi were not inspired by any big or small Dayanand or Gandhi. This is a point of renaissance in Hindu society. The bottom line is-understand ***Moorti Pooja***, but condemn ***Moorat Pooja***. It is bothersome that the progeny of great Swami

Dayanand is being reduced to Lilliputians on the world stage. During my flights of inspiration, I often ask: why, another Dayanand or bigger Dayanand is not born in free India or free-er USA? Extending it to minus infinity in past-why there is no fifth Ved, and why the end of the Vedas, ***Vedanta*** is 'intellectually celebrated', and why Dayanand's crusade 'Back to the Vedas, has screeched down to a halt?? Many Sanskrit scholars, including Pandit Buddha Dev and Vinoba Bhave, have stated that no human being can compose a ***mantra*** matching a Vedic ***mantra***! It has put a capstone on Hindu intelligence and imagination.

During this tsunami of thoughts, I had to go to a dental office, where the following pointers rushed up: The Hindus need to have some structure for nourishing leadership. It is time to foster budding Hindu leadership in homes, offices, and elsewhere. Are Hindus too reverential, obedient towards their parents, teachers, bosses, and leaders? We put false covers over the faults of our leaders, while suppressing our aspirations and ambitions in childhood and youth.

Two years ago, I started a research project with my students on specifically finding aberrations, idiosyncrasies and fault lines in the lives of legendary mathematicians. This ongoing project is called ***Dark Spots on the Moons***. It is based upon the whole idea that even the geniuses have gigantic flaws. If a young person is awed by a genius in a field, then he/she cannot excel his/her mentor in life. This project grounds the heroes in a grand scheme of life. It is never intended to undermine their international achievements. Incidentally, the students enjoy this exercise while changing their lives subtly.

On the ever-changing missions of Arya Samaj, Dayanand's work on untouchability has hardly scratched the surface of Hindu consciousness in the last 100 years. After all, it goes back in ancient times. In the present democratic set up in India, the caste system has raised its dreaded heads. Before partition, in the 1930s, the Muslims demanded that 50% of the untouchables be officially 'transferred' to Islam! Yes, Buddhist, Christians, Muslims and Sikhs have always embraced the untouchables. But the Hindus, by and large, have not yet opened their hearts. Dayanand's work for women's emancipation has only gone too far in the direction of female modeling, but the bride burning, female infanticide and abortions of female fetus are greater challenges for the Arya Samaj today.

Above all, Dayanand ignited the flame of Hindu nationalism in India. The time has come to make it global. Even after 60+ years of independence, the Hindu missionaries are hardly significant in numbers and they have not extended their hands to the Hindu Diaspora. If organized, it has tremendous economic potential too. Granted, private resources were lacking soon after India's independence but now a few Hindus are listed amongst the top billionaires of the world.

As a matter of fact, DAV Education Society can easily start colleges and universities in the entire region of Southeast Asia. During my visits to Cambodia, Indonesia, Malaysia and Thailand, the local people feel forgotten by the Hindus from India. In the aftermath **9/11 Attack on America** and far too many attacks in India by the Islamic terrorists, it is pertinent to review Hinduism globally in every aspect of national life including politics. For drawing new blood from Hindu youth and other religions, it is time to open new doors.

Dec 23, 2010/June, 2011

MEMORIES VIA DEEKSHANAND

A week ago, I learnt about the death of Shyama at age 73. She is the daughter of my mother's younger sister. Incidentally, both sisters were married at the same time, and delivered their first-born daughters, only days apart. Yes, I did have an older sister, named Nirmala, who died of complications of dysentery, at one year of age. But Shyama lived on to see her great grandkids. I met her only three times in life, and the last one was in the summer of 1996 when she was also visiting the Vedic Research Institute of Swami Deekshanand Saraswati, located in Sahibabad, near Delhi. Her husband supervised the expansion and construction of new stories of the institute during 1995-96.

Being mother's younger brother, I continued to address Swami Deekshanand as Mama Ji even after his taking ***sanyaas***. Spending a few days with him was the highlight of my annual visits to India. I browsed Vedic literature in his extensive personal library and discussed various topics. His conversations with his visitors of all shades were no less interesting. Of course, he always welcomed his 'erstwhile' nephews and nieces, since he had restricted his home visits after ***sanyaas***.

During one of these stay, out of nowhere, Shyama asked me, something like, "Satish, have you eaten beef?" Without asking her business, context, or motives behind this question, I simply answered it in the affirmative. Beef truly defines American cuisine and culture. As a matter of fact, on arrival at the US airport after returning from an overseas trip, the first thing I eat is a Big Mac of McDonald's, if insight. In India, for Hindus' reverence for cows, cow slaughter is mostly prohibited, and the sale of beef restricted. I never had an occasion to eat beef in India, nor would do it for the sentiments of friends and relatives.

Years later, I came to know that my beef-eating response was stretched and twisted in all possible manners amongst all the ten cousins from the side of this aunt. It reached to a point of 'pressurizing' Swami Mama Ji of having no ties with me and the Institute. Without being aware of this campaign against, on my part, whenever, Mama Ji would discuss possible names for the trustees, I declined it on the grounds that full justice could be done from the US.

A point of this reminiscence is that memories and legacies of a departed one are meaningful and meaningless, or call it by any pair of opposites. In Shyama's case, her husband was depressed, when I called him. Each one of her children would remember her differently, and so would her neighbors and friends. Swami Mama Ji never brought up this beef incident with me. He knew the answer, as I gave him one in 1966, when point blank, he asked about my drinking alcohol on a specific occasion. Ironically, it was set off by Kusum, Shyama's younger sister! Occasionally, I would tell him that if human characters are to be measured by food habits-like that of meat and alcohol, then most Buddhists, Sikhs, Muslims, Christians and Jews are going to be condemned. His silent response said it all.

Over the years, Mama Ji groomed Kusum, as his successor of the Institute. Being a renowned ***sanyaasi***, he stayed away from legal ownership of any property. Institute was essentially Kusum's. She, following the footsteps of Mama Ji, never married, and turned out to be an eminent Vedic scholar of India. For preserving some cultural continuity, she adopted a daughter of Shyama, and raised and educated her in Vedic environment. But the youth revolted, married, and moved away. Tragically, Kusum suddenly died of cancer in 1997.

Kusum's death broke down Swami Mama Ji's plans and dreams on Vedic research and its propagation. Often, I suggested him to sell off the Institute and endow Rs 25 lakhs each in four Vedic research professorships in the universities of Gurukul Kangri, Delhi, Banaras and Rohtak.

On a momentous day of Jan 01, 2003, when I asked to take his 'last leave', he literally sat me and Rajan, Shyama's first younger brother, down on a sofa. It was at Rajan's residence in Mumbai. He instructed us to consult with each other on the affairs of the Institute. Mama Ji was prophetic, as he died four months later. Rajan is a trustee chairman of the Institute.

It is a common destiny of men that any collection of ideas or things would meet their own destiny. Legally, Shyama's daughter inherited everything belonging to Kusum. What is then a memory and legacy?! It is all very subjective.

Jan 04, 2011

COMMENTS

I am sorry to learn about the death of your cousin. Please accept my condolences.

As for killing cows here are some ***shalokas*** from Vedas. It has nothing to do with being condemned. It is an identity of Hindus, as the 5 Ks are to the Sikhs and not eating pork is to the Muslims. It is an identity which lots of Hindus lose when they leave India. Good or bad, it for an individual to decide, but one does loose the moral force of being a community leader or reformer.

Ghrtam duhaanaamaditim janaayaagne maa himsiheeh. Yajurveda 13.49
Do not kill cows and bulls who always deserve to be protected.
Aare gohaa nrhaa vadho vo astu. Rig-Veda 7.56.17
In Rig-Veda cow slaughter has been declared a heinous crime equivalent to human murder and it has been said that those who commits this crime should be punished.
Sooyavasaad bhagavatee hi bhooyaa atho vayam bhagvantah syaama Addhi trnamaghnye vishwadaaneem piba shuddhamudakamaacharantee
Rig-Veda 1.164.40 or Atharv 7.73.11 or Atharv 9.10.20
The Aghnya cows-which are not to be killed under any circumstances, may keep themselves healthy by use of pure water and green grass, so that we may be endowed with virtues, knowledge and wealth.

What is memory and legacy eventually? All illusions!! **Abraham**

PROFESSIONAL PREACHERS OF HINDUISM

"***WHERE ARE ARYA SAMAJ MISSIONARIES*** . . . ?," thus wrote Dr. Deen B. Chandora in an online discussion on a burning Hindu religious issue. Dr Chandora, a Hindu leader, founded the first Vedic Center in Greater Atlanta area 20 years ago. However, his remark ignited my mind, as it touched a dormant nerve. It goes back to 60 years, when I was a student in Mahatma Hans Raj Arya High School, Bathinda. The school was often visited by Hindu preachers-including Acharya Krishna, known as Swami Deekshanand Saraswati (1918-2003) after the ***sanyaas***. I continued to address him as Mama Ji, as he was my mother's younger brother.

As an established Arya Samaj preacher, Deekshanand was allotted a small quarter in Arya Samaj Dewan Hall, one of the most prominent centers of Arya Samaj in Delhi region. I visited him at least once a year. Over a period of time, he earned his reputation for being the most sought-out preacher of Vedic knowledge in India and overseas. He was a unique combination of a tall physique, visionary looks, Vedic scholarship, and to top it all, he had great oratorical skills.

Deekshanand never married. However, I still remember the names of famous preachers-like, Om Prakash Tyagi and Shiv Kumar Shastri who lived with their families in Dewan Hall. I was friendly with their kids. Now here is a **Preacher Shocker #1**. Neither, these prominent Arya Samaj preachers wanted their kids to follow them as preachers, nor were the kids proud of their fathers making living as preachers. Nevertheless, I was completely unaware of the status of preachers in other religions. I was too young to connect different dots.

Around 1985, Swami Deekshanand moved to his Ashram type Vedic Research Institute that he established in Sahibabad, 10 miles away from Delhi. During annual visits to India, spending a week with him was like an intellectual pilgrimage to ancient Hindu heritage. The institute grew along with his stature.

However, it was strange to me when he stopped talking and doing anything for the new preachers of Arya Samaj. Instead, he envisioned the institute as a residential research center in Vedic studies. A couple of times, I told him point-blank, "You have earned all your name and fame in India and abroad as a phenomenon preacher alone, so you owe a debt to professional Arya Samaj preaching. Train at least one preacher before you Check Out from Planet Earth." But it never registered on his mind. He would simply smile it away. Also, there was no one else, in his inner most circles, who thought like me. This is the **Preacher Shocker #2**.

In comparison with hierarchical religious preachers in Christianity, Islam, Mormonism, and Sikhism, living Hindu preachers can be counted on fingertips. There are two historical aspects-one may be rightly called Dayanand era, since 1875, when he established the Arya Samaj to revitalize Hinduism. The other is the Hindu rule of India-roughly from the 5th century to the end of the 10th century AD.

Swami Dayanand infused fearlessness in Hindu psyche that small cadres of Hindu preachers voluntarily started going around the world for the revival of Hinduism and re-conversion (means Hindus converted to Muslims/Christians-back to Hinduism). Reverse Hindu proselytization is still an act of incredible courage today, as it has been for the last 200 years ago. It is out of fear of reappraisal, as frequently witnessed even in India, that generation of Hindus started believing that people of other religions cannot be converted anew or back to Hinduism. As a corollary, unfortunately, a few converted ones are not fully accepted and integrated in Hindu social folds. Consequently, 25 % of the new converts are known to quit Hinduism and go back to their old religions.

During my travels to Thailand, Malaysia, Cambodia, Singapore and Indonesia, I saw monumental evidences of Hindu preachers who had travelled thousands of miles away from India. Its tangible proofs lie in grand temples devoted to the Hindu trinity of gods, reverence for the legends of Ramayana and Mahabharata, and other cultural affinities and similarities. The dark periods that followed after the 10th century are the result of many physical, intellectual and spiritual holocausts by numerous Muslim and Christian invaders and rulers of India. They came from nearly every part of Middle East and Europe. By the end of the

18th century, the closed Hindu life styles lead to convoluted beliefs like crossing the oceans as sin and social boycotts etc.! Institution of Hindu preaching was eventually buried deep and lost.

The Hindus will come forward to become preachers, only if there are colleges to train them and places to work with dignity. It can only take place if preaching pays well enough to support a family. Individual Hindus and businesses have to band together and open their hearts, minds and purses to support online programs and institutions for preaching. In contrast, look at the power and wealth of an ordinary Christian evangelist even in India. The Hindus have a long way to go. But I always maintain that the Hindus in the US can lead the Hindu Diaspora.

Feb 26, 2011

COMMENTS

Actually India's one of the biggest export to the west is Gurus and Swamis. I am not sure where your conclusion is coming from. **Rahul**

I wrote: Yes, I agree with your observation. Here is my context: Remember a couple of months ago, Deepak Chopra stated that the yoga has no links with Hindu heritage. At the same time, Christian and Muslim theocracies strongly believe it otherwise, and have issued periodic injunctions against yoga.

Another scenario: never ever a guru from India has preached in the prisons and depressed neighborhoods of the US. You know what they come for. I had such discussions with all the gurus who have stayed with us at home. I respect them for whatever they do for Hindu heritage, but up to a certain point. Most of them spread passivity of mind that is OK for the aggressive white race. But the passive Hindus do not need more of it.

Rahul: Deepak Chopra is one small part of equation. Sri Sri Ravi Shankar teaches to prisoners too. So your concern is that Hinduism does not have militant preachers and not preachers in general. I think Hindu preachers have most impact on American/Western middle class than any other non-Christian teachers. Kudos to them. The new age religion, Theo philosophical societies have major impact of Hinduism. Injunctions aside Yoga has become part of main stream America.

I wrote: It seems that we have detracted each other from what I wrote from my experience with a cadre of preachers that have existed in Arya Samaj only. Swami Mama Ji was a student of Dayanand Updeshak Vidyalya, Lahore. Such training opportunities are not even known today. That alone is my thrust.

The preachers who are available are big cheats. Vedic university cheated the people in USA and the world. O P Tyagi visited USA Los Angeles in 86 and formed 9 fictitious Arya Samajs . . . . Bold, honest people like Swami Rameshwara Nand are no longer known to the Arya Samaj. **Madan gupta**

I wrote: Dear Madan Ji As compared with long lasting, grand and powerful organizations and institutions of other religions, Arya Samaj is the only Hindu organization that has a continuous history of over 100 years old. My plea to you and other Hindu leaders is to get involved in the organization, weed out the corrupt elements, **but never weaken the Arya Samaj**, as there is none other !! With regards.

PS: There is no point in splashing Hindu differences to others, if they could be resolved on one-to one basis. It is a post 9/11 world! I am sure you live to the meaning of your name, Madan-as, I have been trying to live up to my name. Thanks.

I do not intend to cause personal hurt, but would like to state that this is a good time to ideologically deconstruct the Arya Samaj movement (and other movements like it incl. e.g. Brahmo Samaj), from a comprehensive Hindu civilizational viewpoint. I believe Arya Samaj had some positive contributions to its credit, and it produced stalwarts of Indian freedom movement and social reformers, but it could not sustain itself as a vibrant movement because of its obtuse ideological foundation. It is a good time to question that conceptual framework.

I am of the opinion that Swami Dayanand Saraswati was responding to the then British onslaught on Hindu culture, but ended up internalizing the basis of that British attack. Overall, I believe, the "reformist" Hindu School of Thought-incl. Raja Ram Mohan Roy, Ishwar Chand Vidyasagar, Swami Dayanand Saraswati et al., accepted the superiority of European religious-cultural framework, and ended up trying to create a Hindu version of their masters/colonialists. Even though this did yield some short-term gains, we as a society lost much in the long run.

I could explain further, but suffice to say that if we have to combat Biblical/Koranic traditions, we will have to find strength in our civilizational heritage and reject the notion of Euro-centrism and Anglo-European superiority. We have to undo the prejudice against murti-puja (for starters). [I am glad that the bulk of Hindu society-the rural masses-did not become Arya Samajis or Bramho Samajis, as it continues to worship Hanuman Ji and Ganesh Ji and Durga Devi.]

The concept of "Hindu missionary" (in the Arya Samajis style) is a borrowed concept from Semitic traditions. There is very little point in becoming a Hindu version of a proselytizer. [Might as well join the original.] Hindu society needs to be reorganized based on its own intrinsic civilizational strength out of native ideology-perhaps new set of ideas-NOT borne out of inferiority complex, as was the case with 19th century so-called Hindu Reform Movements.

Let us think of new ways to achieve our civilizational goals, and not become dogmatic prisoners of our immediate past that was mired in acute ideological inferiority complex. The concept of bachelor/bramhachari Hindu missionary (Arya Samaj) (or RSS pracharak for that matter) is passé and ineffective. Let us think of another way to proceed. Best regards, **Rajiv Varma**

Agreed, first step is to get rid of the hierarchy where only one type can become a priest. The best way to accomplish this is to open colleges with formal degrees. Next, to balance out the centuries, a couple generations of affirmative action wouldn't hurt to give preferential admission to allow all the non-priest caste to admission. That should shake things up, in a way that only American innovation is capable of doing!-**Ketan**

THE SON OF A *GHASEETI!*

A couple of days ago when my younger brother remarked that the first name of the mother of Swami Deekshanand Saraswati (1919-2003) was ***Ghaseeti***, I casually said-yes. He had been reading his biography written by Prem Lata Bhatnagar, my first cousin. His surprise was, perhaps, how come, she had such a funny name? Immediately, my mind switched into a different gear-on Hindu nomenclature, the most comprehensive and inspirational system amongst all the societies in the world. The ***namkaran*** (name giving) is one of the major ***sanskars*** (religious ceremonies) in a Hindu way of life, and it continues to amaze me even at age 70+.

Ghaseeti, a feminine noun in Hindi language, is derived from ***ghaseetana***, a verb; meaning-to drag. Under normal conditions, no sane Hindu parents would name their children-like ***Ghaseeti, Ruliya*** (a lost one)***, Kurra*** (dirt), ***Middu*** (dwarf-ish), ***Chua*** (rat) etc. Yes, such names are given under absolutely abnormal family circumstances. For instance, a friend explained, how her father was named ***Ruliya*** (also means a discarded one). Her grandparents had lost a few babies at birth. They were advised by a family/neighborhood astrologer to place their next newly born child on a roadside for a while and then bring him back home. It would symbolically that the baby was given up by someone on roadsides, and her grandparents found and sheltered him. ***Ruliya*** Ram, born in a household of humble means, turned out to be an affluent contractor in Hoshiarpur.

Swami MamaJi had no direct memories of his mother, as she died a couple of years after his birth. He was named **Krishna** Swarup. It is the first name that has all the magic and power to transform, mold, or track a life. Yes, the first name could be a compass or pole star of life, provided the astrologer is competent enough to understand the planetary configuration with exact time of birth. That is one side of the equation. The other side is choosing an appropriate word capturing the essence of a human life throughout its span.

On a personal note, I often tell that my first name, Satish is my ***naam/ mantra***, a driving force of my life-like most Hindus 'get a ***mantra***' from their spiritual masters/gurus. Hindi word 'Satish' means 'truth personified'. Over the years, it has been influencing me to seek truth and stand by truth as objectivity as possible. Conversely, I try to stand for righteousness of a moment. It may explain my choice of mathematics as my lifetime professional pursuit. The essence of mathematics lies in its deductive reasoning and in the principle of cause and effect.

That is why I gravitate internally towards Arya Samaj, where I find a synthesis of abstract mathematical concepts with formlessness of God, as advocated by Swami Dayanand, the founder of Arya Samaj, a Hindu reformist movement of the 19th century. The rational intellectuals, like E. Kant and J. Krishnamurti, are closer to me. My situational ***Reflections***, being written for the last eight years, are meant to discover, understand, and capsulate truth and factuality at an instant-including ultimately my own self-realization.

The middle names-like Swarup, Chandra, Kumar, Lal, Chand, Sahai, etc. provide forms or vehicles to the first names. Of course, the last name or family name, usually after the middle name, serves the purpose of a public identity of the family. Due to political conditions in India during the last millennium, the Hindus have lost so much of their heritage. Scholars in this field of knowledge will develop when institutions for its study and research are started up.

The Hindi word ***devi*** means goddess, and commonly used as a middle name of girls. The birth of ***Ghaseeti*** Devi must have a story behind her first name-like painful extraction from the womb of her mother, near death experience, or her mother's dream of someone pulling her baby away, etc. In 'abnormal' names, the 'bad' influence is mitigated by special prayers. It is based on my individual observations, and do bear out statistical validity. It is fun and worth testing this hypothesis on individual names.

However, ***Ghaseeti's*** son lived up to his first name-became famous as Acharya Krishna. He had physical charms of Lord Krishna, but never had a ***gopi***, consort, or ever a wife. Not once, he revealed the secret(s) of his incredible control on his sexual urges. Actually, control is not the right word in his case. Amongst other things, he sublimated his passions by not taking salt and sweets during his early adult life. He was a Hath yogi, on his scale. Lord Krishna is known as Yogiraj, the King of the Yogis.

Of course, Swami MamaJi preached on the epic of Mahabharata-always fighting with social dogmas, particularly, untouchability and superstitions, in which the Hindus had shackled themselves for abject survival in their own homeland. Above all, he was an ardent follower of Swami Dayanand Saraswati. Every day, in his moments of deep contemplation, he would say-***Dhanya Ho Rishi*** (hail thee Rishi). It carried over a mystical glow on his countenance.

In 1975, Acharya Krishna was initiated into ***sanyaas*** (Hindu monastic order) by Swami Satya Prakash-once a renowned chemistry professor and first historian of sciences in ancient India. I had the privilege of having met him on several occasions while I was in India and communicated with him from the US, when he published and edited a journal on Vedic Sciences. The sanyasi name, Deekshanand was given by him. What an appropriate name it was! During his ***sanyasi*** span, he truly lived every moment up to this name.

During our Last Meeting from Dec 29, 2002 to Jan 01, 2003, he only breathed the Vedic lores in public and private meetings. When I asked him what major project is left out to finish before breathing out, he spontaneously uttered, ***Ved Gita***. Neither he elaborated his concepts and insights, nor did I inquire for a short time that we were together. But his life had beautifully flamed out and blossomed up into his birth name, Krishna and ***sanyasi*** name, Deekshanand.

May 15, 2003 is the day when his mortal remains were extinguished-called ***Nirvana Divas*** (Day of spiritual liberation), set for the high souls. A significance of reddish color of ***sanyasi*** garb is that he is eternally engulfed in flames-consuming his previous inclinations towards domestic and professional life. That is why biological birthdays are not celebrated for a ***sanyasi***. His 2011-***Nirvana Divas*** is being celebrated in Delhi on coming Sunday. I just got an email announcement. ***Dhanyo Ho MamaJi!***

May 12, 2011

COMMENTS

Hi Satish: Informative and enlightening. Evidently you have pursued research interests in penning this piece. **Moorty**

Dear Bhai Satishji, Sasneh Namaste! I believe the explanation you have given is correct, as in those days, when the people were NOT so affected by the reforms of our Maharishi Dayanand Saraswati. Till he came on the Indian scene, our people were in the habit of giving their children names as was of late respected Swami Deekshanand Ji's mother was.

I belong to Jhansi, I had seen names like "KUDA MAL", "CHURA MAL", "RABRI DEVI", "PISTA", "Kachori", "LADDOO", "IMARTEE", "SETH GHASITA RAM" and so on as in those days people were worshipping Dust /Garbage Dumps etc. Hence, I do NOT see anything wrong in respected Swami Deekshanand's mother's name either.

In our SATYARTH PRAKASH, name certainly has effect on a person's life & I certainly believe so: My father had a name "SHAMBHU NATH" & my mother's name was "SONA DEVI". Both proved TRUE to their names till their respective deaths. I have also named my children names as ***PRATIK***, ***PRAGATI*** & ***BHOOMIKA***. My son is proving as an embodiment or symbol of success, my elder daughter is proving to be a person of perpetual success. Our younger daughter, Bhoomika's had a slow beginning, but is very solid in life now.

Thus, I believe, Swami Deekshanand's name had equal impact on our Vedic dharma & Arya Samaj, true to his name : always giving away or passing his vast knowledge of Vedas to every one without any discrimination etc. **S C GUPTA**

EASY COME-EASY GO!

A week ago, when I heard that the entire building housing the ***Smarpan Shodh Sansthan in Sahibabad*** has been sold for Rs 40 lacs (Rs 4 millions or US $ 80,000) my thoughts flew high and wide. It was not clear whether it included a library of a thousand rare books. Finally, my thoughts landed on a popular Hindi maxim that says: ***chori ka maal, lathi ke gaz***-meaning: stolen goods are sold away at throw-away prices (for getting rid off as soon as possible). The person who told me is a renowned octogenarian Vedic scholar. I had contacted him for an article on Swami Deekshanand Saraswati (1918-2003) for my upcoming book on his life. On evincing more interest in details of the transaction, he feigned away the source of this news. It is immaterial anyway for my ***Reflection***!

Here is a context to this news: ***Samarpan Shodh Sansthan*** (Samarpan/ Vedic Research Institute) was set up by Swami Deekshanand in the 1980s in the honor of his guru, Swami Samarpananand, known as Pandit Buddha Dev before initiated into ***sanyasi*** order. I have very fond memories of meeting him in the chambers of Arya Samaj Dewan Hall during late 1950s. At that time, before sanyas, Swami Deekshanand, popularly known as Acharya Krishna, lived in Dewan Hall too. He shifted to Sahibabad when the ground/first floor structure of the ***sansthan***/ institute was ready. In the next 20 years, it grew up into a huge four-storey building.

During my annual trips to India, spending a few days with Swami Deekshanand in Sahibabad used to be an intellectual retreat of its own kind. Whenever, he envisioned research scholars living there, I stressed upon him a tested model of endowing Rs 20 lacs each in four research chairs in four universities whose Sanskrit departments were closer to him-namely, the ones situated in Delhi, Gurukul Kangari, Banaras and Rohtak. Its interest income would boost the salaries for attracting renowned Sanskrit scholars for undertaking the highest quality of Vedic research in perpetuity. However, once I would return to the US, his mind would go back to square one, as people around him had no clue of sterling research work.

During the last 4-5 years of his life, Swami Deekshanand's mind was completely turned off from day-to-day management of the institute. He just wanted to remain immersed in the Vedic ***mantras***, ideas, lores and ancient wisdom. His last desire was to write a unique book he had named as Veda Gita. For 2-3 years, he ignored his growing heart problem until he was forced to go for a bypass surgery in July 2000. It gave him three productive years.

An intriguing question arises: who is/are the beneficiary (ies) of supposedly sale proceeds of Rs 40 lacs. The sales in India are notorious for black and white money. The building is/was worth Rs 150 lacs by some estimates. It is a complex web only fit for a financial investigator to track down its ownership completely. Here is a reason for it. Swami Deekshanand, being a ***sanyasi,*** not wanting to buy the Sahibabad plot in his name; instead, he bought it in the name of Kusum Lata, his niece. He had groomed her from her teen years to all the way to Sanskrit PhD and to Vedic scholar of repute. She was the heir apparent of this institute. Unfortunately, she died suddenly of cancer in 1997. Swami Deekshanand's heart and plans for the institute were shattered. He channeled his resources mainly in the publication of out-of-print quality Vedic books.

Kusum was very beautiful, but decided not to go for married life, and lived almost like the way Swami Deekshanand did. But to satisfy her motherly instinct, she adopted a daughter of her elder sister and dreamed a similar life of Vedic scholarship for her niece or 'daughter'. But that was not destined to be! The girl probably rebelled, went off her own ways and married.

The irony of life is that she has legally inherited every thing that was in Kusum's name-from Kusum's retirement funds to the ownership of the plot, and perhaps of the structure of the ***sansthan*** standing on it. During last years of life, Swami Deekshanand did form a 'Trust' (registered??) of the ***sansthan***, but I have no knowledge of its role in building Swami Deekshanand's legacy. My exclusion or not inclusion in this 'Trust' is a story for another ***Reflection***. Such are the paradoxes of life!

During the last 10-12 years of Swami Deekshanand's life, money in donations was just pouring in because of his exalted name and lofty publications of the ***sansthan***. I often noticed cheques, drafts and cash lying around undeposited and unprotected. He overlooked his visitors and personal assistants pilfering away petty cash and kind. Furthermore, he ignored, forgot and forgave away lacs of rupees in 'loans' he generously gave away-especially to so many of his near and dear ones.

I sighed to realize as to how a certain cycle of life is completed. Swami Deekshanand was born in anonymity, but died with fanfare. However, his legacy is supreme. As Arya Samaj preacher, he touched the hearts of thousands of people. As Vedic scholar, he inspired scores of them. He was magnanimous. Fallout of all this is that he basically let the ***sansthan*** find its own course.

During my last visit to India, concluded just two weeks ago, I did want to visit the ***sansthan***. In all the inquiries made about it, I got many different stories on its state of affairs. A cousin told me that in order to get entry into, the building I will have to get a key from his brother in Delhi. That ended of my longing to go to Sahibabad, and Delhi too. From Chandigarh, I went straight to Delhi airport.

I am not sad about the building of the ***sansthan***, like I am not sad about the body of Swami Deekshanand. Nonetheless, I am very sad about the loss of the purpose for which it was built. For all intents and purposes, the ***sansthan*** died the day Swami Deekshanand died! However, my biography on his life shall keep his legacy alive for a while, After all, a life is measured by the number of books written about it!

July 25, 2013

MY SANSKRIT AND HIS ENGLISH & PUNJABI

Swami Mama Ji (Deekshanand Saraswati) and I have something in common linguistically. Backing it up a bit, both of us were born and raised in pre-partition Punjab. I was born in Jakhal (1939, now in Haryana) and he in Bhiwani (1918, Haryana too). The states of Haryana and Himachal Pradesh (HP) were carved out of post-partition Punjab in 1966. Imagine the size of pre-partition state of Punjab-it covered the present Indian states of Haryana, HP and Punjab along with the Pakistani state of Punjab, which stretched all the way in the west to Afghanistan.

Anyway, when my father was transferred to Bathinda in 1945, I picked up Punjabi as I started going to school and played out with friends. But our mother of seven kids was very strict against our speaking Punjabi inside the home and even amongst the siblings outside the home too. As a matter of fact, I never heard my parents ever speak a word of Punjabi. But I have compensated this gap by having an equal mastery over Hindi and Punjabi-be it in reading, speaking, writing, and street thinking.

However, Mama Ji never uttered a word of Punjabi in his life, though he studied for five years (1938-1943) in a gurukul right in Lahore, the heartland of Punjabi culture at that time. When I think of it, I tend to say that his vocal cords were just not built to enunciate typical Punjabi sounds. They were meant to speak only Hindi and Sanskrit, and he always sounded melodious then. There was a political overtone too, since he courted arrests in Hindi agitations held in Hyderabad and Punjab.

Such are the reasons that Mama Ji could never learn to read, write, and speak even rudimentary English, though he always wanted to learn it. That is where Sanskrit gets into my picture. In high school, when we were required to choose between science and Sanskrit, it was natural for me to go for science. My younger brother, under the influence of Mama Ji, chose Sanskrit. However, in my 40s, when my intellectual horizons were widening and expanding, I realized that Sanskrit was the most important language-no matter, what an Indian, in particular, wanted to study in depth-be it mathematics, sciences, history, literature and philosophy. The lofty ideas are all compactly coded and preserved in the Sanskrit of the Vedas, Upanishads and other ancient scriptures.

Learning of Sanskrit has long been on my mind; it started 30 years ago. I got elementary books to learn Sanskrit by myself. Mama Ji used to be ecstatic at my papers that I wrote on the importance of Sanskrit in connection with Vedic Mathematics. While in South Africa, he successfully developed a methodology of teaching/learning Sanskrit in 2-3 weeks, but for a number of reasons, Sanskrit kept passing by me.

A particular incident of the 1990s that stands out in my mind is when Rakesh, one of Mama Ji's devotees and state director of DAV educational enterprises, visited him in the ***sansthan*** (institute) in Sahibabad. His entire education was limited to the one he received in a Jhajjar gurukul. But like most Indians, he spoke in Hingish-comprising 60% Hindi and 40% English. Mama Ji was very impressed with his 'mastery' of English. It reflected his inability to learn English-though, he was way past it. On the other hand, during my stays in India, I like to practice in speaking chaste Hindi or Punjabi, and never mix a word of English. After Rakesh left, Mama Ji asked me, "How come you did not respond to Rakesh in English when he was speaking in English?" I was really amused at his unquenched desire of English. Perhaps, it showed a psychological complex he harbored about some superiority of English knowers.

It so happened that Rakesh came over to the ***sansthan*** the next day, and again smattered in English. This time, I spoke in the purest Hindi to the bewilderment of Mama Ji! In my mind, there was no point of my impressing Rakesh or Mama Ji about my fluency in English, when I had already lived in the US for 30 years? Interestingly, this incident flashed my mind this morning out of nowhere.

Here is another side bar to language learning. During his family visits to Bathinda, Mama Ji used to say that Hindi enunciation of we the kids raised in Punjab could never be correct, as it was influenced by Punjabi, which is not an issue for persons born in Hindi regions. However, the linguists and Ear-Nose-Throat (ENT) specialists have discovered that geographical locations have great bearings on the development of vocal cords/muscles, and consequently language enunciation is bound to vary.

For example, all stage singers and performers in multiple languages undertake physical therapy sessions for bringing their vocal cords and lungs to operate accordingly.

Eventually, Mama Ji ploughed all his energies back in Hindi and Sanskrit. At my end, for the last 12 years, I have been 're-learning' English, the medium of my five books so far. Sanskrit has been removed from the list of things to be completed before I die. I am at peace with not knowing Sanskrit. My linguistic goal is to be able to develop my English writing style that is undisputedly acclaimed as mine-having touches of both Bathinda/India and Las Vegas/USA!

Oct 19, 2013

COMMENTS

It seems like that "adopting" Punjabi as your "home" tongue was a reaction to you being prohibited to speak Punjabi at home by your mother. Have you thought about writing the reflections in Punjabi titled as "***Meri Dungi Sochan***" **Rahul**

I wrote: I do write in Punjab, but no longer are there people intellectually alive in my circle, including Sikhs, who know Gurmukhi. Yes, I have addressed gatherings in Punjabi to the surprise of the people. At home, my wife and I speak in Hindi, though her home language was Punjabi. Certainly, a Reflection, the power of Punjabi in my expressions, is overdue.

I had to choose between Sanskrit and Punjabi in 8th grade. I chose Punjabi and am regretting it. I also want to learn Sanskrit, but it is too late. **Rajendar Singal**

I share your childhood experiences with learning Sanskrit. During my boyhood days I was constantly moving due to my father's frequent transfers in Chittoor district of the former Madras province, now in Andhra Pradesh. Apart from my mother tongue, Telugu, I was also getting exposed to Tamil and Kannada. For a few months I was in my grandfather's village in the delta region of Godavari River and Bay of Bengal when I had the opportunity to watch young Brahmin boys being exposed to recitation of Vedas in Sanskrit. That was the extent of my exposure; however, I do recite a few Sanskrit prayers in Sanskrit to Lord Venkateswara daily. Looking back, I wish I had been exposed to Sanskrit, the mother of all modern Indian languages. The literary Telugu is highly Sanskrit-based in its vocabulary. **Moorty**

SECTION III

OTHER EYES

WHAT IS INSIDE SECTION III?

The material in this section also sets this biography vertically and horizontally apart from any other biography. From the beginning of this project, I wanted the biography to be all inclusive. In the present institutional life in the US, 'All Inclusive' is a buzz phrase-meaning to incorporate every kind of diversity under the assumption that heterogeneity brings more power and creativity to a unit than homogeneity does. Traditionally and historically, it has been just the opposite. The laws of physics support a principle that aligned homogeneous forces have far more pulling power than the directional forces of heterogeneity-bringing it to standstill/zero in some scenarios. Anyway, this is a side bar comment.

When I set out to write this biography, I knew that I did not have a large amount of material on Mama Ji's life for a reasonable size book. Since writing his biography was not thought of, I never studied, researched and collected materials on his life, as most journalists do it these days-when assigned to write a biography. Of course, I had ruled out the inclusion of any pictures-making it a signature of my books. Besides, there are no new pictures of Mama Ji-besides the ones included in his 2007-biography written by my cousin, Prem Lata Bhatnagar.

As stated in the introductory ***Reflections***, I decided to solicit write-ups from the relatives, admirers and associates of MamaJi as much as I could trace them. Amazingly, it hardly created any response! I wrote them and called them numerous times, but it was of no avail. One thing is sure that formal writing is not easy even for those who are used to it-particularly, in my age group. Since Prem Lata did not reach out members of the extended family for some reasons, I repeatedly urged them all to put their new thoughts together that were not written up earlier.

The only overwhelmingly positive response came from Dr Usha Sharma, the wife of Jaidev Shastri, MamaJi's first and the most lasting disciple. My younger brother, Suresh sent a large Word file which I had to prune it for adjusting in the framework of the book. He may expand it into a full book on MamaJi's life later on. But I was not to give up on certain individuals, and decided to collect oral reminiscences on MamaJi's life from them. This idea came up to my mind as I often coax my students in history of mathematics course to include pieces of oral history in their hands-on-history projects integral to the course.

Hence, this Section has full-fledged write-ups, transcribed oral histories. Some write-ups are in Hindi-that is the way they were solicited and welcomed. If the write-ups from Indrajeet Dev, Om Prakash Verma, Sushil K. Bhatnagar, Girish Khosla, and Tulsi Ram arrive in due course, then they may be included in an addendum.

Dec 28, 2013

[Chandra Prabha Bhatnagar is my wife of 50+ years. It took a lot or persuasion for her to write the following piece. The point is that I have been calling and pressing people in India and the US for any oral or verbal pieces of their memories associated with Mama Ji's life. So, not having one from my wife would have looked incongruous.

After the birth of our first daughter, she did MA in Philosophy (1967) from India. However, neither she cashed on this degree in India nor in the US. Yes, in the US, she took care of children and grandchildren on a full time basis so lovingly that she has already started reaping the harvest of love and care from all our children and grandchildren. It is a true blessing in fast life styles. Her impressions about Mama Ji are based upon her direct and indirect knowledge during a brief period of 1963-69-before she left India to join me in the US.]

This memory is from the time when we were newly married, means-50 years ago! I was visiting (without my husband) in laws' place-Bhatinda. It was a cold and early morning time. I was still in the bed half awakened and half asleep when I heard some conversation sound coming out of the kitchen. That dialogue was between who and what about. I do not remember now and it is not important either but the melodious sound and most dignified tone of a male person was amazingly attractive! I remember wondering . . . is it a dream or reality? The solid and clear pronunciation of the each word was very impressive!

After a little while Baby-Madhu and Gopal entered in my room and I asked them who came early morning and talking? They told me that their "Mama Ji" from Delhi came to visit them. Then they expressed their happiness over the two boxes of sweets Mama Ji got them from Delhi's special sweet shop! Anyway, after fixing myself, I made an entry in the kitchen too. My mother in law said to me-***"Bahu***, (for bride) pay regards to my younger brother (cousin) from Delhi, he is known as Acharya Krishna-a very well respected name in whole of Arya Samaj society!" I touched his feet and he gave me his blessing. I came back to my room soon, as it was expected in those days from a "***Nai Bahu***" (new bride) in a traditional family.

Anyway, it was enough of the first introductory meeting with the pleasant essence behind! Besides this, his physique was also very impressive and elegant! Right then, he reminded me of the great poet and writer Rabindranath Tagore in looks! With regards.

[Suresh C. Bhatnagar is the first of my five younger brothers. After moving to the US in 1973, he joined the US Army at the advance age of 32. During his initial 3-year contract with Army, he finished MA in counselling. After coming out of the Army, he completed MS in library science from IU, Bloomington. But he never worked as a librarian in the US that he was in India for six years. Before re-joining the Army as education counselor, he worked as a counselor for the Department of Interior in an Indian Reservation in Northern Arizona for two years. He served the US Army mainly overseas-in Korea, Germany, and Afghanistan. He retired in Aug, 2012.

His spiritual pursuits reflect the twists and turns in his professional life. First 30 years of his life were nourished by the tenets of Arya Samaj. In the US, he turned around religiously and devotedly explored Christianity for ten years. While posted in Seoul, Korea, he about turned again to follow Satya Sai Baba of Puttaparthi. He spends most of his retired life in Puttaparthi, and volunteers his time and expertise as needed there. He has authored nearly a dozen books on the Sai teachings, philosophy, and practices.]

MY LEARNING AT HIS HOLY FEET

Swami Deekshanand Ji, who was popularly known as Acharya Krishna before his initiation into the *Sanyasi* (renunciate) stage of life, was my *Maamaa* (maternal uncle). He used to tell me, when I was young, that his love for us is equal to two *Maa's* (*Maa+Maa=Maamaa* or mothers). That is why he was called "*Maamaa*'. Indeed his love for his nephews and nieces was profuse and prodigious. He expressed his love through low, slow and sumptuous tone while conversing with the children and by distributing sweets and fruits to them.

The main aim of his engagement with young children was not to win their adoration, but their transformation of mind for excellence in character building. His teachings were predicated on the tenets of Indian culture, Vedic canons and doctrines, as enshrined in the Vedas, Upanishad, Ramayana, Mahabharata, and Shrimad Bhagavad Gita, and other renowned ancient lore.

He used to tell us that he got title of Acharya because his *Achar* (conduct) is in conformity with his sermons to general public. According to him, those who maintain harmony of thought word and action deserve the title of "Acharya". But those who impart academic instructions to school/college students without maintaining this unity of thought, word and action, are mere "*Adhyaapak*" (teachers), who are concerned with mundane issues.

Saintly people always have their names meaningful, which demonstrate their concurrence with their actions. In other words, their actions signify their names. His name was "Krishna" Like Krishna whose advent was to uproot evil forces and to establish Dharma by propagating the Bhagawad Gita, Acharya Krishna Ji also gave to the world the light of Vedic literature unraveling enigmatic thoughts and esoteric constructs in simple and lucid expositions, with an aim to remove ignorance by its illumination.

The word Krishna has originated from the Sanskrit root "*Krish", "Krishit Iti Krishna*". That means the one who ploughs is Krishna. The heart is the symbol of field. The heart should be cleared of weeds (evil qualities). It should be filled love and compassion. The seeds of the Lord's Name (OM or Pranava or Omkara) should be sown in it. Lord Krishna always encouraged his devotees to develop virtues and eschew vices and sinister and sinuous traits. Likewise, Acharya Ji's mission was also to make a society of noble people (Arya Samaj) by dispelling filthy and foul qualities by cultivating virtues.

There is another explicit explanation of his name, which finds its derivation in Karsh +Na, Krishna is one who attracts people not only by his matchless beauty of his winsome ways, but also he is versatile in transforming the anger of the Gopis and others through his pranks and plays (Leela). Acharya Ji himself became the connoisseur of his followers and admirers because of his towering personality and nectarine-laced speech in conversation and public discourses wherever he went. His power of attraction though his conduct and oratory skill was amazing.

Though he renounced this name of Krishna after his initiation in to the Sanyasi order and assumed the name of Swami Deekshanand. Swami means master or owner. The word "Deekshaa" has been derived from the Sanskrit root "*Deeksh*", which to initiate, to consecrate or dedicate oneself to monastic order. Hence, the word "*Deeksha*" connotes consecration, initiation for ceremonial induction into some sect or order, etc. It is indeed a ceremonial commitment to a religious undertaking for a noble purpose. Swami's Deekshanand was dedicated and committed to spearheading and disseminating noble teachings postulated on Arya Samaj principles and doctrines to create of a society of noble people.

My first contact with Swami Ji occurred when I was hardly seven-year-old. He used to take me to his Gurukul situated at the outskirts of Bathinda at that time and brought me back home in the evening. This small building was donated by Ganesh Pahelawaan (wrestler) for this purpose. Once I asked the meaning of Gurukul. He told me that Gurukul refers to the dormitory-type of academic institution where preceptor and pupils live together day and night. Preceptor keeps surveillance over the activities of his pupils to ensure compliance with established moral conduct and Indian culture. Guru means preceptor and "*kul*" means campus. Hence, it is the campus of a spiritual teacher (guru) where pupils are shaped in spiritual moulds and models for proper physical, moral and spiritual growth. His main emphasis was on self-control, purity of mind, deep knowledge of Arya Samaj principles.

I. WHAT IS OM OR AUM?

His initial teaching at the Gurukul was to recite the mystic mantra "OM" in the morning and evening to awaken our latent potency and prowess, which I chanted as frequently as possible. Later on when I became matured enough he exhaustively explained the significance of OM, which is delineated below.

OM is the sound of the movement of the stars in the firmament. It is the sound that manifested when the dawn of Creative Will stirred the Attributeless into activity. As a matter of fact, every little disturbance of equilibrium produces sound, however minute. So, you can understand that when the Elements (earth, water, air, fire, ether) originated and creation started, the sound of OM was produced. That sound is the primal, the primeval one. No sound is beyond the ken of OM. All sounds are permutations and products of OM. Brahman too is OM.

METHOD FOR CHANTING OM

Gather in some holy place in solitude to repeat the Pranava. Recite OM slowly, contemplating its vast potentialities. The 'A' emerges from the throat, the 'U' rolls over the tongue and the 'M' ends on lips. That is to say, OM which is a composite of A, U and M, is the sum and substance of the Universal Absolute. After 'M' there must be the unheard resonance, which represents the Attribute-less Formless Abstract, the *Niraakaara Parabraman.* The ascending voice of the Pranava or OM must take a curve at 'M' and descend as slowly as it rose, taking as much time as when it ascended, disappearing in silence, which echoes in the inner consciousness.

II. GAYATRI MANTRA

After practicing the intonation of "OM", Acharya Maamaa (Acharya Krishna Ji) exhorted me to learn the Gayatri Mantra and understand its full meaning. He recommended its repetition at least 108 times per sitting. Since I was a middle school student, he advised me that daily chanting of this Mantra with full concentration will sharpen my intellect and heighten my memory.

The Gayatri Mantra occupies a very prominent place in the Hindu religion. Its recitation is regarded as a very sacred and sublime spiritual exercise. It is chanted on all religious, spiritual, holy and social functions, such as birth, wedding, death, and other ceremonies, because of effective potency inherent in its phonetic vibrations and the potent pleading to the Almighty to invoke blessings and boons. Several specific institutions established in India with branches abroad like Gayatri *Maha Parivar* and other denominational sects and groups associated with Hinduism are spearheading the dissemination of the effectiveness and efficacy of the Gayatri Mantra for the benefit of humanity throughout the globe. The Gayatri Mantra, mentioned in the Rig Veda and Yajur Veda, is a simple and sincere prayer to the Almighty to confer bright and brilliant intelligence.

"Gayatri" means that which is sung. What is sung is music only i.e. rhythmic sound. The potency of the Gayatri Mantra is in its sounds and phonetic vibrations. Thus, the correct pronunciation of the Gayatri Mantra is stressed. It is believed and accepted that for any mantra to be effective and beneficial, its pronunciation should be perfectly precise, as any slightest variation of any word can change its sound, meaning and content. The correct utterance of the sound is the basis of the Gayatri Mantra. Wrong pronunciation will vitiate its effects, benefits and desired results.

WHAT DOES THE GAYATRI MANTRA TEACH?

In the Gayatri Mantra, the unity of body, mind and soul is depicted in the first line *'Bhur-Bhuvah-Suvah'*. The next line *'Bhargo Devasya Dheemahi'* means: 'Dispel the darkness'. *'Dheeyo yo nah prachodayaat'* means 'let the effulgence of the Divine remove the darkness of ignorance'. Description of the glory of meditation and prayer are all contained in the Gayatri Mantra. When does a prayer become meaningful? It is only when you stabilize your mind and turn it towards God. The basis for this is to meditate, pray and experience. It is essential to achieve harmony in thought, word and deed. Gayatri teaches this lesson.

The Gayatri Mantra has infinite potentiality. It is a vibrant formula. It has immense powers, the powers that are truly amazing, for the Sun is its presiding Deity. The Gayatri Mantra is a prayer for the development of your intellect, so that you might discriminate between good and bad, between right and wrong. It sharpens the intellect, and then unity in nature will become evident. The most popular mantra (prayer clothed in ritual formula) in the Vedas is Gayatri. It seeks the grace of the Source, the Source of all, and the light to foster one's intelligence.

When a child is ready for schooling, an ***Upanayana Sanskaara*** is performed and he is vested with a sacred thread called "***Yajnopaveet***". The recitation of the Gayatri Mantra is followed by a learned and enlightened guru. The child is asked to memorize the Gayatri Mantra and recite it three times a day; because what a pupil needs more than anything else is keen and sharp intellect. Thus, the Gayatri Mantra is also known as "**Guru-mantra**" because it is taught by the guru or the preceptor to a disciple. Every student in ancient Vedic seminaries was expected to learn this Mantra to enkindle intellect. Thus, the Mantra became more popular than any other mantra of the Vedic lore. Hence, it is sometimes called "**mahaa-mantra**" (the most popular verse).

THREE PARTS OF THE GAYATRI MANTRA

Gayatri is has three parts: 1. Praise, 2. Meditation and 3. Prayer. The first nine words of Gayatri Mantra (***OM, Bhur, Bhuvah, Suvah, Tat, Savitur Varenyam, Bhargo, Devasya***,) correspond to the description (praise) of the Gayatri. ***'Dheemahi'*** pertains to meditation. "***Dhiyo yo nah prachodayaat***" is the prayer to God for steady and pure intellect. The Divine is first praised and meditated upon and then an appeal is made to awaken and strengthen the intellect (***Buddhi)***.

III. VEDIC *SANDHYA*

When I was in the eighth grade, Swami Maamaa Ji once came to our house and spent a few days with us. During that period, he was pleased with me, as I was religiously reciting the Gayatri Mantra and intonation of OM daily, both morning and evening. Then he counseled and cajoled me to start learning ***Vedic Sandhya*** and gifted me a small booklet containing all the mantras of ***Vedic Sandhya***. He taught me how pronounce each word with correct rhythm and accent. Initially, I used to read the mantras from the booklet and gradually I memorized them. He explained that ***Vedic Sandhya*** is a different type of prayer. It is an action by which we conceptualize and concretize the Highest. The process of ***Puja*** must purify one's senses to have a new birth in spirituality and Divinity. Hence, *Vedic Sandhya* became part and parcel of my daily ritual until today.

Sandhya can be performed twice a day-before sunrise and after sunset. There is no harm in having one's own norms, such as mid-day ***Sandhya***. But regularity and discipline play an important part in life. ***Sandhya*** performed as a ritual, hardly takes more than five minutes. The ritualistic ***Sandhya*** has also its own significance. In this type of ***Sandhya***, one merely recites the number of Vedic verses as prescribed.

Congregational prayers in loud tone have instructional and educational advantages. It provides an opportunity of learning the Vedic verses. The chorus recitations (like chorus songs) have an acoustic trance that provides a sort of smoothening rhythm. There is a disciplined way of reciting Vedic verses, which you learn in mass prayers. Additionally, congregational prayers cultivate a community spirit, harmonious feelings and a sense of unity, unleashing a flood of spiritual vibrations purifying the entire area and its surroundings.

IV. UPASANA

While explaining the meaning of Vedic mantra, Acharya Maamaa Ji quoted the following mantra: *OM ya aatmadaa baladaa yasya vishva upaasate prashisham yasya devaah*
Yasya chchhaayaa-amritam yasya mrityu kasmai devaayaa havishaa vidhema//
Rig Veda X-121-2 & Yajur Veda V-13

He elaborated that in the Vedas the term "***Upasana***" has been used in the adoration of God. In the above Rig Vedic mantra, the term "***Upaasate***" indicates adoration.-***Upasana*** is a divine prayer. This is originally a Sanskrit word comprising two parts: "***Upa***" and "***Asana***". The complete meaning is a seat close by. It is used to implicate the rituals in Hinduism to go closer to God or the Supreme Power.

According to Swami Ji, ***Upasana*** refers to sitting near and also being very dear to the Lord. If you are close to the Lord, if you become dear to Him, then you will earn His love. Soon all the bad qualities will vanish away and be replaced by the good qualities that God embodies. Develop your love so that you may get even nearer and nearer and dearer and dearer to God. The easiest way to get close to God is to remember Him in whatever you see, whatever you say and whatever you do. Think only of God and how to get nearer and dearer to Him.

Usually this term "***Upasana***" is used in Hinduism to denote a prescribed method for approaching a Deity/God or getting close to deity. In Vedas some ***Upasanas*** are prescribed where one meditates on all pervading *Brahman* or some aspect of creation such as fire, etc. In other words, ***Upasana*** can be described as a systematic practice of a prescribed method of worship for pleasing and winning the attention of the Deity or it can be a Deity-less practice of austerities meditating upon some aspect of nature as told in some Vedic ***Upasanas***. A devotee would consult the scriptures or any person who knows them thoroughly, to get a prescribed form of worship (***Upasana***) for his Deity of choice or ***Ishta Devata*** and follow it faithfully or dutifully.

Upasana means to be conscious of the nearness to God (***upa*** = near & ***aasana*** = seated, which indicates proximity to the Divine). It implies surrender to God. One who surrenders to His Divine Will, he will never be disappointed and dejected. He would lead to the next one after death. When all lights fail to illumine your path, His light guides you through. Seated in your innermost conscience, He speaks to you, when there is none else to help you.

V. UPAVAASA (FASTING)

When I was in the 8th grade, I used to notice my mother observing fast on Shivaratri, Tuesdays for Hanuman Ji, ***Navami*** and other Hindu religious days. I got intrigued by her fasting ritual by negating food. One day, I expressed my desire to observe fasting on Tuesdays for Hanuman Ji, who is also Ram Bhakta or Ram Das, etc. She felt happy over my overture and told me to refrain from eating grain or cereals. However, eating fruit or drinking milk and tea is an acceptable norm under the fasting process. I continued this fasting until I completed my BA degree. Ruminating at my fasting ritual during my school days, Acharya MamaJi explained the significance of the term: ***Upavasa***".

It is commonly believed by various religious adherents that by keeping fast and praying sincerely to God during the fasting period, God will fulfill their wish and bestow divine blessings. They believe that we should observe fast even if we feel weak and vulnerable. This may seem illogical as fasting weakens one physically. Scriptures confirm that God responds to fasting and prayer by providing protection from harm and victory over the enemy. Fasting and praying is a powerful tool that God has given to us to have our cherished prayers answered positively. Fasting is not a complicated process. Just don't eat food. Refrain from eating food or a specific type of food for a set amount of time per personal conviction or belief.

The fast, called in Sanskrit *"**Upavasa**",* means something far more significant than missing a meal. It means living (***Vasa)***, or living near (***Upa***). With whom?, Near whom? Near and with God. ***Upavasa*** means living in the constant presence of the Lord through ***Nama smarana*** **that** is the real fast, holding fast to Him. During a fasting period, the recitation of the names of the Lord or reading Holy Scriptures will help to purify the atmosphere. As a result, the sacred sound waves get absorbed in the atmosphere.

People take fasting for weight loss and health point of view as well. ***Upa+vasa*** is a combination of withdrawal of all our sense organs from materialistic aspects and direct them to God. When all cognitive senses are directed to God, naturally for a day or part of a day, fasting takes place naturally. Not only the real meaning of fasting confined to abstinence of eatable foods, but what we hear or see too are foods for those respective senses. When all the five senses are restricted of 'foods' for a day or part is real fasting or ***Upavasa.*** Actually, fasting is an automatic process. When we think, see, hear and speak of god only, fasting becomes a reality by default.

VI. YAJNA

When I was a high school student, I went to see Acharya Maamaa Ji (Acharya Krishna) residing at Dewan Hall, Chandani Chowk, Delhi, during my summer break. I spent one month in his holy company. He taught me how to perform daily ***Yajna*** and gave me a book containing all the mantras of ***Yajna*** and ***Sandhyaa***. He taught me how to pronounce each mantra precisely and correctly. He explained their meanings, significance and advantages of performing daily Yajna.

Upon my departure from Dewan Hall to return to Bathinda, he commanded me to perform the Yajna every day. Since its performance needs ghee, ***Saamagri*** (oblation mixture of herbs and other materials), hence I asked him how to arrange money to meet these monthly expenses. He told me he would take care of it. When he came to Bathinda, he talked to my Nana Ji (grandfather) to give me every month five rupees for ***Yajna***, since I used to massage the feet of my Nana Ji (grandfather) daily; he readily agreed to do so. He continued contributing five rupees per month for the Yajna until he breathed his last in 1960. In this way, the commencement of Yajna performance started daily and continued until 1962, when I left Bathinda for higher studies.

The Sanskrit word *"**Yajna**"* has been derived from the root "***Yaj,*** which means to adore, to revere, to organize. Derived from the practice of Vedic times, it is done to make the divine deities and God happy in Hindu temples and homes today. Vedic ***Yajna*** is usually performed by a priest or an expert Vedic scholar by reciting Vedic verses. The essential element in the ***Yajna*** is the sacrificial fire (also called ***Agni)*** into which oblations are poured along with mantra recital, as everything that is offered into the divine fire is believed to reach God instantly. Daily Yajna can be performed by the individual himself, if the person is competent to do so.

Yajna is 'renunciation' or giving up'-for whom? For the Divine! The heart you gave me, I am offering it in return', is the spirit of renunciation. The heart He has given, the feelings He evokes, the wealth He has conferred, the fame He has awarded-these have to be gladly offered back to the Divine. Manu, the ancient lawgiver, has declared that reverential prostration done before mother, father and preceptor is indeed a *Yajna*. When the egoistic pride or greed is absent and when the objective is the good of all, certainly that deed is *Yajna*.

VII. SWAADHYAAYA

Before starting at Government College, Bathinda, I went to Arya Samaj Dewan Hall, Delhi, to see Acharya Krishna during my summer vacations. During my stay there, he exhorted me to do *Swadhyaaya,* which refers to reading of sacred books like Vedic literature, Ramayana, the Mahabharata and the Bhagawad Gita. He explained the significance of the word "*Swaadhyaaya*", which has been derived from the Sanskrit, root *"Su"* (holy, beautiful) + *"Adhi-ee"* (to study for assimilation). *Swaadhyaaya* means study of holy literature for transformation of thoughts and mind to practice good conduct in daily life. He used to lecture me daily on *Swaadhyaaya.*

Swami's main emphasis was on cultivation of virtues to become a noble citizen. In his discourses he advised listeners to cultivate qualities like tolerance, love, sympathy, righteousness, justice and truth. It is impossible to experience Divinity without cultivating human values. The sanctity of human life lies in undertaking righteous actions and developing good character and noble characteristics.

VIII. *SATWIC* FOOD

Swami always told his nephews and nieces to take only *Satwic* food. Do not eat eggs, chicken, fish and any type of meat. By eating meat you develop animal tendencies. Emotions of pain and pangs being experienced by dying animals during their slaughtering process get absorbed in our body and mind to pollute our natural propensities, tendencies Anger, envy, jealousy become powerful in one's personality, thereby making it domineering and dreadful. His inclination toward drinking alcohol becomes irresistible. His desires for damsels or harlots start brewing and surging. He does not mind in indulging in gambling. He does not mind smoking cigarettes and or cigars or chewing tobacco products to enjoy this deleterious momentary pleasure, thereby, inviting dangerous diseases.

By eating fatty food, the cholesterol level is increased causing heart trouble. A simple diet of fruits and vegetables free from salt is the Satvic one, which will prevent heart ailments. Rajasic food, rich in salt and spices, and Tamasic food, consisting of meat, fat and intoxicants, will ruin the health.

IX. SWAMI'S PERSUATION FOR VEDIC STUDIES

When I got admission to college for a baccalaureate degree, Acharya Mama Ji who had assumed a new name as Swami Deekshanand Ji after entering into *Sanyaas* (renunciate) Ashram (stage of life) asked me to select the Sanskrit language as an optional subject to know the multi-faceted dimension of Indian culture and scriptures. I followed his advice and completed my Master's Degree in Sanskrit from Kurukshetra University, Haryana.

After this degree, he coaxed me to do research in Vedic literature. Hence, I got enrolled in M.Litt. degree with Punjabi University, Patiala. The topic for my thesis captioned "Concept of Agni in the Rig-Veda" was assigned by Acharya Mama Ji himself, when I was at D.A.V. College, Jullundur, Punjab. He indeed guided me in my research work. According to him, all deities in the Vedas represent some concepts and natural powers. The Agni concept represents the leadership trait. To illustrate this viewpoint, he elaborated that king is Agni in his kingdom as he leads his people to welfare and security. In the family, father is Agni, as he provides security and sustainability to family members. Hence, Agni is one that leads and guides. The worldly Agni also marches ahead by burning all items coming in its way.

After obtaining my M.Litt. degree, he advised me to do expanded research work on Agni for the Ph. D. degree encompassing all the Vedas. Before my departure from India to USA on immigration visa, I submitted my thesis hurriedly and left for USA in August 1973.

X. A LOAN FROM SWAMI JI

Attainment of my Master's Degree in Sanskrit did not open the door of job opportunities, unless one has a Shastri or Acharya degree or a Ph. D. in Sanskrit. But both the processes augur long paths to reach desired destination. Upon discovering that immigration visa (green card) was being given to those who have a degree/diploma from Delhi University (not from other Indian universities). I promptly applied for admission to the one-year Library Science Diploma program. I was accepted. But I did not have at least one thousand rupees to pay for tuition fee in 1965. I went to Swami Ji in Dewan Hall, Delhi, and asked for a loan of R. 1,000, payable in 1967. He listened to my plan and agreed to give me the required amount next day. Next day I got the money from him, but he pointed that Pundit Buddha Dev Ji, during his consultation with him regarding this matter, pointed out that it was indeed a too much favor for me, in spite of the fact that my other cousins were getting much more financial help from him on a recurring basis. While lending the money, Swami Ji pointed out that the lender of Balbir Bhai sahib (my elder cousin), upon surety from Mohan Bhai Sahib, was charging the interest rate of 30% for that loan. I kept mum without uttering a single word.

As pledged, I paid off the entire loan by the end of 1967, upon getting my employment with D.A. V. College, Jullundur, Punjab. Notwithstanding this payment, I continued paying or donating money whenever I met him, thereby making the total amount more than hundred-fold. Surprised by my integrity, he made a reference to this fact that most of the borrowers who took loans from him hardly paid off the debt, except a few like me and my elder brother Dr. Satish C. Bhatnagar.

XI. OFFER OF MANAGERIAL POSITION

Two years prior to his heavenly departure, Swami Ji wrote me a letter during my assignment in South Korea, and urged me to accept the position of the Manager of his *Samarpananda Shodh Sansthan* at Sahibabad, U.P. I wrote him back that I would personally discuss this matter with him during my next visit. After a few months, I came to Delhi and stayed at Mohan Bhai Sahib's residence at Chitra Vihar. Swami Ji called me on phone and informed that he would be coming there shortly to see me. Within an hour, his vehicle arrived. With a somber demeanor and sweet and subdued tone, he asked if I had thought over the acceptance of his offer to become the Manager of his Research Institute at Sahibabad. After a little pause and contemplation, I replied negatively. He felt shattered over my blank "no". He assertively said that he had himself come to renew this offer expecting its acceptance from me, but not rejection.

Probing further, he asked inquisitively the reasons behind this decline. I told him frankly that my working style is anchored to transparency and integrity to get the assigned mission done expeditiously and ethically. I was afraid that I may encounter head-on collision with a Bhatnagar clan already involved in Sansthan's administration and operation directly or indirectly. This would cause desolation and dissentions and generate pungency and poignancy. His mood became restive and pensive. He left the house with the words "to think over it again calmly"

After his departure, I felt guilty and remorseful, as if I had committed a blunder by hurting the tender heart of Swami Ji. Now by watching the post-Swami Ji era, in view of this fact that his Sansthan had been sold out and his bank balances got depleted, his name from the Sansthan obliterated, I express my gratitude to the Almighty for saving me from ignominy and animosity.

XI. LAST MEETING WITH SWAMI JI

After 6 months, the reports from three examiners, who reviewed my PhD thesis, were received. Two examiners recommended the revision of three chapters. Since I was in USA without books and reference materials, I dropped the idea of revising the text of the thesis by banishing and burying the aspiration of attaining the Ph. D degree from Punjabi University.

The typed text remained dormant for several years. Two years before Swami's Mahasamadhi, during a casual conversation with the Swami Ji, I mentioned about the thesis at his *Samarpananda Shodh Sansthan.* I requested him to review and revise the text as per his pleasure, in conformity with Arya Samaji doctrines and canons. He told me he would do so provided I pay him the full printing cost. I gave him the cheque for one lakh rupees, as demanded by him.

After several months when I came back from USA to see him, during the last meeting, he informed me that the revised thesis had been sent to the printer for printing. After his heavenly abode, I never heard about its printing. Later on, Pundit Jai Dev Shastri told me that my manuscript was with a printer, but he could not recollect the name of the printer. Then Jai Dev Ji too passed away and the whereabouts of the manuscript is still unknown.

It is my desire to get my near PhD thesis published as a tribute to Swami's contributions to Vedic lore. During the last moment of his life, Swami Ji wrote a comprehensive and scholarly foreword for this book, which specks and sparks of the depth of his oceanic knowledge in Vedic studies. In my view, printing of this book will be an apt tribute adding laurels to his burgeoning fame and name. This was indeed his last write-up. I am still eager to retrieve and get it printed, by funding its full printing cost, waiving all claims for its sale proceeds.

CONCLUSION

Swami Ji was indeed a *Saagar* (ocean) of eclectic knowledge (*Atmic Jnana*). All his teachings cannot be abridged in this article. I am thankful to God who allowed me to learn a variety of holy things in his close proximity. I pray to God to shower His blessing, courage and strength to imbibe and practice them to enjoy abiding peace of mind, and engage in welfare activities.

ORAL REMINISCENCES

[Dinesh C. Bhatnagar, age 69, is my second younger brother. He retired from the Indian Railways in 2005 after putting in 38 years into it. He is one of the few individuals who spend chunk of their life in a relationship with a job, person, or place that doesn't give them any satisfaction. Dinesh's heart has been always been in music-showing magic tricks at any gathering, dancing and singing-both light and Punjabi folk. He is so talented that he can entertain any audience for full 75 minutes. But he never took his leap of faith-heart over the head. He has lived his entire life with least amount of writings in any shape or form. Whatever he wrote, it was all in high school! Yes, Dinesh never wrote or replied to my letters either. It is now extended to phone calls too! Life is for sure very interesting with such a variety of persons around you.]

When I contacted him to recall his memories of Swami Mama Ji, the right from the top of his heard, he quickly reeled down the following incidents. The first one is his attending our cousin's marriage in Yamuna Nagar in 1972. Swam Mama Ji had come over to perform it. During the wedding sermon, he stressed the importance of marriage for every man. As a matter of fact, he went to the extent of mandating marriage for everyone. He believed that the ***grahsta ashram*** is the backbone of all the four ***ashrams***. Dinesh then could not help asking him point blank- "MamaJi, How come you have not married yet?" Mama Ji just brushed his question aside.

Later on, when Dinesh wanted Mama Ji to perform his wedding ceremony, Mama Ji said, "Since your marriage party will have meat and alcoholic drinks, so I won't be able to come. Dinesh said, yes that will be the case. Both lived up to their vows. Jaidev Ji, Mama Ji's first disciple came over to BTI and performed Dinesh's wedding in Feb, 1973.

Dinesh also recalled Mama Ji courting arrest during a Bathinda agitation on protecting the land belonging to a cow shelter (***goshala***). However, he was taken out of town and released in a far off village Nathana near Bathinda. Another memory embedded in his mind was of Mama Ji's love for sweets. On his way to Delhi from Bikaner, he used to bring sweet

Bengali ***rasgullas*** and spicy ***bhujia*** from Bikaner, as the train always passed through Bathinda.

Also, he recalled Mama Ji's uncommon swimming style in Sirhind canal-not splashing water with feet or flaying it with hands-his was a peaceful style!

Oct 14, 2013

ORAL REMINISCENCES

[Pramod K. Bhatnagar, age 67 years, is my third younger. He joined the workforce in India at a relative young age of 19 years-after finishing one year course of stenography from a newly started Industrial Training Institute in Bathinda. Before immigrating to the US in 1979, he served for several years in the Income Tax Department and State Bank of Patiala. All along, he took evening classes to finish his BA and MA (Public Administration). Working hard and long hours have become his second nature, and no amount of failures has blocked his ambitions. He stopped writing poetry (both in Hindi and English) after moving to the US. For the last 25+ years, he has been working in Las Vegas Hilton and doing real estate business.]

On the recollections of Swami Mama Ji, Pramod told me that he was hardly 15 years old (1961) when our father gave him a railway travel pass and let him go to Delhi alone-a distance of nearly 300 KM. It is unthinkable on the parts of today's parents-whether in India or in the US. The train journey was not a big thing, as father may have asked some of his railway acquaintances to help Pramod, if needed. The real test of his confidence was his coming out of crowded and Old Delhi railway station and going to Dewan Hall, where Mama Ji lived. He still remembers the rickshaw ride that brought him from the station about a mile and half away.

During one of his annual trips to Delhi, he accompanied Mama Ji and Jaidev Ji to Meerut, where Usha lived with her parents. Mama Ji wanted Jaidev Ji to meet the girl and give his approval for marriage. Jaidev Ji was too shy and asked Pramod to give his opinion! It is another scenario that is unthinkable in today's sexually uninhibited societies in India and the US.

Pramod told me that he had left meat eating at the instance of Mama Ji, but resumed it when he lived with us in Shimla for a year (1963-64) of his college. I did not know that I had such an unspoken influence. During Dewan hall stays, his memories of Mama Ji are of going out to buy fresh vegetables every morning and cook them nicely. Pramod never enjoyed eggplants the way our mother used to cook at home, but Mam Ji's preparation of eggplants, he relishes them even to this day.

During Mama Ji's visit to Bathinda, as a kid, Pramod remembers sweets and ***bhujia*** he brought for the kids, and taking the kids for long morning walks to Sirhind canal. He also reminiscenced Mama Ji's views on death. He has vivid memory of the last rites that Mama Ji performed at the death of our maternal grandfather in 1961, and of our father in 1971. I missed both the funerals for one reason and the other.

Actually, Mama Ji told me that out of the eighteen ***sanskars*** (ordained religious ceremonies) prescribed during a life time of the Hindus, the ***Antyeshati sanskar*** (the last rites ceremony) is the loftiest one in spirits. He would come in his elements especially during its performance.

Oct 15, 2013

ORAL REMINISCENCES

[Shashi, 65 years old, is my third younger brother. With sheer hard work and patience, he has built a good electrical business and name for the family. He exemplifies my favorite life theme that education is not limited within walls of schools and colleges. Those who believe in it, Indians by and large, miss out the grandeur of their lives. If one is keen to learn anything then one can do it-though it may take long. Shashi did not finish even high school, but he mastered the electrical wiring trade with his hands. Subsequently, with some family support and his ability to take advantage of opportunities, he has made us proud. He is settled in Bathinda and lives together with his enterprising son and his family.]

Shashi also recalled Mama Ji's bringing lot of quality sweets and ***Bhujia*** during his passages through Bathinda. It really tells the power of food on the minds of the people-young or old. The historic tradition of ***Langar*** in Sikh gurdwaras serves this purpose too-enjoying a fully cooked meal. Of course, there is a lot more to it-like, collective thinking and social engineering are behind the ***Langar***.

Mama Ji was fond of good food-whether it came to eating or cooking. He went one step further by serving delicious food to his visitors. During the conversation with Shashi, I asked his wife too, if she remembered anything about Mama Ji since their marriage in 1978. She recalled a vivid conversation between Mama Ji and my mother. Mother, being two years older, simply addressed him as Krishna. During that specific visit, Mama Ji politely explained to mother that Krishna had 'died' after the sanyas. For every one now, Swami Ji is the only way to address him. Mother listened and did not say a thing. But, I never heard her addressing him Swami Ji in a conversation with others or otherwise. Well, genetically it sure has rubbed to me, as I continued to address him as Mama Ji. However, mother's one younger sister, who too was older than Mama Ji by a few months, started addressing him as Swami Ji.

ORAL REMINISCENCES

[Ashwani Kumar Bhatnagar, 59 years old, is my fifth younger. He is one of the few persons whose life, most likely, would have been wasted away, had he stayed back in Bhatinda (BTI). Bad company and bad habits had started taking a toll on his life. He did not pass the 8th grade exam. But after coming to the US, he has thoroughly learnt every imaginable handy man's job-including painting, plumbing, electrical, landscaping, carpentry and mechanist, etc. Lately, he has been with the maintenance department of the world famous Bellagio Hotel and Casino since its opening in 1998. His collection of high quality tools gives him as much pride as the college diplomas give to a formally educated person.]

Being the youngest amongst the brothers, Ashwani's memories are of the affectionate nature of Mama Ji, who showered love on him. Mama Ji telling Ashwani not to address him as Mama Ji had no effect on Ashwani, as he kind of enjoyed teasing him by calling him Mama Ji. He did not have too many meetings with Mama Ji, as he never went to Sahibabad. Moreover, he left India in 1985.

Ashwani's vivid recollections are of his going to the BTI railway station to meet Mama Ji. After the ***sanyaas***, he stopped visiting the homes of his erstwhile relatives. During extended train stopovers at BTI station, he would send out a word at home on his arrival. The family members would then rush to meet him in the train or in some nearby waiting area.

It is rightly said that like an ocean is made of drops of water, so is a human life-made of simple memories.

[Madhu Anal, known by her nickname, Baby in a small family circle, is our only sister of six brothers. She is 17 years younger than I. In her life, she has known many places, people and things in two ways-firstly, while living under the shadows of one of her six older brothers; and secondly, in her own independent manner. Knowing Swami Mamaji is no exception to this rule either. Her ties with him are way different than that of mine.

It also speaks of the great persona of Mama Ji and our individual prisms of observing life around us. When I told her to prepare a write-up for the book, she readily agreed. Every few days, when I would check on its progress, she would tell me-"still not done". Finally, after 6-7 weeks, she turned it in a sheaf of 30 sheets. It is the most interesting description of the story of her life which intersected with the life of Mama Ji. Perhaps, she could write her own book on his life.

Once Mama Ji told me that a wealthy Arya Samaji of Jaipur wanted to donate a big parcel of land on Jaipur-Delhi highway for establishing a school. Mama Ji thought of Baby for this project. At that time, Baby and Anal, her more than a life partner, were running four different kinds of schools in Agra. Well, Baby surprised and disappointed Mama Ji, and others too, when she decided to leave India in 1992. She has not looked back! Giving surprises is next to her nature.

Her write-up is all in Hindi and is inserted the way it was received. By the way, she passed Hindi ***Prabhakar*** examination after passing her BA. It is usually done the other way around.]

मामा : "मा" प्रारम्भ "मा" अन्त

मेरे बड़े भाई (श्री सतीश भटनागर) ने कहा, "बेबी मामा जी के साथ अपने अनुभव लिखना।" अपने बड़े भाई को बहुत अधिक प्यार करती हूँ, उन्हें ना कैसे कह सकती थी?

माँ गायत्री का स्मरण तथा महान् गायत्री मंत्र का गायन करते हुये, स्वामी मामा जी के साथ वसंत ऋतु के फूल के समान बिताये गये कुछ पलों के संस्मरण का श्री गणेश कर रही हूँ।

सबसे पहले उस ऋषि को प्रणाम जिन्होंने माँ के भाई को 'मामा' नाम दिया। ऋषि ने निश्चय ही अनुभव किया होगा कि माँ का भाई (अपनी बहन के) मासूम नन्हे बच्चे को बेमिसाल प्यार देगा और तभी संगीतमय मीठा शब्द 'मा मा' का ईजाद हुआ होगा। शायद ऋषि ने चाँद में भी मामा के सदृश्य शीतलता का अनुभव कर उसे चँदामामा नाम दिया हो।

वनस्थली विद्यापीठ हो या समर्पण शोध संस्थान मामा जी मेरी प्यारी कुसुम दीदी (स्व०) को अक्सर कहा करते थे "बेबी दिल से काम करती है" आज दिल से प्रयास कर रही हूँ उन्हीं संस्मरणों को लिखने का।

पंजाब में जन्म, कान्वेन्ट स्कूल की प्राथमिक शिक्षा, वनस्थली विद्यापीठ की माध्यमिक शिक्षा पंजाबी यूनिवर्सिटी की उच्च शिक्षा तथा अमेरिका में प्रवास ने जीवन में ऐसा ताल-मेल उपस्थित किया है कि सही अर्थों में मैं भाषाविहीन हो गयी हूँ। मामा जी का संस्मरण अपने पारिवारिक बोल-चाल की भाषा में लिखने का प्रयास कर रही हूँ जिसमें व्याकरण एवं वाक्य विन्यास की त्रुटि सहज व स्वाभाविक होगी जिनका संपादन भी यहाँ सम्भव नहीं है। भाषागत दोष के लिये प्रारम्भ से ही क्षमा प्रार्थी हूँ।

'बाल निवास' घर में ज्योंहि खुशी की आवाज़ सुनायी देती मामाजी आ गये, मामा जी आ गये, मैं भाग कर मामा जी से लिपट जाती। मम्मी तो रसोई में होती थी पर वो भी उठ जाती "भैया आ गये"। मामा जी के मुँह से "बेबी" शब्द की ध्वनि आज भी गूँज रही है। मामा जी के साथ हमेशा बहुत सुन्दर आसमानी रँग की बड़ी सी बाँस की टोकरी होती थी। जो बचपन से ही मुझे जादू का पिटारा लगता था। मुझे याद है मामाजी मम्मी को आगरा का पेठा, कराँची का हलवा/सोहन हलवा नीली टोकरी से देते। मसाले वाली चटपटी काजू मुझे अपने हाथों से देते। आगरा की दालमोठ। बीकानेरी भुजिया। सोहन हलवा, शुद्ध घी के बेसन के लड्डू उनके प्रिये भक्त के बनाये होते थे। स्टील के डिब्बे से निकालकर मामा जी जब बंगाली सफेद रसगुल्ला देते तब मेरे भाई भी बहुत खुश होते। मुझे याद नहीं मामाजी ने बिना नीली टोकरी के कभी सफर किया हो। मैं नीली टोकरी से भी बहुत प्यार करती थी। मामाजी के हाथों में जादू था वो मुझे नीली टोकरी से उतना अपने हाथ से देते जितने से मेरा मन।जीभ तृप्त हो जाये। मामा जी के साथ मैंने ट्रेन में कई बार सफर किया। मेरे बिना माँगे नीली टोकरी से खाने को देते रहते। गुड़ की रेवड़ी, गुड़ की गजक, नमकीन बिना छिलके की मुंगफली, स्टील के चमकदार डिब्बे से बेसन के लड्डू सभी कुछ नीली टोकरी से निकाल कर देते थे। एक बार मैंने मामा जी से पूछा 'नीली टोकरी से आलू के पराठे भी निकलते हैं" मामा जी जोर से हँसे पर मुझे याद है मामा जी की नीली टोकरी से सिर्फ मेरे लिये अनारदाना डालकर मसाले वाले आलू के पराठे शुद्ध घी में (बचपन में मैं ध्यान नहीं देती थी घी। तेल किस में बना है) बना उसी नीली टोकरी से निकाल कर दिये थे। बड़ी होने पर देखा, मामा जी व कुसुम दीदी सूखी सब्जी सरसों तेल में बनाके भोजन शुद्ध घी के खाते थे।

एक बार मैं स्कूल से आई, और मामा जी की नीली टोकरी देखकर बहुत खुश हो गयी और मम्मी से पूछा मामा जी कहाँ हैं? मम्मी कहती यूनिफॉर्म पहले उतार कर और हाथ धोकर आ, तेरी पसँद की कढ़ी, चावल, खुरे आलू बनाये हैं। भैया को भी पसँद है। मैंने कहा नहीं, पहले मामा जी जो देंगे पहले वो खाऊँगी तब लँच करूँगी। मम्मी कहती मामा जी तो अभी घर नहीं हैं, प्रवचन/सभा में गये हैं, पता नहीं कब आयेंगे। मम्मी कहती थी मैं खाने की चटोरी हूँ। पर उस दिन मैंने कहा "नहीं मामा जी को आने दो तब खाना खाऊँगी। मम्मी की मैं जान थी। मम्मी शाम की चाय के साथ मेरे लिये दाल का पराठा बनाया और कहा खा लो बेबी। मैंने कहा नहीं। मुझे याद है बड़े भाई के कमरे में बाऊजी ने मैथ (Math) कराया। होमवर्क करवाया पर मेरे भीतर तो यही चलता रहा कि मामा जी कब आयेंगे। पहले तो नीली टोकरी में खाने का ध्यान था। अब रात होने लगी मामा जी कहाँ हैं? क्यों नहीं आये? मैं मम्मी के पास सोने आ गयी और मम्मी से पूछा 'मामा जी मेरे पैदा होने पर आये थे। मम्मी ने कहा- जब तू आने वाली थी, मैंने तेरे बाऊजी से कहा- अबकी बार आपकी बहन मेरी मदद करने नहीं आयेगी। मेरी बहन रामा आयेगी। आपकी बहन बेटे लाती, मेरी बहन बेटी लायेगी। कहती तेरी रामा मौसी आयी और जब तेरा जन्म हुआ, तेरी मौसी गायत्री मँत्र का जप कर रही थी। उसने तुझे अपना दूध भी पिलाया। तेरे मामा जी ने तुझे गोदी में ले सर सूँघा, प्यार किया। मुझे याद है मुझे उतना अच्छा लगा। मामा जी ने मुझे बचपन में उठाया। मैं कब सो गयी पता नहीं। पर जब मैं उठी नीली टोकरी गायब। मम्मी ने बताया कि मामा जी तो गये। मुझे सोते में प्यार कर के गये। मैंने उन्हें बताया 'बेबी ने कुछ नहीं खाया', तेरे लिये नीली टोकरी से बहुत कुछ खाने को दे गये। पर मैंने नहीं खाया, मुझे लगे मामा जी ने क्यों अपने हाथ से

नही दिया ? एक मासूम बच्चे की प्यार की तपस, मामा जी
जैसे ऋषि को ना पहुँचे यह असम्भव है। इतना याद है
कि मम्मी कहती तेरी अच्छी अच्छी फ्रॉक जूते मोजे
आदि सामान रख रही हूँ तेरे मामा जी आ रहे हैं वो
तुझे रामा मौसी के पास धौलपुर ट्रेन से ले जायेंगे।
मैं तो इतनी खुश लगा मामा जी के साथ ट्रेन में। मामा
जी और मैं, कौन सी स्टोरी सुनाऊंगी। मामा जी आये। यह
पहली बार था, मम्मी ने मुझे अपने से जुदा कर मामा जी के
साथ भेजा, पर मम्मी को पता था, मामा जी मुझे बहुत प्यार
करते हैं। मम्मी उनकी बड़ी बहन + प्यारी बहन बीबी है, बीबी
की जान को वो लेकर जा रहे हैं। ट्रेन मे याद है, मुझे फर्स्ट
क्लास का केबिन, मामा जी, मैं बीबी नौकरी, दो सेवक।
मैं अपनी बातें मामा जी को सुनाती रही। बचपन से ही
मेरे बड़े भाई और प्रमोद भाई मुझे राखी पर जन्मदिन
पर अंग्रेजी की पुस्तकें देते थे। मामा जी को छोटेपन से मेरी
अंग्रेजी की स्टोरिज। मैने कई बार स्कूल की शरारतें भी
मामा जी को बताती थी, मामा जी जोर से हँसते थे "पगली"
उनका मेरे लिये प्यार से लबालब जिवन्त शब्द रहा।
बड़े भाई ने Mother Goose Classical Fairy Tale Book
दिया था, तो वो मोटी बुक धौलपुर साथ लेकर गयी।
मैं मामा जी के पास किताब लेकर गोद मे बैठ गयी मुझे
Green Peas Princess कहानी अच्छी लगी, जब मामा जी को
सुनायी, कहते तू तो अपने भाईओ की शहजादी है और बड़े प्यार
से सर पर हाथ फेरते हुये कहते तू बीबी की प्यारी व लाडली है।
तेरे सब भाई तुझे कितना प्यार करते हैं, मामा जी ने कहा
"तेरी इस मोटी किताब कि हरे मटर की राजकुमारी जो है वो तो
सिर्फ अपने माँ बाप की लाडली है, तू तो अपने सभी भाईओ
पूरा परिवार की राजकुमारी है, बीबी की तो इतनी लाडली है
महारानी है, तू तो बोल नियारा' घर की रौनक है। अच्छी

तरह यह बात मेरे बाल मानस में बैठ गयी कि मैं Green Peas Princess हूँ जिन्हे मामा जी अति प्यार से "पगली" कहते हैं। (यह एहसास मुझे हमेशा बना रहा) धौलपुर स्टेशन पर मुझे याद है, मामा जी ने मेरा हाथ पकड़ा और कहा बेबी जब बहन 'रामा' के घर पहुँचेंगे तु चुप रहना। रजेन्द्र भाई साहब रेलवे मे बड़े आफिसर थे बहुत बड़ा बंगला था। 'बाल निवास' की तरह यहाँ भी मुबिक शोर 'मामाजी आगये', मामा जी आ गये। सब मामा जी से मिले, मौसी ने पूछा भैया यह बच्ची कौन है? मामा जी ने कहा मेरे परिचित की। मैं तो चुप थी क्योंकि मामाजी ने कहा था। मामाजी को घेरकर सब खुशी से भीतर चले गये। मैं अकेले रूम मे 5 मिनट या 10 मिनट बैठी रही, मौसी जी दौड़ती पर्दे को हटाती बेबी बेबी कहकर मुझे सीने से लगाया, पीछे मामा जी व मेरे सभी भाई बहनें आयी। सब इतना प्यार करे बेबी। मौसी जी बोली 'बीबी' ने इसे कैसे भेज दिया? मामा जी के शब्द याद है कहा जब कहा परिचित की बेटी है तो इस नन्ही सी बच्ची की किसी को परवाह नहीं, जब पता लगा बीबी की भतीजी की राजकुमारी आयी है, तो देखो अब मुझे भूल गये। मौसी जी का, राजेन्द्र भाई सा० और भाभी, शशी दीदी, उमा दीदी, राकेश भाई, बब्बू भैया, गुड्डू भैया का इतना प्यार मिला। मामा जी तो प्रवचन / सभा आदि मे चले गये थे। याद नहीं शायद 10 दिन रही पर मेरे को जब वापिस भाठेडा जाना था, मेरे लिये साटन कपड़े का हल्के पीले रंग का चुड़ीदार पजामा कुर्ता शायद किसी बहन ने सिला था। मामा जी कहते देखते नहीं बेबी कैसे बढ़िया फ्रॉक पहनती है। यह क्या बना दिया? मुझे अच्छी तरह ध्यान है भाभी ने रेडीमेड ड्रेस वो फ्रॉक दिलवाये। मामा जी तब खुश हुये। यह मेरा मामा जी का रिश्ता था।

एक बार पता नहीं कैसे मुझे पता लगा कि मामा जी आने वाले हैं। मैं तो बस प्लानिंग करूं, मामा जी हमेशा जादुई टोकरी से मेरी पसंद की चीज निकालकर मेरी पसंद का निकालकर खाने को देते हैं, मैं क्या दूं। मेरे शशी भाई बिजनेस काम से दिल्ली गये थे और मेरे लिये latest फैशन का स्कूल बैग जो Aluminium का बहुत सुन्दर अटैची जिसमें मेरी सारी Books, Notebooks आ जाती थी लाकर दिया था। मुझे याद है, स्कूल में मेरी Class के सभी बच्चों ने पूछा था कहां से यह लिया है। मैंने कहा मेरे भाई दिल्ली से लाये हैं बाद में एक दो बच्चों के पास तथा 1 साल में तो सभी बच्चों के पास ऐसा बैग आ गया था। मुझे लगा कि मामा जी की जादुई टोकरी की तरह मैं अपने स्कूल के सूटकेस में से मामा जी को निकाल कर कुछ दूं। मैं जब घर आयी, मम्मी तो इतना गुस्सा हुआ कहां गयी थी। तेरी स्कूल की बस तो कबकी चली गयी। मैंने मामा जी को देखा और दौड़ती उनके पास गयी। मम्मी तो गुस्से में थी कहा पहले इससे पूछो। मामा जी ने इतना प्यार से पूछा- बेटी कहां से आ रही है। मैंने कहा- मामा जी आँख बंद कीजिये। मम्मी तो पता नहीं क्या क्या कर रही थी, पर मामा जी ने आँखे बंद किया और मैंने अटैची में से Cadbury Milk चाकलेट निकालकर मामा जी के हाथ में रखकर कहा, मामा जी आँखे खोलो। मामा जी ने कहा, बेटी कहां से लाई? क्या है? मैंने कहा मामाजी आप हमेशा अपने झोला से जादुई टोकरी से सब को खाने को देते, मुझे लगा कि मैं भी आपको दूं चॉकलेट"। मामा जी बोले बेटी पैसे कहां से आये बाजार कैसे गयी? मैंने कहा- बस से उतरी रिक्शा वाला दिनेश भाई को जानता था शशी भाई को भी। बस से उतर कर रिक्शे पर बैठ कर धोबी बाजार गयी। शशी भाई साहेब के दोस्त दिल्ली से यह चाकलेट मंगवाते हैं, पैसे की जरूरत नहीं। मामा जी इतना हँसे कहते 'पगली" मामा जी का मेरे प्रति अटूट विश्वास कि मैं गलत सोचती नहीं तो करूंगी कैसे?

एक बार भठिण्डा में ही शायद मम्मी ने मामा जी से शायद कुछ कहा होगा, मेरे कान्वेन्ट स्कूल में पढ़ना, जीसस को गॉड की तरह मानना, ~~मुझे नहीं पता~~ मैं गले में चेन उसमें क्रॉस पहनती थी। मामाजी आये जीतो टोकरी का प्रसाद सब को मिल गया, मुझे ध्यान है, मैं उनके पास बैठी थी, जब कभी मन किया Sweet गणेशा Belly को प्यार भी करती, मामा जी पर बहुत लाड आता दाढ़ी भी सहलाती, मम्मी गुस्से में टोकती क्यों ऐसे करती है? मामा जी ने पूछा 'बेबी तु गले में यह क्रॉस क्यों पहनती है? मैंने कहा मामा जी मम्मी इसे तुनतुना कहती, दिलवी है। अब तो गोपाल (मेरा छोटा भाई) भी पहनता है। मामा जी ने फिर प्यार से पूछा 'बेबी क्यों पहनती है? मैंने कहा मामा जी आप भी सफेद धुले कपड़े एकदम सफेद पहनते हैं, जीसस भी। आप के भी लम्बे बाल हैं, जीसस के भी। आपके भी लम्बी दाढ़ी जीसस के भी। आप भी इतने सुन्दर, गोरे गुलाबी गाल हैं, जीसस के भी, मुझे आप बहुत अच्छे-सुन्दर लगते हो जीसस एकदम आप जैसे। मामा जी इतना जोर से हँसे, कहते "पगली"

मैंने देखा कि मम्मी की इच्छा या बात, मामा जी हमेशा आदर व प्रेम भाव से मानते थे। जब मेरी बड़ी भतीजी गौरी का जन्म हुआ, नाम संस्कार, मुंडन संस्कार मामा जी ने बहुत धूम धाम से वैदिक ढंग से किया। मामा जी इतने मिठास से बोलते थे जितनी मीठी तो चीनी भी नहीं। जो हलवाई पुड़ी बना रहा था उसे मामा जी ने बड़े प्यार से कहा 'भाई पुड़ी एक तो फूलनी चाहिये और पुड़ी का स्वाद तभी है जब आटे में नमक ही अजवाइन हो, कढ़ाई में घी जब खौलने लगे तभी गोल छोटी लोई की पुड़ी बना कर डालो। शायद यह भी कहा था पलटना नहीं, पर याद नहीं, मुझे इतना पता है, मेरी मम्मी तो ऐसे ही सिखाती थी। मामा जी का सुनकर मुझे लगा, पुड़ी बनाना आ गया। ऐसे ही मामा जी का सलाद काटना। आलू, सेब, प्याज को जब छिलते थे, मुझे तो जादू लगता था। एक बार छिलका उतारना शुरू

करते डिलायमन सा बनाकर खतम करते। जब मैं उमर से बड़ी हो गयी संस्थान में अनन्त जी, कुसुम दीदी भी थी मामाजी रसोई के बाहर बरामदे में आराम कुर्सी पर पकौड़े की तैयारी के लिये धनिया इतनी सफाई, महीन सुन्दरता लिये कैसे काटते थे समझ में नहीं आता। मैंने कहा मामा जी मुझे सिखाये आलू छिलना। उन्होंने जोर से हँसते हुये कहा 'बेबी का रसोई से क्या काम? तु तो प्रेम से खा। मामा जी भरमें करेले बनाते थे गजब के। कड़वा तो होता नहीं था। करेला में कुछ भी डालते थे। 1980 में जब मैं पहली बार बिहार अपने परिवार में गयी, बड़ी दीदी जीजा जी से कहा 'भरवा मसाले वाले करेले, मैं बनाऊँ, मेरे मामा जी जैसा, कुछ भी वो डालते हैं सब हैरान। खैर। मामा जी के हाथों में जादू है, हृदय से खाना जो भी पकाते वो पूजा भाव से, प्रेम से खिलाते जिसका आनन्द ही कुछ और होता। मेरे करेले तो कड़वे, नमक इतना तेज, मैं तो जीभ पर भी नहीं रख पायी। अब एहसास होता है मामा जी की मिठास प्रेम से खिलाने का आनन्द, जो प्रसाद बन जाता था।

दीवान हॉल: मेरे मामा जी का घर :- ढेर सारी सीढ़ियाँ चढ़ने के बाद इतनी बड़ी छत पर मंदिर के गुम्बद के नीचे मेरे मामा जी का घर। छत इतनी बड़ी रात में आकाश के सब सितारे चन्दा मामा सब दिखते। यहाँ मैं हर साल गर्मी की छुट्टियों के बाद स्कूल के पहले दिन जाती, अपने class Mates से कहती मुझे याद है, हमें डायरी लिखना होता था "about my Summer Vacation' तो मैं पुरे दो पेज मामा जी को अपने English Essay में लिखती तो English Subject की Sister कहती Is your mamaji a Prince? मैं कहती 'He is King' you have to go and visit his place opposite to Red Fort" but you have to climb 500 steps" जब मामा जी को मिलने मोहन भाई साहेब के साथ मम्मी और मैं जाती थी मम्मी कहती

इतनी सिढीयाँ? मम्मी तो एक बार ही जाती थी। बचपन में तो सिढीयाँ मुझे याद थी पर अब ठीक से याद नहीं। मामा जी के पास हमेशा कोई न कोई सेवक जरूर रहता था और मामा जी हमें कुछ न कुछ गरमा गरम खिलाना चाहते थे जबकि मम्मी हमेशा मामा जी के पसंद का खाना लेकर जाती थी। मुझे याद है मामा जी कहते " अरे भाई जबतक स्टोव की नीली लौ ना जले, स्टोव पर बरतन रखोगे तो काला हो जायेगा। फिर बरतन रगड़ते रहना चमक नहीं आयेगी। मैंने यह भी सिख लिया, पर मामा जी का धैर्य रसोई में यह साधना अभी तक चल रही है। जब मैं मम्मी के साथ गर्मियों की छुट्टी में दिल्ली आती मोहन भाई साहेब मुझे मामा जी के पास दीवान हॉल लेकर जाते। मैं गाने का अपने शब्दों में पैरोडी बनाकर सुनाती।

स्कूल में एक बार Essay में लिखा, दिल्ली में दो चीजें सबसे ऊँची कुतुब मीनार एवं मेरे मामाजी का घर दीवान हॉल चाँदनी चौक में चार खुली छत पर। you have to climb 500 steps एकदम Red Fort के सामने। मेरे क्लास में 30 बच्चे थे, They all believed that my mamaji is King but in my heart he really is (not was) King. मुझे याद है दोपहर में कोई मिलने वाला नहीं होता था, मैं तो उछलती-फुदकती मामाजी को गाने का पैरोडी बनाकर सुनाती और मामा जी हँसते। मामाजी खड़ी गरमा गरम काला गुलाब जामुन etc नीली टोकरी से निकालकर खिलाते। दीवान हॉल में मामा जी का कमरा साथ में एक और कमरा, सिर्फ पुस्तकें। मामा जी तो शोध etc में व्यस्त रहते, No toys, No TV, No my age children, but it was paradise for me, because of my mamaji's pure love. दीवान हॉल में मैं जब पहुँचती थी हमेशा मामा जी प्यार से कहते 'बेबी तो बहुत प्यारी लग रही है'। मैं चहकती

बोलती अपनी फ्रॉक के बारे में कौन सा भाई लाये हैं" अधिकतर दिनेश भाई साहिब / मोहन भाई साहिब / Bombay से शशी भाई साहिब latest design की फ्रॉक/शू मैचिंग socks लाते थे, मुझे ध्यान है मैं सोचती मामा जी के पास पहनकर जाना है, मामा जी कितना खुश होंगे। तब लगता था, मामाजी को मेरी फ्रॉक, शू, हेयर क्लीप ok अच्छा लगता है, पर मामा जी को तो मैं तब भी उनकी 'Green Pea Princess लगती बिना आयरन की हुयी खादी की सफेद सूत पहनती।

एक बार मामा जी अपने साथ मुझे जालंधर ले गये। डा० विद्यावती का, पता नहीं कितने एकड़ का विशाल बगीचा बड़ा घर जहाँ मैं मामाजी के साथ सात-आठ दिन रही थी। मामा जी महायज्ञ करवा रहे थे। पूरा परिवार मामा जी का भक्त, मामा जी के लिये इतना प्रेम, अपने हाथों से शुद्ध घी का पीन्नी (लड्डू) के लड्डू लाते। मामा जी की नीली टोकरी कैसे नमकीन, मिठाई, मेवे से भरी रहती है यह मेरे मन में कभी नहीं आया। मुझे लगता था जादू के पिटारे में अपने आप आती हैं क्योंकि मामा जी इतना अपने हाथों से बांटते थे, आज लिखते वक्त लग रहा है नीली टोकरी कैसे भरी रहती थी। मैं उमर से बड़ी होती रही, पर नीली टोकरी के प्रति वही भाव बने रहे। कैसा है यह खेल? जालंधर में इतना विशाल यज्ञ स्थल देख मैं हैरान होती। मामा जी कितने प्रेम से एक-एक से मिलते, आशीर्वाद देते, कभी उनके चेहरे पर थकान नहीं देखा। मामा जी को पता था सब मेरा कितना ध्यान रख रहे हैं पर तब भी मुझे ध्यान है सोने से पहले, सर पर हाथ रखते, सहलाते। मामाजी को सफाई अति प्रिय थी चादर तकिया-कोई सिलवटें नहीं। मुझे याद है, मामा जी एक बार कहा बेबी सोने जा रही है, पर बहुत अच्छे कपड़े पहनी है, मैंने कहा मामा जी, यह अच्छे कपड़े नहीं, Night Suit है। इतना जोर से

हँसे और कहा 'पगली'। मुझे कभी एहसास नहीं हुआ कि मामा कितने famous status लोगों के VVIP हैं। पर आज लगता है कैसे मामा जी इतने व्यस्त सामाजिक धार्मिक जीवन में मेरी छोटी-छोटी बातों को ध्यान से सुनते और मुझे प्रेम से भर देते। मैं उनकी Green Tea Princess थी।

एक बार पंजाब में ही कोई शहर नाम याद नहीं, इतने सारे यज्ञशाला शायद 54 या 108 हवनकुंड बने थे और सब पर शायद पति-पत्नी बैठे थे, कुछ लोग सिंहासन जैसी Chairs पर बैठे थे। मामा जी का बहुत सुन्दर राजा की तरह मंच। प्रथम दिन जब कोई आयोजक मुझे मंच के ऊपर ले गये, मामा जी ने उन्हें बड़े प्यार से कहा नहीं यह आपके परिवार की बच्ची है, आपके परिवार के साथ बैठेगी। मामा जी का भाव तब तो समझ नहीं पायी अब समझ में आ रहा है। इशारा था, योग्यता हो तो मंच पर बैठना शोभनीय है न कि रिश्तेदार होने के नाते। I love it.

वनस्थली विद्यापीठ: जालंधर सुरेश भाई के पास जनवरी 1, 1970 को बाबूजी की अचानक मृत्यु हो गयी। मामा जी का अपनी बहन के प्रति प्रेम करुणा हमेशा मैंने महसूस किया। मामा जी जालंधर आये। मम्मी ने मेरे भाईओं से कहा बेबी को वनस्थली विद्यापीठ में पढ़ाने के लिये। तो स्वयं मुझे वनस्थली विद्यापीठ लेकर जायेंगे। मामा जी ने कहा बेटी कुसुम वनस्थली विद्यापीठ कालेज में ही पढ़ रही है। वनस्थली विद्यापीठ भारत का बहुत ही प्रतिष्ठित शिक्षा संस्थान है। बेबी को वनस्थली विद्यापीठ का माहौल व होस्टल अच्छा लगेगा तो बेबी का एडमिशन वहीं हो जायेगा। मामा जी के साथ मम्मी और मैं ट्रेन से दिल्ली, दिल्ली से जयपुर, वहां से वनस्थली विद्यापीठ पहुंचे। इतना विशाल संस्थान, 5वीं कक्षा से पीएचडी तक

की पढ़ाई। मम्मी को तो कुसुम दीदी की शालीनता प्रेम से मिलना, तथा बेबी मेरी देख-रेख मे रहेगी कहना बहुत अच्छा लगा। हम मामा जी के परिचित नाम ध्यान नहीं, उन्हे मैं, दीदी मम्मी शायद मामा जी भी "ग्रेमा" जी कहते थे उनका two bedroom क्वाटर हमारा घरौंदा बन गया। मम्मी तो बहुत प्रसन्न हुयी। कान्वेन्ट स्कूल मे मम्मी को लगता था Co education है, मेरे लिये अच्छा नही। मामा जी ने हमेशा मम्मी के खाने की रसोई सफाई की प्रशंसा की। मम्मी साथ के साथ किचेन साफ करती थी व गर्मा गर्म खाना मामा जी को खिलाने का व खाने का काम बहुत शौक से करती थी। क्वाटर के पीछे खुला स्थान, वहाँ बहुत पेड़, हरियाली तथा बहुत से मोर पँछी मुझे आज भी याद है। मम्मी कहती भैया कितना अच्छा मोर, और पँछी व हरियाली यहाँ है। हम सब बाहर चटाई पर और मामा जी आराम कुर्सी पर बैठे थे, मामा जी ने पूछा 'बेबी तुम्हे पँछी जानवर पसंद है, मैंने कहा हाँ' मामा जी ने कहा - अपनी जीभ स्वाद न पाने के लिये इनके प्राण तो नहीं लेगी? मैंने कहा कभी नहीं, मै तो मीट खाती नहीं। मामा जी तुरत बोले पूछ बीबी से। जब मीट बनता है, उसमे आलू बीबी डालती है, और तू सोचती है कि तेरे लिये आलू की मसालेदार सब्जी बनी है। मैने मम्मी से पूछा मम्मी ऐसा करती हो ? मै गुस्सा हो गयी थी फिर मम्मी ने कहा हाँ, फिर मम्मी मामा जी से बोली 'भैया पता नहीं कैसे घर मे शादी हो, ससुराल मे बनाना पड़ा etc मुझे याद है मैंने पैर पटक कर कहा - मैं शादी नही करूंगी। मामा जी हँसते रहे, मम्मी ने कहा भैया बेबी को अब ऐसे कभी नहीं खिलाऊँगी। मामा जी का संकेत जो मै समझी। इस प्रभु की सुन्दर नगरी मे हम खुशी स्वतंत्र निर्भय जीना चाहते हैं, तो कैसे निरपराध, भयग्रस्त जीव की हत्या कर स्वा

कभी हम निर्णय करनामय हो सकते हैं? वहीं से मामा
जी मम्मी को वापिस दिल्ली ले गये।
मामा जी जब आते, कुसुम दीदी और मैं मामा जी के
चारों ओर प्रेम आश्रयाना मुझे लगता था मामा जी जितने
दिन वहाँ रुकते हम दोनों वहीं रहते। दीदी का तो अध्ययन
पढ़ाई, शायद वेद के गहरे सूत्र की होगी क्योंकि मामा जी
बहुत पढ़ाते थे दीदी को मोटी-मोटी ग्रंथों से। कई बार
दीदी कहती अब नहीं तो मामा जी बहुत स्नेह से कहते, बेटी
कुसुम बस 'यह संगीतमय इतना शब्द है' या कि नहीं, मुझे
कभी कुछ नहीं कहा। मैं ही अपने स्कूल की कुछ घटना सुनाती
तो जोर से हँसते और कहते 'पगली'। नीली टोकरी से अपने
हाथों से निकालकर 3-4 बार कुछ न कुछ देते रहते। दीदी को
मैंने नमकीन-मीठा कभी खाते नहीं देखा क्योंकि वो बाजार का
बना कुछ नहीं खाती थी। दीदी से मुझे इतना प्यार हो गया-
उनकी सादगी, सफाई व सुन्दरता और जीवन के व्रतों का पालन
पर मैं तो कुछ आलसी 'मामा जी की पगली'। जब मम्मी चली
गयी मैंने जिद किया- दीदी रात का खाना आपके साथ खाऊँगी
और सोऊँगी भी आपके पास। दीदी ने कहा नहीं, समझाया
भी। मैंने कहा "No" तो दीदी ने मामा जी से कहा। मामा जी
तो जोर-जोर से हँसते कहते, इस मामले में मुझे नहीं फँसा।
मैंने खाना नहीं खाया। स्कूल अगले दिन बिना खाये गयी। एक
दिन 'डिनर' ना करने से ही प्यारी दीदी का बाल ब्रह्मचारी हृदय
पिघल गया। दीदी को पता था कि I love food. चटपटे
नमकीन नीली टोकरी से खाना। मामा जी हँसते दीदी फिर मेरे
साथ खाती। जब भी हम साथ होते रात सोने के लिये दीदी कहती
सोजा पर छूना मत। मैंने कहा दीदी मैं तो कमर में हाथ डालकर
सोती हूँ। मामा जी के Sweet गणेशा Belly को भी तो प्यार
करती हूँ। मुझे याद है दीदी कहती 'देखो यह क्या बना है मैंने

बताया - मामा जी के भारी तोंद का नाम मैंने रखा
है 'Sweet गणेशा Belly'। मामा जी और दीदी तो
इतना हँसे, दीदी तो लोटपोट, मामा जी ने तब हँसते हँसते
कहा 'पगली' I know मामा जी को आनन्द आगया। मेरी
हरकतें या बातों से जो भी हो दीदी का मुझसे बहुत प्यार
रहा। जब मैं गोद में होती मुझे "हीरो" कहती थी। दीदी
कहती ठीक है सो जा और प्यार से अपनी बांहें मुझपर रखती।
मामा जी के साथ मैं जहाँ कहीं भी गयी, रात में सोते में
सर पर हाथ से सहलाते थे, आज सोचती हूँ वही उनका आशीर्वाद
होता होगा। एक बार मामा जी ने दीदी से कहा 'बेबी कुसुम
बेबी से तुम्हे स्नेह हो गया, मातृत्व जान जाना बुरा नहीं तू
बेबी को गोद ले ले। मामा जी तो शाखा प्रवचन आदि में रहते
थे, दीदी शायद मेरी लोकल गार्जियन थीं। एक बार मैं घुड़सवारी
सीखने में Pony से गिर गयी। दीदी को तुरंत खबर गयी (मुझे
तो अब एहसास हो रहा है कि दीदी और मामा जी वनस्थली
के महान प्रतिष्ठित व सम्मानित विद्वानों में से थे, तब तो सिर्फ
मेरे मामा जी, मेरी दीदी और मेरे लिये मामा जी की मोटू
की बोलो लेकरी ही सबकुछ था) मैं वनस्थली के हास्टल
के बेड पर थी। हास्पिटल की गाड़ी से 3 लोग (ड्राइवर नहीं जोड़कर)
और दीदी मेरे साथ मुझे जयपुर लेकर गये। वहाँ वनस्थली
के हम Students ही जाते थे। X Ray वगैरह हुआ। कोई fracture
नहीं था। सिर्फ मोच थी। दीदी तो पूरा समय अपने मंत्र
जपती रहीं और मेरा हाथ पकड़े रहीं। मुझे पता नहीं मामा
जी को दीदी ने क्या कहा, पर अगले दिन हम मामा जी के
सामने में मामा जी के साथ थे। दीदी को एक ही चिन्ता 'मौसी
जी को मैंने वचन दिया था, बेबी मेरी देख-रेख में रहेगी' मामा
जी के आने पर दीदी की आँखों में सुकून के आँसू भी आ गये थे।
मैं दीदी के एकदम करीब बिस्तर पर लेटी थी, मैंने कहा मैं
ठीक हूँ, मामा जी ने दीदी से हल्दी तेल etc का लेपलगवाकर

स्वयं अपने हाथों से मेरे पैरों की तरफ लगाया। कहते बेबी तो दौड़ेगी। उड़ान भी भरेगी। पर लोगों को अभी पता चलेगा। मैंने कहा - मामा जी, मैं तो Gliding सीखने जाती थी, पर Instructor ने कहा मेरा वज़न कम होता है, मामा जी इतने ज़ोर से हँसे कहते पगली हवाई Gliding करते कुछ गड़बड़ होता तो। मामा जी को दीदी ने कहा - मामा जी आप बेबी से कहें तो आपको पूछ कर कुछ करे। मामा जी इतने ज़ोर से हँसे कहते बेटी कुसुम बेबी मैं तो कर लेगी, तब बतायेगी। मुझे याद है दीदी ने कहा - यह तो बिगड़ने के लक्षण हैं? मामाजी ने कहा बेटी कुसुम 'बेबी कुछ गलत करेगी नहीं' मामाजी के ये 5 शब्द मेरे लिये मंत्र बन गया। यह 5 शब्द मेरे लिये निस्वार्थ प्रेम की रेखा (लक्ष्मण रेखा) रही।

एक बार दीदी ने काली स्कर्ट Printed Red flower का टॉप मेरे लिये राजस्थानी टेलर से बनवाया (राजस्थानी में शॉपिंग, टेलर आदि सभी सुविधायें थीं) मैं अगले दिन उसे पहनकर स्कूल गयी। सबने कहा मैं बड़ी सुन्दर लग रही हूँ। मुझे पता नहीं क्या सूझी मैंने मामाजी से पूछा दीदी हमेशा सफेद कपड़े खादी की क्यों पहनती हैं, कब से पहनती हैं आदि आदि। मामा जी ने बताया दीदी जब 9th-10th class में थी तब उन्होंने सफेद कपड़ा पहनना शुरू किया। मैंने कहा मामाजी, आज दीदी जब कॉलेज से आयेगी, मेरी इच्छा है उन्हें Black स्कर्ट Red flower Top पहनने को कहूँ। मामा जी तो इतने ज़ोर से हँसे कहते 'पगली' मुझे याद है कहते तू यह खाली नौकरी से। मैंने कहा नहीं आज तो ख्वाब है दीदी को रंगीन ड्रेस में देखना, और आप कहते हैं कि दीदी ने तो कभी रंगीन कपड़ा नहीं पहना। दीदी को कैसे मनाऊँगी Only for one moment, मामा जी कहते तेरा गोरखधंधा हो जाय। मामा जी के झमेला, गोरखधंधा आदि कॉमन शब्द थे। गर्मी का मौसम था, मामा जी ने ठंडाई या पेय पदार्थ बनाया था। दीदी

शाम को आयो। दीदी कॉलेज में खादी की साड़ी पतली रंगीन
बॉर्डर वाली पहनती थी, सर्दी में सफेद शुद्ध खादी का और खादी
का ही दुपट्टा। मैंने बहुत प्यार से कहा दीदी, एक बार मुझे
Black स्कर्ट तथा Printed Red Flower Top पहनकर दिखाओ।
दीदी ने कहा होरी तेरा दिमाग खराब है, दीदी ने यह भी कहा
बेबी मुझे पता है तु अब खाना नहीं खायेगी। दीदी ने मामा जी
के रूम में जाकर कहा - बेबी की जिद्द ठिक नहीं। मामा जी ने
कहा तुम दोनो का झमेला, मुझे कोई मतलब नहीं, पर मुझे
इतना पता है, आज रात अध्ययन चौपट। दीदी कहती - नहीं
अध्ययन तो करूँगी बेबी को करने दो जिद्द। मामा जी ने कहा
बेटी कुसुम तेरा मन पढ़ाई में लगेगा नहीं। मामा जी हँसते बोलते
रहे, दीदी ने शायद दिखाने के लिये खाया, मैंने तो खाया नहीं।
अगले दिन Thursday था वनस्थली में Thursday off होता था
पढ़ाई नहीं। (अब पता नहीं) छुट्टी का दिन था मुझे पता नहीं क्या
सुझी, मैंने प्रातः अपने आपको Toilet में बंद कर लिया। मुझे
इतना याद है, धूप थी, Toilet बाहर था Indian Style। दीदी
ने बहुत बार दरवाजा खटकाया और कहा बेबी, दरवाजा खोल
बाहर आ। मैंने एक बार कहा - आप हाँ कहोगी तब आऊँगी। दीदी
की आवाज गुंज रही है, छोटी गलत बात पर जिद्द ठिक नहीं। मैं चुप
होकर शायद 1 घंटा या 1½ घंटा बन्द रही, दीदी ने जब हाँ कहा मैंने
फिर दरवाजा खोला। मामा जी की हँसी की आवाज उनके कमरे
से सुनी। मैं और दीदी अपने रूम में आये। दीदी ने मुझे Black
top, Red flower Printed स्कर्ट पहन कर दिखायी। दीदी इतनी
सुन्दर लग रही थी मैं उनके गले से लिपट कर इतनी रोयी और
दीदी से कहा अब मैं कभी आपको तंग नहीं करूँगी, मैं भी आपके
तरह सफेद कपड़े पहनुँगी। मामा जी को रोते - रोते बताया कि
दीदी मुझे इतना प्यार करती है, हम दोनों मामा जी के पास मामा
जी के गोद में प्रेम के आँसू बहा रहे थे। (दीदी वही आपने सफेद खादी
रूप में मुझे माँ सरस्वती लगी, वो आकृति दीदी को भूलती नहीं।

मामा जी ने दीदी के सर पर हाथ रखकर कहा माँ की इच्छा का भाव बहुत ऊँचा, तेरा बैबी के प्रति प्रेम लगाव तू इसे गोद ले ले।

वनस्थली में मामाजी ब्रह्ममुहूर्त में उठते। दीदी आसन प्राणायाम और ध्यान करती। कई बार मामाजी दीदी को ध्यान की प्रक्रिया बताते, पर मुझे कुछ भी नहीं कहते। दीदी ही मामा जी से कहती आप बेबी से कहो कि वह भी जल्दी उठे, अपनी पढ़ाई करे। मुझे याद है मामा जी के शब्द 'बेबी को जब लगेगा, वह ब्रह्ममुहूर्त में उठेगी, ध्यान आसन सब करेगी।

दीदी सर की मालिश बड़ी अच्छी करती थी, मेरा तो Boy cut हेयर स्टाईल था पर दीदी के बहुत सुन्दर लम्बे काले बाल, दीदी ने मुझे सिखाया कैसे सर में तेल लगा मालिश करना है। एक बार मैंने मामा जी से कहा - आज मैं आपके सर की मालिश करूँगी। मामा जी ने कहा - यह क्या बवाल शुरू करना है? मामा जी का एक शब्द 'बवाल' भी हुआ करता था। मामा जी मुझे ना तो कहते नहीं पे जब मैंने मालिश किया, मामा जी खुशी से मीठी आवाज में कहा - बेबी ने यह गुण कहाँ सिखा? मैंने कहा दीदी से।

मुझे मामा जी की खादी की बड़ी सी सफेद बनियायन जिसकी बड़ी सी विचित्र पाकेट होती थी मामा जी के Sweet गणेश Belly पर बड़ी अच्छी लगती थी। मैंने मामा जी को दिवान हॉल व वनस्थली में पहने देखा। मैं दीदी से सब तरह की बात करती थी तो एक दिन दीदी से कहा - मेरा मन मामा जी की बनियायन पहनने का करता है। दीदी कहती छोरी तेरा तो दिमाग एकदम खराब है। दीदी ने मामा जी से कहा - मामा जी तो 'पगली' कह हँसते रहे। उन्हीं दिनों वनस्थली के वार्षिक उत्सव की तैयारी जोर शोर से चल रही थी। अपनी कक्षा से मुझे नाटक के लिये चुना गया। मेरा रोल याज्ञवल्क्य

शायद राजनेता का था, वो नेता मोटी तोंद वाला। मैंने मामा जी से कहा - मुझे नाटक में मोटी तोंद वाला राजनेता बनना है, आपकी Sweet गणेशा Belly बनियायन चाहिये। मामाजी तो इतना हँसे, दीदी कहती यह ठीक बात नहीं। मैं तेरे ड्रेस की व्यवस्था कर दूंगी। मैंने कहा मामाजी की बनियायन पहनकर रोल में जान आ जायेगी। खैर मामाजी का तो प्रश्न ही नहीं, पर मुझे तब बड़ी खुशी हुयी, जब मामाजी रंगशाला मेरा नाटक देखने आये। दीदी की तो साधना थी नाटक क्रिया का देखना। बाद में दीदी ने कहा - बेबी अब यह बनियायन तु रख, मैंने कहा क्यों? कहती तेरे को फिर जरूरत पड़े। मैंने कहा - मामाजी मेरे पास, जब जरूरत पड़ेगी फिर ले लूंगी, रखने की क्या जरूरत? याद है मामा जी बोले - देखना इसका ढंग और विश्वास। मामा जी VVIP स्थान पर बैठे थे। मेरी बेस्ट फ्रेन्ड और रूममेट, शोभी जो उ०प्र० के मुख्यमंत्री श्री कमलापति त्रिपाठी जी की ग्रेंड डाटर, वो भी मामाजी के साथ बैठे थे। आज मुझे लग रहा है कि तब मेरा कोई अहंकार भाव नहीं था, बस यही खुशी कि मामाजी आये। मुझे अच्छा अभिनय करने का पुरस्कार भी मिला पर मुझे याद है, मैं तो मामाजी को देखकर इतनी खुश कि मंच से सीधे कूदी और उनके पास आकर उनसे गले लगी। मुझे सबके सामने मामाजी ने कहा 'पगली'। मेरा बेस्ट रिवार्ड तो मामा जी का रंगशाला में आना था नाटक देखने।

मामा जी के साथ कहीं भी रही (भटिण्डा को छोड़कर) प्रातः हवन प्रतिदिन करती थी। हवन की तैयारी मैं बहुत प्रेम से करती थी। दीदी को देख मामाजी कहते - बाद में बेबी सफाई कितनी अच्छी करती है, बीबी का यह गुण आया है। मामा जी को सफाई बहुत प्रिय था। भारत में ऋषियों ने मानव जीवन के हर पहलू पर गहरी खोज की है। माँ बनने की क्रिया का प्रथम चरण "मासिक धर्म" कितना सुन्दर शब्द। मामाजी को मैंने

बताया - बड़े भाई साहब का अमेरिका से English में पत्र Monthly / Period पर इतना शिक्षाप्रद पत्र आया तो Warden ने, जिसे English का ज्ञान था उससे पढ़वाया और उसे Hostel के सभागृह के Notice बोर्ड पर उसे लगवाया। मामा जी कहते तेरा भाई तो बड़ा ही ज्ञानी है। मामा जी open Mind के थे, तथाकथित पंडितों के तरह अंध विश्वासी नहीं थे। वैज्ञानिक सोच के थे। मेरा मन प्रसन्न होता मैं हवन में बैठती। पेट दर्द आदि होता और स्कूल बन्द होता तो मामा जी के हाथ का गरमा गरम काढ़ा भी मिलता।

दीदी को जब मैं गर्मी की छुट्टियों से वापिस आकर बताती थी मैंने कौन सी मूवी देखी तो दीदी कहती चोरी सिनेमा देखती है। मैं कहती मुझे बहुत अच्छा लगता है मूवी देखना, बाहर खाना। दीदी मामा जी से कहती यह सुधरेगी भी कभी? मुझे याद है मामाजी कहते बेबी तो साफ सुथरी है। दीदी कहती - फिल्मी गीत गाती है, मामा जी कहते भजन भी तो गाती है। दीदी तो बहुत अच्छा गाती थी। मुझे याद है दीवान हॉल में मैंने मामा जी को बताया कि मैं मोहन भाई साहब की शादी पर Dance करूंगी, मम्मी ने मुझे Dance स्कूल में डाला है। मामा जी बड़े खुश होकर कहा - मुझे दिखायेगी। मैंने कहा मामा जी फिल्मी गीत है। कहते कोई बात नहीं। मैंने 'कंकड़िया मार के जगाया, कल तू मेरे सपने में आया' मैंने पहले थोड़ा Dance दिखाया और बोली मामा जी पूरा dance दिखाऊंगी। मामा जी हँस के बोले 'पगली'। मामा जी का 'पगली' Yes, Very good यह हमारी भाषा रही। मामा जी ने मुझे हमेशा प्रोत्साहित किया। मामा जी हमेशा Broad Mind और open hearted रहे।

वनस्थली में मामा जी से एक गुण मिला 'तलवों की massage करना' जो अभी तक मैं प्रयोग करती हूँ। मामा जी के साथ वनस्थली में लगता रहा मामा जी माँ की तरह २ बेटियों की परवरिश समर्पण भाव से कर रहे हैं।

मामा जी का सन्यास 1975: मम्मी से पता लगा मामा जी सन्यास लेंगे। दिल्ली रामलीला मैदान मे मामा जी के सन्यास का विशाल आयोजन था। मुझे समझ में नहीं आ रहा था। सन्यास? पता नहीं किसने कहा अब मामा जी घर नहीं आयेंगे, सफेद कपड़े नहीं पहनेंगे। बाल बड़े नहीं रखेंगे, मुंडन होगा। मेरी तो कल्पना से ही रोना निकला। मैं जाना नहीं चाहती थी पर मम्मी ने कहा जाना है। मुझे इतना याद है, इतनी भीड़, हमलोग तो मंच के एकदम साथ, शायद परिवार के है इसलिये ले गयी थी। मैं खामोशी से कोई देखे नहीं रोती रही। मामा जी को No hug \ No hug to Sweet गणेशा Belly, No गोली टॉफी No पगली, मुझे आज भी ध्यान है। सन्यास नाम। गेरुए कपड़े के बाद मामा जी हाथ जोड़ कर मम्मी के पास आये। मम्मी रो रही थी। मैं तो जैसे खो गयी। शब्द नहीं पर मामा जी की आँखें मुझे देखे, पर मैं पीछे हो गयी, शायद कुसुम दीदी के पास, उनका हाथ पकड़ कर खड़ी हो गयी। मामा जी का सन्यास लेते, मामा जी की Fairy Tale की Green Princess पगली भी कहीं गायब हो गयी। It was very painful for me. मामाजी का सफेद एकदम दूध जैसे never any दाग ओके कपड़े पहने देखना सफेद रंग पसंद रहा। बचपन की छाप कितनी गहरी व ऊंचाई लिये होती है जैसे नीला सागर नीला गगन।

मुझे याद नहीं किस वर्ष मम्मी के साथ मामा जी के समिपन शोध संस्थान गये। मोहन भाई साहब लेकर गये। मामा जी वैसे ही Sweet गणेशा Belly, हाथी वाला, मामा जी को मैं दौड़ कर हग (hug) किया। मामा जी के मुंह से 'पगली' सुन, मैं मैना की तरह चहकने लगी। मुझे मामा जी ने एकबार भी नहीं कहा बोलो मुझे स्वामी जी कहना मामा जी नहीं। लेकिन मम्मी भी भैया भैया बोल रही थी। कुसुम दीदी व मोहन भाई साहब स्वामी जी कह रहे थे। मामा जी से मैंने कहा मैं आपको पत्र लिखूंगी। मुझे याद है स्वादिष्ट पकौड़े वाली कढ़ी

चावल, हरी धनिया वाली सूखे आलू की सब्जी। मामा जी को कितना ध्यान रहा कि हमें क्या पसंद है, सबसे अच्छा लगा।

मामा जी ने जब कहा- 'बेबी मेरे कमरे से नीली टोकरी तो लाना" मुझे तो इतनी मस्ती आयी Sweet गणेशा Belly को hug किया, मामी कहती- बेबी इतनी बड़ी हो गयी, पर मामा जी हँसे जोर से और धीरे से कहा 'पगली'। मुझे ध्यान है, मैं इसलिये मस्ती में नहीं आयी कि मामा जी अपने हाथ से नीली टोकरी से मेरे पसंद की Snacks देंगे, पर यह खुशी की नीली टोकरी जैसी है। बस इतना पता है मामा जी ने कहा 'बेबी यहीं कुसुम बेटी के साथ कुछ दिन रहेगी। एक सपना सा लगे, मामा जी दीदी के साथ इतने बड़े संस्थान में ? यहाँ 5-6 सेवक भी थे।

मामा जी को मैंने जब भी पत्र लिखा उसका उन्होंने हमेशा Reply दिया। बाद में किसी से लिखवाते थे। मामा जी के मोती जैसे अक्षर, कभी cutting नहीं, सीधी लाइन। मामा जी को गाँधी आश्रम से पत्र लिखा। विनोबा जी के आश्रम जब पत्र लिखा मामा जी का आशीर्वाद आया। मेरा सौभाग्य, मैं एक युगपुरुष ऋषि के ब्रह्म मंदिर में हूँ, अनूठा अनुभव मिलेगा।

1979 मैंने 3½ साल बाद मामाजी को पत्र लिखा। कुसुम दीदी ने पत्र अपने हाथ से मामाजी के शब्दों को लिपीबद्ध किया। पत्र का भाव उनका आशीर्वाद दिल से था कि मैं उत्तम जगह पर हूँ पर मेरे मतलब की बात ' उन्होंने कहा- संस्थान पर उनके पास कुछ दिन रहूँ, कुसुम दीदी भी है।

1980 मैंने मामा जी को अनल जी के बारे में पत्र लिखा कि सामाजिक और राजनैतिक दृष्टि से लोकनायक जय प्रकाश नारायण से जुड़े हुये Active, Activist हैं। मामा जी ने किसी से लिखवा कर उत्तर दिया था कि जब भी अवसर मिले हम दोनों संस्थान आयें। मुझे शुरू से ही रहा अनल जी को, मामी मामाजी बड़े भाव हृदय से स्वीकार करेंगे। अपनी बेबी की खुशी के लिये नहीं बल्कि अनल जी के अपने गुणों के कारण। मैंने मामा जी के बारे

मैं अनल जी को देखती रही। निरूनी भीतर प्रसन्नता थी। हम दिल्ली में थे हम दोनों खादी पहनते थे। मैंने क्या कहा, अनल जी white सूट रेडिमेड खरीद कर लाये। मैंने कहा किस के लिये? कहने तुमने कहा था सूट चाहिये, मैंने कहा कितने का है किस Shop से खरीदा? अनल जी ने बताया कनॉट प्लेस Snow White से Rs 625.00 का। प्रथम बार मामा जी की अनल जी से मुलाकात होनी थी। मैंने उस सूट को पहली और अंतिम बार पहना। इतने मंहगे सूट को पहनने की हिम्मत नहीं हुई। और सूट खादी का था भी नहीं। 19 साल बाद अमेरिका में यह सूट मैंने अपने मित्र Carol को उपहार में दिया। अनल जी की पहली भेंट मामा जी के साथ संस्थान पर यह सूट याद दिलाता था, मामा जी के निर्मल स्वच्छ हीरा की तरह सफेद वस्त्रों की।

मामा जी को अनल जी ने पैर छूकर प्रणाम किया और मामा जी ने आशीर्वाद दिया। मुझे इतना ध्यान है मामा जी व अनल जी देर तक बातें करते रहे। मामा जी ने खाना खिलाया, फिर कहा रात भी यहीं रुको। प्रातः हवन में साथ रहे। मामा जी अनल जी से राजनैतिक एवं सामाजिक चर्चा करेंगे जैसा मैं सोचती थी पर ऐसा कुछ भी नहीं हुआ। बहुत गहरे वेद सूत्रों के विषय में चर्चा होती रही। रात में मैंने अकेले जब मामा जी विश्राम को जा रहे थे मैंने जैसे ही कहा मामाजी, मामाजी जोर से हँसे - कहने मुझे पता है तू क्या पूछेगी? ध्यान है मैं गले लग गयी। मामा जी ने कहा 'पगली' जा सो जा। मामाजी अनल जी से अत्यधिक प्रभावित हुये। उनको आभास हुआ कि अनल जी अतीव विवेकशील व्यक्ति हैं। मुझे इतना भीतर अच्छा लगा। मामा जी अनल जी का अपना एक अलग अनूठा रिश्ता बना। हर साल हम 8-10 दिन तो मामा जी के साथ रहते ही थे। कई बार गर्मी की छुट्टियों में मेरी प्यारी कुसुम दीदी भी होती थी। मामाजी, अनल जी दीदी वैदिक काल, वेद मंत्रों etc पर चर्चा की चर्चा होती रहती। दीदी ने एक बार मामा जी से कहा स्वामी जी आप इन दोनों को संस्थान / आर्यसमाज / वेद का कुछ कार्य

संस्कृत और हिन्दी में चलेगा। मुझे याद है मामा जी ने तब भी यही कहा "यह दोनों आर्य समाज / संस्थान से भी ऊपर सही मार्ग पर हैं। वेद माता का काम तो ये अमेरिका में करेंगे बीज डल चुका है"

मेरा दीदी के प्रति वैसा ही प्रेम था, जैसा वनस्थली में मामा जी ने देखा, दोपहर या रात एक [illegible] दीदी के पास मैं लेटे-लेटे बात करती। मामा जी आते प्यार से हम दोनों के सर पर हाथ फेर, मुस्कराते अपने कक्ष में चले जाते। मामा जी की मुस्कराहट, मामा जी का होना, ठंडी हवा के झोंके की तरह मन को शीतल कर जाता था।

१९९४ में अमेरिका से जब मैंने मामा जी को पत्र लिखा कि मेरी इच्छा है १९९४ में जब मैं भारत आऊँगी, आप अनल जी के साथ वैदिक ढंग से पूरे मंत्रों के साथ विवाह करायें। मामा जी ने बहुत उत्साह दिखाया। अनल जी तो उन दिनों संस्थान में मामा जी जैसे कहते वैसा कर रहे थे। मामा जी इतना उत्साह दिखाया, दिल्ली गुरुकुल के छात्रों को वेद मंत्रों के गायन के लिये आमंत्रित किया। मामा जी ने विवाह स्थल, वेदी स्वयं से चयन किया। भोजन का मेनू मामा जी की पसंद की मिठाई etc, पीले फूलों (गुलाब) से मामा जी ने पूरे विवाह मंडप को सजवाया। जब मैं मामा जी से मिली जितना मुझे उत्साह था, उससे अधिक प्रसन्नता व उत्साह मैंने मामा जी में देखा। मुझसे कहा - क्या अनल जी खुशी से पीली धोती कुर्ता विवाह के समय पहनेंगे? मैंने कहा मामा जी, अनल जी हम दोनों से प्यार करते हैं, मान सम्मान, औपचारिकता का सम्बन्ध वो नहीं रखते, अनल जी हमारे खुशी में खुश होंगे। जब मैं अमेरिका में ही थी तभी पत्र के माध्यम से जो मंत्र / प्रश्न पति पत्नी (हाँ) उच्चारण करना था व संकल्प लेना था मैंने मामा जी से कहा कि उसे हिन्दी में समझना, मामा जी ने प्रेम से समझाया। जब माँ बनने का धर्म निभाना व परिवार बढ़ाने का संकल्प मंत्र आया (मंत्र ध्यान नहीं) मैंने मामा जी से कहा - मैंने तो विनोबा जी के सामने पवनार आश्रम में ब्रह्मचर्य का व्रत ले चुकी हूँ और

भार सौंपे। मामा जी की प्यारी हँसी जोर से कहते 'बेटी कुसुम यह संस्था में बँधने वाले लोग नहीं।" मामा जी के प्रति अन्ना जी का मात्र आदर भाव नहीं था। बौद्धिक जिज्ञासा। प्रश्नों का गहरे तल पर चर्चा, मंथन तो था ही पर लगाव अपनापन और प्रेम भी मैंने महसूस किया। अन्ना जी कितने भी व्यस्त हो मामा जी के पास २/३ दिन संस्थान में रुकते ही थे। कई बार मामा जी की लिखा-पढ़ी etc काम होता तो वो अधिक भी रुकते। मैं अक्सर साथ होती थी। मामा जी ममतामयी माँ की तरह नाश्ता, लंच, डिनर सब का स्वयं रसोई में आकर देखते। मामा जी को कढ़ी बहुत पसंद थी। मुझे तो इतना आनन्द आता था जब वो उस आदमी की class लेते, जो कढ़ी बनाता था, रसोई में।

१९८२ में "आसाम आंदोलन" की वजह से हम मामा जी के पास संस्थान नहीं गये, पर मामा जी ने किसी से लिखवाकर पत्र भेजा था 'अन्ना जी के नेतृत्व में चल रहे आसाम आन्दोलन को हमारा आशीर्वाद।" मेरे लिये यह बहुत बड़ी बात थी।"

Nov '९२ में मम्मी और मैं अमेरिका जाने से पहले मामा जी से मिलकर आये। मामा जी को मैंने कहा - मैं हवन कुंड (लोहा) हवन सामग्री लेकर जा रही हूँ। मामा जी को पता था, मैं रोज हवन नहीं करती थी। गांधी आश्रम, पतवार आश्रम, अन्ना जी के साथ, Activist लोगों के साथ तो मेरा जीवन ही हवन था। पर आज मैं सोचती हूँ, मामा जी को हमारा भविष्य दिख गया होगा। उन्होंने कभी मुझे नहीं कहा 'हवन करना' जबकि मैंने सुना है वो कितने लोगों से हवन करने को कहते थे। मामा जी ने कहा अमेरिका में हवन करने की दिक्कत आये, लकड़ी के घर हैं, तो घी का दीपक जलाकर मैं अपनी साधना कर सकती हूँ। १९९३ में जब मैं भारत आयी मामा जी के पास मैं रोज चहक रही थी जी, जी, जी। इतने सारे अमेरिका के अनुभव मामा जी पूरे ध्यान से सुने। एक बार फिर कुसुम दीदी ने कहा 'स्वामी जी, बेटी से आप कहें भारत/USA में यह प्रचार का काम English में करे। मेरा कर्म

हमने अगरवाल में विवाह किया, भाई मुन्नालाल जी ने हमारे ब्रह्मचर्य व्रत का आशिर्वाद देते हुये गाँधी आश्रम में 1980 में folding चरखा उपहार स्वरूप दिया था। और तब से ही हम अपने व्रत का निष्ठापूर्वक पालन कर रहे हैं। मामा जी इतने गद्गद हुये और बड़े प्यार से कहा बेटी आ इधर और सर पर हाथ रखो। मैं तो दोनों हाथों से उनके Sweet गणेश Belly का स्पर्श किया। मंदिर व पूजा स्थल मेरी मम्मी का, उनका वाल्मी निवास' व हम बच्चे में रहा। मम्मी रोज पूजा करती थी, खुद ही मिठाई बनाती थी बेसन के लड्डू, जब गणेश भगवान के लिये बनाती थी मुझे बचपन से लगता था गणेश भगवान जी का पेट मेरे मामा जी जैसा है। बचपन से ही मम्मी जब कहती भगवान को हाथ जोड़, मुझे बाकि भगवान का तो ध्यान नहीं, पर मामा जी गणेश भगवान हैं, गणेश Sweet Belly। बचपन में मेरे जो भी करीब थे, किसी का भी पेट निकला नहीं था, तो मामा जी की गणेश Sweet Belly ही को गोद लगती रही।

मामा जी ने अनल जी को भी आशिर्वाद दिया। मामा जी के संरक्षण में प्यारी कुसुम दीदी, उषा भाभी, जयदेव भाई, मुन्ना जी, एक और विद्वान शास्त्री जी ने पूर्ण वैदिक परम्परा से विवाह सम्पन्न कराया। उषा भाभी ने स्वयं रचित सुहाग का गीत गाया, मामा जी ने अपने आशिर्वचन में कहा था बहुत कुछ, पर मुझे एक लाईन याद है "बेटी श्रृंगार तो करती नहीं, मजा तो तब है जब अनल जी (पति) अपने हाथों से सिंदूर लगाये। मामा जी की बात दिल में बैठ गयी। सिंदूर तब से अनल जी ही लगाते हैं। हनुमान जी की तरह लाल माथा हो जाता है, पर मुझे यही अति सुन्दर श्रृंगार लगता है।

प्रतिवर्ष मैं अमेरिका से भारत जाती और मामा जी से मिलना होता और मैं अपने अनुभव मामा जी को सुनाती। शायद 1995 में जब भारत आयी, पता लगा मेरी प्यारी दीदी को Blood Cancer है, और उपचार की सारी सीमायें टूट चुकी थी। दीदी और मामा जी Bombay में राजेन्द्र भाई के घर पर थे। अनल जी और मैं दोनों दीदी से मिलने Bombay गये। मुझे तो इतना रोना आये, आँसू थमे नहीं। मामा जी ने गले लगाया, सर पर हाथ रखा,

पर बोले कुछ नहीं। 6-7 दिन हम वहाँ रुके। मैं पूरा समय दीदी के साथ रही। दीदी के अंतिम शब्द "मेरा जीवन शेष है तो मिट्टी भी औषधी बन जायेगी, जीवन समाप्त है तो दवा भी मिट्टी बन जायेगी।" मामा जी को तो मैंने शांत, स्थिर सागर की तरह देखा और महसूस किया कि मामा जी भीतर से भी शांत थे।

कुसुम दीदी के शरीर त्याग के उपरान्त, अनिल जी, मामा जी के साथ और जुड़ गये। जब भी मामा जी को, जैसे भी मामा जी अनिल जी का साथ चाहिये था वह संस्थान जाते रहते।

जुलाई 1997 मामी के मृत्योपरांत मामा जी का भाण्डुप जाना। बड़े भाई साहेब ने बताया, मामा जी जब बोले तब बड़े भाई भी रो पड़े थे। मैं तो थी नहीं, पर मुझे लगता है, मामा जी के भीतर से उस वक्त जो शब्द निकले होंगे वो वैसे ही जैसे माँ के वात्सल्य से अपने औलाद के लिये कुछ निकलता है, भूख, प्यास, मन की अस्थिरता सबको पूर्ण कर देता है।

मैं मामा जी को हमेशा पत्र लिखती थी, उनका हर पत्र का उत्तर आता। मोती के तरह सुन्दर अक्षर। कभी भी line उपर नीचे नहीं। कभी Cutting नहीं। 1996 में बरसात का पानी हमारे पुरे कॉलोनी के घर-घर में 2-3 फीट तक घुस गया। हमारे घर Aroma में भी घुस गया था। हम उस समय आगरा अपने घर पर नहीं थे। पिता जी की बीमारी एवं अचानक देहान्त के कारण हम गाँव गये थे। हमारे सारे पत्र भी शायद पानी में गल गयी। जिराकी जीजी ने दो सुन्दर मटकी बना दी।

अनिल जी 2001 में अमेरिका आ गये। स्वयं मामा जी, अनिल जी के लिये अपनी अस्वस्थता के उपरान्त भी अमेरिका प्रस्थान से पूर्व विशेष हवन एवं अपना आशीर्वाद दिया। 2001 अंत में ही हम दोनों अमेरिका से वापिस आकर मामा जी से मिले। मामा जी बहुत खुश हुये, कहा अमेरिका से तो लोग 5-6 साल से पहले आते नहीं। अनिल जी 9 माह में आ गये? जब मैंने उन्हें बताया कि मम्मी को हम रोज अमेरिका से फोन करते

थे। 11 सितम्बर को पता चला कि मम्मी अचानक Comma मे चली गयी है। और अभी दरभंगा Hospital मे है। इधर सितम्बर 11 को अमेरिका न्यूयोर्क मे World Trade Tower पर आतंकी हमला और सारी Flights Cancel। ज्योंहि Flights प्रारम्भ हुआ हम भारत दिल्ली आये। दिल्ली से Flight से ही पटना और Taxi से सीधे माँ के पास Hospital मे। माँ हास्पीटल बैड पर 5-6 दिन से पूरे Coma मे। परिवार के सभी लोग आ गये थे। अनल जी के ही आने का सब को इंतजार था। पर जैसे जैसे ही अनल जी ने अपने हाथों से माँ के चरणों का स्पर्श किया माँ की आँखे खुल गयी। डा० हास्पीटल के स्टाफ व सारा परिवार हैरान। माँ बोली बउआ घर चलो और आश्चर्य ढंग से उठ कर बैठ गयी। और उसी दिन हास्पीटल की कागजी कार्यवाही पुरी कराकर अनल जी माँ को दरभंगा घर ले आये। जब मैं मामाजी को सारी बातें विस्तार से बता रही थी, मामा जी हमेशा की तरह एक एक बात ध्यान से सुनते रहे। मामा जी ने कहा अनल जी के मन मे माँ के प्रति भक्ति, समर्पण देख मन गदगद हो गया।"

2002 मे जब हम आये हम ज्यादा दिन माँ के पास ही रहे। मामा जी के पास मात्र 2 दिन रुके। मामाजी दोपहर को कहते है बेबी को Ice Cream खिलाते हैं। मैं इतने जोर से हँसी और कहा भी मामाजी Ice Cream खैर भी Ice Cream मुझे बहुत पसंद है। मामाजी ने अपने हाथ से प्लेट मे Ice Cream डाल दिया तथा दोनो दिन 2 टाइम मामा जी ने खिलाया। मामा जी को मैंने कभी नहीं कहा- क्या चाहिये पर उन्हे पता लग जाता था। यह रहस्य मैं अब समझ रही हूँ।

अरे एक बात तो मैं भूल गयी, जब मैं छोटी थी मैंने मामा जी से कहा प्रमोद भाई ने "Florence Nightingale True Story Book दी है। मैं भी बड़ी होकर नर्स बन सेवा का

काम करूँगी। No शादी। मामा जी मुस्कुराते हुये बोले - शादी तो बेबी तेरी होगी, है पर तु खुद अपना वर खोज लेगी। मुझे नहीं पता मामा जी को ज्योतिष विज्ञान का भी ज्ञान था।

अमेरिका "अमृतम" में हमारे प्रेमी लोग गणेश जी की मूर्ति ही अधिकर लाते हैं, मुझे तो लगता है, मामा जी का Sweet गणेश Belly यही है।

जैसे मेरी मम्मी माँ में समा गयी, मामाजी अन्ना जी में समा गये, मेरी नौकरी अमृतम की रसोई 'मिठास' में समा गयी. सत्संग हो, 24 घंटों का का गायत्री यज्ञ हो शिव का अभिषेक हो, श्रद्धा भोज खतम ही नहीं होता।

मामा जी अपनी पगली Green Peas Princess को इतने गहरे विशाल सागर में बिना गोता लगाये ही मोतियों से भर दिया।

बचपन का रिश्ता व प्यार वैसा ही होता है जैसे चीनी का दूध में घुल जाना। और मैं भी चीनी की तरह दूध में घुल गयी।

माँ, मामाजी की पगली।
Green Peas Princess
बेबी

[Baba Anal, 61 years old, had won the head and heart of Mama Ji to an extent that was far greater than any other person I know of. He is a social thinker, legal expert, and politcial activist. Through the 1990s, he voiced his views in his Hindi monthly, ***Anal Kann***-published from Agra. Yes, Baba is his legal first name. For years, he has been living up to its image in popular Indian perception of a wise man, spiritual leader, and an ultra caring person.

During the 1990s, Mama Ji wanted a live-in person who could run his institute, and assist him in research and publications. Thus, young Swami Chakransh from Agra joined Mama Ji on the recommendations of Anal. Interestingly, years earlier, Chakransh, then in his early 30s only, had insisted on being initiated into ***sanyaas*** by Anal! However, Swami Chakransh left Mama Ji after a year for a higher public call from within.

In the 1970s, Anal, in his close circle of friends, was called by a nickname Baba for his leadership role in the ***Youth Struggle Brigade*** of India. It was further cemented for his pivotal leadership role during a peaceful-turned-violent agiation in Agra for the settlement of 400 flood displaced persons. After moving to the US in 2001, when the time came for taking the US citizenship, he officially changed his name to Baba Anal. Anal, which has been his pen name since college days, was chosen for his last name.

Anal and I were with Mama Ji in Sahibabad, when Mama Ji started having non-stop angina pains, a condition of which he had been aware of for over a year. It was on Anal's persuasion and patience that Mama Ji finally agreed to undergo cardiac tests the very next day, and subsequently to an open heart surgery in a Delhi hospital. It all happened in July 2000. Anal stayed with Mama Ji throughout the hospitalization. Before his departure for the US in Jan, 2001, Mama Ji performed a very special ***yajna*** for his safe journey and successful life in the US.

For the last eight years, Madhu and Anal have been performing many Vedic ***sanskars***, ***homa*** ceremonies, free ***pranayam*** instructions, monthly ***satsangs***, annual celebrations of 24-hour ***Ramayan*** recitation, ***Shivratri*** and ***Gaytri-thon***, and much more. All these events, under aegis of the American Hindu Association, are held at the ***Amritam***, the name of their dwelling. Out of town monks and guests are regularly welcomed to stay with them.]

AGREEMENT & DISAGREEMENT WITH SWAMI MAMAJI

When I write about Swami Mama Ji, it is all about the projection of the image that is stored in my brain as memories. These memoirs were accumulated during my stay with him. My memories only reflect the image, not the real personality of Mama Ji. My relationship with Swami Mama Ji was at two fronts; one was family relationship and the other spiritual relationship. In any relationship, we create and project the images of one another that may be physical or/and psychological. Normally, all family relations are affected by pressure and demand, but fortunately our family relationship with Mama Ji was based on selfless interactions-not on demands.

As Mama Ji, he was beyond comparison. He was very soft spoken and loving. His unending smile is unforgettable. I never saw him getting angry. I do not know and I never wanted to know whether his love and affection was personal to me or because of my relationship with the Bhatnagar family. Undoubtedly, Mama Ji was a hero of my wife.

In 1994, when Madhu decided to have a traditional Vedic marriage, I conveyed this message to Mama Ji, who was delighted to know it. He gladly took over all the responsibilities from A to Z. The way our marriage ceremony was arranged and performed by Mama Ji and Kusum Didi, it was the only one of its type. Everyone present in the ceremony was surprised at the role of Mama Ji and Kusum Didi. It was the first and the last special marriage ceremony directly managed by two great souls.

In July, 2000, Satish Bhaisaheb (my brother in law) and I visited Mamaji. From there, it was an unplanned visit to ***Prabhat Ashram***, near Meerut. That turned out a very hectic day. In the evening, we found that Mamaji was restless with severe chest discomfort. I never saw Mama Ji in such a helpless condition.

We discussed the situation with Mama Ji and he agreed to consult his Vaidya/family doctor next day. I accompanied him for his checkup with Vaidyaji. After discussion with Vaidyaji, I convinced Mama Ji for getting checked up at the Heart Institute. Without further delay, I took Mama Ji to one of the best Heart Institute of India in Delhi. Mama Ji was thoroughly examined and his angiogram showed that he was heading towards a severe heart attack. Thus, an open-heart surgery was unavoidable.

He was admitted to the hospital. I had enough money for his surgery, because Mama Ji had given me 4-5 signed checks for any emergency. It was not disclosed to anybody. Now it was the time for me to inform all relatives and disciples of Mama Ji. I was really surprised that some of the family members were not in favor of his heart surgery. However, I am really thankful to Dr. Ravi Bhatnagar who convinced others.

Mama Ji also asked me to call Jai Dev Ji for getting the cash that was in a locked box at the ***sansthan***. It was another surprise for me that more than Rs. 1,35,000.00 was in that box. We never needed that. Everything went smoothly at the hospital. I remained in the hospital till Mama Ji was there. Earlier, Mama Ji wanted to collect all (about 15 lacks) his loaned money from his relatives with my help, but I totally refused to get involved in it.

After his release from the hospital, one of his disciples took Mama Ji to his home for post-surgical care. Incidentally, there were three disciples of Mama Ji who vied with each other to pay off the total hospital bill in amount of about Rs. 3.65 lacs. However, only one could get this honor, privilege or opportunity!

While Mama Ji was recovering and getting back to his normal health at another disciple's home, I told Mama Ji of my plans of going to America. He instructed me to see him a day before departure for America. Thus, on my arrival, Mama Ji arranged a grand ceremony of Homa (Havan) and blessed me.

Mama Ji was very open, respectful and friendly towards me and had great trust in me. He discussed all financial and ***Samarpan Shodh Sansthan*** issues with me. Only one thing, I could not understand that why Mama Ji did not want to hand over the ***Samarpan Shodh Sansthan*** powers to his most honest, faithful and loyal disciple, Jai Dev Ji.

At spiritual level, Swami Deekshanand and I were almost opposite to each other. For me, "Sanyas" in itself is liberation from worldly and material affairs, and spirituality brings freedom in real life. Death is not when life (body) comes to an end, but when there is no answer; there is no way out.

Swamiji was in his own prison of self-centered activities and was caught in his own thoughts of Arya Samaj and its deadly daily routine of habits and activities. Mama Ji was aware of the fact that his path does not lead anywhere. He knew that there was no escape and no amount of running away would ever resolve this problem.

During our spiritual talks Swamiji innocently admitted about the adulteration in the Vedas, He had some doubts and unanswered questions about "***Manusmriti***" and "***Satyarth Prakash***". Swamiji told me that because of his age and affiliation with Arya Samaj, he could not talk about those things in public. This was nothing but a fear caused by vested self-interest. For me, Swamiji died that day-well before his bodily death.

Swamiji's great weakness was his family relationships that caused pressure and demands on him. He was a religious person, but even in religious world, his self-interest was dominant. He did not learn a lesson from the premature death of Kusum Didi. I believe that his near and dear relatives took all the advantage of his fear and disadvantages of his love and compassion towards them.

I do not know what happened to ***Samarpan Shodh Sansthan***. Its fate was dark and its death was inevitable after the death of Swamiji, who was an extra ordinary intelligent religious person who was caught in the world. He could not explore his own extraordinary capacity of his brain. He had some original ideas to work on, but they never came even in the form of an experiment.

Our Agreement ends with the death of Mamaji, but Disagreement will continue with his Soul until it finds peace!

[Vinod Behari Bhatnagar, age 71, is my first cousin. His mother, now 90 years old, is ten years younger than my Late mother. In the exteded family, Vinod remains an ardent follower of Arya Samaj-no matter where he was posted in the course of his sevice as an auditor of Railway workers union. Curenlty, he is leading a retired life in Indore, and is lucky to have a son and grandson live under one roof-a blessing in today's fast life. He alwlays holds an office and remains active in the Malharganj Arya Samaj. Both of his sons are also regular members.

During India visits, spending a few days with him become memorable. One reason is that he synchronizes a family frunction with my visit. Latley, he is going to a limt by asking me to take Sanyaas in his Arya Samj ***mandir***. I have not said yes or no to him. But what a life if some thing unexpected is not done!

Vinod speaks in chaste Hindi, but his handwriting style is very free and unresrticed that it is impossible to read it unless one knows his mind. In this regard, Baba Anal graciously helped me out by re-writing of three write-ups. They are of Usha Sharma, Madhu Anal and Vinod Bhatnagar.]

वेदज्ञान मार्तण्ड स्वामी दीक्षानन्द जी

स्वामी दीक्षानन्द जी सन्यास के पूर्व आचार्य कृष्ण के नाम से जाने जाते थे। यदि भारत में यज्ञ का मर्मज्ञ कोई था तो आचार्य जी का नाम प्रथम पंक्ति में था। 1958 में दीवान हाल में पहली बार गया। आचार्य जी के पास 15 दिवस रहा। उनका स्वभाव बहुत अच्छा था। वे सदैव छोटे बड़े को 'जी' शब्द से सम्बोधित करते थे। मैंने उनके जीवन में सबसे बड़ी बात पाई, वे समानता का व्यवहार करते थे। मैं कई बार उनसे मिला था। आचार्य जी को सन्यास स्वामी सत्य प्रकाश जी ने दिलाया था। सन्यास के समय उन्होंने कहा था 'मेरे परिवार का कोई, बच्चों का यज्ञोपवीत करायेगा तो मैं उसमें अवश्य उपस्थित होऊंगा, अन्यथा नहीं।

स्वामी जी के सन्यास के 10 वर्ष पश्चात मैंने अपने दोनों बालकों का यज्ञोपवीत कराया। स्वामी जी को बुलाया था, किसी कारण से स्वामी जी नहीं आ सके, और किसी अन्य स्थान पर परिवार में पहुंच गये।

कुछ दिन बाद किसी कारण से मैं दिल्ली गया। वहां डा० सतीश भटनागर जो मेरे भाई भी हैं, अमेरिका से भारत आये थे, उन्होंने इच्छा प्रगट की कि मैं उनके साथ साहिबाबाद चलूं जहां स्वामी जी का स्थान 'समर्पण शोध संस्थान' है। वहां पहुंचने पर स्वामी जी ने सहज भाव से कहा 'आओ विनोद जी भोजन करो'। मैंने कहा मैं भोजन नहीं करूंगा, आपने अपने वचन को तोड़ा है आप मेरे यहां यज्ञोपवीत में नहीं आये। स्वामी जी ने कहा 'जब कभी आपके यहां इन बालकों का कोई संस्कार

होगा, मैं अवश्य उपस्थित होऊँगा। समय के साथ बालकों के विवाह का समय आ गया। समय की गति डा० सतीश जी पुन: मिल गये और बोले चलो नांदेड़ चलना है, वहाँ स्वामी जी आ रहे हैं। गुरुकुल के कार्यक्रम में मैं भी वहाँ पहुँच गया और स्वामी जी से अनुरोध किया कि 20.2.2003 को चि० लोकेश का विवाह होना है। स्वामी जी ने सहृदय से कहा 'मैं अवश्य आर्शिवाद देने आऊँगा। विवाह की तिथी से दो दिन पूर्व स्वामी जी को ज्वर आ गया। बम्बई से कैप्टन देवरत्न आर्य जी का फोन आया कि स्वामी जी को ज्वर बहुत अधिक है वे नहीं आ सकेंगे। कुछ ही देर बाद पुन: फोन आया, स्वामी जी भाई राजेन्द्र जी के साथ आ रहे हैं। मैं उस समय इंदौर आर्य समाज का मंत्री भी था। स्वामी जी की तबियत बहुत खराब थी फिर भी वे आये अपना आर्शिवाद दिया। जो शब्द उन्होंने विवाह मंडप में कहे वे आज भी कानो में गुंजते हैं। अतएव मैं कहना चाहुँगा स्वामी जी अपने वचनों पक्के थे।

उन्होंने "समर्पण शोध संस्थान" की स्थापना सु श्री कुसुम लता जी आर्य के लिए की थी। दुर्भाग्य से ईश्वर ने उन्हे हमसे छीन लिया। वह संस्थान आज समर्पण शोध संस्थान न रहकर 'चम्पागर' संस्थान रह गया है। उनकी जो भावना थी वह पुरी नही हो सकी। मैं समाज का छोटा कार्यकर्ता रहा। जब मैं आर्य समाज रतलाम का मंत्री था, मैंने स्वामी जी को बुलाया था, वे आये थे। उन्होंने सदैव कार्य कर्ताओं का सम्मान किया।

मुझे अच्छी तरह से याद है, उज्जैन के सिंहस्थ पर्व पर स्वामी जी अखण्ड भारत आर्य प्रतिनिधि सभा के

कार्यक्रम में आये थे, मैं उस समय सभा मंत्री था, स्वामी जी ने इच्छा प्रगट की, हम सभी पंडालों में जाएं एवं बात करें एकता की। सबने कहा स्वामी जी यह संभव नहीं होगा। स्वामी जी की सोच सबको एकता सूत्र में बाँधने की थी।

आर्य समाज के सम्मेलनों में जहाँ संगठन में स्फूर्ति एवं उत्साह का संचार होता है, वहीं स्वामी जी सबसे मिलकर साथ चलने की भावना रखते थे। अनेक पुराणिक सन्यासी स्वामी जी का आदर करते थे। कई बार स्वामी परमानन्द जी को उनसे वार्तालाप करते देखा था।

स्वामी जी सिद्धांतों के धनी थे। एकबार इंदौर आने पर मैंने उनसे इच्छा प्रगट की, मिलीट्री से रिटायर्ड श्री शर्मा जी की इच्छा है आपसे सन्यास लेने की। उन्होंने तत्काल बताया मेरी शर्त है 'विद्वान हो या मेरे पास छः माह रहे' तभी मैं सन्यास आश्रम में प्रवेश करा सकता हूँ। श्री शर्मा जी इन्दौर में तैयार हो गये यह बात १९९० की है। वानप्रस्थ दिलाया गया तथा वे स्वामी जी के साथ दिल्ली चले गये, उनके पास रहे।

आज स्वामी जी हमारे बीच नहीं है, किन्तु उनका मार्गदर्शन हर आर्य समाज के लिये, उनके परिवार के लिये आवश्यक है। मेरी इच्छा एवं भावना है, की आत्म समर्पण शोध संस्थान की स्थापना जिस उद्देश्य के लिए थी वह पुनः स्थापित हो।

विनोद बिहारी भटनागर

[Usha Sharma, 72 years old, is the wife of the Late Jaidev Shastri, who, during his teen years, became the first gurukul disciple of Mama Ji when he was known as Acharya Krishna. Jaidev had, perhaps, taken a secret oath of allegiance to Acharya Krishna and later on known as, Swami Deekshanand Saraswati. Interestingly enough, Usha, was 'recommended and suggested' by Mama Ji as Jaidev's wife.

However, she charted a course of life, which was independent of the influence of her scholarly father, brother, husband, and even Mama Ji. From hardly any formal education before marriage, with a kind of vengeance, she finished high school, college, and earned PhD in Sanskrit from Delhi University. After teaching in Delhi high schools for a few years and raising two children, she went to Mauritius for three years to strengthen Arya Samaj in the island. For similar reasons, she toured the US for a few months.

Besides meeting Aryan Samaj obligations in the community, she distributes her time with her IT son in Gurgaon and an IT daughter in Banglore.]

: श्री स्वामी दीक्षानन्द जी : -

ऋषि विश्वामित्र सदृश्य व्यक्तित्व

लेखिका : आचार्या डा० उषा शर्मा 'उषस्'

यत्र मनसा धीरा: वाचक्रत ।

अत्रा सखाय: सख्यानि जानते ।

तत्रैषां लक्ष्मी निहिताधि वाचि ।

(जहाँ मीठी वाणी का व्यवहार होता है, वहाँ कल्याणकारिणी वाणी रसना बाणी रसना पर विराजमान रहती है।)

<u>मेरा स्वामी जी से परिचय</u>: मेरे पिता इलैक्ट्रिकल इंजीनियर थे। मैसूर के राजमहल पर जो बिजलियों का पूर्ण श्रृंगार है, वह मेरे पिता के प्रधानत्व में हुआ था। माँ कहती थी उस समय के राजा श्री कृष्णराज ओडियर ने दो काश्मीरी शाल सच्चे सोने की जरी से कढे उपहार में दिये थे। बाद में उन्होंने स्वेच्छा से सेवा निवृत्ति ले ली थी।

सन 1958 में हमलोग बेंगलूर से मेरठ आ गये। मेरठ में मेरे बड़े भाई डा० धृतिशील विश्वेश्वरानन्द वैदिक रिसर्च संस्थान से पी० एच० डी० (Ph.D) कर रहे थे। मेरे भाई का संकल्प था कि जब तक 'ऊषा' की शादी नहीं होगी मैं अपनी शादी नहीं करूँगा।

मेरे पहले नम्बर के बड़े भाई त्रिवेन्द्रम (केरल) में हिन्दी सचिवालय में लेक्चरार थे। उन्होंने मेरठ में इन्द्रराज को पत्र लिखा कि मेरी बहिन के लिए वर ढूँढे। उन्होंने पंडित बुद्धदेव विद्यालंकार (स्वामी समर्पणानन्द जी) से कहा। तब वे सन्यासी नहीं थे।

मैं उस समय संस्कृत विद्यालय से मध्यमा (सम्पूर्ण) कर रही थी। सायंकाल का समय था अचानक पंडित जी घर आ गये। पिता जी होमियोपैथी औषधालय चलाते थे और वे औषधालय पर थे। माँ पिता जी को बुलाने गयी। इस बीच पंडित जी ने संस्कृत में बातचीत की। पिताजी ने आतिथ्य में गौ दूध प्रस्तुत किया, "अब इसके घर में पियेंगे" कह कर चले गये।

<u>प्रथम दर्शन</u>: अप्रैल का प्रथम पक्ष, श्री आचार्य कृष्ण जी (स्वामी दीक्षानन्द जी), श्री जयदेव जी तथा श्री प्रमोद भटनागर के साथ लगभग 4 बजे आये। प्रमोद जी सतीश जी के ही छोटे भाई हैं;

पिताजी बड़े प्रसन्न व विह्वल थे। उन्होने उनके आने से पहले ही अमरूद कटवा कर रख दिये थे, जो काले से हो गये थे, मैं ही लेकर गयी और वापिस आ गयी। संयोग की बात थी, आचार्य जी की स्वीकृति थी। इधर प्रमोद जी को नौचंदी देखने की तीव्र इच्छा - हाँ कर दो भाई साहेब, हाँ कर दो भाई साहेब कह कर शास्त्री जी को मजबूर किया, पर शास्त्री जी कच्ची गोलियाँ नही खेले थे, वे आनाकानी कर रहे थे। बाद मे पता चला, आचार्य जी ने शास्त्री जी को आग्रह करते हुये कहा - यदि यहाँ नही करोगे तो फिर तुम्हारे विवाह पर नही आऊँगा। फिर भी कोई बात नहीं हुयी। फिर बतायेंगे कहकर चले गये।

पँडित बुद्धदेव जी ने शास्त्री जी के चाचा को पत्र लिखा, क्योंकि शास्त्री जी के पिता नहीं थे। उनका उत्तर पँडित के नाम से हमारे पते पर आया। बात लगभग निश्चित थी। परन्तु आचार्य जी या शास्त्री जी का कोई उत्तर नहीं था। (शादी के बाद सुना था कि आचार्य जी कह रहे थे कि डाक्टर साहेब भौंकते रहे, हमने कोई उत्तर नहीं दिया) मेरे पिताजी का संकल्प था जो मुझे संस्कृत में पत्र लिखेगा उसको ही उषा का हाथ दूँगा। पर दोनों ने ही मेरे पिताजी को संतुष्ट नहीं किया, दोनों ही बहुत अभिमानी थे। 20 जुलाई 1960 को विवाह हो गया, और मैं आर्यसमाज दीवान हॉल विदा होकर 21 जुलाई 1960 को आ गयी। 9 बजे के करीब श्री सत्यकाम भटनागर टैक्सी में बिठाकर हमें अपने घर किदवई नगर ले गये।

मुझे पता था कि हम महाराष्ट्र अपने गाँव जा रहे हैं। माँ ने कहा था कि कुछ पहनकर मत जाना। सफर में सादा ही जाना। मुझसे किसी ने कुछ नहीं कहा — एक साधारण सी साड़ी पहनकर सारे जेवर ट्रंक में रखकर चल पड़ी थी।

<u>विचित्र दिवस</u>: किदवई नगर में श्री माता जीने एक ही थाली में हमारा खाना लगाकर दिया। मैंने ले जाकर शास्त्री जी के सामने रख दिया। शास्त्री जी ने सारा खाना खा लिया, जाकर खाट पर बैठ गये। मैं खाली झूठी थाली देखती बैठी रही। शास्त्री जी बोले - खालो यहाँ तुम्हे कोई खाने को नही कहेगा। मैंने पहली बार किसी पराये पुरुष को सिर उठाकर देखा। मैं एकदम स्तब्ध रह गयी। बरतन रख आई।

लगभग 4 बजे माता जीने कहा - और साड़ी जेवर कुछ नहीं लाई? मैंने कहा - सब ट्रंक में रखे हैं, किसी ने कुछ नही बताया कि कहाँ जा रहे है?

माता जीने अपनी साडी दी, गजरा मंगाया, खुद वेणी बनाई, तैयार किया कि लोग बहू को देखने आयेंगे, एक परिवार को छोड़कर कोई नहीं आया। शाम हुई, माता जीने शास्त्री जी से कहा बहू को कहीं घुमाकर ले आओ - वे बोले कहाँ जायेंगे? पर कहीं पास ही मे ले गये। माताजी का पुत्र राजा केवल छ: मास का था, मैंने उसको गोद में लिया और चले गये।

दुसरे दिन हम दीवान हॉल आ गये। रात्री की गाडी थी सामान बांधा, आचार्य जीने पूछा - आज खाना कौन बनायेगा, मैंने कहा, मैं बनाऊँगी। आचार्य जी ने पूछा क्या बनाओगी? मैंने कहा - जो आप कहेंगे। पहले बताये अमरूद के कारण आचार्य जी सोचते थे कि मुझे कुछ नहीं आता। अत: वे बोले, खीर कैसे बनती है। मैंने बता दिया। बोले अच्छा बना। मैंने सब्जी आदि बनाई, बोले पराठा खायेंगे। मैं ने पराठा तिकोने वाला बनाया, बोले गोल बना, मैंने बना दिया। बोले जलेबी वाला बना, वह भी बना दिया। फिर बोले कटोरी वाला बना, वह भी बना दिया, फिर बोले, चौकोर बना वह भी बना दिया, तब बोले सीख जायेगी।

पिताजी बड़े प्रसन्न व विह्वल थे। उन्होंने उनके आने से पहले ही आमरूद कटवा कर रख दिये थे, जो काले से हो गये थे, मैं ही लेकर गयी और वापिस आ गयी। संयोग की बात थी, आचार्य जी की स्वीकृति थी। इधर प्रमोद जी को नौवंदी देखने की तीव्र इच्छा - हाँ कर दो भाई साहेब, हाँ कर दो भाई साहेब कह कर शास्त्री जी को मजबूर किया, पर शास्त्री जी कच्ची गोलियाँ नहीं खेले थे, वे आनाकानी कर रहे थे। बाद में पता चला, आचार्य जी ने शास्त्री जी को आग्रह करते हुये कहा - यदि यहाँ नहीं करोगे तो फिर तुम्हारे विवाह पर नहीं आऊँगा। फिर भी कोई बात नहीं हुयी। फिर बतायेंगे कहकर चले गये।

पंडित बुद्धदेव जी ने शास्त्री जी के चाचा को पत्र लिखा, क्योंकि शास्त्री जी के पिता नहीं थे। उनका उत्तर पंडित के नाम से हमारे पते पर आया। बात लगभग निश्चित थी। परन्तु आचार्य जी या शास्त्री जी का कोई उत्तर नहीं था। (शादी के बाद सुना था कि आचार्य जी कह रहे थे कि डाक्टर साहेब झींकते रहे, हमने कोई उत्तर नहीं दिया) मेरे पिताजी का संकल्प था, जो मुझे संस्कृत में पत्र लिखेगा उसको ही उषा का हाथ दूँगा। पर दोनों ने ही मेरे पिताजी को संतुष्ट नहीं किया, दोनों ही बहुत अभिमानी थे। 20 जुलाई 1960 को विवाह हो गया, और मैं आर्यसमाज दीवान हॉल विदा होकर 21 जुलाई 1960 को आ गयी। 9 बजे के करीब श्री सत्यकाम भटनागर टैक्सी में बिठाकर हमें अपने घर किदवई नगर ले गये।

मुझे पता था कि हम महाराष्ट्र अपने गाँव जा रहे हैं। माँ ने कहा था कि कुछ पहनकर मत जाना। सफर में सादा ही जाना। मुझसे किसी ने कुछ नहीं कहा - एक साधारण सी साड़ी पहनकर सारे जेवर ट्रंक में रखकर चल पड़ी थी।

सन 1963 की छुट्टियों (गर्मी की) में हम गाँव गये थे। अम्मा (हमारी सासजी) की मृत्यु 6 जून को हुई थी। उन्होंने मेरे लिये चाँदी के हाथों के कड़े छोड़ गयी थी। मैं उन्हें ले आई थी। माता-पिता मेरे बड़े भाई सत्यपाल जी घर ठहरे थे, मैं दीवान हॉल में कड़े हाथ में लिए थी, आचार्य जी ने पूछा कि क्या है? मैंने कहा - चाँदी के कड़े हैं, अम्मा मेरे लिए दे गयी थी। पूछा इनका क्या करेगी? मैंने कहा - अम्मा बैंगलूर जा रही है, उनसे थाली बनवाऊँगी। आचार्य जी ने जोर से हुंकार भरी - बोले चाँदी की थाली का क्या करोगी? मैं कुछ नहीं बोली।

थाली बनकर आ गयी थी। बहुत सुन्दर, बादामी शेप की, बीच में लम्बा मयूर बना था। पेट में मोटी चाँदी भरी थी। चारों ओर कंगूरे बने थे। आचार्य जी सौन्दर्य के पुजारी थे। उज्ज्वला का 1965 में जन्म हुआ था, वह 21 दिन की थी, सुधीर पौने तीन वर्ष का था। सुधीर का मुण्डन, उज्ज्वला का नामकरण किया, हमने दक्षिणा में 21 रुपये, धोती खद्दर की कुर्ते का कपड़ा, एक नारियल उस थाली में रखकर दिया। जब सारे चले गये, मैंने थाली न देखकर पूछा? थाली नहीं दिखाई दे रही है? बोले आचार्य जी माँगकर ले गये।

शास्त्री जी के मन में मेरे प्रति हीन भावना ही थी, हालांकि मैं तबतक विशारद, प्रभाकर तथा शास्त्री का प्रथम वर्ष कर चुकी थी। कभी मैं उनकी सद्भावना ले नहीं पाई। राजन भाई साहब की शादी थी। तीन-चार दिन दीवान हॉल में सबकी सेवा की। नौकरों की तरह काम कराया, जब शादी पर जाने की बात आयी, मुझे ले जाने से इंकार कर दिया। इस बात का मुझे बहुत दुःख हुआ। मैंने पूछा क्यों नहीं ले जा रहे हैं? कुछ नहीं बोले, उठकर चले गये। आचार्य जी खाने पर बैठे बोले - सबके पास अच्छे अच्छे कपड़े

आभूषण सब कुछ है, तुम्हारे कुछ नहीं है। हालांकि जो विवाह में मिले थे, वह थे, परन्तु मेरा अपमान करना था। मैं अपने अपमान से थक चुकी थी। मैंने बिना झिझक के कहा— देखिये मुझे विवाह कर के लाये हैं, भगाई हुई नहीं हूँ अगर मेरे पास नहीं हैं दिलायें, अगर दिला भी नहीं सकते तो स्वाभिमान से रहें, अगर स्वाभिमान भी नहीं तो मुझे अपने घर में ही रहने दें, मैं अन्दर से इस अपमान को स्वीकार न कर सकी थी। उस समय तक मेरे पास कोई भी डिग्री नहीं थी। (मैंने तभी से पढ़ना शुरू कर दिया) आचार्य जी को शायद बहुत महसूस हुआ, वे बोले- चलो तैयार हो जाइये, मैं ले चलूँगा। और ले भी गये। तब से मुझे कपड़ों से नफरत हो गयी। भटिण्डे वाली बीबी के घर दौड़कर कहीं नहीं गयी, वह भी सतीश भाई साहेब के पुत्री के नामकरण पर गई, जबकि बीबी बहुत बीमार हो गयी थी। उसके बाद फूफा जी जब नहीं रहे तब गयी। फिर प्रमोद भाई साहेब की शादी में गई, तब तो मेरे सारे जेवर ही चोरी चले गये।

सन 1969 मेरी हरियाना में नौकरी लग गई थी। 1972 में मैं दिल्ली मे सर्विस प्रारम्भ कर चुकी थी। आर्य समाज में भी पूरी तरह प्रतिष्ठित हो गयी थी। तबतक आचार्य जी सन्यास ले चुके थे। दीवान हाल जाना बन्द हो गया। शास्त्री जी ही हमेशा अकेले जाते थे। स्वामी जी यदा-कदा उत्सवों पर मिल जाया करते। कभी-कभी मैं उनके लिए भोजन बनाकर ले आया करती थी। कभी-कभी जयपुर जाते समय भी पाथेय बनाकर दे आती थी।

जोधपुर में एक खेजल्हा गांव है, वहाँ सात दिन का उत्सव था। उस समय तक स्वामी जी कुसुम बहन जी को Ph. D. करा चुके थे, अनुभव हो गया था, मैंने भी उनसे

कहा – कि मुझे भी Ph. D. के लिये कुछ बताईये, उन्होंने छूटते ही कहा – तू स्वाहा - स्वाहा छोड़ दे, मैं सहायता करूँगा। "स्वाहा" और "इदन्नमम्" तो मेरा जीवन है, आज भी उसी के सहारे चल रही हूँ, सारा विश्व मेरा अपना है, उसे कैसे छोड़ सकती थी, मैंने कुछ नहीं कहा। बाद में मैंने अपने प्रयत्न से सब कुछ कर लिया।

एक बार मुझे किसी ने कहा – कि आपके पिता जी का लिखा ओउम् संकीर्त्तन स्वामी जी ने अपने नाम से छपवा दिया और उसकी प्रति भी लाकर दी, मुझे अच्छा नहीं लगा। मैंने लाजपतनगर के आशाराम जी को कड़ाके का पत्र लिखा, क्योंकि शंकर मार्केट के प्रेस में छपा था। उसके द्वारा उन्हें पता चला, हमारे घर पर आये। मैंने यथावत् श्रद्धा से भोजन कराया, मैं आकर अपने बिस्तरे पर सो गयी। मेरे जीवन की सबसे बड़ी विडम्बना यह है कि भारत में रहते हुए मेरा अपना कमरा अपना बिस्तरा कभी नहीं रहा। इसी कारण मुझे अपने चार बच्चों का नुकसान उठाना पड़ा। खैर शास्त्री जी ने (मेरे पति) आकर कहा - स्वामी जी बुला रहे हैं, मैं गई, स्वामी जी ने कहा – जो गलती हो गयी उसका क्या किया जा सकता है? – मैंने आँखों मे आँसु लेकर - या भरकर कहा – स्वामी जी, मेरे पिता धन से बहुत गरीब थे, यही मेरा दहेज था, उसे भी मेरा रहने नहीं दिया। अब उसका यही हो सकता है किसी पत्रिका में संशोधन करके छपवा दें, स्वामी जी ने ऐसा नहीं किया, पुस्तक का मुखपृष्ठ बदलकर, कुछ प्रतियाँ मुझे भेज दीं।

सबसे अन्तिम दर्दनाक घटना: मेरे भाई सत्यपाल वेद-शिरोमणि सन्यास लेना चाहते थे। 19 मई को उन्हें सन्यास लेना था। उन दिनों मैं कन्या गु० कु० में सेवा करती थी। स्वामी

जी ने मुझे बिना सूचना के शास्त्री जी को वानप्रस्थ दे दिया। मुझे बताते तो कभी मना न करती, पर उन्होंने मुझे नहीं बताया। मेरे बड़े भाई साहब का पुत्र ओमी अमेरिका से आ रहा था। वह बेंगलूर से रेलगाड़ी में आ रहा था, मैं नई दिल्ली स्टेशन पर उसकी प्रतीक्षा कर रही थी। मेरा पुत्र सुधीर आया, झट आकर कहा – पिता जी ने तीन-चार दिन हुए वानप्रस्थ ले लिया। मेरे पैरों के नीचे से धरती निकल गई।

19 को स्वामी जी ने मेरे भाई को सन्यास देना था। गुरुकुल गौतम नगर में ग्यारह कुण्डों का यज्ञ था। ग्यारह प्रतिष्ठित पुरोहित थे। उनमें से एक शास्त्री जी थे, उसी पर मैं अपने भाई के साथ बैठी थी। स्वामी जी ने अपना गौरव दिखाया। जयदेव जी आओ यज्ञकुण्ड आसन पर बैठो – मेरी तरफ आवाज देकर बोले – उषा बेटी तुम भी बैठो – जयदेव जी वानप्रस्थी हो गये। मैंने झट कहा – स्वामी जी मैं अभी गृहस्थी हूँ, मैं उनके साथ नहीं बैठूँगी। यज्ञ प्रारम्भ होने वाला था, स्वामी जी फिर बोले – हमने आपको बहुत ढूँढा आप नहीं मिली। यह दूसरा अपराध था, सन्यासी के लिए अक्षम्य और जघन्य अपराध। एक नादान पतिव्रता नारी को धोखा देना था। मैंने रोषभरकर कहा – मेरे भाई सन्यास ले रहे हैं – मैं भी आज से तैयारी में लग जाऊँगी। स्वामी जी ने कहा – "न स्त्री स्वातंत्र्यमर्हति" ये वाक्य दो तीन बार दोहराए। मुझसे यह सुना नहीं गया – मैंने झट स्वामी जी के सामने से माईक छीन लिया – मैं ने कहा – अगर जयदेव जी वानप्रस्थ लेते – और आपलोगों ने मुझे मैत्रेयी समझा होता तो उनको घर से सादर विदा करती परन्तु यहाँ स्थिति ही अलग है – मेरे भाई हैं जो मेरे पिता के स्थानापन्न हैं, आप हैं, जिन्होंने विवाह कराया था, ये मेरे पति के रूप में थे। तीनों

ने मेरा खूँटा उखाड़ दिया, कौन कहता है कि मैं स्वतंत्र नहीं हूँ। फिर उसके बाद स्वामी जी का, श्री जयदेव जी का सदा-सदा के लिए सम्बन्ध समाप्त हो गया। श्री जयदेवजी दो महीने बाद घर वापिस आ गये। कौन रखता है, आज के इस समय में? श्री जयदेव जी न घर के रहे न घाट के, पर मैंने कभी कुछ नहीं कहा - सेवा करती रही, समय पाते ही मैंने 31 जुलाई 1988 को स्वेच्छा से सेवा निवृत्ति लेकर नैरोबी चली गई। फिर लन्दन, फिर मॉरीशस फिर लन्दन फिर मारीशस वापिस आ गयी। वहां 2006 तक गुरुकुल की आचार्या रही। 2007 में मैं अमेरिका गयी वहां से फिर मॉरीशस वापिस आ गयी और 2009 तक लेक्चरॉर के रूप में कार्य किया। दर्शन, हिन्दी, संस्कृत का प्राध्यापन करती रही। 2009 को शास्त्री जी का निधन हुआ, मैंने पूरी श्रद्धा से स्वयं अन्तिम संस्कार किया। अपने उत्तरदायित्व को शिथिल नहीं होने दिया। मेरे पुत्र सुधीर और पौत्र शतक्रतु ने पूरी सेवा की।

स्वामी जी के अन्तिम दर्शन : सुना था स्वामी सत्यम् (मेरे भाई) और कैप्टन देवरत्न जी ने उनके आश्रम पर अपना आधिपत्य कर लिया था। मुझे 11 सितम्बर 2001 को मॉरीशस आना था। मेरी एक पुस्तक राधा प्रेस में छप रही थी, उसको लेने के लिए मैं गयी थी। वहीं स्वामी जी के दर्शन हुए। उनके आँखों में आँसू थे। बोले - बेटी मैं उसी दिन मर गया, जिस दिन तेरे भाई ने आश्रम को छीन लिया। मैं क्या मरने के बाद देखूँगा? ये लोग उसका क्या करेंगे? मुझे मेरे पिता याद आये, मेरी आँखों में भी आँसू आ गये। मेरे पिताजी भी भाईयों से तंग होकर ऐसा कहते थे। यही मेरा और उनका अंतिम दर्शन था।

1. मानव परमात्मा की अत्युत्तम प्रजा है। उसकी कोटि को तीन भागों में बांटा है, प्रथम, मध्यम और उत्तम। मेरे पास या इर्द-गिर्द तीन उत्तम कोटि के पात्र हैं। एक ऋषि विश्वामित्र की भाँति, स्वामी दीक्षानन्द जी, क्योंकि विश्वामित्र जिस वस्तु को अपने योग्य समझते थे, उसे अपनी मुट्ठी में भर लेते थे। ऐसे ही पुरी विद्वता महान विद्वानों के विशेष पंडित श्री बुद्धदेव जी विद्यालंकार (स्वामी समर्पणानन्द जी) की विद्वता पुरे मस्तिष्क में भरकर सकेशी बन गये थे, जिससे कोई और उस जंगल में घुसकर निकाल न पाये।

2. श्री आचार्य जयदेव जी शर्मा थे, जो वसिष्ठ की कामधेनु के समान थे, जिसकी रस्सी स्वामी दीक्षानन्द जी के हाथों थी, वे जब भी जहाँ भी चाहते खींच ले जाते थे। कामधेनु का काम सिर झुका दूध दोड़ देना मात्र था।

3. उषा- जो सोची वसिष्ठ के पुत्र के समान थी, जिसके पिता इतने बड़े इलैक्ट्रिकल इन्जीनियर होने के बाद भी ऋषियों की भाँति निस्पृह थे। माता तो पिता के स्नेह से खिंची - एकदम समर्पित थी। उनका नाम पद्मावती था, परन्तु उनके समर्पण के कारण पिताजी त्यागिनी देवी कहते थे। माता का स्वभाव मुझे मिला है, परन्तु मेरे पिता की भाँति पति का सम्मान नहीं मिला, क्योंकि कामधेनु की रस्सी विश्वामित्र के हाथ में थी। माता पिता, या पति-पत्नी का आत्मिक स्नेह उनकी प्रजा के लिये महत्त्व नहीं रखती क्योंकि शाखायें तनो से बहुत ऊँची और दूर चली जाती है। तनों की महिमा भी समाप्त हो जाती है।

आइये इन तीनों की विशिष्ट चर्चा करते हैं।

स्वाभाविक रूप से सभी मानवों में सत्वगुण, रजोगुण विशिष्ट रहता है, तो स्वामी जी में भी था। सत्वगुण के कारण

अत्यन्त स्वाध्यायशील थे। पतञ्जलि बताये विधि के अनुसार "ऊहा" विधि विशिष्ट थी। मानव जन्म से ही माता और पिता के द्वारा तथा आचार्य के द्वारा प्रशस्त होता है, वही आगे चलकर विद्या द्वारा प्रशस्त होता है। मुझे जैसे पति श्री जयदेव जी द्वारा ज्ञात हुआ, इन तीनों से स्वामी जी वञ्चित थे, केवल महावीर चाचा जीने इनकी जिविका चल सके अत: कुछ कार्य सिखा दिया था। आगेचलकर स्वामी जी का० गुरुकुल मे और लाहौर मे श्री आचार्य प्रियव्रत जी के उपदेशक विद्यालय से कुछ शिक्षा प्राप्तकर सके। सन 1944 मे आचार्य प्रियव्रत जी के पास ही से श्री जयदेव जी भी (मेरे पति) श्री आचार्य प्रियव्रत जी के कहने पर भटिण्डा उपदेशक विद्यालय में श्री आचार्य कृष्ण जी के पास आ गये। उनके विद्यालय में कोई विद्यार्थी न था, श्री जयदेव जी के साथ गुरुकुल होशंगाबाद मध्यप्रदेश से श्री मनोहर, श्री अमृतराव तथा श्री रामकृष्ण भी आये थे, परन्तु वे अधिक समय न रहे, चले गये। केवल जयदेव जी रहे।

समय का पता नही, पण्डित बुद्धदेव जी भटिण्डा गये. दोनों ही को साथ अपने प्रभात आश्रम में ले आये। प्रभात आश्रम के जीर्णोद्धार मे लग गये, वहाँ विद्या प्राप्त करने का सौभाग्य नही मिला। अत: 1958 मे प्रभात आश्रम छोड़कर आचार्य जी दीवानहाल की उपर बुर्जी मे रहने लगे, और जयदेव जी बल्लभगढ के पास गदपुरी गुरुकुल में उपाचार्य बनकर आ गये। तबतक वे विशारद और पंजाब यू० से शास्त्री कर पाये थे।.1958 में ही हिन्दी आन्दोलन में जेल गये। इन्ही दिनों हम भी बेंगलूर से मेरठ आ गये। आचार्य जी को विद्याध्यन का समय नही मिला। अत: प्रवचनादियो अपने विषय की स्थापना "ऊहा" विधि से प्रस्तुत करने लगे। वाणी में माधुर्य था, स्वाध्याय भी अच्छा था, विश्व

हो गया। इधर मुनिया दीदी का छोटा पुत्र दुर्घटनाग्रस्त हो गया, और मृत्यु भी हो गयी, उन्ही दिनों कुसुम भी बम्बई में राजन जी के घर में चल बसी। स्वामी जी टूट गये। एक दिन अकेले में राजेन्द्र नगर साहिबाबाद समर्पण शोध संस्थान में चिन्तित बैठे थे। मैंने पूछा - "स्वामी जी क्यों उदास बैठे हैं", कुसुम जी की याद आ रही है?" बोले - उसका निर्माण बड़े विशेष ढंग से हुआ था। स्वामी जी का उद्देश्य था, कि स्वामी जी नैष्ठिक ब्रह्मचारी हैं, कुसुम भी रहेगी, उसकी दत्त पुत्री भी रहेगी। पर यह हो नहीं पाया। निशि ने शादी कर ली। सुनते हैं कि वह जयपुर यु० में लगी है। राजेन्द्र नगर, गाजियाबाद की सम्पूर्ण सम्पत्ति की वही मालकिन बनेगी, क्योंकि वह भूमि कुसुम के नाम की है। एक विशेष बात - चमूपति जी के पुत्र श्री लाजपत राय जी, स्वामी जी के अत्यंत प्यारे थे विद्वान थे, उन्होंने कुसुम जी के शोध पत्र में बहुत सहायता की थी। स्वामी जी 6 माह साउथ अफ्रीका तथा मॉरीशस में थे। उस समय लाजपत जी वनस्थली में अतिथिशाला में रहते थे। कुसुम ने माता की तरह उनकी सेवा की, परन्तु स्वामी जी को अच्छा नहीं लगा, तब मैंने ही कहा - आपही ने तो कहा था, - वे विद्वान बहुत हैं, और निराश्रित भी, उनकी सेवा होनी चाहिए। अब क्यों नाराज होते हैं।

2. <u>कामधेनु</u> श्री जयदेव जी - जैसे पहले ही बताया उनकी रस्सी स्वामी जी के हाथ में थी। जो स्वामी जी कहते थे वह उनके लिए शिरोधार्य था। उदयपुर में आचार्य नरेश के प्रतिवर्ष स्वामी जी के साथ कुसुम और जयदेव जी जाते थे, एक सप्ताह रहकर, स्वामी जी कुसुम को जयदेव जी के सहारे छोड़ आते थे। यही कारण था उनको वानप्रस्थ देने का। संस्थान का कोषाध्यक्ष बनाया था, वहाँ का धन कोई भी चुरा लेता था स्वामी जी चुप हो जाते थे। जयदेव जी भी कुछ नहीं कहते थे। एक बार जयदेव जी मेरी गोदी में मरा बच्चा की अन्त्येष्टि के बाद ही उनके साथ चले गये

थे, कभी करुणा के दो आँसू दोनों की आँखों में नहीं थे।

3. <u>मैं स्वयं वशिष्ठ की पुत्री:</u> मेरे पिता कभी इन दोनों को पसन्द नहीं थे। सदा मद्रासी है, कुछ नहीं आता का ताना दे देते थे। जब मैं पढ़ गयी तो मुझसे उदासीन रहने लगे। कभी प्रवचनों में स्वामी जी से सामना होता तो बड़े लोगों के तरफ मुड़ जाते। स्वामी जी मेरे Ph. D के विषय में कुछ भी बताने से मना कर दिया था। कुछ ऐसी घटनाएं हुई जिनको बताने की इच्छा नहीं है।

सामान्यत: मानव की प्रकृति दोहरी होती है, समाज के लिए अलग और परिवार के लिए अलग—

<u>स्वामी जी का मातृवात्सल्य:</u> राकेश भटनागर स्वामी जी के भांजे केवल 15 वर्ष के थे। सुधीर लगभग डेढ़ या दो वर्ष का था, स्वामी जी हमारे घर आये, सुधीर को अपनी छाती पर उल्टा लिटाकर बोले— जयदेव जी आपने कभी सुधीर को ऐसा लिटाया था? देखें कैसे चिपका हुआ है। मैं जब भी रमा बीबी के जाता हूँ, बच्चे सभी मेरे साथ सोने को मचलते हैं।

सन 1968 में मेरे घर एक नन्ही परी आई थी। दूसरे ही दिन स्वामी जी आये। धाई ने उसे नहलाया, स्वामी जी गोदी में ले लिया, अभी नाभि भी नहीं निकली थी, उसे देख बहुत प्रसन्न हुए। परमात्मा की प्रशंसा प्रारम्भ कर दी।

सन 1991 में स्वामी जी फिर मेरे घर आये, सुधीर का चार महीने का बेटा था। मैंने उनकी गोद में दिया। पूछा क्या नामकरण किया? मैंने कहा - शतक्रतु है - बोले "क्रतु" बुलाना, कंधे से लगाकर थपकी दी।

ये कुछ परिचय स्वामी जी का है जो मेरे जीवन से घुला हुआ है। स्वामी जी प्रेम के पुजारी थे। इससे बड़ा सम्बन्ध भला मेरे साथ क्या होगा।

[Satish Chandra Gupta is an octogenarian and dedicated Arya Samaj leader in Mumbai. He runs a successful business and often travels around the world. I met him in 2004 in Tampa Florida when he came from India to attend the annual sammelan (conference) of Arya Samaj in North America. He is one of the first Indians who have bravely supported my idea of building a Hindu Holocaust Museum in India. Below is an extract from his email detailing his reminiscences of Swami Deekshanand.]

Though I may have been so young or just a child, but our house was a 365-day open house for all Arya great scholars of that time. Our Vedic scholars also used to take pride by staying at our humble house in Jhansi, but unfortunately I have no memories of Swami Deekshanand Ji, your respected MamaJi till 2001, when I met him for the first time in Mumbai during international Arya mahasammelan. I was specifically deputed to receive him & drive him in my car from Dadar railway station to sanyaas ashram. Shri Girish Khosla Ji had also arrived by the same train, and also honored me to travel with me in my car up to Santa Cruz & to your MamaJi to sanyaas ashram, vile Parle West.

Though I had met your MamaJi for the first time, but his personality with long flowing white beard were so prominent spreading ***"abha"*** all around that I needed no photograph etc. to recognize him, and receive him. It was my 2nd time when I had gone to receive some great person without any introduction or photo etc. but it had not taken even a minute to me to recognize such great person as your MamaJi was.

The Late Swami Deekshanand Ji, as far as I know, had come to Mumbai in 2001 to attend our International Arya Mahasammelan. Soon thereafter, he was appearing on Indian TV giving his talk on Vedic Dharma (Arya Samaj) daily for about 10 to 15 episodes, each for about 15 to 30 minutes.

He was very close to late Capt. Deo Ratan Arya & hence I suppose, he must be equally close to Captain's other people, like Dharam Pal Arya, Vinay Arya, Raj singh etc. who inherited or claim to inherit Captain's legacy of Arya Samaj & which is the 3rd Sarvadeshik Arya Pratinidhi Sabha Group claiming for its name.

[Chitranjan Saawant is an octogenarian retired Brigadier from the Indian Army. He was decorated with the honor of ***Vishishtha Sewa*** medal for exemplary service in the army. Born in 1932, he is a dedicated Arya Samaj leader in India]

SWAMI DEEKSHANAND SARASWATI: AN EMINENT SCHOLAR-SPEAKER

Indeed an impressive personality he was both in appearance and in scholarly parleys. There was hardly a soul who met him and returned without gaining Vedic knowledge. Although I had heard his scholarly discourses in various annual functions of different Arya Samajis of Northern India, it was in the Dun valley that I have had an opportunity to know him from close quarters. After many meetings with him and person to person interaction I found that I had gained tremendously spiritually. Thereafter I yearned to have his spiritual company whenever an opportunity came my way.

Dronsthali Arsh Kanya Gurukul, Kishangang canal road, Dehra Dun is the name of the place where I have had an opportunity to hear him morning and evening in the Sabhagar during the three day annual function of the Kanya Gurukul.

Dr Ved Prakash Arya, kulpita and founder of that august institution, as well as Acharya Dr Annapoorna Ji were successful in persuading Swami Deekshanand Ji to come to the Doon valley and interact with the large number of Arya Samajis who assemble there year after year for the last one decade or so. Swami Deekshanand Ji mentioned in one of his informal chats that generally he ascertains the credibility of the institution and assesses the quality and number of listeners of his discourses before giving his nod to his active participation. However, in this case he was convinced of the sincerity of the hosts and their genuine interest in furthering the cause of Vedic education and hence agreed to be a part of the mission of Dayanand Saraswati. Indeed Swami Deekshanand Saraswati was a true crusader to preach the Vedic Dharma as enunciated by Swami Dayanand Saraswati.

I was elated when Swami Deekshanand Ji sent a message that he too would like to attend the TV documentary show on Maharishi Dayanand that the Doordarshan Delhi Kendra had produced and I had scripted and done the running commentary in Hindi. The documentary comprised a number of bytes of the Delhi based eminent Aryas and the whole thing was put together rather hurriedly. On seeing the TV documentary Swami Deekshanand Ji was rather disappointed. Being a gentleman to his finger tips, he made no scathing criticism on the spot in the presence of the large audience but suggested mildly that some more Research was needed to put up an impressive show. Indeed that was his inoffensive but effective way of speaking his mind on a given issue. Truly it was expected of an Arya Sanyasi not to lose his cool. Swami Deekshanand was always a calm, cool and collected man of a personality that made deep impressions on all those who came in contact with him.

Besides reading, writing and publishing his own thoughts, Swami Deekshanand Ji took upon himself to republish books of sterling worth written by Arya Samaj leaders of yore. "YOGESHWAR SHRI KRISHNA" written by pt. Chamupati, M.A. Acharya of Gurukul Kangri, Haridwar was a fine biography of our beau ideal and morale booster, Shri Krishna Chandra Ji. The book was popular when published first time but had gone out of print later. Swami Deekshanand Ji took upon himself to republish it and sell at a subsidised price to enable all sections of the society to buy and own a copy. Likewise he published some other works of importance too.

Swami Deekshanand had founded an Ashram in Sahibabad near Noida and operated from there. He had no resident students or disciples there as that would have hindered the smooth flow of Prachar Karya that he was engaged in. Before his demise, he had gifted the Ashram and his rich library to the Savadeshik Arya Pratinidhi Sabha, Delhi and requested its Pradhan, Capt. Deo Ratna Arya to carry on the mission of Dayanand from there as he had been doing heretofore. I regret to say that after his demise, things were not the same.

Swami Deekshanand Ji was in great demand by eminent colleges and universities too to preach the Vedic Dharma and help the youth in staying on course. Many adverse influences, both homemade and imported from the West, were instrumental in letting the young boys and girls go astray. Swami Deekshanand Ji made his contribution to the cause and bringing the youth back on rails.

Swami Deekshanand Ji was invited by Dr Ashok Chauhan at the inauguration ceremony of the Amity University to shower his blessings and exhort both the high and mighty as well as the common man to stay on course and resist being swept away by the glamour of riches and flashy way of life. The educationists had listened to him with rapt attention and were benefitted by his short but sweet discourse. Swami Deekshanand Ji had been suffering from acute back pain for some time. One day I ventured to ask him how the pain started in his well looked after body, mind and soul. He mentioned of a minor accident when the driver of a car sent to fetch him for an important function jumped across speed breakers in his car-cum-flying machine. That did an untold damage to his spine in that advanced age. Life was never the same again.

Swami Deekshanand Ji is not with us in this world today but I am confident that his soul must have found another deserving body to carry on the good work for the humanity that he had been doing heretofore.

SECTION IV

SPARKLERS

WHAT IS IN SECTION IV? (PART I)

This section contains excerpts of a few letters that I wrote to Mama Ji and more of his letters received in reply. They are certainly not all the letters which we wrote to each other in life time. However, these are the ones which have survived somehow or the other. It may be worth reiterating that throughout life, I have loved writing letters and enjoyed reading letters including those of historical figures. For me, letters form as important a genre of literature as poetry, dramas, novels, and stories etc. do to the others.

Since the 1950s, I have saved all the letters received for 40 years. While I still continue to save the rare ones which trickle in. Twenty years ago, I started re-cycling the old ones in many creative ways-like sending them back to the writers on new-year days, birthdays, anniversaries, and on such personal occasions. This 'reincarnation' of dead and forgotten letters makes a new kind of delight. Furthermore, it provides a unique moment of introspection of life lived thus far. No letter was ever trashed. Initially, collecting letters and organizing them was never intended, but it came about as an obvious corollary of not throwing letters away. Of course, the collection is limited to the letters written to me only.

My enjoyment of letter writing has elevated to a yogic level, called Letter-Yoga, one of the many paths of yoga. Yoga means union. A union being between two entities, so which two are defined in yoga? At one end is clearly the individual, and at the other end is the Infinity, the Infinite-call it God, god, or the projection of one's ultimate potential, as it is always advancing from each point of actualization or realization. And, there are infinitely many paths connecting the two entities-according to one's potential and environment.

I have experienced transcendent moments in writing letters to a few individuals, and Mama Ji is one them. At times, I felt diving deep into myself while riding over a vehicle of letter writing. Letter writing is no different from body sculpting with various weights and training equipment. One easily understands body building, as progress therein is noticeable and measurable. Letter writing can be intensely one-to-one that for its duration the writer alone can grasp over a total experience. The writee's response (writee means a person whom a letter is written) is a measure too.

MamaJi's personal and professional life was not stable like that of mine in terms of being at one place for a while. He was travelling all the time in the course of his public and private commitments and schedules. As his popularity increased, his leisure time decreased. Normally, he would reply to my 3-4 letters in one shot. Mama Ji's hand writing was extremely beautiful, a model of calligraphy. He had such an emotional control over his hand that even when he was writing hurriedly, the beauty of script was not sacrificed.

This section adds another unique feature to this biography. Let me add that only a person who has a sense of history would save correspondence, make copies of letters before mailing them out, and keep them organized. In this respect, the Hindus have devalued their history both at the individual and collective levels. There are political reasons for it. Anyway, my letter collection goes back to the days when there were no fax, copying and scanning machines. Carbon papers used to be an important part of stationery.

In all, there are nearly 30 letters-all in Hindi. In size, they range from one, a 40-year old post card to quite a few letters running into 10-16 pages. I may add that some of the letters were lost in flood waters when we lived in Ambala Cantt (1980-82), and a few in moving from of one place to the other every 3-4 years.

Dec 30, 2013

WHAT IS IN SECTION IV? (PART II)

This section is a mine for the understanding of the mind of Swami Deekshanand Saraswati in near totality. His two dozen books only tell the mind of a scholar. In the beginning stages of this book, this section was not even thought of; was missed entirely; was not even on a remote horizon. When a good thing happens like this, I call it a beauty of not planning-different from non-planning. My basic nature of doing things is spontaneous. The book was almost done after Section III that I suddenly noted a couple of MamaJi's old letters written to me. They were so good that I rummaged through my folders of letters and dug out 26 of them including copies of four of letters that I had written him. Yes, I have an old habit of saving some important hand-written letters.

During the course of our common life span, I have exchanged lots of letters with Mama Ji. Obviously, some are lost in my cross continental movements of households and changing of homes. Personally, I never destroy any letters. Once I gave a good look at all the surviving letters, I realized two things. One, the functioning of a literary mind cannot be captured by any other medium except through his/her letters. Two, a bunch of letters provide a proof of a level of confidence and mutual trust.

MamaJi's letters are master pieces of calligraphy, ideas and vision of his work. Neither he was ever jealous of any one, nor did he compete with any one. His 1998 letter is so uplifting in the present US context when an 18-year old daughter is suing her parents with all kinds of allegations. On the other hand, his letters portray my ties with him so lofty and sublime.

From my archives, MamaJi's first letter is of June 23, 1962 and the last letter of June 16, 2002-forty years apart. These letters contain a lot of history, philosophy, metaphysics, Vedic lores-including his travels, achievements that he gladly shared with me. Three days of Dec, 2002 that we spent together in a gurukul 50 KM from Nanded and 18-hour train journey From Nanded to Mumbai would remain unforgettable for many counts. We had sensed the finality of our earthly ties when we took leave of each other on Jan 01, 2003-five month before his Departure.

At one time I thought that I will crop and prune the contents of letters, add my comments in English for the benefits for those who do not know Hindi. But I quickly realized that it would destroy the essence and beauty for everyone. The contents are inseparably meshed up. Hence, they are here as they were. Those who know Hindi will have a feast of ideas on them, despite their having written to me! There is an element of universality of ideas expounded in most letters. The underlines in the letters are all mine. It is my habit of highlighting a part of any text that resonates with me. It is worth noting that in a few letters, the entire page is underlined. Reason: it is so marvelous!

The longest letter that MamaJi wrote, in reply to mine, is in 12 pages. I matched it with 10 pages! Such a correspondence is unthinkable in the present high-tech tweet age. For me, writing such a letter is really meditative as the mind gets focused on one person. The rounding up the ideas becomes easier. Also, included is a 1974 report of an external examiner of Kusum's doctoral dissertation. MamaJi proudly carried it and showed it off to his visitors. He was very proud of Kusum's research work as he was equally engaged in it. It gave him a lot of intellectual confidence on the originality of his ideas, which became a turning point in his life's pursuits. He did not want to be known as a ***pracharak*** (preacher) only.

During 1998-2000, MamaJi had developed cardiac problems. Its onset was indicated much earlier by his loose grip on a pen that drastically changed his handwriting in terms of the size of letters, loops and flair. Since 1996, he started dictating long letters to his assistants. I was with him in Sahibabad in July 2000 when he suffered a heart attack. After a lot of convincing, he agreed to go for an open heart surgery.

The letters are arranged in a chronological order. There are glimpses of a lot of history in them. For example, the post card that used to be for 6p in 1960s is now priced for 50 p and an inland letter has gone up from 10 p to Rs 2.50.

In a few letters, he has spelled out his preaching circuit-visiting so many places. Prior to 1980s, the trains were the only means of transpiration. Physically, it is not easy even for the young, when one has to spend 1-2 days in a train.

March 07, 2014

। ओ३म् ।

आर्य समाज दीवानहाल देहली
२३-८-६२ ।

प्रिय सतीश !

सस्नेह आशीर्वाद ।

आशा है तुम सर्वथा प्रसन्न होगे । तुम्हारा पत्र २० की शाम को मिला समाचार ज्ञात हुए । मैं सदा ही इस प्रयत्न में रहता हूं कि मुझ से जो बने सबकी सेवा करूं और इसे अपना कर्तव्य समझता हूं । आपको यह नहीं सोचना चाहिए कि कभी पहिले तो पत्र नहीं डाला आज काम जो है लिख रहा हूं न जाने वह क्या समझेंगे । न कुछ समझने की बात है यदि कोई अपना कर्तव्य समझे तो कोई विवाद नहीं रहता मुझ से यदि किसी का कार्य सम्पन्न हो जाए तो इससे बढ़ कर और कल्याण होगा । आप किसी प्रकार का विचार मन में न लाएं । अब लीजिये समाचार ।

(१) मैं २१ की शाम को श्री रामचन्द्र जी शास्त्री से मिला उनसे समय निश्चित किया कि प्रि० शान्ति नारायण जी से कब मिलने चलना है उन्होंने २२ की शाम का समय निश्चित किया ।

~~(२) २२ की शाम को मैं और श्री रामचन्द्र जी शास्त्री~~
प्रि० साहिब से मिले जो कुछ उन्होंने कहा वह निम्न प्रकार है

(क) प्रिंसिपल साहिब को जब याद दिलाया तो उन्हें आपकी याद आ गई । और उन्होंने आपका नाम 'सतीशचन्द्र रस्तोगी' याद कर लिया । साथ ही यह भी कहा कि उन्हें चाहिए कि देहली के किसी भी कालिज से want निकले वहां प्रार्थना पत्र अवश्य दे दें जैसे करोड़ीमल कालिज हिन्दू कालिज, रामजस कालिज इत्यादि और मैं सभी स्थानों पर इन्टरव्यू में होता हूं कहीं न कहीं ले लूंगा ।

(ख) यदि पंजाब में रहना चाहें और किसी College से want निकली हो और आप रहना चाहें तो वे कहते थे कि वहां भी लगवा सकता हूं ।

(ग) उन्हें चाहिए कि वह मुझ से सम्पर्क बनाए रखें जब देहली में आएं तो मिल लें यदि पहिले भी मिल लेते तो अभी तक यह कार्य सम्पन्न हो जाता ।

(घ) यह भी कहा कि मैं उनकी Application फाइल से निकलवा कर देखूंगा और उचित कार्यवाही करूंगा ।

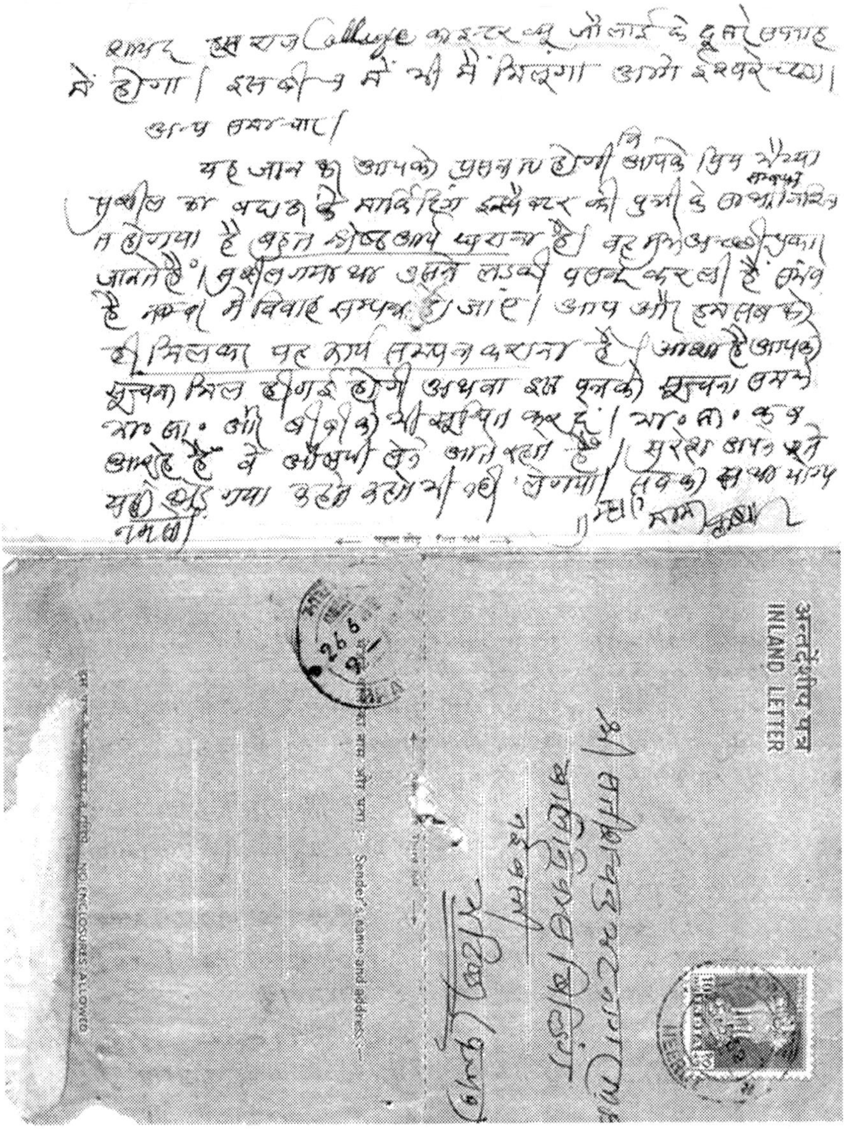

में होगा। इस बीच में भी मैं मिलूंगा आगे ईश्वरेच्छा।
अन्य समाचार।
अन्तर्देशीय पत्र
INLAND LETTER
Sender's name and address
NO ENCLOSURES ALLOWED

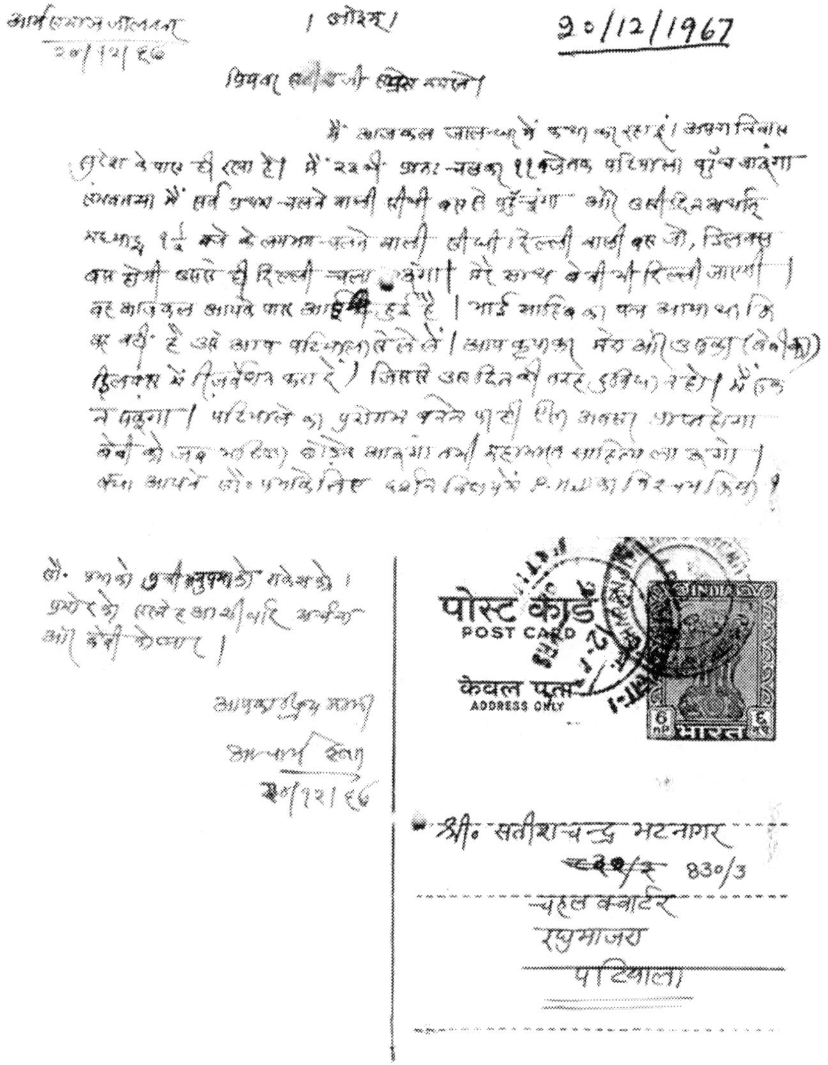

आर्यसमाज जालन्धर
२०/१२/६७

। ओ३म् ।

20/12/1967

प्रियवर [illegible] जी सप्रेम नमस्ते।

मैं आजकल जालन्धर में काम कर रहा हूं। [illegible]

[illegible]

श्री० सतीशचन्द्र भटनागर
830/3
चहल क्वार्टर
रघुमाजरा
पटियाला

पटियाला
16 जून, 1948.

आदरणीय मामा जी सादर प्रणाम

आशा है कि आपको मेरा पहला पत्र मिल गया होगा। मुझे पता चला है कि आप मेरे जाने के एक दिन बाद ही जालन्धर रवाना हो गये थे। फिर तो शायद मेरा यह पत्र आपको और एक दो रोज़ बाद ही मिलेगा जब आप नौकरी आदि के काम से लौट आयेंगे। यह पत्र लिखने का मेरा एक विशेष आशय है। लिखना कि मैंने आपको दिल्ली मिलने पर बताया था कि इस बार मैंने अमरीका जाने का निश्चय किया है और आशा है कि आप बड़ों के आशीर्वाद और शुभ कामना से मेरा यह मनोरथ सफल हो जायेगा। एक समस्या है किराये के लिये पैसों की भी जो कि लगभग 5000 हैं। 3000 का तो मैंने बन्दोबस्त कर लिया है और बाकी का प्रबन्ध करना है। तो माता पिता के बाद मैं आप ही से आशा करता हूँ तो केवल आप से और उसके बाद तो कुछ मित्रों या दूसरे साधनों से ही प्रयत्न करूँगा। लेकिन मेरा पूरा भरोसा है कि नौबत नहीं आयेगी। तो मुझे आपके 2000

तब की आशा का रक्खी है। आवश्यकता मुझे 15 अगस्त तक पड़ेगी और न क्योंकि परसों मद्रास से अगस्त तक करने का है।

हां एक प्रार्थना है और कहना कि यह मेरी एक बात के बारे में बहुत करके किसी के जिम्मे न करना और खुद भी यह पत्र मिलते एकदम छोड़कर [illegible] देने की कृपा करना।

आपका

[illegible]

[illegible]

। ओ३म् ।

आर्य समाज दीवानहाल
२५ । ४ । ६७

प्रिय सतीश। सस्नेह नमस्ते।

मैं परसों ही बाहिर से आया तो आने पर आपका पत्र मिला। यह जान कर अत्यन्त प्रसन्नता हुई कि आपको अमेरिका की इण्डियाना यूनिवर्सिटी ने गणित के उपाध्याय पद के लिए बुलाया है।

मेरे से जो भी सहयोग होगा दूंगा। आज ही प्रातः श्री शान्ति नारायण जी से बात हुई थी। उन्होंने कहा है कि उन्हें बुला लो, वह सारे कागज़ात लेकर आएं। मैं स्वयं चलकर उनका कार्य कराऊंगा। अतः आप पटियाला जाने से पहले यहां आकर मिल लें। मैं यहां ३० अप्रैल तक हूं फिर बाहिर चला जाऊंगा।

मेरी सदा ही मंगल कामनाएं साथ हैं।

तुम्हारा हितैषी
आचार्य कृष्ण

आर्य-प्रतिनिधि सभा मध्य दक्षिण

। ओ३म् ।

१३-८-६८

प्रिय सतीश। सस्नेह आशीर्वाद।

अभी अभी सेवक ने लिफ़ाफ़ा लाकर दिया, खोलने से पहले ही दिल्ली और आपका नाम पढ़कर प्रसन्नता हुई। पत्र पढ़कर तो अत्यधिक हर्ष हुआ आप अपने लक्ष्य पर बढ़ रहे हैं। परमात्मा आपको सर्वत्र सफलता प्रदान करें।

मैं २५ को आपकी प्रतीक्षा में था जब सायं तक आप नहीं आए और पत्र मिला तो अब मिलने की तो आशा रही ही नहीं थी अन्यथा आपके हाथों में ही देने का विचार था मैंने सोचा कह भेजता हूँगा २५ को आएंगे तो आपको ही दे दूंगा पर पत्र मिलने के पश्चात् विवश होकर मोहन को ही दे आया उसने भी बड़ी मुश्किल से गाड़ी पकड़ी यह सब उसने सुना ही दिया होगा।

आपने आभार माना यह छोटे होने के नाते तुम्हारी विनय है अन्यथा यह तो मेरा कर्तव्य था मुझे तुमने अवसर दिया कि मैं अपना कर्तव्य पालन कर सका यह किसी पर अहसान थोड़े ही है। बस यही खेद रहेगा कि जाते समय मैं आपसे नहीं मिल सका।

मैं २४ (24) अगस्त तक हैदराबाद रहूंगा और जिस दिन आप कुंभिगटन पहुंचोगे मैं बम्बई पहुँचूंगा काश कि कुछ भी इशारा हो जाता तो कुछ पहिले का ही प्रोग्राम बना लेता। अस्तु अब क्या विवशता है।

२५ से ३० अगस्त तक आर्य समाज परली बैजनाथ जि. बीड़ (मराठवाड़ा) रहूंगा

३१ से ५ तक शोलापुर रहूंगा बम्बई से १० घण्टे की यात्रा है परन्तु मेरे दोनों समय का प्रोग्राम है इसलिए जाकर आना कठिन है। वहाँ का पता c/o प्रो० ओमकुमार जी दयानन्द कालिज शोलापुर रहेगा ठहरना आर्य समाज में होऊंगा। कस्तूरबा मार्केट शोलापुर) मार्केट के पास ही आर्य समाज है।

६ को बम्बई उसी दिन प्रस्थान ८ से १२ c/o आर्य समाज गुना (मध्य प्रदेश)

यदि आप देहली के दिनों में से कटौती कर सकें तो सम्भव है शोलापुर
के लिए समय निकाल सकें (पत्र) अर्थ में परेशान होने की आवश्यकता
नहीं।

बम्बई में आप कहाँ ठहरेंगे यह कुछ पता नहीं वहाँ श्री
किशन सहायजी (महावीर सहाय जी के छोटे भाई) हैं, उनसे
अवश्य मिलना सम्भव है कि पहले भी मिले हो यदि नहीं भी
मिले तो भी मिलना क्योंकि वह भी काफ़ी रह कर आए हैं कुछ
उनके अनुभव से भी लाभ उठाना वह बहुत ही मिलनसार हैं
सम्भव है आपके पास उनका पता न हो तो मैं लिख रहा हूँ।
V.S. Bhatnagar Wardon & Co Ltd Mezagaon.
Bombay 10. Tel. No. 370306. ।

संभवतया आप वहाँ कुछ के चाचा जी के यहाँ ठहरें जहाँ भी हो
अपना पता अवश्य लिखें।

बहिन जी की भेजी राखी आपके पत्र के साथ ही मिल गई
बात यह हुई कि वह राखी का लिफ़ाफ़ा देहली दीवान
से ५ अगस्त को चेम्बूर आर्य समाज के प्रधान
पत्नी लेकर चले कि आचार्य जी वहाँ कथा कर रहे हैं
मैं शीघ्र पहुँचकर दे दूँगा पर हुआ ऐसा कि अति
वर्षा से गाड़ी का मार्ग रुक गया और वह बम्बई पहुँच न
सके कि मैं बम्बई से चल दिया फिर उन्होंने
अलग लिफ़ाफ़े में लिफ़ाफ़ा डाक से भिजवाया
जो कल १२ को मिला आज दो आमद उठाने आयद
पत्रों से आई लेकिन ठीक आई। शेष सब
कुशल मंगल है। सब को आशीर्वाद कहना
मेघी को प्यार बच्चों को बहुत बहुत प्यार
अशोक आनन्द को सस्नेह आशीर्वाद —

भवदीय शर्मा
आचार्य बृहस्पति

ओ३म् आर्य समाज सान्ताक्रुज बम्बई ५४
२८ - ३ - ६८

प्रिय पुत्र सतीश! सस्नेह आशीर्वाद

हैरानी की बात होगई कि तुम्हारा पत्र मिला। कि जब मैं अभी कुल १ महीने के आये, अर्थात् दूसरा जन्म धारण किये ३० दिन बीते थे, तुमने २८ दिसम्बर को लिखा था और पत्र २६ जनवरी को मिला, जो कि आपने [illegible] २१ जनवरी को लिखा था आज।

अब आपको साथ सम्बोधन न करना चाहिये क्यों कि अब [illegible] मुझे और [illegible] दयानन्द हो गये, पुराने रिश्ते समाप्त और नये रिश्ते बन हो गये, आप मुझे श्री स्वामी जी महाराज लिख सकते हैं, मैं तो सभी को पुत्र कहकर बुला सकता हूं।

हां तो आइए हम कुछ पीछे चलें, जब कि आप जानते हुए थे कि मेरी दक्षिण अफ्रीका जाने की योजना बन रही थी, आप जानते कि मैंने [illegible] को प्रातः ६ बजे डरबन के लिए उड़ान भरी और उसी रात्रि को १० बजे डरबन पहुंच गया, मेरे साथ श्री पं० नरदेव [illegible] जी शास्त्री थे, ३, ४ को विश्राम किया [illegible] को हमारा सार्वजनिक अभिनन्दन हुआ जिसमें मुझे उत्तर में दो शब्द कहने थे और मैं तो हिन्दी में ही बोलता [illegible] भी [illegible] में मेरा भाषण समाप्त हो गया, श्री [illegible] जी इंग्लिश में बोले, लोगों ने मुझे घेर लिया कि आपने हमको [illegible] बदल दिया, कि हिन्दी भाषी यहां [illegible] नहीं होगा हमें तो यह लगता है कि जो [illegible] भी आपको मिलेगी [illegible] पहले आए, किसी को न मिली होगी, लोगों ने आग्रह किया कि हम [illegible] (क्योंकि [illegible] यही [illegible] को सुनना चाहते) हैं, वास्तव में मुझे तो उन्होंने यज्ञ कराने के लिए बुलवाया था कि मैं यज्ञ करूंगा [illegible] इंग्लिश में भाषण दे दिया करेंगे, अब हुआ ये कि मेरे [illegible] दो [illegible] आ पड़े, यज्ञ भी प्रवचन भी, कुल ३४, भाषणों के पश्चात् तो यह हाल हुआ आर्य समाज से बाहर के संगठन (हिन्दू) बुलाने लगे, अभिप्राय यह कि हम ३४ दिन दक्षिण अफ्रीका रहे २१ [illegible] नगरों में घूमे और [illegible] भाषण हुए डरबन सनातन धर्म सभा में और [illegible] भाषण हुआ तो इतना [illegible] हुआ कि

उन्होंने लंदन यूनिवर्सिटी के अधिकारियों को लिखा कि यूनिव-
र्सिटी में हिन्दू प्रीस्ट की चेयर रिक्त है, भारत से आचार्य आए
हैं उन्हें उस पर नियुक्त कर लिया जाए, हिन्दू जनता की ओर से
[illegible] से प्रार्थना है कि वह उन्हें उस पद के लिए रख लें
मेरा पता दिया गया था मैं आर्य समाज के स्थान के गृह पर
इसका यूनिवर्सिटी से फोन आया कि श्री आचार्य जी
को ले कर आए, मैं गया मैंने अपनी विवशता बतलाते
हुए कहा कि न तो मेरे पास कोई डिग्री है और न अंग्रेजी
ही जानता हूँ उन्होंने कहा हिन्दू प्रीस्ट के लिए ये सब जानना
आवश्यक नहीं उन्हें संस्कृत आनी चाहिये, मैंने
कहा कि मैं थोड़ी संस्कृत जानता हूँ इस पर
भी उन्होंने कहा कि आप संस्कृत ले कर आइए।
मैंने यह कहकर जान छुड़ाई कि संन्यासी नौकरी नहीं करते
तो भी उन्होंने प्रार्थना पत्र दिया कि इस पद को खाली रखें
जो अब तक मेरे पास है मैं चाहता हूँ कि उस स्थान पर
गुरु भेजा जाए मैं दिल्ली जाकर उस का लिखूँगा।
और वह फॉर्म भेज दूँगा अभी वह [illegible]।
14 अक्टूबर 196[illegible] को लंदन से लौटकर मॉरिशस आए
वहाँ दस दिन प्रचार कार्य किया। मैं एक कातूरल गया, मैंने
वहाँ 'यज्ञोपवीत धारण करो' आन्दोलन चलाया सर्वसाधारण
देता हुआ प्रेरणा देता रहा था परिणाम यह हुआ कि आर्य
दिन जिस दिन पूर्णाहुति होनी थी प्रातः 8 बजे से यज्ञो-
पवीत लेने वालों का जो तांता आरम्भ हुआ वह सायं
6 बजे तक चलता रहा, ये हाल था कि एक लाइन
लगी हुई थी, बस बीच में 1½ घंटे का वक्त टाइम
निकाला था अन्यथा यज्ञोपवीत का तांता टूटा नहीं
दो हजार व्यक्तियों ने यज्ञोपवीत पहने थे कि
सब को मैं स्वयं अपने हाथ से पहनाता था इसलिए

इतना समय लगगया यह प्रभु कृपा है जो प्रभाव छोड़ा वह
स्वयं अनुभव करने की बात है, इस सब का क्या वर्णन करूं, कहां
तक करूं, लौटते समय हवाई अड्डे पर मुझे एक चीनी का [illegible]
कर दिया. और मेरे समस्त सामान को सहित [illegible] ने
दिया, अब मैं पुनः अगले वर्ष दक्षिण अफ्रीका जाऊंगा।
क्या ही अच्छा होता कि आपने मुझे इंग्लिश पढ़ा दी होती
तो मैं भी आज स्वामी विवेकानन्द की भांति सारे विश्व
को आर्य बनाने निकल पड़ता। और आपने संस्कृत पढ़ा दी
होती तो क्या ही अच्छा होता, आप भी [illegible]
करते, अस्तु आप इस बात को तो यहीं छोड़ देते हैं

अब आइये भारत लौट आएं हम 24 अक्टूबर
को बम्बई एयरपोर्ट पर उतरे और 31 को दिल्ली पहुंचे
वहां जाते ही आर्य समाज स्थापना शताब्दी के लिए जुलूस
जो 25 से 28 दिसम्बर 1975 दिल्ली में होनी थी
मैं उस का संयोजक बनाया गया था इसलिए उसके
जुलूस की [illegible] देश विदेश से लोग आएंगे
तो 2-3 लाख व्यक्ति जमा होंगे लेकिन जो अनुमान था
कोई [illegible] अनुमान से दो गुणे व्यक्ति आगये इतना
लम्बा भारी जुलूस था जो 25 तारीख को जलूस
था वह तो अभूतपूर्व था। इस पर्व के आयोजनों का महत्व
जयन्ति पर निकाले और निर्वाण के शताब्दी जलूसों
[illegible] निकाले गये जलूसों से भी अधिक था
जब आपातस्थिति के कारण हम D-A-V- संस्थाओं
को सम्मिलित नहीं होने दिया गया अन्यथा तो
यदि पंजाब और राजस्थान, यू.पी. की संस्थाएं यदि
सम्मिलित होतीं तो अद्भुत दृश्य होता अस्तु
जलूस पर लाल किले पर यह छाप पड़ी कि आर्य समाज एक जीवित
संस्था है अब मरी नहीं, [illegible] उत्सव
बड़े बड़े सम्मेलन हुए। वेद सम्मेलन का पाठ सामाजिक
इसलिए कर रहा हूं कि उसके पुरोधा [illegible]
थे सार्वदेशिक ने निश्चय किया कि सारे देश के

ने विद्वानों को जो वेद के विद्वान हों सम्मानित किया
जाए, आपको जान कर यह अत्यन्त हर्ष होगा कि
उन नौ वैदिक विद्वानों में आपकी बहिन डा० कुसुम
का भी नाम था। जब पहले पहल नव भारत में पढ़ा
तो आश्चर्य में रहा कि क्या स्वप्न तो नहीं
कुछ आश्चर्य भी था क्योंकि देश के धर्म देव
डा० (श्रम), उदयवीर जी जैसे विद्वान जिनकी
आयु 80 के निकट है और कुसुम जो अभी बच्ची है
उन लोगों के साथ सम्मान ले गई है पर कुसुम
तो कल की छोकरी है, सोचता रहा कि यह तो पक्ष-
पात है, पर सार्वदेशिक ने उसके शास्त्र पढ़ने
को देखकर उसे सम्मानित किया था, ठीक था।
आप अनुमान नहीं लगा सकते कि उस की वैदिक साहित्य
में रुचि की कहीं उपलब्धि है, और आप पूर्ण विवरण
रिपोर्ट पढ़ें तो दंग रह जायें कि है इतना बड़ा काम
किया है। परमात्मा उसे आशीर्वाद दे कि वह इसी प्रकार
और कार्य करे। 23 अगस्त को उसका कार्यक्रम होगा
था और उसी दिन उस बच्ची को उपाधि से अलं
कृत कर दिया गया। मैंने सुना था कि यदि हिन्दू
होती तो उसे भी पुरस्कार मिलता। आज किसको
सही। (201) रुपये 1 शाल और 10 ग्रन्थ भेंट किए गये थे।
अब कुछ मेरे समाचार को भी लीजिए
जिस प्रकार रविजी के घर में पुत्र जन्म की खुशी होती है
वही प्रसन्नता आज आर्य जगत में मेरे सत्यार्थप्रकाश पर
भी आर्य समाज में समझा रहा है कि मैं सत्यार्थ
लेकर कुछ पाठकों लाउंगा मैं कुछ दिनों में जाकर
यह लेख मैदान में आन पहुंचा है। यह तो लेखपत्र
मोहन ने लिखा ही होगा कि पटियाला के कतिपय सदस्य
उनके सम्मानित हुए लोगों की भीड़ में तो

(५) टालते थे, मुझे तो संन्यास लेने में जुट जाना पड़ा था, भोले लोग चाहते तो तुम्हारे रास्ते जाते और मोह के कारण हो गया होगा, लेकिन मोह के नाते बाद में इसलिए लेकिन अब के पास है, आपने आपको मिलना है, मैं तो यहां से भी चलता का हूँ यह तमन्ना है, अन्यथा तो इतना ज्यादा काम कम हो जाता है। अब आपको [illegible] ख्याल नहीं होगा कि मैं पत्र नहीं लिखता, मैं इन्सान से इसलिए को आप [illegible] सूरत [illegible] कर जो कहा है अच्छा हो, यदि यह पढ़कर आपके पास मिलकर देखें। देख लेना।

अब आइये संन्यास आश्रम की ओर। इस आश्रम का क्या महत्त्व है आप इस तरह से पूछ रहे हैं, जैसे मैंने आपको संन्यास लेना हो। मुझे जब [illegible] ने संन्यास की दीक्षा दी, तो उन्होंने कहा कि न तो आप अपने किसी सम्बन्धी से मिलने जायेंगे, न घर जायेंगे, न उस गांव में ही जायेंगे, जहां के आप रहे हों, न उनकी दी हुई कुछ लेंगे, न पहनेंगे। और इस पर मैंने नतमस्तक हो कर स्वीकृति दे दी। फिर जब मैंने समापन [illegible] दिया तो उस समय कहा कि मैं [illegible] जब आप में से कोई [illegible] ले कर संन्यास लेगा इस पर [illegible] ने कहा तो हम आपको बुलवा लेंगे, तो मैंने सोचा कि आपकी [illegible] लिस्ट में अपना नाम लिखवा रहे होंगे। मैं क्या लिखवाऊँ तो आइए अभी टापिक पर।

पहले संन्यास शब्द का अर्थ समझ लो इसमें
पड़ा हुआ सम् उपसर्ग 'ठीक ठीक' का 'पूर्णतया'
का अर्थ देने वाला है न्यास का अर्थ है त्याग
ठीक ठीक त्याग, पूर्णतः त्याग, पूर्ण तया
किया त्याग हो तो इस का दूसरा अर्थ समझो
सन्न्यास। सन्न्यास न्यास कहते हैं
धरोहर को सत कहते हैं, उत्तम पात्र को तो
जो धरोहर पूर्वजों से तुम्हें प्राप्त हुई है
उसे किसी सत् पात्र को देकर स्वयं मुक्त हो
जाए अब तक तुम उसके न्यासी (ट्रस्टी)
थे तो अब समय आ गया कि ट्रस्टीशिप
भी छोड़ दो। जो तुम्हें पूर्वजों से धरोहर के
रूप में जमीन जायदाद चल अचल सम्पत्ति
मिली हो उसे छोड़ने का समय आ गया है
उसे छोड़ो ठीक तौर का त्याग तब होगा जब
उत्तम पात्र को धरोहर संभाल देंगे वरना
सब छोड़ने पर भी यहीं के बने रह जाएंगे
न जाने कितने उस जायदाद को बेचा करेंगे
बनाएंगे या बर्बाद करेंगे ये काम मरने के
बाद तो होते ही हैं उस समय तो मृत्यु स्वयं
सन्यास दिलवा देती है इसमें क्या विशेषता है
विशेषता तो इसमें है कि तुम स्वयं छोड़ दो
दूर से छुड़वाया न जाए स्वतः छोड़ दो।
चल अचल सम्पत्ति धन रुपया पैसा छोड़ने का नाम

वास्तुपक्ष है और विवेक, विवेक, ज्ञान के
छोड़ने का कारण संस्कार है। निश्चित रहे विवेक ऐसी
वस्तु है जिसे आग नहीं जलाती चुराया नहीं
जाता धन इसका अभिप्राय यही है कि बाप से
लेने के बाद यह समझ आया है कि उस विवेक से कोई
व्यापार या कमाई न करोगे और विवेक मुआवजे
के दाम करोगे और कोई ऐसा ज्ञान का रहस्य
न होगा जिसे आपने अपनी व्याख्या समझकर
छुपा रखा हो वह छुपाओगे नहीं वह फाइलें
जो आपकी रोजी रोटी का कारण बनते थे आज
मैं बच्चों, याद से दे दूंगा चुराओगे नहीं
छुपाओगे नहीं। जब विवेक, ज्ञान, दिशा
का भी त्याग कर दिया है तब संन्यास ले सकते हैं
मैं समझता हूं कि जमीन जायदाद तो मैंने
पहले ही नहीं रखी, रहा पैसा जिस दिन
संन्यास लेना था बैंक से 50 रुपये थे निकल-
वाए और उस दिन की दक्षिणा देने में काम
आए, जिस दिन मैं यह संस्कार हुआ। रही
विवेक की सम्पत्ति जो मुझे महर्षि दयानन्द
और पं० बुद्धदेव जी से प्राप्त हुई थी उसको
सत्संगों में जयदेव जी, सत्यप्रकाश जी, राजेन्द्र
लक्ष्मीकान्त जी, मोहन जी, तुम्हारे भाई सुरेश
को और तुम्हारी बहिन कुसुम को बांट दी
अब और बात है कि किसका कितना भाग था और

(८)
कौन कितना ले पाया। इस प्रकार कोई भी
व्यक्ति व्यापार सम्पत्ति रूप धरोहर आपने पुत्रों
में न्यायत बाँटे, पितृ ऋण से मुक्त हो जाता है।
और विद्या ज्ञान और शिक्षा का न्याय करके गुरु
के ऋण से मुक्त हो जाता है। और यदि संन्यास
में सम्पूर्ण भाग स्व सम्पदा त्याग कर सके तो उसका
दान करता रहे और लोगों को मोक्ष मार्ग
पर चलाता रहे, तो ऋषियों के ऋण से मुक्त
हो जाता है तभी मुक्ति मिलती है अन्यथा नहीं
जन्म रहे और मुक्ति कैसे जाए, सब भी आत्मा पर है
जब तक तीन ऋण रहते हैं तब तक कर्म भी
जनेऊ के तीन तार रहते हैं यहाँ इन्हें उतार
दिया जाता है। मानो उसने कपड़ा छोड़ के
उतार दिया। याद रहे जीते जी मरना
वानप्रस्थ है और जीते जी जलना संन्यास है।
इसीलिए संन्यासी के वस्त्रों का रंग अग्नि
का रंग रखा जाता है मानो वह कहता है कि
मैं जीते जी आग में बैठ गया हूँ। तुम्हें पता
होगा कि पिता के मरने पर बिरादरी उसके
बेटे के सिर पर पगड़ी बांधती है जिसे पगड़ी
की रस्म कहते हैं, यह क्या सूचित है, मरने के
बाद पुत्र के सिर पगड़ी बंधी तू ? क्या और गुरु
जीते जी! अपने हाथों से बांध और अपने

(८)

तुम्हें याद होगा कि तुम्हारे नाना जी की मृत्यु के उपरान्त
बाबू राम स्वरूप के सिर पगड़ी बांधी गई थी यद्यपि बड़े भैया
जीते जी नाना जी ने कभी पगड़ी बांधी नहीं उन्हें
ऐसा ख्याल नहीं था कि लड़के लायक नहीं हैं कि जो
पगड़ी की लाज रख सकेंगे जीते जी नहीं छोड़ी। अन्त
को मृत्यु ने छुड़वा ही लिया, इससे क्या खूबी
कि मृत्यु छुड़वा ले या इन्द्रियां शिथिल हो जाने
लगें क्यों न छोड़ दें, इसलिए छोड़ने की ख्वाहिश
बड़ा प्यारा काम है।

सतीश! आओ जरा सोचें कि आखिर सब कुछ
छोड़ना न होगा, मरना न होगा, जलना न होगा।
मरने के बाद छोड़ा तो क्या छोड़ना हुआ,
मरने के बाद मरना हुआ तो उस मरने का क्या महत्व
जीते जी मरना माना है उसका महत्व है।
मरने के बाद चिता पर चढ़ा दिये गये तो क्या?
जीते जी चिता पर चढ़ना और जलना है।
या तो यह हो कि छोड़ना न होगा मरना न
होगा, जलना नहीं होगा, पर जब यह अवश्य
होना ही है तो देखो कि अब क्या?

मैं एक और बात पूछता हूँ कि गौतमजी
का नियम है कि हर व्यक्ति ५० वर्ष में
सार्वजनिक छोड़ दे तो क्या मतलब यहां की चीजें
तो छोड़ दें और वहां की, सोना हाट की, साथ
ही गद्दी से चिपक जाए, ऐसा आजकल है
तो क्यों नहीं सब जगह त्याग हो जाए, बल्कि-

दिखकनमान है डाक्टर ~~अ~~ इंजीनियर सर्विस से
रिटायर होगया फिर बाजार में दुकान खोल कर
बैठ गया। अब क्यों इजाजत हो वह बेरोज़-
गारी बढ़ाता है, नौजवानों के हक छीनता है
सरकारी सर्विस के अयोग्य व्यक्ति यहां
दुकान पर बैठने को कैसे योग्य होगया और
राष्ट्रपति प्रधान मन्त्री भी नेता तक के
लिए यही बात लागू होनी चाहिये कि
कोई भी व्यक्ति ५८ वर्ष का होते ही
सब जगह से रिटायर हो जाता है तो
विश्व में शान्ति का राज्य स्थापित हो
जाए। संसार में आपाधापी, व राजनीति
बूढ़ों युवकों के झगड़े, स्वार्थी लोगों के
झगड़े तभी तक है जब तक यह निकम्मी
व्यवस्था है, रिटायरमैंट तो होती है
स्वतः रिटायर हो जाए तो कितना अच्छा
हो, बस इन सभी समस्याओं का हल एक
मात्र वानप्रस्थाश्रम से है।
प्रश्न होगा कि तुमने बूढ़ों को रोज़ी
दी और इनको को बेरोज़गार कर दिया क्या
इससे राष्ट्र पागल नहीं होगा है उत्तर दिया
नहीं राष्ट्र अब बूढ़ों को तो पेन्शन दे रहा है

मेरा पता स्वामी दीक्षानन्द सरस्वती आर्य समाज दीवान हाल
दिल्ली ६

वह तो दुरुपयोग कर रहे हैं उनका सरकार से (55)
पैसा ले रहे हैं और इधर जनता को लूट रहे हैं
वह तो सब से बड़े अपराधी हैं। उनकी सम्पत्ति
ज़ब्त कर लेनी चाहिये सम्पत्ति ज़ब्त करके
कम्युनिज़्म है सम्पत्ति को सभी लोगों का
आराम व्यवस्था है।

फिर प्रश्न होगा इतने बूढ़े बेरोजगार नहीं
तो बेकार तो हो जाएगा यदि बेकार पड़े रहे
तो कल तो सरफाइये तोड़ेंगे या कुछ न कुछ
खुराफात करेंगे। नहीं कुछ नहीं करेंगे। यह
सभी सरकार के अपने निःशुल्क सेवक हैं
और कहेंगे कि जो यौवन की पीढ़ी, जो गृहस्थ
में गुजर है, अर्थात विद्या है, उसे दान करेंगे।
अर्थात विद्या दान देंगे बस सरकार उनके
पास विद्यार्थी जुटा देगी और राष्ट्र
की शिक्षा निःशुल्क चल पड़ेगी और गरीब
लोग पढ़ सकेंगे। अर्थात दान पुण्य और पात्र
पढ़ेगा दोनों तपस्वी और त्यागी होंगे।
इनकी भी आयु वृद्धि होगी, यदि वृद्ध लोग काम
पर ही लग रहे तो उनकी आयु क्षीण हो जाएगी
उनकी आयु वृद्धि के लिए उनके पास बच्चे
छोड़ दिए जाएंगे वह बच्चों से वात्सल्यता
का व्यवहार करेंगे प्यार प्यार से पढ़ाएंगे
अपनी आयु बढ़ाएंगे। अपने देश को हराभरा

(12) हृदय का यदि माता काका को अपने बच्चों
से पोते पोतियों दोहते दोहतियों से अधिक
प्यार होता है नाना की आयु का तकाजा है
यदि मैं एक जगह रखे जाएं जब इस एक
जगह रखे जाने का नाम गुरुकुल है।

सोचो राष्ट्रपति राधाकृष्णन सर्वोच्च
छात्रों का विश्वविद्यालय के दर्शनशास्त्र के
बैठे तो देश के युवक अनपढ़
आते और कितने ही राधाकृष्णन छोड़ जाते
अब राष्ट्रपति बन कर क्या बनाया बड़ा
सम्मान तो और कुछ नहीं, जब तक उन
औरों से नहीं ते न रहेंगी जातियाँ तब
तक कुरीतियों की लड़ाई जारी रहेगी
महात्मा की आकृति सब भारत का बैठे हुए
व्यक्ति के कारणों में नेहरू पटेल आगे आ
हो जाते, तो नेहरू पटेल बनकर की अपेक्षा
महात्मा गांधी अधिक प्रसन्न रहते
नेहरू पटेल नहीं बनते न नेहरू न पटेल
उन परम्परा को रखो कारण ये महात्मा की भूल
पाखंडियों छोड़ देते तो देखते देश का
नक्शा होता महात्मा गांधी होता सम्भव

[illegible]

<u>REPORT</u>

I have read with pleasure and interest the thesis entitled 'Purusha Sukta Ka Vivechanatmaka Adyayana' Submitted by Kumari Kusum Lata Arya for the degree of Doctor of Philosophy (Ph.D.) at the University of Rajasthan.

Divided into 10 chapters, the thesis covers a profound study of the Purusha Sukta. The first chapter introduces the different points of view of the principal Vedic Commentators (viz. Sayana, Shaunaka, Uveta, Mahidhara and Dayananda Swami) on the meaning of the Purusha Sukta. The difference in the number of the Mantrasof the Purusha Sukta in all the four Vedas is pointed out with plausible answers. The second chapter enumerates the various etymologies of the word 'purusha' on the basis of Vedic and Classical authorities. This has helped the candidate to determine the nature of 'purusha'.

Chapter III represents the central idea of the 'Purusha Sukta', wherein the Yajna-Purusha-Paramatman has been well established. The fourth chapter forms the core of the present thesis. It is very ably written. The treatment of the Philosophical doctrines prepares the structure to study Vedic cosmology. Truly, several scholrs have already contributed to this aspect, however, it is gratifying to note that the candidate has been able to make significant contribution in this chapter. The interpretation of Pura, Dashangula, Bhumi, Virat and Prishadajya are quite interesting. On the basis of the philosophical doctrines the candidateshas studied the Vedic Cosmology in the fifth chapter. The various intriguing questions regarding the theories of creation such as the basis of consciousness, and the manifestation of Purusha in the beginning of creation have received critical treatment on the basis of Yathapurvavada and Yathatathyavada. The nature and form of Yajna has been studied in the sixth chapter. The candidate has thrown fresh light to understand the nature of Purusha as identical with Yajna. The three principal and foremost dharmas of Yajna, the meaning of Sarvahut; the symbol of Deva Puja, dana and sangatikarna, and the meaning of several disputed words such as Pashu, Alambhana, Sanjnapana and Avadana have been interpreted with added material. The candidate has further made an attempt to study the concept of Pancha-pashu and Panch-Medha.

To complete the study of Vedic cosmology, the candidate has dealt with 'Apaurushaya Janana' in the seventh chapter. The central idea of the Purusha Sukta is to propose the 'Samaja Purusha'. Therefore, in the 8th chapter the origin of Varna-Vyavashta according to Karman has well been traced and an outline is proposed for a neo-social order. The ninth chapter discusses the concept of Apavarga. The end of human life remains incomplete by the enjoyment of worldly pleasures. It has been correctly stated here that the final goal of human life is to achieve immortality in the form of salvation. Therefore this chapter dealswith the concept of Moksha and the nature of the object of knowledge. The last chapter enumerates the results and findings of the present thesis.

It seems on the surface that the present work is simply a study of the Purusha Sukta but in reality the candidate has gone very deep to study the Ancient India (social Philosophical and cultural) values; the thesis represents an understanding of Vedic literature and allied br anches of classical Sanskrit Literature. I congratulate the candidate for this comprehensive study of the purusha Sukta with fruitful results. The thesis attests candidate's judicious mind, capacity of critical analysis, and an understanding of the modern methods of scientific research. It is written in faultless and literary Hindi and is worthy of publication in its present form. The candidate has made valuable contribution to the field of Vedic Studies. I recommend to the authorities of the University of Rajasthan that Kumari Kusum Lata Arya be awarded the degree of Doctor of Philosophy (Ph.D.) on thebasis of this work. A Viva Voce examination may however be held if the rules permit.

University of Rajasthan
Jodhpur

Report on the thesis entitled 'PURUSH SUKTA KA VIVECHANATMKA ADHYAYANA' submitted by Miss Kusum Lata Arya for the award of Ph.D.

I have examined the above mentioned thesis. The thesis deals with, apart from the main subject, a wide va-riety of other topics connected with the Purusha Sukta.

The treatment of the subject is very systematic and clear. The following topics are presented in a new light.

1. PURUSH SUKTA KI MANTRA SANKHYA PAR VICHAR: in Chapter-1
2. PURUSHA SUKTA AUR SHODASHA KALAYEN: in Chapter-2
3. PURUSHA SUKTA MEN DARSHANIK TATTVA: in Chapter-4
4. VRIKSHA VANASPATI, PASHU, MANUSHYONKA UTPATTI KRAMA, YUVA MANUSHYON KI UTPATTI: in Chapter-5
5. MEDHA PRAKARANA in Chapter-6
6. Shardra in Chapter - 8

Other topics are also presented in very clear terms. The language is good and there are no mistakes.

The candidate has taken great care and pains in going about her work. I recommend her for the award of the degree of the Ph.D.

Osmania University
HYDERABAD

3. Yes. When published it will be very useful for the students of Veda in general and of Purusha Sukta in particular.

[illegible]

①

लालबेगल
11 जून, 1976

नानाजी; मर गये! यह स्वीकार करना कितना कठिन है। आपको भी यह कई बार आभास हुआ होगा कि जब किसी प्रियजन की एक मृत्यु हो जाती है तो कितने दिनों तक सपनों में या चेतन अवस्था में भी उसका आकार सामने चलता फिरता नजर आता है। और यह एक लम्बे समय का प्रभाव होता है कि जब दिल और दिमाग उसे अपने से दूर खिंचे हुए मानते हैं तो यही हाल मेरा है। न मैं मानसिक तौर पर पहिले तैयार था और न अभी तक इसके लिए समर्थ हूं। नाते, सम्बोधन की इन बारीकियों में इतनी गहनता कहाँ है। यह तो किसी सम्बन्ध के शुरुआत में तो अवश्य कुछ भाव रखते हैं पर जो इतना लम्बा एकतरफा वार्तालाप का रहा हो वहां रह ही क्या जाता है। पर जैसा मैंने लिखा कि आप मुझे आगे इसी प्रकार मिलते रहे तब मैं अवश्य उसे दिल से स्वीकार कर लूंगा चाहिए।

तो अब आपकी यह चिट्ठी पढ़ी तो पुकारा पहुंचा तो इसी समय स्वाभाविक हो चला पर मैंने विचारा नहीं। और वह मैं तो सच्चा रहा गया कि २ विचारों में जो आज तक भी नहीं आ रहे। यहां एक विचार था कि मैं भारत आकर और [illegible] उनके [illegible] का समय अपने साथ [illegible] रख सकूं। पता नहीं यह सब आपके लिए कितना भारी या सम्भव होगा। और भी कई बातें दिमाग में आ रही थी पर सोचा कि यह पत्र आपका इतना दिल दिमाग को [illegible] देने लायक था तो पीछे दिल के संतुलन आ जाने तक मैं [illegible] हुआ। ठीक तो [illegible] पत्र लिखते समय भी [illegible] है पर वह [illegible] लिखती नहीं है [illegible]। लगभग २ माह बीत गये हैं जब यह आपका पत्र मिला था।

तो प्रश्न है कि मैं किस बात के बारे में पत्र लिखूं। आपका जो दक्षिण अफ्रीका और योरोप का संक्षिप्त वर्णन है वह बड़ा ही अच्छा लगा। एक बात अब यह ध्यान आती कि अब भारत के बाहर भी आप अपने धर्म को आवश्यक समझने लगे हैं। इसके दो बड़े लाभ हैं एक तो बाहर वाले जब अपने विचारों के आधार निष्पक्ष समीक्षा देखेंगे तो उसका इतिहास, संस्कृति, राजनीति पहलुओं पर भी पड़ेगा। क्योंकि धार्मिक का परिवर्तन समूहों में एक अद्भुत परिवर्तन लाता है। दूसरे जब घर वाले (या देश वाले) देखते हैं कि बाहर वाले आपको इतना मान और सम्मान देते हैं तो उनके विचारों में भी अधिक परिवर्तन आने लगता है।। यहां खोज का खतरा भी है क्योंकि जो इसी देश के और बाहर भी कार्यकर्ता होते हैं उनमें एक प्रकार की धर्म ईर्ष्या पैदा होने लगता है। और महर्षि महेश योगी के शिष्य। विदेशों में इसका जो बड़ा कार्य हो रहा है तो भारत में उन कई लोगों ने कई दृष्टि से ही समझते हैं। मैं यह तो मानता हूं कि इतना कार्य इतना महान नहीं है जितना विदेशी समझते हैं पर वह निरा ढकोसला भी है।

हां मुझे इस पत्र से यज्ञोपवीत के बारे में पता लगा और किसी महत्व जानने की कुछ उत्सुकता इसके देखकर भी हुई। आपको याद है शायद एक दिन पहिले मैंने कहा था कि यह क्या विचार लगता है तो आपने मुझे समझाया सारा विचार संस्कार का अर्थ सिखाया था और अगले दिन में इस विधि को मानकर के जाना था मैंने कहा। तो अब जब भी मैं देश लौटूंगा तो अवश्य ही यह यज्ञोपवीत धारण करवाऊंगा!

सब उसके बीच जनेऊ धारणा मैं सोचें इतने महान विचार
है यह कैसा भारतीय परम्परा के प्रति मस्तक नमन
का कृत्य लगता है।

इसी बीच मैं लिख दूं कि उसी समय मैंने आपके का
भी एक फोटो कापी सुरेश को भेज दी थी। राकेश (लता)
की शादि जो यहां एक संभ्रान्त लड़के के २२ मई को हुई
है। तो हम सब लोग जून में और एक सप्ताह सुरेश
के पास आ रहे। उसे आपका भेजा हुआ प्रार्थनापत्र
तो अभी तक नहीं मिला था पर वह आपकी चिट्ठी
लिखने वाला अवश्य था। उसकी पत्नि की ओर
आपीयों का इसे कुछ पता नहीं था आजकल वह
~~एडजामीनरों~~ की ~~रिपोर्टों~~ की ~~इन्तजार~~ में है। देखो
वे कैसी आती हैं और उसका वह नतीजा पता
देता है कि नहीं।

और पूछनी बात जो इसी बीच में के लिखनी है यही है
कि क्या सच आपको अंगरेजी न आने के बन्धन
महसूस हुआ था। क्या आपने कभी (तो) अनुभव भारत
में भी किया था? केरल और मद्रास के लोग हिन्दी कम
जानते हैं। बंगाल और आसाम और नागा प्रदेश के लोग
पूर्व में रहते हैं। तो वहां क्योंकि नहीं अंगरेजी से काम
चलाया जाता। जो हमारा विचार पूर्व में है वह
आपके प्रभाव की अधिक आवश्यकता है ताकि
उन विदेशों में जहां केवल अंगरेजी ही बोली जाती है।
आप आगे लिखें कि भारतीयों को यहां तो आपको भारी
अधिक पुराने और सम्बन्ध मिलेगी बजाय
उसके अगर आप सिर्फ इनके अंगरेजी सीखें और
हिन्दुओं (भारतीयों) में प्रचार करें। वह काम आप जितनी

चिन्मयानन्द को भी करने दें। मैं आपकी इनकी बातमें बड़ा सत्य है कि आज मैंने ~~कि~~ संस्कृत पढ़ी होती तो मेरे विचारों में इस समय तक काफी परिवर्तन आ गया होता। तीन साल पहिले मैंने रूसी भाषा सीखी थी जो संस्कृत से बहुत अधिक मिलती थी। तो मैं बार २ यही कहा करता था कि आज मुझे संस्कृत आती होती। यह संस्कृत के लिए न होती तो मैं बहुत शीघ्र रूसी ~~संस्कृत~~ सीख जाता। क्योंकि जिन विद्यार्थियों संस्कृत थोड़ी सी भी आती थी उन्होंने बड़ा अच्छा किया था। तो यह तो बातों में से बात निकल आई जिसका इस चिट्ठी की बात से कोई सम्बन्ध नहीं है। पर इतना अवश्य है कि अब मैं संस्कृत को सीख नहीं सकता। और लगता है कि अगर सिखाने वाला कोई अच्छा विद्वान हो तो मैं तीन मास में संस्कृत के ग्रन्थ पढ़ने लगूंगा। तो यह बात भी आप याद रखना।

बाकी मुझे कुसुम के बारे में सुन कर बड़ी दुःखी हुई कि उसे आर्यसमाज ने इतना आतंकित किया है। इसमें प्रेरणा और सहायता आपकी भी है। वरना तो उसकी तो आपका किया है था। यह ठीक है [illegible] जानती कि कितना किस का था और कितना [illegible]। पर जिस प्रकार से किया [illegible] गया वह भी तो विचार योग्य बात है न।

ठीक है इन दो लड़कों ने [illegible] आर्यसमाज को [illegible] को अपना प्रत्युत्तर दिया। फिर क्या? मेरे विचार से [illegible] आर्यसमाज के लोगों की [illegible] कि [illegible] अकालियों और मुसलमानों की तरह अपनी पार्टी के [illegible]। उन्होंने क्या [illegible] सोचा है। इसका परिणाम यह हुआ कि [illegible]

पार्टियों पर सरकार रहे वर्षोंतक लगाते रहा कुछ आर्य
समाजी भी लोकदल में आगये। आर्य समाज के नेताओं
को राजनीति में सीधा नहीं कूदना चाहिये और शिवकुमार
शास्त्री और प्रकाशवीर शास्त्री ने किया। यह मामला
गलत परम्परा है। उन्होंने जनता से वोट लिये और वहीं
सरकें ली और लग गये दूसरे काम। यह एक पार्टी
मैदान में जनता के विश्वासघात से कम नहीं है। तो
आपके / उस विवरण से ऐसा लगा कि आप तो अब
आर्य समाज के वे नेता आधार बना कर शहीद हो गये।
शहीद होना पवित्र है पर होने वाले में पूरा योगदान हो
उस कार्य का।

आपने लिखा कि आप कुछ दिनों के बाद जौहर
बूट लेकर मैदान में आने वाले हैं तो मैं इसका अर्थ
पूरी तरह से नहीं समझ सका। लगता है यह कोई
सामाजिक – राजनीतिक उथल पुथल का कोई रूप है।
अगर कुछ भी ऐसा है तो मैं उसके पक्ष में नहीं।
आपने जिस क्षेत्र में इतना नाम और प्रभाव बनाया है
आप उसी में एक नई सरवेता को जन्म दे सकते
हैं। सत्ता की कुर्सी न तो लाया है और न लायेगी!
जैसे अकबर का काम राज करना था न कि नये
धर्म की स्थापना करना। उसी का दीन-ए-इलाही
अकबर के साथ ही समाप्त हो गया। इसी तरह राज
कार्य भी सन्यासी के लिये नहीं। फलस्वरूप किसी
व्यक्ति या पार्टी को भी दिलाना आपकी भी
परीक्षा। उसमें ठीक तरह से सिद्ध नहीं होता। जहाँ
तक हो सके मैं इस जौहर बूट को बिल्कुल भी न समझा हूँ
तो कभी समय पाकर अब अवश्य लिखना। आशा

जैसे आपने लिखा तो अब तो आप इस ख़त में वो [illegible]
होंगे। हां मुझे याद आया कि इतिहास में जो पदमिनि
ने खिलजी के समय जो जौहर प्रथा थी तो वह उनमें
तो वह अपनी सहेलियों के साथ आग में कूद पड़ी थी तो
आज इस प्रकार की कोई बात है तब तो हाल कर सकती है
जो मैंने आपको लिखी है। बहरहाल मुझे औरत के अवश्य रक्षित
करावे। तो बीच पत्र में आपने सन्यास और वानप्रस्थ का
जिकर किया था तो लगता नहीं मैं कर रहा हूं। लेकिन
लिखा कि मैंने पिछले पत्र में आपसे ऐसे पूछा था और
मैं स्वयं ही सन्यास लेने वाला हूं। इसमें कोई शक भी
नहीं और सच तो यह है कि हर मनुष्य में एक
थोड़ी समय २ पर आती है जब वह पाप कर के
पूरे सन्यासी की भूमिका में बदल जाता है मुझे
याद है आप जी भी कभी २ ऐसे बहुत करते थे। फिर
और बात है जब आदमी गृहस्थी और घरेलू समस्या
ओं से तंग आकर वह कुछ समय के लिये अपने भागना चाहता
है व इस वातावरण से। मेरा यह अभिप्राय नहीं है
और हर आदमी अभिलाषा होना समझते भी हैं सन्यास
के लिये। और ऐसी कई महात्मा जो सच्चे सन्या-
सियों भी हुई हैं वह भी कर्म के माध्यम। तो यहां
फिर मेरी अपनी बात सन्यास का सच्चा पहिले
वानप्रस्थ तो मेरा एक सुन्दर २ स्थान है ही।
यहां आकर कितनी प्राकृतिक सम्पदाएं नजर आती
हैं मुझे जो अब और देशों में भी हरियाली नजर आती
है जिन बीच मनुष्य का मन एक भौतिक स्वभाव
है। बीच इतना सा फिरकनी, एक अलकनन्दा, गंगा जी
और भागीरथी का मिलन हो जाता है। तो यहां जो

सो देखते हुये दिमाग में कभी २ कुछ उलझनयाहट आ जाती है
कि लगता तो आपके [illegible] उपन्यास का अर्थ समझ आया है पर
लिखना कौतुक है कि दिमाग कहीं ऊंची २ हवाओं में उड़ने लग
जाता है। परन्तु दरअसल सच तो यह है कि आपके विचार
की मान्यतायें ब इतने महान हैं कि जो हैरानगी होती
है और विचार जो असाधारण हैं उनके पीछे यह आपके जो
या विशेष शब्दों को बल देता है। आपकी हैरानगी कि [illegible]
मेरा [illegible] लगता है हर किसी किताब को पढ़ने में दिल नहीं
करता। या मुझे पता है कि कुछ टॉपिक पर क्या बात लेखक लिख
सकता है और या मुझे लेखक का पता है कि उसका
लिखने का उद्देश्य क्या है। और यही देखने में आता कि लेखक
जो लिख रहा है उसको उसमें न दिलचस्पी है और न अनुभव। कुछ
अजीब खोखलापन और बोझ नज़र आता है मुझे लिखे
शब्दों में अक्सर। इसमें कोई और मतलब नहीं लिखने का
कि मैंने दो सालों में केवल आपकी ही किताब पुस्तकें ५ बार पढ़ी
हैं और या पंडित जी के प्रवचन गीता पर प्रवचन जो
मैं कुछ व्यस्ततावश समाप्त नहीं कर सकता पर उसमें मज़ा
अवश्य है।

तो आपने यह लिखकर कि डॉ. मेरा नाम भी बालप्रवच-
देने वालों में लिखकर यह समझा कि मैं कोई गया/नहीं
बल्कि आप। अब आपका यह कर्तव्य बन जाता है कि
आप मुझे उन्नति के पथ में आगे सदा ठीक से दर्शन कराते
रहें ताकि समय आने पर मैं केवल तैयार हो न हूं बल्कि
उस समय तक काफी आगे जा चुका हूं। तो इस पत्र लिखने
का मेरा यह विशेष अनुरोध है कि आप इस सम्बन्ध में
कि क्या क्या होना चाहिए लिखकर सूचित करें।

२. रही उपन्यास में सामाजिक पहलू क्या २ हैं। पहले

तो प्रश्न का उत्तर है कि क्या सन्यास लेने की एक ही निश्चित है। मतलब क्या हर जाति के लिये सन्यास आवश्यक है चाहे वह क्षत्रि, ब्राह्मण, वैश्य और शूद्र हो? मेरे विचार में ऐसा कई शास्त्रों में यह उल्लेख मैंने नहीं पढ़ा कि किसी शूद्र जाति के या औरत ने भी सन्यास ली हो, वैसे ही सन्यास धारण करना भी किसी-2 व्यक्ति को ही रजामन्द है। मैं यह बात लिख रहा हूँ और मुझे कोई नहीं इन बातों का अधिकार दे। यह बात सभी एक जैसा महसूस करता हूँ तो आपको उत्तर मिल गया है, आपका समाधान भी हो जायेगा। अगर बिल्कुल गलत हुआ तब भी ठीक, और ठीक लिखा तो ठीक है ही!

जब जैसा मैं सामाजिक स्तर पर लिखने जाता था पर एक बात मैं कह दूं कि मुझे सबसे अच्छी बात लगी क्योंकि ~~किसी वैराग्य~~ भुलाने की जो केवल सन्यास लेकर ही भुलाया जा सकता है। सब इस पर न तो मैं बड़ी देर तक सोचता रहा कि कितना चोटी का यह सूत्र है। विज्ञान आज ~~[illegible]~~ इतने के मशीनों को देख कर कम्प्यूटर के कारनामों को देख कर एक बार लगता है कि शायद वह सीमा आ गई और इसके बाद इससे अच्छी मशीन नहीं बनेगी पर कुछ ही समय के बाद उससे भी अच्छी मशीन नजर आ जाती है। मनुष्य का ~~मस्तिष्क~~ यह मशीनों को सुधारने के कामों में कमी नहीं लेता। यह लोग मशीन बनाने की मशीन हो गये लेकिन हम 'आदमी' हैं! हमारे विचारों के जो एक से एक चोटी के सार और सूत्र देकर जो महान ही लोग हुए हैं वह अद्भुत हैं। है तो मेरा यह कहना भी गलत होता है पर फिर यह सोचते हुए कि हमारे शास्त्रों का भंडार इतना विस्तृत है कि मुझे जीवन में केवल गिने चुने लोग ही नजर आये हैं जिन्होंने उनका एक अंश मात्र को ही लाभ

शब्दों के गुलाम हों। वैसे बात तो। की व्यथा निकल गई है पर
यह कहकर फिर वापिस आता हूं कि सब धर्म शास्त्रों का
निस्तार और बड़प्पन तो क्योंकि हिन्दुत्व में एकता का प्रतीक
है इसके इलावा और कोई भी ऐसा चिन्ह नहीं है और अगर है
तो वह इन्हीं का बाह्य रूप है।
मैं इतना लिखने के बाद सोने की तैयारी करने लगा। इतने
पीछे राकेश की पत्नी ने जिसका नाम भी उर्मिला है
मेरे से पूछा कि भाईसाहब क्या आप कोई ग्रन्थ
लिख रहे हैं आजकल। तो मैंने फिर उसे सारी बात
बताई। मैंने चिट्ठियां तो मैंने आज 30-40 पन्ने की
कई बार लिखी हैं लेकिन किसी का किसी से मुकाबला
नहीं। ऐसा भी होता है गद्य की भांति विज्ञान-व्याख्या
के ग्रन्थ भी लिखा जा सकता है पर मेरा अभिप्राय
केवल इतना है कि आपके पत्र द्वारा मैं एक नया
संचार करते हैं और फिर मैं लिखने के पश्चात् में
आजाना चाहता हूं क्योंकि मैं बातचीत में अपने
अपने विचार इस तरह से प्रगट नहीं कर पाता
जितना निश्चिंत होकर लिख कर सकता हूं। पर
अब मैं इस पत्र को यहीं समाप्त करता हूं। इसके
दो कारण हैं कि एक आपके पास इतना समय
नहीं होगा कि और इस लम्बे पत्र को पढ़ सकें
इत्मिनान से सारा जो कि ऊपर से चुटकियों से
भरा हुआ है और असर भी शायद न हो नहीं है। इसके
लिए बार बार और लिखने वाला था वह है नमस्कार
और सन्मान की सामाजिक समस्याओं के हल की
ओर। ऐसा मुझे लिखना है। शायद आप, आगे
जब कभी और लिखें तो बड़ा ही अच्छा हो।

मैं तो यही चाहूँगा कि आप जल्दी से जल्दी फिर दिल्ली से बाहर बम्बई या कहीं और प्रवास के लिये जायें और फिर पहले की तरह समय निकाल कर पत्र लिखें। इसके मैं यही तरह समझता हूँ कि जो महात्मा आपने इस पत्र में लिखा है वह सब हाल भर के लिए काफ़ी है।

जो आपकी आज्ञा मेरी और पुस्तक स्वाध्याय सर्विस और अध्ययन सर्विस के इसका छपी हों तो आप उन्हें भिजवाने की कृपा करें। और मोहन भा: की चिट्ठी 29 मई को मिली थी जिसमें लिखा है कि मुझे भारत में रही और लिखा था और इसकी कि मैं आपकी कोई भिजवाऊँगा जो पता न जाने कब पहुँचेगी। तो आप उसे आग्रह करना कि वह हिसाब कोई तो वह आपकी सेवा निकाल दे बाकी फिर भेजते रहें। शायद वो ही आपकी पुस्तकें भिजवा देंगे।

और सब ठीक चल रहा है। मनुष्य चाहे तो जीवन से कितनी ही शिकायतें कर सकता है हर मोड़ पर। पर उनका अंत कोई है नहीं। इसलिए इतनी कि अजीब सी जीवन के प्रति लहर और लहर सी उठती है और शायद कभी ये उठती रहें भी यह सब इसी से लेकर उठे अब यही जीवन के देखने की बात है। जब आप तो दिल्ली के पास आये नहीं तो जल्द भी कोई अफ़सर मिले तो उन्हें मेरा पत्रव्यवहार बतलाकर परिचय करो।

सरस्वती

आखरी प्रश्न। आपने ठाठ स्वामी दीनानाथ जैन पुनाइक का अवश्य लिखें।

आपका पुत्र
निर्दोश।

ओ३म्

प्रिय सतीश! सस्नेह आशीर्वाद — पीटर मैरीत्स बर्ग [illegible] 51

आशा है तुम सपरिवार सानन्द होगे। तुम्हारा लास वेगास से [illegible] का लिखा पत्र [illegible] समय मिल गया था। मैं इतना अधिक व्यस्त था कि चाहते हुए भी शीघ्र उत्तर न दे सका। आज भी निश्चय करके जुट गया कि कुछ भी कार्य हो सर्वप्रथम सतीश को पत्र लिखूंगा। वास्तव में तो मेरा तब से पत्र लिखने का विचार था कि जब से [illegible] आया हूं। [illegible] दिल्ली से चलते समय [illegible] इसलिए [illegible] प्रिय मोहन को लिखा कि वह पता भेजे [illegible] निकले कि [illegible] महीने के पश्चात आपका और सुरेश का पता भेजा है जब कि आपका पत्र पहले मिल गया। इसलिए कुछ देरी की बात इसलिए नहीं थी कि मैं स्वयं आपको पत्र लिखने वाला था, और पत्र व्यवहार में आप आगे [illegible] रहे हो।

जैसा कि तुमने लिखा कि [illegible] मेरे [illegible] लिखने की तो सदा [illegible] है। लेकिन मेरी भी स्थिति यही है और इसलिए [illegible] लिखने बैठा हूं। और आशा है [illegible] कि आप भी [illegible] कंजूसी नहीं करेंगे।

आपने पूछा कि आपका कार्यक्रम पहले की तरह व्यस्त है। सतीश क्या बताऊं पहली बार तो मैं १ महीना १० दिन के लिए आया था पर इस बार तो [illegible] के लिए आया हूं इसलिए इस समय की व्यस्तता अपने ढंग की है और उस समय की व्यस्तता अपने ढंग की थी, यहां की स्वर्ण जयन्ती भी सब जगह [illegible] तूफानी दौरा था। प्रतिदिन २, ३, कभी कभी ४ लेक्चर भी देने होते थे। पर इस बार की व्यस्तता सबसे अलग है। [illegible]

तुमने प्रिय मोहन से सुन लिया होगा कि मैं कि [illegible] (अफ्रीका) में [illegible] मृत्यु का निमंत्रण हो, जैसे मृत्यु के समय व्यक्ति [illegible] उस शरीर को भी छोड़ना पड़ता होता है जिसने इतने दिन [illegible] अस्तु [illegible] सब काम छोड़कर चल दिया और जब यहां पहुंचा कि इतनी क्या आफत आ रही थी कि [illegible] और टेलीफोन पर टेलीफोन करके परेशान कर दिया तो आप [illegible] कि एक समाज का अध्यापन चलाना था। [illegible] लगा कि यह काम तो कोई भी [illegible] सकता है। मैं और [illegible] महीने [illegible] सकता था। [illegible] क्या किया जाए [illegible] बुलाया है तो क्या योजना है [illegible] कि आप लेक्चर देंगे यहां वहां जाकर। मैं मन सोचने लगा कि किन पागलों के पल्ले पड़ गये हो चलो अब अपनी योजना [illegible] चलना चाहिए। प्रिय सतीश क्या बताऊं सारे आर्य समाजों की यही स्थिति है, चाहे विदेश हो या देश हो। कोई योजना अव्वल तो है नहीं यदि कदाचित् कोई [illegible] तो उस पर कोई चलना नहीं चाहता। इससे उन्नति नहीं [illegible] होती है। उसी पुराने ढर्रे पर चलने में वह खुश रहते हैं। यदि कोई व्यक्ति कुछ नवीन करना चाहता है तो उसे [illegible] जाती है या उसे [illegible] के लिए [illegible] रहना चाहिए।

मैंने संन्यास के पश्चात इस सम्बन्ध में कुछ [illegible] निश्चय किया था मेरे [illegible] मथुरा [illegible] आर्य समाज हिल गया उसकी अनुकूल और प्रतिकूल प्रतिक्रियाएं हुईं। मैं एक लेक्चर श्रद्धानन्द शताब्दी के अवसर पर [illegible] का उपराष्ट्रपति श्री [illegible] की अध्यक्षता में [illegible] भाषण था। मेरा [illegible] था [illegible] और ६० वाले पद छोड़ो। [illegible] कुर्सी छोड़ो। क्या [illegible] ६० [illegible] से [illegible] हो राष्ट्रपति भी हो प्रधानमंत्री भी हो ये क्या [illegible] रहे। मेरा कहना था बेटा होने पर पद लो पोता होने पर छोड़ो इस प्रकार से विचार स्वयं समाप्त होंगे। बूढ़े [illegible] का, [illegible] का, नई पीढ़ी [illegible]

2.

नई पीढ़ी का विचार, राष्ट्र की शिक्षा का प्रश्न और सब से अधिक बूढ़ों की सेवा का प्रश्न। कोई भी राष्ट्र बूढ़ों को पेन्शन दे सकती उनके लिए होम बना सकती है परन्तु उन्हें सेवा और स्नेह कहां से मिलेगी और सब से बड़ा वह लाड प्यार वात्सल्य किस को दिखाएगा पोतों से प्यार करने के दिन गये यह समस्या बच्चों से प्यार करने का हो गया है मनु से मनो विज्ञान को समझ कर ८ और ६० वालों का घर छोड़ने और नया घर जिसके वही सदस्य होंगे सब पोते और सब बाबा, या पोते बाबा का शिष्य गुरु के नाम से बुलाया जाएगा और उस घर का नाम गुरुकुल होगा। जैसे कन्या के दो घर होते हैं एक पिता का और दूसरा पति का ठीक इसी तरह हर व्यक्ति के दो घर होंगे बच्चों के लिए एक पिता का और दूसरा बाबा का (गुरुकुल) और हर वृद्ध के लिए जहां एक पुत्र का घर होगा वहीं दूसरा पोते का कर्म... तरह हर पुत्र दोनों घरों का फेरा करता रहेगा। ८ वर्ष तक पिता के घर ८ से २२ तक बाबा के घर २२ से ६० तक पिता के घर और पुनः ६० से बाबा बनकर पोते के घर। मनु ने इन दोनों व्यक्तियों को एक जगह इकट्ठा करके जहां उपर लिखी समस्याओं का हल दिया था राष्ट्र की बेकारी समस्या का हल भी दिया था। आप भी सोचेंगे कि मैं क्या लिख गया। यह उस दिन का आलाप था तुलना स्वामी श्रद्धानन्द जी को उनकी जन्म शताब्दी पर एक गुरुकुल के अध्यापक के नाते मैं इससे बढ़कर और श्रद्धांजलि क्या हो सकती थी कि आर्य समाज जनता अपने ८ साल के बेटे और ६० साल के बापों को घर से निकाल गुरुकुल को आबाद करें। श्रद्धानन्द का गुरुकुल (कांगड़ी) बाजार हो रहा है। यह भाषण उस समय दिया और उपराष्ट्रपति की उपस्थिति में जब कि इन्दिरा का आपात्कालीन स्थिति के नाम पर दमन चक्र चल रहा था ... ताड़ित था। इससे जहां आर्य समाज के लीडरों की गद्दी कांप गई (वहां) कुछ स्वामी, पुरोहितों विद्वानों में जान आ गई। उसी समय अलग विद्वानों ने मीटिंग करके मेरा धन्यवाद किया और कहा कि हम समझ रहे थे कि विद्वान मर गया है परन्तु हमें आज पता चला कि महर्षि दयानन्द के वंशज अभी लड़ रहे हैं उसी समय विद्वानों की परिषद की जिसका मुझे संरक्षक बनाया। उसके पश्चात आर्य समाज की लीडरशिप ने मेरी बड़ी कदर की सोची। पर रास्ता कैसे लेना। अस्तु यह सब लिखा है इसलिए लिख रहा कि यहां की आर्य समाज भी सोई पड़ी है। अतः सब परिस्थिति का अध्ययन किया। यहां के लोग भारत की भांति चमड़ी और शकल से इण्डियन लगते हैं परन्तु आम भारतीय की तरह ओलिम्पिक में सराबोर हैं। संस्थाओं के नाम पर दुकानदारी है। यहां के पुरोहितों की योग्यता इतनी ही है कि गायत्री मन्त्र भी शुद्ध नहीं लिख सकते अन्य साधारण व्यक्तियों की बात क्या। सब लोग रोमन स्क्रिप्ट्स में वेद मन्त्र पढ़ते हैं। हां आर्य समाज की वाटिका में पुरानी पीढ़ी के कुछ हिन्दी समझ लेते हैं जिनमें मेरे भाषण होते हैं। अन्यथा मेरे जैसे व्यक्ति की यहां कोई दाल नहीं गल सकती थी।

(२)

यह भी एक आश्चर्य मिश्रित हर्ष की बात है कि दक्षिण अफ्रीका के पिछले ५०
वर्ष के इतिहास में एक मात्र मैं ही वह व्यक्ति जो हिन्दी माध्यम से 5 |
भाषण करता और हिन्दी माध्यम से ही पढ़ाता है। हां तो मैं लिख रहा था
कि यहां की परिस्थिति को देखकर मैंने यह योजना बनाई कि वैदिक धर्म
को आर्य समाज की चार दीवारी से बाहिर लाना चाहिए। इसके लिए १ महिला
श्रेणी प्रातः १० से १२। दूसरी संस्कृत श्रेणी (जिसमें नागरी अक्षरों में ही)
वेद मन्त्र, गीता, रामायण आदि पढ़सकें) सायं ४ से ६ और तीसरी पारिवारिक
सत्संग रात्रि ८ से १० तक। इसका बड़ा चमत्कारिक परिणाम हुआ। संस्कृत
क्लास में तो यूनिवर्सिटी के स्टूडेन्ट भी आते रहे उनका कहना था कि हमने
यूनिवर्सिटी में ३ वर्ष में वह नहीं सीखा जो यहां १ महीने में सीखा। रात्रि के
आयोजन जो पारिवारिक सत्संग के रूप में होते हैं उनमें बाहिर के व्यक्ति भी आते हैं
यहां के लिए यह पहला अवसर था कि पारिवारिक सत्संग, पुरानी विचार चाहते कि
आर्य समाज में व्याख्यान हों, तो रात्रि का प्रोग्राम पारिवारिक सत्संग का न कर
व्याख्यान हो जाते थे और हां प्रातः और सायं के तो नियत चलते ही रहे।
डर्बन नगर का एक उपनगर जिसका नाम चार्ल्स टाउन है में लगातार १ महीने तक
यजुर्वेद ब्रह्म पारायण यज्ञ होता रहा, यहां २ लाख हिन्दू रहते हैं। ३ नवम्बर पूर्णाहुति
के दिन ११ यज्ञ कुण्ड बनाये गये और उसमें ५० कपल जोड़ों ने यज्ञ पति बनकर
यज्ञ किया। सरकार की ओर से टीवी का आयोजन भी था उस रथ का प्रदर्शन
इण्डियन प्रोग्राम में दिखाया जायगा।

मैं दिसम्बर १९८४ के आरम्भ में डर्बन से पीटर मैरिट्ज़बर्ग
आगया और यहां का २।। महीने का प्रोग्राम चल रहा है। यहां ने जनता रूपी भूमि उपजाऊ
है इसमें डाला हुआ बीज फल लायेगा। मैं इसी आशा से दो बार १०, १० दिन के लिए पहले भी
आगया हूं मैंने पहले ही से प्लानिंग करली थी कि ग्रामीण भी स्त्रियों में बड़ा प्रभाव और
युवकों में काम करना है। सो आप जानते ही हैं यहां दिसम्बर में अवकाश का समय होता है।
यहां १६ दिसम्बर से २२ फरवरी तक का आयोजन बनाया है २२ फरवरी इसलिए कि महाशिव-
रात्रि पर्व है इतवार का दिन है उसदिन इस सेशन (सत्र) की पूर्णाहुति होगी। इसका
नाम संस्कृत-संस्कृति-स्वाध्याय-सत्र (S.S.S-S) रखा है। इसमें ८० व्यक्ति
प्रतिदिन भाग ले रहे हैं। दो क्लासें १ - प्रातः १० से १ बजे तक दूसरी रात्रि को
७ से १० तक चलती हैं। प्रातः कुमार कुमारियें संस्कृत पढ़ते हैं मन्त्र सीख रहे हैं
आपको आश्चर्य होगा कि कुमारों ने संस्कृत इतनी शीघ्रता से ग्रहण की कि भारत के
व्यक्ति भी नहीं ग्रहण कर पाते १½ महीने में अ आ से आरम्भ कर १० वीं क्लास
की संस्कृत सीख गये हैं। शिवरात्रि के दिन ५१ यज्ञ कुण्डों में यज्ञ होगा उसमें
यही व्यक्ति चारों वेदों के ५०० मन्त्रों का पाठ करेंगे। इसलिए इन्हें १०० मन्त्र शुद्ध
लिखने, शुद्ध पढ़ने सिखा दिए हैं। ५० श्लोक सिखा दिए हैं। यह सब हिन्दी और
नागरी अक्षरों के माध्यम से हो रहा है। रात्रि को ७ से १० तक की क्लास में दिन
भर के थके अध्यापक व्यापारी वकील और २० के लगभग युवक इस प्रकार ६०
व्यक्ति भाग ले रहे हैं। इसको दो भागों में बांटा है एक जो १६ दिसम्बर से आ
रहे हैं और एक वो जिन्होंने यह देखकर साहस किया कि और उन्होंने १ महीने
में इतना सीख लिया हम क्यों नहीं सीख सकते। इसलिए दो जगह क्लास लगानी
होती है। जो भाई बहिन १६ दिसम्बर से आ रहे हैं उनके विभाग कर दिए हैं
हर ग्रुप को एक एक वेद के १०० मन्त्र इस प्रकार संख्या को मिलाकर ४ ग्रुप
हो गये हैं कि जिन्होंने १०० १०० अलग अलग मन्त्र अभ्यास कर लिए हैं। इस वर्ग
का चुन कर यहां के दैनिक पत्र ने एक दिन पूरी क्लास सहित इण्टरव्यू लिया

४

जिसकी कॉपी संलग्न है। इसके साथ साथ २४ जनवरी की रात्रि को एक संगीत सम्मेलन रखा गया है। जिसमें डर्बन और यहां के संगीतज्ञ भाग लेंगे इसके लिए मैंने भारत से चलते समय ही लगभग ६० गीत टेप करा लिए थे और कुछमें भी चुन चुना लेता था तो उसके आधार पर १०० नये गीत भजन यहां के भिन्न भिन्न संगीतज्ञों को दो महीने पहले से दिए हैं जिसे वह तैयार कर रहे हैं पहली बार नये गीत सुने जाएंगे होंगे क्योंकि आर्य समाज, वेद, दयानन्द और प्रभु भक्ति के। आप सोचेंगे कि आप यह सब क्यों कर रहे हैं तो सुनो मेरा विचार यहां एक गुरुकुल खोलने का था यहां वहां की सरकार ने मुझे ३ वर्ष रहने के लिए छूट दी तो एक गुरुकुल की स्थापना तो करने का संकल्प है। इसके लिए भारत से एक अन्य विद्वान को बुलाने का निश्चय हुआ है। जिन्हें भारतीय रुपया ढाई हजार मासिक और एक क्वार्टर देने का निर्णय कल कमेटी में हुआ है। आप उन विद्वान को जानते हैं उनका नाम प्रताप सिंह/ श्री० पं० विद्यानन्द वेद वागीश है। नाम तो सुना होगा मन्दस्थली में बेबी और कुसुम इनके पास ही रहते और पढ़ते थे। आपकी भतीजी भी १ महीना उनके पास रही थी। उनसे मैंने दो महीने पहले ही पत्र व्यवहार कर लिया था वह आने को तैयार है। मैं चाहता हूं कि मेरे दक्षिण अफ्रीका छोड़ने से पहले वह यहां आ जाएं। गुरु के अन्तिम विधि को मुझे छोड़कर जाना होगा। मेरे लिए भी प्रसन्नता हो रहा है कि और समय कटा लिया जाए। यदि यहां गुरुकुल जैसे कार्य की स्थापना का लक्ष्य रहेगा तो ही रहूंगा अन्यथा मैं वापिस चला जाऊंगा। मैंने अपना सारा अपने प्रोग्राम लिख दिया है। अब आप समझ सकते हैं कि मैं पत्र क्यों नहीं लिख सका और यह शोक कृपया होता है कर नहीं सकता। आज दूसरा ३० जन० का दिन है।

आप भारत गये और दीवान हाल की जीवनी भी करा आए राकेश और भाई गुड्डू से मिले इसके लिए धन्यवाद यह आपका स्नेह है। मुझे इसका बड़ा खेद रहा कि मैं यदि १ सप्ताह और रुक जाता तो कितना अच्छा होता आप से प्रत्यक्ष में मिल लेता सम्भवतः प्रभु को यह स्वीकार नहीं था। अच्छा ही हुआ, अन्यथा यह पत्र व्यवहार न होता अब इसका आनन्द अलग ही है। ईश्वर ने चाहा तो आप यहां मिलेंगे या मैं वहां मिलूंगा। जब आप गुड्डू से मिले होंगे तो उसने मेरे द्वारा १ महीना पहिले स्थापित किए ट्रस्ट का कुछ जिक्र किया होगा। मैंने सन्यास के पश्चात यह योजना बना ली थी कि गुरु वर्य पं० बुद्धदेव जी के नाम पर एक रीसर्च इन्स्टिट्यूशन खड़ी करनी है। यही उसकी स्थापना का आधार था। यह स्पष्ट है और किसी से छुपा नहीं कि डा० कुसुमलता ने अपना पूरा जीवन दयानन्द, आर्य समाज और वेद के अर्पण किया है और आरम्भ वेद के रिसर्च से हुआ क्यों न एक रिसर्च संस्था बनाई जाए। इसलिए 'समर्पण शोध संस्थान' (S.S.S) के नाम से एक संस्था बनाई है जिसकी

सैक्रेटरी स्वयं मुझसे है, प्रेजिडेंट श्री पं० शिव कुमार जी शास्त्री हैं। कोषाध्यक्ष श्री 55
पृथ्वीराज जी शास्त्री हैं। ट्रस्टी श्री जयदेव जी श्री रघु जी, श्री सत्यानन्द जी -
श्री सत्य प्रिय जी (डा) एम.ए. पी.एच.डी. हैं। रामगोपाल जी भी एक ट्रस्टी हैं। मेरा
सारा पुस्तकालय उसके नाम है। जो अब ५० हजार का तो होगा ही। और संस्थान
की ओर से जिन दो बृहद् ग्रन्थों का अभी अभी प्रकाशन हुआ है जिसे गुरु ने
आपको दिखाया भी होगा। वैदिक साहित्य में बेजोड़ हैं रहेंगे, इन पर दूसरे पर
पचास हजार रुपया व्यय हुआ है। शायद तुम्हें यह पता न हो कि सन् १८७५ में
जब आर्य समाज स्थापना शताब्दी हुई थी उस समय भारत के ५ विद्वानों को
सम्मानित किया गया था उनमें कुसुम का भी नाम था वही एक स्त्री थी कि
जिसे पण्डिता की उपाधि से अलंकृत किया गया था। उसने इस छोटी आयु में
अच्छी उन्नति की है मैं अत्यन्त प्रसन्न हूँ कि न केवल मेरी परम्परा अपितु श्री पं०
बुद्धदेव जी की शोध परम्परा को रिसर्च ट्रेडीशन को अपना लिया है आजकल वह
वनस्थली में विद्यालय जो वेद का पृथक से है उसकी आचार्या है और साथ
ही साथ वहां श्री गुरु जी के शतपथ भाष्य का भी सम्पादन (एडिटिंग) कर
रही है जो आगे ट्रस्ट की ओर से छपेगा। पं. बुद्धदेव जी के ग्रन्थों के प्रकाशन
पर ही डेढ़ लाख का व्यय आएगा। आपको यह जानकर प्रसन्नता होगी कि कुसुम ने
इस वर्ष 'वेदाचार्य' जो वेद की हाइएस्ट डिग्री है प्राप्त कर ली है सारे भारत
में यह तीसरी महिला होगी कि जिसने वेदाचार्य परीक्षा पास की है।
वेद विद्यालय के आचार्य पद पर रहने के लिए 'वेदाचार्य' होना आवश्यक है
सो उसने मुझे बताए बिना ही इसकी परीक्षा दे दी। यदि समय हो तो उसे एक
बधाई पत्र भेज देना मतलब है कि जवाब देने में सुस्त है। उसका पता
डा० कुसुमलता आर्य एम.ए. पी.एच.डी., वेदाचार्य आचार्या वेद विद्यालय वनस्थली
विद्यापीठ वनस्थली (जयपुर राजस्थान) भारत रहेगा। मुझे प्रसन्नता है कि वह
अपने कार्य अच्छी प्रकार संभाले हुए है। और यह ट्रेडिशन समाप्त न हो अपनी
भानजी (शास्त्री की बेटी को) बनारस संस्कृत और वेद पढ़ने भेज दिया है।
मेरे मस्तिष्क में यह योजना न जाने कब से थी शायद तब से जब कि मैंने
सुरेश को संस्कृत अध्ययन में डाला था और सोचा था कि परिवार का कोई पुत्र
इस कार्य को संभाले परन्तु पुत्र ने नहीं तो किसी पुत्री ने संभाल लिया
और सारा जीवन देने से तो वह भी पुत्र सदृश ही है। मैं अब निश्चिन्त
हुआ अब कोई चिन्ता। आप लोग भी जहां रहते हैं कुछ न कुछ इस परम्परा
की रक्षा करते ही हैं। देखो अभी भारत आने पर जो सुरेश ने ६ सहस्र का
दान दिया वह संस्थान के खाते में जमा होगा यह भी एक परम्परा की
रक्षा का तरीका है। आप भी सदैव ऐसा सोचते और करते रहते हैं।
मैं यह स्पष्ट अधिकार पूर्वक कहूंगा कि यह संस्थान वैदिक साहित्य
के शोध और प्रकाशन में उत्तम कार्य करता रहता। इसमें पूर्ण सहयोग

देते रहना अथवा विदेश से आप न आते तो दूसरियों में तुम्हारा नाम रहना था। अब भी यदि यह बात बाधक न हो तो मैं अगली मीटिंग में इस प्रस्ताव को रखकर पास करा दूंगा। आप इस पर अपने विचार लिखना।

संस्थान में इस समय चार (व्यक्तियों ने) उच्च कोटि के विद्वानों ने शोध कार्य के लिए अपना अमूल्य समय दे रखा है। अभी अभी प्रकाशित (?) पुरुष सूक्त के विवेचनात्मक अध्ययन और ऋग्वेद मण्डल [illegible] का इंग्लिश अनुवाद हो रहा है। जिसे श्री डा० लाजपतराय जी एम-ए कर रहे हैं। शब्दकल्पद्रुम (?) (पुनर्मुद्रण) का सम्पादन कुसुम कर रही है। एक वैदिक पद निर्वचन कोष का निर्माण व्याकरणाचार्य श्री पं० सुरेन्द्र जी दिल्ली निवासी कर रहे हैं। वैदिक चिन्तन की [illegible] की उद्धरणों की एक पुस्तक का निर्माण श्री पं० [illegible] आर्य कर रहे हैं।

सन् 1983 में ऋषि दयानन्द की मृत्यु को और सत्यार्थ प्रकाश निर्माण का हुए 100 वर्ष हो जायेंगे। उस समय भी विशाल शताब्दी मनाई जायगी। उसके उपलक्ष्य में मैं अभी से संस्थान के आधीन सत्यार्थ प्रकाश के 14 समुल्लासों का भाष्य करवाने की योजना बना रहा हूँ। यह कार्य भी आरम्भ हो रहा है। इसके लिए 14 विद्वान जुड़ेंगे जिन्हें मासिक भी देना होगा। इस समय भी संस्थान एक हजार मासिक व्यय कर रहा है।

यदि यहां गुरुकुल खोलने की योजना बनी तो 1 वर्ष और भी रहूंगा अन्यथा भारत चला जाऊंगा। वहां संस्थान को दृढ़ करना, शोध करना करवाना। सत्यार्थ प्रकाश भाष्य करवाना। एवं आर्य समाज में आ रही गिरावट को रोकना और इसमें नये जीवन का संचार करना। [illegible] और [illegible] करने वाली योजना को सफल बनाना उसके लिए देश भर में साधना शिविरों का चलाना [illegible] की स्थापना करना। संस्कृत भाषा का सर्वत्र प्रचार करना यह उद्देश्य है और ईश्वर ने [illegible] जीवन दिया तो इस में अपना [illegible] दूंगा।

आशा है इस बार भारत जाने पर तुम कुसुम से श्री जयदत्त जी उनकी पत्नी [illegible] जी आदि से मिले होंगे। यदि नहीं मिले होंगे तो उन्हें खेद रहा होगा। मैंने प्रिय जयदत्त जी को P.H.D के लिए प्रेरित किया है पर वे तो हिलते ही नहीं। उनकी पत्नी वेद के उषा सूक्त या उषा देवता का अध्ययन नामक विषय पर शोध करने का विचार कर रही है। मैं अभी 10 दिन पहले उन्हें पत्र द्वारा प्रेरणा दे चुका हूं।

(7)

तुमने लिखा कि 'दिल यही कर रहा है कि आगामी गर्मियों के दिन आपके साथ गुजारूं, सच बताओ कि आप को मन्जूर होगा कि नहीं', तब मन में मेरे एक अजीब तरह का उफान सा उठ जाता है. और मुझे विश्वास है कि ठीक सम्पर्क और वातावरण में वह ठीक दिशा में चलेगा, फिर पत्र के अन्त में आपने लिखा एक सुझाव रखा है कि जिससे आप विश्वविद्यालय में अध्ययन के प्रोफेसर हो जा सकें। सतीश भला यह भी पूछने की बात है कि आप को मन्जूर होगा कि नहीं। यदि मेरे सम्पर्क से आप का कुछ हित होता हो तो क्या नहीं हो मुझे क्या आपत्ति हो सकती है। परन्तु क्या मेरे सम्पर्क की आपको अब आवश्यकता है। अब तो वह स्टेज रही नहीं वह तो कभी की पार हो गई। जब तक भारत में थे तब तक थी और यथा सम्भव मिलती भी रही है। फिर एक कहावत है कि 'घर का जोगी जोगना बाहर का जोगी सिद्ध' सो हम तो ठहरे घर के जोगी का संन्यास लेने से यदि मैं बाहर का सिद्ध हो गया हूं तो यह अहोभाग्य है यदि आप मेरे सम्पर्क में आएं। देखना अब समय कहां रहा है कि आप आएं और मेरा सम्पर्क मिल सके। क्यों कि पहले तो दक्षिण अफ्रीका में आना कठिन और आने की बात हो तो महीनों इस में बीत जाएं कि वीजा मिले व [illegible]। अर्थात जब आपके आने का समय हो तो पुराने पंछी का कहा जाए कि उड़ जाओ और हमें उड़ जाना पड़े। यह तो अभी आकाश पुष्प की सी बात है अर्थात ख्याली पुलाव है। आप अपने सभी सर्टिफिकेट्स फोटोस्टेट कॉपी बनवाकर भिजवाना। मैं यहां के विश्वविद्यालय में प्रयत्न करूंगा।

सतीश एक और भी बात है कि मेरे सम्पर्क में तो कोई नवीन बात नहीं है। मैं तो सांचे ढांचे पला ढला व्यक्ति हूं। हमारी आपकी पटरी का कुछ दूजा का कांटा बदल जाता है। मुझे तो यह भौतिक और वैज्ञानिक उन्नति एक मर्यादा तक ठीक लगती है उस से आगे तो यह सर्वनाश का मार्ग है। आज का व्यक्ति एक मात्र मशीन बन कर रह गया जैसे कारखाने की मशीन का चलाने वाला सबके पाप चलाता है और अथवा पर ... दबा का स्टाप कर देता है वही सब का हाल है आज का व्यक्ति कितना परेशान है व्यग्र है, फिर भी आप जानते हैं जितना विज्ञान ने विश्व को समीपता का भौतिक समीपता का देह की समीपता की उतना ही आत्मिक दृष्टि से हम एक दूसरे से दूर हो गये हैं। यहां तो योरुप में तो एक का दूसरे पड़ोसी का कुछ भी पता नहीं कि कौन मरा कि कौन जिया दर असल इसलिए मुश्किल हो रहा है। परन्तु भारतीय दर्शन (हिन्दू धर्म) तो एक दूसरे की आत्मा का अपनी आत्मा समान में समझना तक ही क्यों प्राणी मात्र तक में आत्मा के दर्शन करने का आदेश देता है। (यस्मिन् सर्वाणि भूतानि आत्मैवाभूद्विजानतः तत्र को मोहः कः शोकः एकत्वमनुपश्यतः)। योरुप की अभी आंख नहीं खुली है वह प्राणी मात्र में तो क्या मनुष्य में आत्मा नहीं समझता उसका भी शोषण और हत्या, मच्छर मक्खी की तरह मानने में हो रही लगती। फिर दिव्यता पुरुषों की तो बात ही क्या? 200 वर्ष पूर्व योरुप के लोग स्त्री में आत्मा नहीं मानते थे उनके साथ पशुओं का सा व्यवहार करते थे। अब उनकी समझ में आया कि स्त्री में हमारी ही जैसी आत्मा रहती है। उसे भी हमारी ही तरह दुःख दर्द होता है। उसे भी पीड़ा होती है। अभी योरुप का यह सीखना है कि अन्य पशुओं में भी हमारी ही तरह की आत्मा है। उनको भी

पीड़ा होती है वह भी रोता है वह जुबान नहीं रखता कहीं अपील नहीं कर सकता २८
आज वह भी हमारी तुम्हारी तरह न्यायालय में जा सकता होता तो वहाँ
से यही न्याय मिलता कि माँस खाने वालों ने इसकी हत्या की है कि अनन्त
जन्मों तक फाँसी देते रहने चाहिए। तुमने बुद्ध के समय में अंगुलिमाल का
नाम सुना होगा वह लोगों की अंगुलियाँ काटता था और गरम गरम लहू को पीता
था सब डरते थे इसलिए उस जंगल में प्रजा का कोई व्यक्ति न जाता था लेकिन
एक भगवान बुद्ध लोगों के मना करने पर भी वहाँ पर चल दिए उस राह को
स्टेट ने अभी तक कैसे मुक्त कर रखा है उसको क्यों नहीं कैद किया उसे देखकर
लालच आ गया कि चल दिए अंगुलिमाल ने देखा आज अच्छा माल आया है कोई दीवाना
इधर आ निकला है मेरी फेर में आ फँसा है। वह सिर के समीप पहुँचा और हाथ
कि भगवान बुद्ध ने अपना हाथ उठा कर रोक दिया न जाने क्या हुआ वह तो
पत्थर की मूर्ति सा बन गया। बुद्ध ने कहा कि अंगुलिमाल सुना अन्तिम घड़ी और
मरने वाले की अन्तिम इच्छा पूर्ण की जाती है तो अब मेरी अंतिम घड़ी है क्या मेरी भी
अन्तिम इच्छा पूर्ण करोगे अंगुलिमाल ने कहा कि हाँ करूँगा तो बुद्ध ने कहा
कि अंगुलिमाल सामने के पीपल के पेड़ से एक पत्ता तोड़ लाओ। अंगुलि
माल सोचने लगा कि सचमुच कोई पागल है चलो मान लो बात अपनी क्या जाता
है वह पत्ता तोड़ लाया। भगवान ने कहा अंगुलिमाल अब एक बात और मान
लो कि इसे वहीं जोड़ आओ और इस इच्छा को पूरा करके ही मुझे मारो काटो
खून पीओ अंगुलिमाल चुप था क्या पत्ता जोड़ा भी जा सकता है क्या
इसी पर अन्तिम इच्छा पूरी किए बिना हत्या करूँगा बोला भगवन्
यह जोड़ा नहीं जा सकता। बुद्ध ने जान लिया कि इसके उद्धार का समय आ गया
है। बुद्ध बोले अंगुलिमाल अगर सचमुच तुम जोड़ नहीं सकते तो तुमको तोड़ने
का क्या अधिकार जिसमें तुम जान नहीं डाल सकते उसके प्राण हरने का क्या
अधिकार बस इतना कहना था कि वह धाड़ मार कर रोने लगा और बुद्ध के चरणों
में गिर गया बुद्ध चल पड़े नगर की ओर अंगुलिमाल उठा और कहता चला
है। लिया मुझे छोड़ कर कहाँ जाते हो। मेरा उद्धार करो। आज सारा भारत
देखिया अंगुलिमाल क्या है भारत जो बुद्ध का घर अहंकार था वह भी
अंगुलिमाल के पीछे चल पड़ा है कि इस अंगुलिमाल का उद्धार कौन
करेगा। तुम उस देश के वासी हो जिसमें गंगा बहती है, उस में गीता
गायत्री का गान गाया जाता जहाँ राम कृष्ण, बुद्ध, महावीर, दयानन्द गांधी
जन्म है तुम उस देश के व्यक्ति हो कहाँ और तुमने क्या
किया है तुम तो अंधेरों में खो गये अपने बच्चों को अंधेरों में खो
रहे हो और परमेश्वर को भुलाने में भी मुस्कराते मना रहे हो। क्या इसलिए
कि जिस रंग में हम रहते हैं उसी में तुम भी आ जाओ। सतीश कुमार
अगर तुम्हारे अनेक बच्चों का नाम, भला होगा क्योंकि वह नाराज

(२)

सेबो इआत, ईट ट्रिंक वी मैरीकी, सैट सपाटे बी, जिन्दगी क्रिता संदेशे ९
इस से अधिक क्या? क्या इसके अलावा होगी पील होगा क्या यही जीवन का
उद्देश्य है!! यदि यही मनुष्य है तो संसार में अनेकों [redacted] भी होते हैं जो बाहर
में चहते हैं किसी सुन्दरी की गोद में रहते हैं आनन्द करते भी करते हैं तो
हम मनुष्यों का भी यही जीवन है। आप तो रवीन्द्र, रामकृष्ण, अरविन्द
विवेकानन्द आदि भारतीय मनीषियों को पढ़ते हैं क्या रवीन्द्र की गीतांजलि
के पद्य कभी गुनगुनाते हैं। उनका जन मन गण गीत भारतका राष्ट्रीय गीत
बन गया। गीतांजलि का एक गीत विश्वगीत बन जाना चाहिए। आवश्यक
आज यह है कि आओ हम एक ऐसा संसार बनाएं कि जहाँ "चित्त भय शून्य मन में
भय न होगा आतंक न होगा जहां लोगों के मस्तिष्क खुले होंगे, (सहज होंगे)
(अन्धे माइन्ड बाउन्ड न होंगे) जहां बराबर टीका सब का मुक्त ज्ञान प्राप्त
लेना होगा। जहां राष्ट्रों की बनावटी दीवारें को कभी की तोड़ दी
जाएंगी और विश्व एक घोंसले = NEST की भांति होगा। जहां यह
सारा विश्व और उसके दिन रात बच्चे की भांति सरल होंगे। जहां
श्रम करने में थकान महसूस नहीं होगी जहां निरन्तर पूर्ण से पूर्णता का विकास
होगा। जहां के लोग अपने व्यक्तित्व कमल पत्र पर रखी बून्द की भांति स्वच्छ
और अलिप्त रखेंगे। जहां वाणियाँ अन्तःकरण रूपी स्रोत से प्रस्फुटित होगी।
जहां भौतिक भूल से (मैटिरियलिस्टिक मद) से लोगों की बुद्धि नष्ट नहीं होगी।
और जहाँ मनुष्य मनुष्यता के शिखर पर पहुंचेगा। ऐसे दिव्य स्वर लोक में
विश्व का मानव प्रतिदिन आँखें खोला करेगा।" यह मैंने हमारे संस्थान के
शोधकर्ता प्रो० पं. लाज जी के गीतांजलि के संस्कृत अनुवाद का अर्थ लिख
रहा हूँ मिलाइए गीतांजलि E 35। मैं भावुकता से बहुत कुछ लिख गया हूँ।
अच्छा सतीश! यह बताओ क्या आपने अब भी मांस खाना नहीं छोड़ा
है आप सोचेंगे कि इस संन्यासी को क्या हो गया है। यह मनिया मुझे सदा से रहा है
सच बताना अपनी आत्मा से पूछना कि क्या मांस मनुष्य के खाने की चीज है जिह्वा
के स्वाद के लिए अपनी बाहुस की रक्षा का भला ही आप गलत लाजिक दे कर आत्मा
सन्तोष का प्रश्न गहराई से जाकर सोचेंगे तो सत्य यही है कि मांस मनुष्य का भोजन
नहीं है। याद होगा भटिण्डा के वे दिन जिन दिनों मैं आपके सम्पर्क से गुजर रहे
थे। जब जब खान विषयक बात उठती थी तो यदि
उत्तम प्रकार डालना चाहता था जब जब खाना विषयक बात उठती थी तो यदि
और भाई साहिब और आप भी यही कहते थे कि यही खान के बारे में कुछ न कहिए।
और जब मेरे भी संस्कृत पढ़ने विषयक बात उठती थी तब भी यही सुनता था
और जब मेरे अब को संस्कृत पढ़ने विषयक बात उठती थी तब भी यही सुनता था
नहीं क्या हमारे बच्चे ही रहेंगे है कि यह संस्कृत पढ़े मैं सोचता था कि
इनके भाग्य कैसे खराब हैं। सच सतीश जिसने संस्कृत नहीं
पढ़ी वह कभी मानवता के शिखर पर पहुंच ही नहीं सकता। जिसका आहार
ठीक नहीं उसका विचार और व्यवहार भी ठीक नहीं रह सकता। अब तो आप लोग

इन कालिमा होगा अब तो छोड़ देना चाहिए। अब योरप अमेरिका आदि देशों में
मांस छोड़ने का आन्दोलन चल रहा है। मैं बहुत सोचता हूँ कि आप लोग या
आप जैसे भारतीय युवक उन देशों में भारत की क्या सभ्यता सिखाते हैं। जब
कोई भारतीय संस्कृति के बारे में पूछता है तो आप क्या कहते होंगे क्योंकि
यह सब थ्योरी मात्र है कहीं प्रैक्टिस में तो है नहीं। यह सब [illegible]
की बात है। मैं यह सब कड़ा सा लिख गया इसलिए कि स्पष्ट कहता हूँ कि
कुछ दिन आपके सम्पर्क में रहने को मन करता है। ऐसी मेरी यह कोई [illegible]
[illegible] दे सकता हूँ और जो देने को है उसे वह लेना नहीं चाहते अस्तु
बहुत लिख दिया और भी बहुत कुछ है।

मैं बहुत बार अपने से प्रश्न करता हूँ कि इन युवकों को क्या हो गया
कि विदेशों में जाकर रहना बसना शुरू कर दिया भला जिस देश का अन्न जल
खाकर बड़े हुए जब सेवा का अवसर आया तो विदेश चल दिया क्या
यही देश भक्ति है क्या आप जैसे युवकों के लिए [illegible]
खाई थी। गान्धी, नेहरू, सुभाष, पटेल के त्याग तपस्या का यही परिणाम है?
हम विदेशों की गुलामी [illegible] है। यह तो नहीं कि वहाँ से लौट
कर भारत में आकर उसकी सेवा करो। यह उलट बात [illegible]
और आप जीवन अनुभव करते हैं कि [illegible] हैं। अन्यथा अपने [illegible]
सम्पन्न था सोना था। लंका जीतने के पश्चात लक्ष्मण ने श्रीराम से कहा कि
यहीं बस जाएँ। तब श्रीराम बोले "अपि स्वर्णमयि लंका न मे लक्ष्मण
रोचते। जननी जन्मभूमिश्च स्वर्गादपि गरीयसी। क्या कभी [illegible]
के इन अमर वाक्यों को पढ़ा है।

पत्र बहुत लम्बा हो गया है अब इन शब्दों के साथ समाप्त करता हूँ। [illegible]
वाला पत्र [illegible] के साथ है। वह कहाँ है आपने लिखा था कि वह आपकी जान
जानकारी में है। सो आप ही उसका पता पर भिजवा दें। [illegible] पत्र में भी जानकारी
तो लिखी है परन्तु कोई यह नहीं बताया कि वो क्या कर रहा है। आज [illegible]
[illegible] क्या कर रहा है उसकी पत्नी [illegible] कि नहीं
मैंने उससे भी पूछा है। [illegible]
आपका [illegible] का कार्य [illegible] सेवा [illegible]
अपनी पत्नी और बच्चों को आशीर्वाद देना। मुझे अगले पत्र और
अपने [illegible] आदि नीचे लिखे पते पर भिजवाना।

Swami Deekshananda Saraswati C/o M. S. Satyapal Ji
Capital Fruit MARKET 104 Retief Street Pieter maritz Burg
3201 NATAL (South Africa)

आपका सदैव मंगलाभिलाषी
दीक्षानन्द सरस्वती
1-2-6[illegible]

27/7/81

तपोवन आश्रम
मालापानी रायपुर रोड
देहरादून

ओ३म्

प्रिय सतीश! आशीर्वाद

मैं १८ जौ० को तपोवन पहुँचा तो
आपके पत्र पड़े मिले। मुझे बड़ा खेद है कि
आप आए भी और भेंट न हो सकी। इस वर्ष
मैं १२ अगस्त तक यहीं हूँ। बहरों तक जाना पड़ा
यदि एक व्यक्ति जयपुर से कार लेकर आए भी
चल गये अन्यथा अवश्य मिलता।
सितम्बर का पूरा महीना दिल्ली में रहूँगा।
अगस्त के १४ से कहीं बाहर जाना है।
यह जानकर प्रसन्नता हुई कि प्रिय
सुरेश भी सपरिवार भारत आया हुआ है।
उसे मेरे शुभाशीर्वाद सूचना दे देना।
मैं ८ जौ० से १८ जौ० तक दिल्ली आई-
फ्लू से पीड़ित रहा अन्यथा मैं १० जौलाई
को अवश्य देहरादून आ जाता। आज
प्रिय केवी (मंजू) का पता लिखकर भेजना।
सबको यथायोग्य नमस्ते बच्चों को प्यार।

भवदीय मंगलाभिलाषी
स्वामी दीक्षानन्द

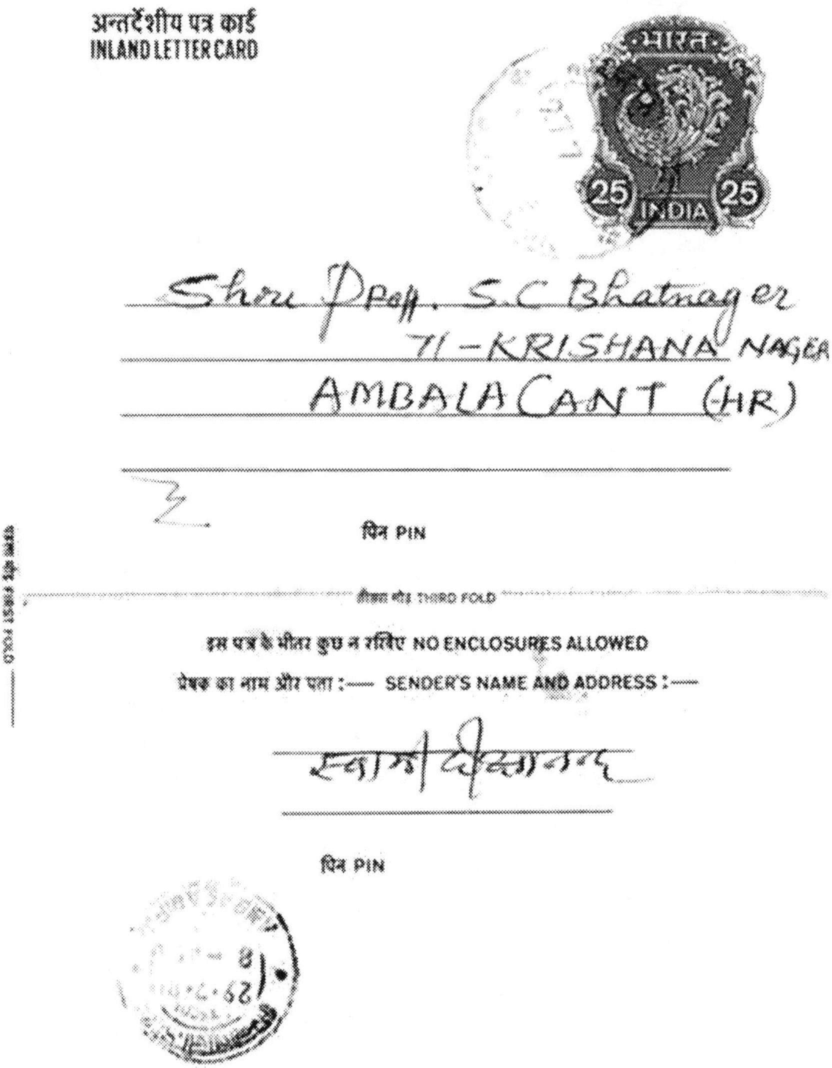
अन्तर्देशीय पत्र कार्ड
INLAND LETTER CARD

भारत
25 INDIA 25

Shri Proff. S.C Bhatnager
71-KRISHANA NAGER
AMBALA CANT (HR)

पिन PIN

तीसरा मोड़ THIRD FOLD

इस पत्र के भीतर कुछ न रखिए NO ENCLOSURES ALLOWED

प्रेषक का नाम और पता :— SENDER'S NAME AND ADDRESS :—

स्वामी विवेकानन्द

पिन PIN

ओ३म्

समर्पण शोध संस्थान

SAMARPANA SODHA SAMSTHANA

A Trust and an Institute dedicated to oriental research

संस्थान के उद्देश्य

शोध

TRUSTS OBJECTIVES

Research

प्रकाशन

Publications

क्र० सं०
Ref. No.

समर्पण शोध संस्थान, नई दिल्ली ११०००५
NEW DELHI 110005

30-6-86

प्रिय सतीश सप्रेम आशीर्वाद।

१ — तुम्हारा लास वेगास से ? जून का लिखा हुआ पत्र समय पर मिल गया था और फिर आते समय जो भारत से पत्र लिखा था वह भी मिला था। खेद यही रहा कि चलते समय कोई भेंट न हो सकी, ठीक है कि मैं रोहतक सम्मेलन में चला गया था परन्तु आपके लिए रोहतक कोई दूर नहीं था आ ही जाते और यदि संस्थान में चक्कर लगा लेते अथवा सरोज जी से फोन पर पूछ ही लेते तो कम से कम कुसुम से तो मिलना हो ही सकता था वह ३ मई से २५ जून तक गाजियाबाद संस्थान में ही रही फिर मैं भी नहीं रहा भयंकर गर्मी में भी शोध कार्य में लगे रहे। पुस्तकों का कार्य चलता रहा और कुछ नहीं तो नए नए शब्दों के चिन्तन, मनन, अध्ययन होते रहे और आनन्द रस पान करते रहे। यदि उन्हीं दिनों आप भी आ जाते तो आपके रस में भी कुछ वृद्धि होती। प्रसंगतः एक बात तो लिख देना उपयुक्त होगा।

२ — यह तो आपको पता ही है कि ब्रह्म का निजनाम ओम् है, इसी ओम् को योगदर्शन में 'प्रणव' (तस्य वाचकः प्रणवः) उसका वाचक प्रणव है। ब्रह्म प्रणव है। उसे प्रणव क्यों कहते हैं इसलिए कि हमारी स्तुतियों का पात्र एकमात्र वह ही है। प्र उपसर्ग (संभवतः इंग्लिश में प्रीफिक्स) है और नव का अर्थ है स्तुति अर्थात् प्र-नव प्रकृष्ट स्तुति प्रश्न है कि स्तुति किस लिए इसलिए कि वह नव है सदा [illegible] और नव ही रहेगा। अतः नव शब्द का अर्थ है नया ब्रह्म वह सत्ता है जो कभी पुराना नहीं होता सदा नया रहता है, एक रस रहता है, कोई परिवर्तन नहीं होता, और पूर्ण रहता है इसलिए सदा नया सदा पूर्ण सदा एकरस ब्रह्म तत्त्व को बोध कराने के लिए गणित के १ अंक से बढ़कर और मिसाल हो भी क्या सकती थी क्योंकि गणित में १ अंक ही ऐसा है जो सदा नया रहता है, जो एक रस रहता है, जो सदा पूर्ण रहता है। इसलिए ब्रह्म को १ अंक से उपमा देने के लिए पतंजलि ने बोला प्रणवः। और फिर उसे ० = शून्य = [illegible] से उपमा दी गई। हम सन्ध्या में प्रतिदिन बोलते हैं ओम् खम् ब्रह्म अर्थात् ओम् क्या है ख है शून्य है, ब्रह्म महान् है। ख का अर्थ आकाश है शून्य है उसे पूर्ण कहने के लिए १ (नव) कहा और उसे व्यापक कहने के लिए ० = शून्य = खम् कहा। बस गणित के मूल यही दो अंक हैं १ और ० सृष्टि के मूल भी यही प्रणव और खम् हैं। जिन ऋषियों ने ब्रह्म को १ और ० से उपमा दी तो क्या उन्होंने गणित का मूल नहीं खोज निकाला था उन्होंने ब्रह्म को भी खोजा और गणित को भी खोजा। मैं १६, १७ [illegible] ब्रह्म और गणित की तुलना [illegible]। इसे आप विस्तार देना।

३ — संस्थान में एक दो विद्वानों को लाने के विषय में आपसे चर्चा होती रही थी उनमें १ नाम श्री वेदपाल जी का था। मुझे याद नहीं कि उनसे भेंट हुई कि नहीं? वह अब २२ [illegible] को काम पर आ गये हैं और बराबर शोध कार्य कर रहे हैं। उन दिनों यदि आ सकते तो बड़ा ही अच्छा रहता वे संस्कृत पढ़ने में [illegible] है आपको उनसे मार्गदर्शन मिलता और प्रेरणा भी।

Dedicated Oriental Research

४– प्रिय सुरेश २२ जौलाई की रात्रि को संस्थान में ही रहा। खूब बातचीत होती रही। साथ में मोहन और [illegible] भी आए थे वे तो चले गये थे परन्तु सुरेश वहीं रहा। उसको भी संस्कृत और वेद पढ़ने के लिए उत्साहित किया। दो पुस्तकें संस्कृत शिक्षण सम्बन्धी और [illegible] ले गया है। [illegible] को निकाल दी है। अपने एम. फिल. के अन्तिम साल के थीसिज को अपने वैदिक [illegible] से [illegible] रहा था और उसके प्रकाशन के लिए पैसा भी देने को तय्यार है। अब उसके शोध कार्य को भी देखूंगा। परमात्मा करे कि उसे संस्कृत के प्रति [illegible] मिले। मुझे २२ को सोनीपत यज्ञ के लिए चला जाना था और उसे २३ को कोलम्बो के लिए इसलिए २२ को ही मेरे हो गई मुलाकात हुई।

५– आपके साथी श्री प्रोफेसर निगम जी द्वारा भेजा २०० का चैक मिल गया था वैसे तो मैंने फोन पर उन्हें धन्यवाद कह दिया है परन्तु अभी मिलना नहीं हो सका है। चाहता हूं मिलूं परन्तु [illegible] व्यस्त रहना होता है कि क्या बताऊं फिर साहिबाबाद से तो निकलना मुश्किल है क्योंकि [illegible] बताऊं [illegible]। इससे पता चलता है कि आपको संस्थान से कितना स्नेह है। परमात्मा करे कि आपका यह स्नेह उत्तरोत्तर बढ़ता रहे और संस्थान के [illegible] में आपका भी भाग बना रहे। आपने दिल्ली रहते हुए प्रो. निगम का कोई जिक्र नहीं किया अन्यथा तभी मिल लिया होता। मुझे यह जान कर प्रसन्नता है कि बेटी और दामाद को मेरी छोटी सी पुस्तिका उपहार सर्वस्व पसन्द आई।

६– इस से पहले भी मैं प्रिय भगवानदेव जी को फोन कर चुका था। पत्रिका योग मन्दिर (विश्व योग संस्थान) मेरे सामने रखी है उसके जौलाई ९८ के अंक पृ. 14, 15 पर आपका लेख Mathematical in the vedas and yoga आपके चित्र सहित छपा रखा है सोचता हूं कि इस अंक को भिजवाऊं कि [illegible] अथवा उसका फोटोस्टेट पत्र भेजने तक [illegible] पत्रिका ही भिजवा दूं। यदि [illegible] से आपको भारत आने में सहायता मिलती है तो एक आध लेख और भी भिजवा दो इसे भी छपवा दूं। आपके इस लेख को कुछ कुछ मैंने भी पढ़ा है, परन्तु इस से वैदिक गणित का उद्धार किस प्रकार होगा। [illegible] से कैसे काम चलेगा आपको तो सब कुछ नया सोचना होगा नई व्याख्याएं करनी होंगी। कुछ चमत्कार करना होगा। क्या तुमको पता है कि अथर्ववेद में सृष्टि की आयु दी है कि ये कितने वर्षों तक रहेगी। हमें इस से कुछ प्रयोजन नहीं कि सृष्टि कितने समय रहेगी हमें तो यह देखना है कि उन्होंने गणित के बिना वर्षों की गणना कैसे कर ली।

७– एक आर्य जगत का सम्पादकीय भेज रहा हूं जिसमें संस्कृत के प्रति विदेशियों का कैसा अनुराग था और अब स्वतंत्र भारत में उसके कर्णधार उसकी क्या दुर्गति कर रहे हैं। सुना है कि लंदन में एक गोरे लोगों का ऐसा विद्यालय है जहां संस्कृत मीडियम से पढ़ाया जाता है। [illegible] इस लेख में लिखा है कि १८२४ में [illegible] ने कलकत्ता में संस्कृत विद्या विद्यालय की स्थापना की। उसके [illegible] जाने पर लार्ड मैकाले की [illegible] का क्या प्रभाव पड़ा यह वर्णित है। संस्कृत में ही [illegible] है।

८– आपका लेख भिजवा रहा हूं। १ अगस्त से १ महीने के लिए [illegible] के दौरे पर जा रहा हूं। परिवार में सभी को आशीर्वाद कहें। मेरे योग्य कार्य लिखें।

अनेक आशीर्वादों के साथ
[illegible]नन्द
२०।७।९८

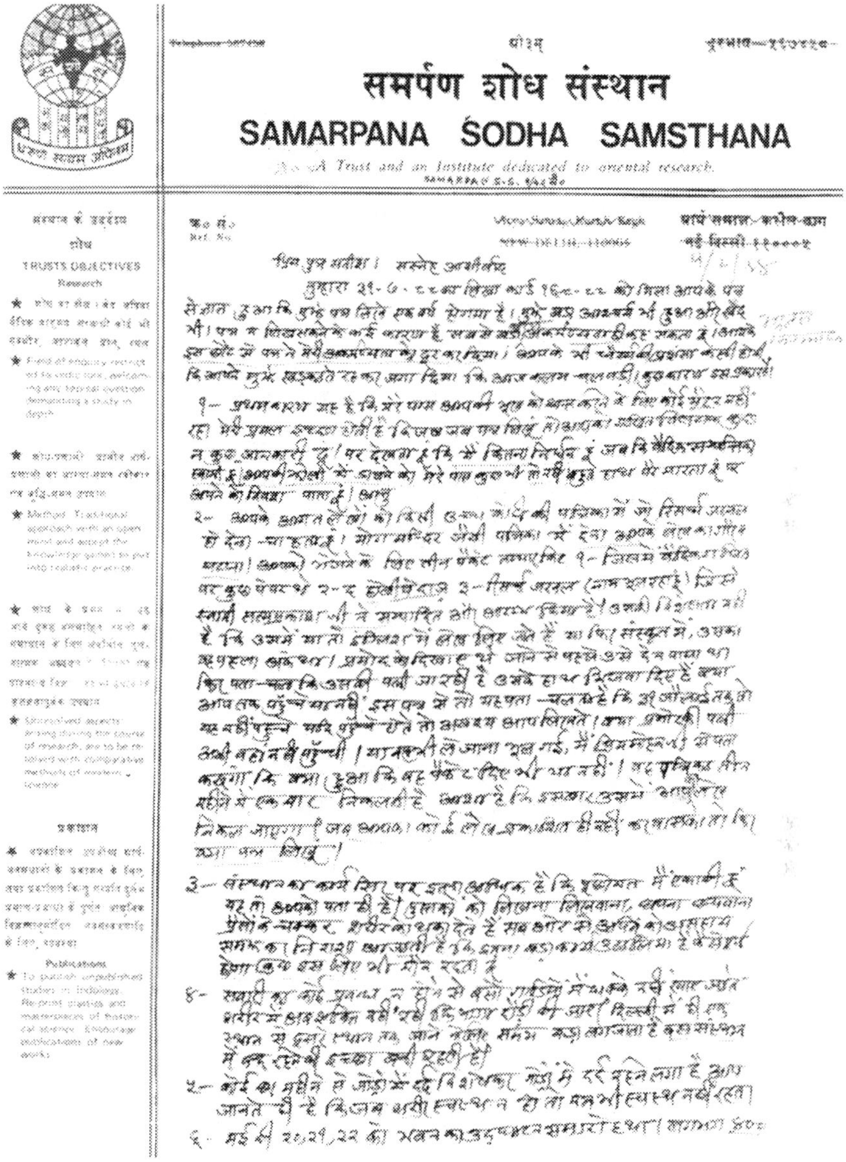

ओ३म्

समर्पण शोध संस्थान

SAMARPANA SODHA SAMSTHANA

A Trust and an Institute dedicated to oriental research.

संस्थान के उद्देश्य

शोध

TRUSTS OBJECTIVES

Research

★ Field of enquiry restricted to vedic lore, welcoming any topical question demanding a study in depth.

★ Method: Traditional approach with an open mind and accept the knowledge gained to put into realistic practice.

★ Unresolved aspects arising during the course of research are to be resolved with collaborative methods of modern science.

प्रकाशन

Publications

★ To publish unpublished studies in Indology. Re-print classics and masterpieces of historical science. Encourage publications of new works.

क्र० सं०
Ref. No.

प्रिय पुत्र सतीश। सस्नेह आशीर्वाद

तुम्हारा 31-7-88 का लिखा कार्ड 16-8-88 को मिला आपके पत्र से ज्ञात हुआ कि तुम्हें पत्र लिखे एक वर्ष हो गया है। मुझे बड़ा आश्चर्य भी हुआ और खेद भी। पत्र न लिख सकने के कई कारण हैं, [illegible] हूँ। आपके इस कोड से पत्र ने मेरी असमर्थता को दूर कर दिया। आपके [illegible] कि आपने मुझे झकझोर कर जगा दिया कि आज [illegible] नहीं। कुछ कारण इस प्रकार हैं।

1- प्रथम कारण यह है कि मेरे पास आपकी भूख को शान्त करने के लिए कोई मैटर नहीं रहा। मेरी प्रबल इच्छा होती है कि जब जब पत्र लिखूं तो आपको [illegible] कुछ न कुछ जानकारी दूं। पर देखता हूँ कि मैं कितना निर्धन हूँ जब कि वैदिक [illegible] आपकी झोली में डालने को मेरे पास कुछ भी नहीं, [illegible] पाता हूँ। अस्तु

2- आपके [illegible] को किसी उच्च कोटि की पत्रिका में जो रिसर्च जनरल हो देना चाहता हूँ। योग मन्दिर जैसी पत्रिका में देना आपके लेख का गौरव घटाना। आपको भेजने के लिए तीन पैकेट बनाए थे 1- जिसमें वैदिक [illegible] पर कुछ पेपर थे 2- [illegible] 3- रिसर्च जनरल (नाम भूल रहा हूँ) जिसे स्वामी सत्यप्रकाश जी ने सम्पादित और आरम्भ किया है। उसकी विशेषता यही है कि उसमें या तो इंग्लिश में लेख लिए जाते हैं या फिर संस्कृत में, उसका वह पहला अंक था। प्रमोद को दिखाए थे जाने से पहले उसे दे भी दिया था फिर पता चला कि उसकी पत्नी आ रही है उसके हाथ भिजवा दिए हैं क्या आप तक पहुँचे या नहीं। इस पत्र से तो यह पता चलता है कि 31 जौलाई तक तो वह नहीं पहुँचे यदि पहुँचे होते तो अवश्य आप लिखते। क्या प्रमोद की पत्नी अभी वहाँ नहीं पहुँची। या वह भी ले जाना भूल गई, मैं [illegible] से पता करूंगा कि क्या हुआ कि वह पैकेट दिए भी या नहीं। वह पत्रिका तीन महीने में एक बार निकलती है आशा है कि इस बार उसमें आपका लेख निकल जाएगा। जब आपका कोई लेख प्रकाशित ही नहीं करा सका तो फिर क्या पत्र लिखूं।

3- संस्थान का कार्य सिर पर इतना अधिक है कि चूंकि मैं एकाकी हूँ यह तो आपको पता ही है। पुस्तकों को लिखना लिखवाना, छपना छपवाना प्रेसों के चक्कर, शरीर को थका देते हैं सब ओर से अपने को असहाय समझ कर निराशा आ जाती है कि इतना बड़ा कार्य कैसे पूर्ण होगा। इस लिए भी मौन रहता हूँ

4- सवारी का कोई प्रबन्ध न होने से बसों गाड़ियों में धक्के नहीं खाए जाते शरीर में अब शक्ति नहीं रही। दिल्ली में ही एक स्थान से दूसरे स्थान तक जाने में कितना समय [illegible] है [illegible] में बन्द रहने की इच्छा बनी रहती है।

5- कई महीने से जोड़ों में दर्द विशेषकर घुटनों में दर्द रहने लगा है आप जानते ही हैं कि जब शरीर स्वस्थ न हो तो मन भी स्वस्थ नहीं रहता।

6- मई में 20,21,22 को भवन का उद्घाटन समारोह हुआ। लगभग 800

व्यक्तियों का भोजन था। गुरुकुल कांगड़ी के भूतपूर्व आचार्य श्री प्रियव्रत
जी पधारे उन के हाथों उद्घाटन हुआ (२० मई को)। बड़ा आकर्षक पण्डाल
आदि सब वाले मैदान में बड़ा शामियाना लगा था। बड़ा यज्ञ किया और
उसी यज्ञाग्नि को लेकर सबने भवन में प्रवेश किया। अखण्ड सर्व वेद पाठ
यह कार्यक्रम प्रात: १२ बजे तक नीचे हॉल में हुआ। फिर २० को २ से ४ बजे
तक गोष्ठी (सेमिनार) हुई जिसका विषय था "पं० बुद्धदेव जी की वेदों
ब्राह्मण ग्रन्थों को विशेष देन"। विश्वविद्यालय के संस्कृत के हैड और
लेक्चरर्स लोग आए थे। उन्हें पण्डित जी का साहित्य पहिले से ही दे दिया था
जिसे पढ़कर वे अपने अपने पेपर लिख कर लाए थे।

२१ मई को प्रात: ९ से १२ और दोपहर २ से ४ तक दो गोष्ठियों में
ब्राह्मण ग्रन्थों (लिट्रेचर) की वेद भाष्य में क्या उपयोगिता है
इसी प्रकार की गोष्ठी २२ को भी हुई जिसका विषय था कि
प्राचीन, प्रकार संस्कार
वेद का आविर्भाव किस प्रकार हुआ। अत्यन्त प्रभावशाली कार्यक्रम
रहा। सभी ओर से सहयोग था। परिवार के सदस्य सभी अपने अपने
बच्चे आए थे २१, २२ को रसोई उन्होंने संभाल ली। कुसुम तथा बच्चे
न आए, हुई थी इस लिए सत्यकाम का काम करते रहे। लोगों के मुख
विवाह आदि पर इकट्ठे होते हैं सत्यार्थ के सब वेद सम्मेलन में इकट्ठे
हुए। राजन्ने अदिति के लिए ४ व्यक्ति जो जवान थे जिन्होंने मैदान
की सफाई घर की सफाई बरतनों भाँडों की सफाई आदि में हाथ
बटाया। इस प्रकार यह उत्सव उत्तम रहा। कुछ लोगों को परिश्रम भी
मिला।

मैंने संस्थान के लिए १० लाख की अपील की थी जिसमें प्रो० ओ०
सिंह जी के परिवार अर्थात् पं० बुद्धदेव जी के पुत्री शान्ता ने एक लाख
रुपया दान की व्यवस्था की। एक समय था कि यही पुत्री हम को गालियां
देती थी कि ये हमारे पिता जी को लूटने में लगे हैं। वही अब एक लाख का दान
दे रहे हैं। यह सब साधना, तप, श्रद्धा निष्ठा सत्यता का फल है।

6 – आपको पता ही है कि यहां श्री वेद पाल जी शतपथ भाष्य के कार्य में संलग्न हैं उनपर लगभग 2000 रुपया मासिक व्यय आ रहा है और श्री पं० राम नाथ जी वेदालंकार सामवेद भाष्य कर रहे उन्हें 1000 रुपया मासिक उन्हें घर पर ही भेजता रहता हूं। तीसरे श्री पं० जगदेव जी गुरु-गामाकले (मेरे शिष्य) भी संस्थान में आ गये हैं। उनसे भी कार्य लिया जा रहा है। इस प्रकार संस्थान यथा शक्ति उन्नति कर रहा है। आप भी उसके सहयोग में भागीदार बनते हैं। अभी प्रमोद भी 2 हजार का सहयोग दे गया है। सुरेश भी आया था वह भी अपनी आहुति डालता ही रहता है और अधिक क्या लिखूं। गणित विषयक कोई लेख मेरे पास नहीं आया। गणित विषयक मैटर भी तलाश मिलने पर अवश्य भेजूंगा। अपनी बुद्धि की कसरत से कुछ निकाल पाता हूं लिख देता हूं पहिले भी लिखा था। वैदिक धर्म में एक प्रसिद्ध सूत्र है मंत्र है। ओम् खम् ब्रह्म। इसके कई अर्थ हैं। इसका अर्थ ओ३म् और आकाश (खम्) दोनों महान् हैं। ओम् ईश्वर का वाचक है और खम् आकाश का जो प्रकृति के मैटर का वाचक है इन दोनों के मेल से सृष्टि होती है। यह इस सूत्र का आध्यात्मिक (स्प्रिचुअल) अर्थ है। इसका गणित विषयक अर्थ है कि गणित में भी 1 और 0 (जीरो) महान् हैं। ओम् का अर्थ है 1 और खम् का अर्थ है (0) शून्य अर्थात् जीरो। यह एक सूत्र अध्यात्म में महत्ता को बताता वहीं गणित में 1 और 0 को महान बताता यही है ओम् खं ब्रह्म सूत्र का अर्थ। परिवार में सभी छोटे बड़ों को बच्चों को यथायोग्य नमस्ते है

शुभैषी
[illegible] आनन्द

Telephone [illegible] ओ३म् [redacted]

सम्पूर्ण शोध संस्थान
SAMARPANA SODHA SAMSTHANA

A Trust and an Institute dedicated to oriental research.

संस्थान के उद्देश्य

शोध

TRUSTS OBJECTIVES

Research

★ [illegible]

★ [illegible]

★ [illegible]

★ [illegible]

★ [illegible]

★ [illegible]

प्रकाशन

★ [illegible]

Publications

★ To publish unpublished [illegible]

क्र० सं०
Ref. No. [redacted]

प्रियपुत्र [illegible] आशीर्वाद — 30/9/88 [illegible]

आशा है तुम सपरिवार स्वस्थ एवं सानन्द होगे। इस से पूर्व एक पत्र 24 सितम्बर को लिखा [illegible] होगा [illegible] कुछ ही दिनों में मुझे [illegible] इसके साथ [illegible] [illegible]।

मैंने आपका लेख डा० श्री स्वामी सत्य प्रकाश जी की पत्रिका में छपने को भेजा था (जिसका जिक्र भी पहले पत्र में कर चुका हूँ) उसकी प्रतिक्रिया में उन्होंने जो नोट दिया है उसे भिजवा रहा हूँ। अब आप इस आधार पर अपनी जिज्ञासा को मिटा सकते हैं। उनका पता स्वामी सत्य प्रकाश जी महाराज c/o आर्य प्रतिनिधि सभा मन्दिर मार्ग, नई दिल्ली - 110001 होगा। उन्होंने इन वैदिक गणित सूत्रों के विषय में स्पष्ट लिखा है कि इनका कहीं उल्लेख नहीं अथर्ववेद के साथ में इनका सम्बन्ध [illegible] द्वारा उनसे सम्पर्क बनाए रखें।

यह हो सकता है कि हम वेदों से गणित न निकाल पायें क्योंकि उनकी शब्दावली (टेक्निकल वर्ड्स) को न समझ पाते हैं परन्तु इसमें सन्देह नहीं कि उन्हें अर्थ ज्ञान था अन्यथा वेदों में गणितीय उक्तियों का अर्थ कैसे समझ पाते। तुम्हें याद होगा कि जब तुम पहली बार संस्थान आये थे तो मैंने अथर्ववेद के पहले मन्त्र पर चर्चा की थी जिसमें त्रिषप्त (तीन सात) का उल्लेख है कि तीन और सात = दस से अथवा तीन गुणा सात 21 से विश्व के समस्त रूपों को धारण किया हुआ है। 1- सूर्य के मुख्य तीन रंग और फिर सात रंग इन सब ने मिलकर इस विश्व के समस्त रूपों को धारण किया है 2- संगीत के 3 सप्तक प्रसिद्ध हैं सा, रे, ग, म, प, ध, नि। ये सात शुद्ध - मृदु - और तार स्वरों से सारे संगीत शास्त्र को समेटे हुए हैं। इस प्रकार अनन्त [illegible] छुपे हुए हैं। मान लिया कि वेद [illegible] गणित नहीं परन्तु जिसने भी यह मन्त्र रचना की यह गणित के 3 और 7 में विश्व का [illegible] पाता है [illegible] नहीं अनन्त [illegible] हैं जो

अनन्त रहस्यों को छुपाए हुए हैं।

Telephone 567458   ओ३म्   दूरभाष—५६७४

समर्पण शोध संस्थान

SAMARPANA SODHA SAMSTHANA

A Trust and an Institute dedicated to oriental research.

संस्थान के उद्देश्य

शोध

TRUSTS OBJECTIVES

Research

★ [illegible]

★ Field of enquiry restricted to vedic lore, welcoming any topical question demanding a study in depth.

★ [illegible]

★ Method: Traditional approach with an open mind and accept the knowledge gained to put into realistic practice.

★ [illegible]

★ Unresolved aspects arising during the course of research, are to be resolved with comparative methods of modern science.

प्रकाशन

★ [illegible]

Publications

★ To publish unpublished studies in Indology. Re-print classics and masterpieces of historical science. Encourage publications of new works.

क्र० सं० / Ref. No.   Brought by Prof [illegible] on 25/1/84

4/42 सै० 5 साहिबाबाद 201005

~~Arya Samaj, Karol Bagh, NEW DELHI 110005~~ ~~आर्य समाज, करोल बाग, नई दिल्ली ११०००५~~

प्रिय पुत्र सतीश सस्नेह आशीर्वाद।

आशा है तुम सपरिवार सानन्द होगे। आपका पत्र यथा समय मिल गया था। पत्र मिलने से ४ ही दिन पूर्व मैंने तुम्हें एक पत्र लिखा था जिस में श्री स्वामी सत्यप्रकाश जी की आपके लेख पर टिप्पणी थी। तुम्हें मिल गया होगा और तुमने श्री स्वामी जी से सीधा पत्र व्यवहार कर समाधान कर लिया होगा। वैदिक गणित के नाम पर जो शंकराचार्य जी के नाम से अथर्ववेदीय सूत्र कहे गये हैं वे अथर्ववेद में नहीं हैं, यह तो हम भी निश्चय कर चुके थे फिर प्रश्न होता है कि ये सूत्र कहाँ से लिए गये अथवा शंकराचार्य जी के स्वयं निर्मित हैं कुछ भी हो ये वेद में नहीं हैं, फिर तो हम वैदिकों के लिए एक चैलेंज है कि क्या वेदों में गणित के विषय में कुछ है भी कि नहीं? जब कि ऋषि महर्षियों का यह मन्तव्य है कि "वेद सब सत्य विद्याओं का पुस्तक है" यह हमारा [illegible] है और इस पर अनुसन्धान करना है।

पता चला है कि श्री महेश योगी वेदों के विभिन्न विषयों पर [illegible] में बनाए शोध संस्थान में शोध कार्य करा रहे हैं। जो गणित पर विशेष कार्य कर रहे हैं उनका पता निम्न प्रकार है यदि सम्भव हो तो आप सीधा पत्र व्यवहार कर जानकारी हासिल करें। मैं भी प्रयत्नशील हूँ कि उनसे मिलूँ और जो जानकारी मिले आपको लिख भेजूँ।

पता —— उनका पता नहीं मिल सका, अगले पत्र में लिख दूंगा

एक लेख आर्य जगत में गणित विषयक छपा था उसमें शून्य पर विवेचना है भिजवा रहा हूँ। उसी पुस्तक पर आप संस्थान के लिए दस लाख की अपील भी कर देंगे। मैंने जो प्रयत्न किये [illegible] वह भी मिल [illegible] थी।

एक प्रसन्नता की बात यह है कि पिछले दिनों श्री स्वामी आनन्द बोध जी (पू. लाला रामगोपाल जी) संस्थान पधारे थे उन्होंने निरीक्षण किया और अत्यधिक [illegible]

और कहा कि यह कल्पना भी नहीं की जा सकती कि
कोई अकेला व्यक्ति इतना बड़ा कार्य कर सकता है
कौन कहता है कि आर्य समाज मर रहा है। जहाँ
वेदानन्द जैसे संन्यासी विद्यमान हों ऐसा सार्व
देशिक पत्रिका ने भी जोड़ दिया। आप जानते ही
हैं कि वे मेरे कितने बड़े विरोधी रहे हैं परन्तु अब
वही सब तक अपने भाषणों में संस्थान का उल्लेख
करते हैं। मुझे गीता का यह श्लोक कि न हि कल्याणकृत् कश्चित्
दुर्गतिं तात गच्छति याद हो आया जिस का अर्थ है कि कल्याण
मे कामना से किया गया कार्य कभी हानि को नहीं पहुँचता।

आगे की यह पंक्तियाँ मैं भटिण्डा में प्रियदिनेश के घर पर २३ जनवरी
को प्रातः ४ बजे लिख रहा हूँ पता चला है कि कल ही गार्गी विदेश
जाने वाली है उससे मिलने और छोड़ने दिनेश की पत्नी कल २४ को प्रातः
वाली गाड़ी जनता से दिल्ली जा रही है यह पत्र उसे ही दे रहा हूँ
कि जिस से गार्गी के हाथ परसों ही मिल जाए। वैसे मुझे अभी
मिले आपके पत्र से ज्ञात हो गया था कि गार्गी २४ जनवरी को आने वाली
है। यही सोचा कि मेरा पत्र तो न जाने कब पहुँचा होगा सो
आज अभी पूरा कर देना चाहिए मैं भी कल २४ को उसी गाड़ी
से दिल्ली जा रहा हूँ कोशिश तो करूँगा कि गार्गी से मिल सकूँ
परन्तु लगता कठिन ही है। पत्र तो पहुँच ही जाएगा।

मैं २० को पुरी एक यज्ञ की पूर्णाहुति पर आया हुआ था जहाँ एक
जैन व्यक्ति ने चारों वेदों का यज्ञ ४० दिन से आरम्भ किया हुआ था
सो २२ को प्रातः पूर्णाहुति हो गई और २ बजे वापस गाड़ी से चल
कर सायं ४॥ भटिण्डा पहुँच गया। यहाँ गुरुकुल में कुछ पुस्तकें
फरीदकोट से इस संस्थान के लिए आई रखी हैं उन्हें ले जाने के
लिए आया हूँ। इस बहाने दिनेश से सबसे मिलना हो गया यहाँ
आने पर एक शोक समाचार मिला कि रुचि के श्वसुर का अचानक
हार्ट अटैक होने से पिछले इतवार को अजमेर में देहान्त हो गया

आपको सम्भवतः यह सूचना मिल गई होगी कि मैं पिछले
वर्ष अक्तूबर में जब अमेरिका गया तो वेदों के विद्यालय का भी दौरा किया। वेदों
और अनल के कार्यों को देखकर मन को अत्यन्त प्रसन्नता हुई। [illegible] यश और प्रसन्न
भी हुए जिससे वेदों और अनल को अत्यन्त प्रसन्नता हुई परमात्मा उन्हें
दीर्घायु प्रदान करे।

आपके सभी पत्र ठीक समय पर मिलते हैं मैं ही समय पर
उत्तर नहीं दे पाता अभी श्री स्वामी सत्यप्रकाश जी से मिल नहीं पाया हूँ।
मिलने पर ही सब समाचार लिखूँगा। भाभी से पता चला कि निम्नलिखित
आपकी रीढ़ की हड्डी में बहुत दर्द रहा और परेशानी रही आगे पत्र में लिखें कि
अब क्या हाल है लिखना। अधिक क्या लिखूँ। शुभाशीर्वाद सहित

तुम्हारा
वेदानन्द

6 जून, 1989

DEPARTMENT OF
MATHEMATICAL SCIENCES

UNIVERSITY OF NEVADA, LAS VEGAS
4505 MARYLAND PARKWAY • LAS VEGAS, NEVADA 89154 • (702) 739-3567

स्वामी मामाजी, सादर प्रणाम

[illegible]

[illegible]

[illegible]

[illegible]

[illegible]

समर्पण शोध संस्थान

SAMARPANA SODHA SAMSTHANA

A Trust and an Institute dedicated to oriental research.

संस्थान के उद्देश्य

शोध

TRUSTS OBJECTIVES

Research

★ शोध का क्षेत्र : वेद अथवा वैदिक वाङ्मय सम्बन्धी कोई भी गम्भीर, आवश्यक प्रश्न, स्वल्प [illegible]

★ Field of enquiry restricted to Vedic lore, welcoming any topical question demanding a study in depth

★ शोध-पद्धति : प्राचीन आर्ष-प्रणाली का [illegible]

★ Method: Traditional approach with an open mind and accept the knowledge gained to put into [illegible] practice

★ [illegible]

★ Unresolved aspects arising during the course of research, are to be resolved with comparative methods of modern science

प्रकाशन

★ [illegible]

Publications

★ To publish unpublished studies in Indology. Re-print classics and masterpieces of historical science. Encourage publications of new works.

क्र० सं०
Ref. No.

Arya Samaj, Karol Bagh
NEW DELHI-110005

आर्य समाज, करोल बाग
नई दिल्ली-११०००५

तिथि २४-३-९० 7/4/90

प्रिय पुत्र सतीश ! सस्नेह आशीर्वाद

आशा है तुम सपरिवार स्वस्थ एवं सानन्द होंगे। आपका पत्र सदा मिल गया था और पहले पत्र भी सदा समय मिलते रहे। आपकी शिकायत भी वाजिब है कि मैं उत्तर नहीं देता। परन्तु यह आक्षेप ठीक नहीं कि मैंने एक बहाने का रास्ता निकाल लिया है कि उत्तर ही न दो स्वतः आपने आप पत्र का लिखना बन्द कर देगा। नहीं प्रियवर! ऐसा नहीं क्या आप ऐसा सोच सकते हैं कि मैं ऐसा चाहूंगा भी नहीं कदापि नहीं, फिर ऐसा क्यों?

बात ऐसी है कि इतने काम उठा लिये कि समय नहीं निकाल पाता और उसका प्रभाव लेखन पर पड़ता है। पत्र व्यवहार भी ठीक से नहीं हो पाता जो जीवन में आवश्यक है। इस न लिखने के कारण कितने ही आरम्भ किये ग्रन्थ बीच में ही पड़े रह जाते हैं। छपने वाले ग्रन्थों के प्रकाशन किया, लिखने में ही समय चला जाता है। पुस्तक छपने में देर हो जाती है। उसका एक मात्र कारण होता है कि [illegible] काम में कमी न रहने देना। अस्तु

अब आप भारत कब आ रहे हैं "इस बार आने की सोच कर भी आना स्थगित रहा। ऐसा क्यों"? तुम्हारा संस्कृत अध्ययन के आगे बढ़ा अथवा रुका हुआ है बिना संस्कृत अध्ययन के वैदिक वाङ्मय की रिसर्च असम्भव है। मैं स्वयं भी अपनी संस्कृत से सन्तुष्ट नहीं हूँ, हाँ मेरा चिन्तन और [illegible] इस प्रकार होती है कि रिसर्च में जो काम आती है वह लोगों में कम पाई जाती है वह सारा समय सोचने और युक्तियों के ढूँढने में ही निकल जाता है। लिखता हूँ फिर सोचता हूँ कोई नई बात समझ में आती है तो पिछला लिखा काट कर नया लिखता हूँ। मैं चाहता हूँ कि आप संस्कृत के शुद्ध ज्ञाता बनें मैं नहीं जानता कि आपको पिछली बार "संस्कृत शिक्षण सरणी" पुस्तक दी कि नहीं जिससे [illegible] शीघ्र सीखी जाती है। (यह पुस्तक आपको मिली या नहीं यदि नहीं तो भिजवा दूं)

आप को पत्र लिख चुका था उसके बाद [illegible] आपका आठ तारीख १०-३-९० का पत्र मिला बड़ी ही प्रसन्नता हुई और [illegible] पत्र में आपके दो पत्रों का उत्तर होगा।

अपने विषय में.......

मैं सामान्यतः ठीक चल रहा हूँ लेकिन गोड़ों का दर्द बराबर बढ़ रहा है अपने गोड़ों पर चढ़ाने का एक घुटने का [illegible] रबर का [illegible] [illegible] रहा वैसे ही लगा रहा है। [illegible] ठीक रहेगा। [illegible] का हाथ [illegible] हूँ। [illegible] ठीक काम कर रहा [illegible] [illegible] [illegible]

पुस्तकें जिनको आरम्भ की हुई हैं वही पूरी नहीं हो पा रहीं। पूरी हो जाएं तो उनके प्रकाशन का प्रश्न है। आपको यह जानकर प्रसन्नता तो होगी कि इस मास २ को मुझे मेहरचन्द महाजन डी.ए.वी. कन्या महाविद्यालय में दीक्षान्त भाषण के लिये बुलाया गया जहां पिछले वर्ष निर्मलानन्द (चिन्मय मिशन के जी को) बुलाया गया था और उस से पहले वर्ष श्री दलाई लामा को इस प्रकार यह गौरव स्वामी दीक्षानन्द को मिला। उनका यही कहना था कि इस बार भी दीक्षान्त सर्वोत्तम रहा। मैं करीब १ घण्टे बोला, लगभग ६०० छात्राओं ने दीक्षा ग्रहण की। आज की डाक में आपके पत्र के साथ वहां के चित्र भी प्राप्त हुए हैं जब आप भारत आएंगे तो आपको दिखाऊंगा।

दूसरी शुभ सूचना यह है कि १५ दिसम्बर १९९९ को मुझे स्वतन्त्रता सेनानी मान लिया गया परिणामतः ८० से अब तक का १६ हजार रुपया और ६५० रुपया मासिक पैन्शन भी मिलने लगी। और सब से बड़ी बात यह है कि रेलवे का पास सारे भारत वर्ष का I श्रेणी या II A.C. का मिला है कहीं भी कभी भी यात्रा कर सकता हूँ और एक सहयात्री को उसी क्लास में साथ ले जा सकता हूँ। अब जब आप भारत आयेंगे तो जहां जाना होगा साथ साथ जायेंगे।

कुसुम के बारे में

पुत्री कुसुम वनस्थली में पूर्ववत् पढ़ा रही है। ठीक अपने मार्ग [illegible] से सफलतापूर्वक चल रही है। अभी उसका अवकाश [illegible] हुई जनवरी पहली तारीख से होगा शायद यहीं आना होगा। आजकल डी.लिट् के लिए ऋग्वेद के १ मण्डल के १६४वें सूक्त के १–५२ मंत्रों वाले सूक्त का शोध कार्य आरम्भ किया है। पुरुष सूक्त पर तो कई विद्वानों की उत्तम उत्तम व्याख्याएं आई हैं इससे उत्साहित होकर अस्यवामीय सूक्त जो वेदों का सब से विस्तृत सूक्त है शोध करने को कहा। देखो क्या होता है। अब उसके [illegible] शोध करने वाली का नाम रजिस्टर हो रही है।

संस्थान के बारे में —

संस्थान का कार्य प्रगति पर है मैं सन्तुष्ट हूं। संस्थान की ओर से श्री रामनाथ जी विद्यालंकार सामवेद का संस्कृत-हिन्दी दो भाषाओं में अनुवाद कर चुके हैं वह २००० पृष्ठों का ग्रन्थ छपकर तैयार होगा। उस पर अनुमानिक व्यय दो लाख रुपया होगा। लगभग ३०० पृष्ठ छप भी चुके हैं। प्रति पृष्ठ की छपाई ६० रुपया है।

दूसरा कार्य श्री पं. वेदपाल जी द्वारा शतपथ का १म काण्ड पूरा होगया और वह भी छपने दिया हुआ है २५० पृष्ठ आ गये हैं। उस पर भी ६५ हजार का व्यय आने की सम्भावना है।

तीसरा कार्य श्री पं. [illegible]पति जी एम.ए. द्वारा लिखी हुई उर्दू पुस्तकों का हिन्दी अनुवाद करा रहा हूं एक पुस्तक का नाम है वैदिक स्वर्ग वह छप कर तैयार होगई है १५ दिन तक बाजार में आ जायेगी।

चौथा कार्य बरेली में एक विदुषी पण्डिता सावित्री देवी जी हैं कि जो शतपथ के दूसरे काण्ड का कार्य कर रही हैं। यदि कुसुम को भी एक शोधकर्त्री मान लिया जाए तो ५ विद्वान इस समय जो मुझे मिले हैं तो ५ व्यक्ति शोध कार्य में लगे हुए हैं।

भावी योजनाएं —

पुरुष सूक्त की भांति ही वेदों के मुख्य मुख्य २०, २५ सूक्तों पर कार्य करने का विचार है शोधकर्त्ता नहीं मिलते क्या किया जाए। मैं तो [illegible] से लगा हुआ हूं। आपने लिखा है कि भवनों के निर्माण में समय और धन का व्यय न करें। आप ठीक [illegible] ऐसा ही है और कुछ [illegible] मेरे लिए तो सर्वोपरि शोध कार्य है। और [illegible] जीवन रहते रहते [illegible] स्थापित करना चाहता हूं कि वह आर्य समाज के क्षेत्र में सदा

Telephone 5763026 ओ३म् दूरभाष 5763026

समर्पण शोध संस्थान

SAMARPANA SODHA SAMSTHANA

A Trust and an Institute dedicated to oriental research.

क्र० सं०
Ref. No.

Arya Samaj, Karol Bagh
NEW DELHI, 110005

आर्य समाज, करोल बाग
नई दिल्ली ११०००५

संस्थान के उद्देश्य
शोध
TRUSTS OBJECTIVES
Research

★ Field of enquiry restricted to vedic lore, welcoming any logical question demanding a study in depth.

★ Method: Traditional approach with an open mind and accept the knowledge gained to put into realistic practice.

★ Unresolved aspects arising during the course of research are to be solved with comparative methods of modern science.

प्रकाशन
Publications

★ To publish unpublished studies in Indology. Reprint classics and masterpieces of classical science. Encourage publications of new works.

स्मरणीय रहेगा। मैं दिसम्बर और जनवरी १५ तक के लिए बम्बई और पूना चला गया था एक तो टेस्ट मैच देखना होगा, और दूसरे पूना के शोध संस्थानों में जाना उनके द्वारा किये जा रहे शोध कार्यों का प्रकार और लेखा जोखा देखा वहाँ हो रहे कार्य को देखकर तो मैं दंग रह गया। हमारा कार्य तो कुछ भी नहीं। परन्तु उनके संस्थानों को आरम्भ हुए ६०, ८० वर्ष होगये हैं जबकि हमें १० वर्ष ही हुए हैं। रवि की छुट्टियाँ थी इसलिये वह भी इस बार कुमार राजन् भी बरली वाले बम्बई गये हैं वह और उसका परिवार भी इस बार पूना में अतः प्रतिदिन सायंकाल १ घण्टा सभी बैठते और प्रवचन सुनते रहे। बड़ा अच्छा रहा। दिन में रवि अपनी गाड़ी में शोध संस्थानों में ले जाता जहाँ हम अपने शोध के लिए ग्रन्थ देखते। उसी प्रसंग में एक व्यक्ति से भेंट हो गई जहाँ जो पिछले ६० वर्षों से वेदों में ज्योतिष शास्त्र की खोज में लगे हैं। यह तो तुम को पता ही है कि ज्योतिष का मूल गणित शास्त्र है, परन्तु उनका सारा काम मराठी में है मैं उनका एक ट्रैक्ट जो इंग्लिश में है आपको के साथ भिजवा रहा हूँ। उसे समझिए मैंने समझने की कोशिश की किन्तु उनकी बात मेरे आज नहीं लगी और न पूना में ही कोई व्यक्ति उसे महत्व देता है। फिर भी आप विचार करें। उन्होंने किसी दक्षिण के संस्कृत के एक ग्रन्थ का हवाला देते हुए नागरी वर्ण माला को गणित में संख्या मानते हैं और उसका सब अपनी शोध का आधार रखा है लगभग ८०० पृष्ठों का हाल लो। फोटोस्टेट करा लाया हूँ एक मराठी विद्वान को हिन्दी करने के लिए दिया है हिन्दी होने पर कुछ पता चलेगा। उसका कुछ मानना इस प्रकार

नञावचश्च शून्यानि संख्या कटपयादयः।
मिश्रे तु पान्त हल् संख्या न च चिन्त्यो हलस्वरः॥

क ख ग घ ङ   च छ ज झ ञ
ट ठ ड ढ ण   त थ द ध न
प फ ब भ म
य र ल व श   ष स ह क्ष ळ

१ २ ३ ४ ५ ६ ७ ८ ९ ० = यदि मंत्र में कटपय में से कोई अक्षर होगा १ का वाचक होगा, ख ठ फ र २ अंक का, ग ड ब ल ३ अंक का, घ ढ भ व ४ अंक का, ङ ण म श ५ अंक का, च त ष ६ का, छ थ स ७ का, ज द ह ८ का, झ ध ९ का, ञ न ळ ० का। अब यदि मंत्र का शब्द नाम है तो न का अर्थ होगा ४ और म का अर्थ होगा ५ = ४५ संस्कृत में अंकों की ~~गिनती~~ दायें से बायें को होती है तो यह ४५, ५४ समझा जायेगा। अतः नाम का अर्थ (५४) 54 होगा।

Dedicated Oriental Research

इस प्रकार सारे वेद मंत्रों के अक्षरों के गणित के अङ्क समझ कर अर्थ करना और उस पर आकाशीय खगोल विज्ञान ज्योतिष शास्त्र को समझाना आश्चर्य जनक है। अभी मेरी समझ में तो नहीं आया। उनका एक इंग्लिश में लिखा ग्रन्थ रामगोपाल के हाथ भिजवा रहा हूँ, उसे समझने का प्रयत्न करना फिर जब आप भारत आएंगे तो पूना-नगर के उन सज्जन से मिलेंगे।

ये सब खोज इसलिए चल रही थी कि पुत्री कुसुम को अस्यवामीय सूक्त पर डी० लिट् का शोध कार्य करना था अन्यथा तो उससे परिचय का प्रश्न ही नहीं था। जब उन दिनों सूक्त पर खोज जारी थी उस पर पूरा कार्य हुआ डा० वासुदेव शरण अग्रवाल का ग्रन्थ मिला परन्तु वह इंग्लिश में था दिल्ली आकर उसे मैंने खरीद भी लिया नाम है The Thousand Syllabled Speech (सहस्राक्षरा वाक्) VISION IN LONG DARKNESS कुसुम के शोध प्रबन्ध से कोई ड्योढ़ गुना बड़ा ग्रन्थ। यदि आप इसे देखना चाहें और पढ़ना चाहें और यदि पढ़ सकें तो इसका हिन्दी कर सकें तो यह ग्रन्थ राम गोपाल के हाथ भिजवा दूं। यह पत्र कल ही डाक से भिजवा रहा हूं सम्भवत: आपका उत्तर तब तक आ जाएगा। मैं भिजवाना चाहता हूं कि आप संस्कृत और वेद विज्ञान का आनन्द ले सकें। महर्षि कृत संस्थान के विषय का आशा है आप इससे प्रसन्न होंगे।

पुत्र राजन् रवि विषय के भी...

इस बार संन्यास (सन् ७४) के पश्चात् पहली बार तुम्हारे परिवार में आने का अवसर मिला तो पाया कि हर कोई अपने-अपने स्थान पर आर्यसमाज का कार्य कर रहा है। राजन् रेलवे मजदूर संघ में इतना लोकप्रिय हो गया कि सेन्ट्रल रेलवे मजदूर संघ का प्रेसिडेन्ट बन गया और अपने प्रभाव से मजदूरों में आर्यसमाज को पहुँचाने का प्रयत्न किया। अभी पिछली सितम्बर में मुझे और बहिन शान्ति जी को बुलाकर १ सप्ताह का यज्ञ, कथा, और प्रवचन कराए। मैंने वहां एक गायत्री यज्ञ राष्ट्रभृत यज्ञ का आयोजन किया जो बड़ा प्रभावशाली रहा। परिणाम स्वरूप पूर्णाहुति वाले दिन लगभग ६० व्यक्तियों ने यज्ञोपवीत लिया और गायत्री जाप का व्रत और बीड़ी सिगरेट आदि व्यसनों को छोड़ने का व्रत लिया। प्रतिवर्ष ही इस प्रकार का प्रचार करवाने का व्रत लिया यह सब कार्यक्रम मथुरा में हुआ जहाँ कृष्णा नगर के आर्यसमाज के प्रधान पद से बड़ा कार्य कर रहा है।

रवि की बदली लेह हो गई है अत: वह लेह में जब भी मिलिट्री में राम नवमी कृष्ण जन्माष्टमी आदि पर्व मनाए जाते हैं तो वही यज्ञ करवाता और उन पर प्रवचन करता है। इधर दिल्ली में सुनिता एक प्रकार से मुक्त होकर आर्य समाजों में प्रचार कार्य करने लगी है। उसके बड़े लड़के का विवाह होकर उसके पास १ पुत्र है। अत: सुनिता गृहस्थ के भार से कुछ मुक्त होकर इधर ध्यान दे रही है।

राकेश ने एक कार्ड-कम्पनी खोली है उसका कार्य बहुत अच्छी प्रकार चल रहा है। पुत्री अपना प्राइवेट स्कूल चला रही है। सब होते हुए सभी आर्यसमाज के कार्य से जुड़े हुए हैं। आप जो इतने तन्मय होकर वैदिक गणित में लिख रहे हैं उससे मुझे बड़ा हर्ष है। विवेक और अनिल जो कार्य कर रहे हैं वह अपने ढंग का है। सब प्रकार मिलकर सारा काम कर रहे हैं। गीता का यह श्लोक 'न हि कल्याणकृत् कश्चित् दुर्गतिं तात गच्छति' हे अर्जुन कल्याणकारी भावना से किया काम कभी दुर्गति को प्राप्त नहीं होता।

Telephone 567458 ओ३म् दूरभाष—५६७४५८

समर्पण शोध संस्थान

SAMARPANA SODHA SAMSTHANA

A Trust and an Institute dedicated to oriental research.

संस्थान के उद्देश्य

शोध

TRUSTS OBJECTIVES

Research

★ Field of enquiry restricted to vedic lore, welcoming any literal question demanding a study in depth.

★ Method: Traditional approach with an open mind and accept the knowledge gained to out into real-life practice.

★ Unresolved aspects arising during the course of research, are to be re-solved with comparative methods of modern science.

प्रकाशन

Publications

★ To publish unpublished studies in Indology. Re-print classics and masterpieces of historical science. Encourage publications of new works.

क्र० सं०
Ref. No.

Arya Samaj, Karol Bagh, New Delhi-110005 — आर्य समाज, करोल बाग, नई दिल्ली-११०००५

संस्थान में अब टैली फोन भी लग गया है. यदि दिल्ली से फोन करना हो तो 8/ पहले लगाना होता है। फोन नं० 63026 घुमाना होता है। यदि हो सके तो किसी के आते जाते के साथ एक टैली फोन का चोंगा जिससे संस्थान में कहीं से भी आसानी से प्रयोग में लाया जा सके भिजवा सकें तो मुझे बड़ी सुविधा हो जाएगी। अन्यथा तो चढ़ने-उतरने में बड़ा कष्ट होता।

आपके द्वारा भेजा गया 4 हजार का चैक मिल गया था। चैक पर केवल नाम लिखें दिल्ली गाजियाबाद आदि कुछ भी न लिखें नाम के आगे पीछे कुछ न लगाएं न स्वामी न सरस्वती। मेरे नाम दो हो गये और दो अकाउंट खाते हो गये 1 तो भगीरथ पैलेस चान्दनी चौक में दीक्षानन्द के नाम से दूसरा गाजियाबाद में कृष्ण स्वरूप के नाम से, पैंशन इसी नाम से मिली है अतः इसी नाम का खाता है। तीसरा संस्थान के नाम का खाता है उस पर केवल समर्पण शोध संस्थान लिखें आगे पीछे कुछ न लिखें न दिल्ली न गाजियाबाद। संभव है आपको न पता हो कि मैंने आजीवन सदस्य (लाइफ मैम्बर) बनाने की योजना बनाई है। आजीवन सदस्यता का शुल्क सारे जीवन भर का कुल एक हजार है इस प्रकार के एक हजार सदस्य बनाने हैं जिससे 10 लाख (दस) फिक्स हो जाएगा उसके ब्याज से ही संस्थान चलता रहे मेरे बाद भी काम न रुके। अब तक लगभग साढ़े तीन सौ सदस्य बना लिए हैं। साढ़े छः सौ और बनाने हैं। साल दो 1, 2 साल में पूरा कर दूं।

यह जान कर अत्यन्त प्रसन्नता हुई कि आप वर्ल्ड कान्फ्रेन्स में जो टोकियो में हो रही है उसमें वेदों विज्ञान पर आपका शोध लेख सुनना मान लिया है यह हमारे संस्थान का भी काम है। मुझे जितनी प्रसन्नता है उतनी किसी को शायद हो।

पिछले दिनों एक संस्कृत के उत्कृष्ट विद्वान् विदेश जाने की योजना बना रहे थे मैं बड़ा प्रसन्न था कि आपका उनसे सम्पर्क होगा और आप संस्कृत सीख सकते हैं। वह वीजा नहीं मिल सका क्या कोई उपाय हो सकता है वह इस समय जयपुर में संस्कृत प्रोफेसर लगे हुए हैं। क्या उनको कहीं आपके पास विश्वविद्यालय में लगा सकते हैं यदि वह आ जाएं और सम्पर्क स्थापित हो जाए तो आपकी संस्कृत की समस्या हल हो जाए।

Dedicated Oriental Research

आजकल मॉरिशस से ५० व्यक्ति भारत यात्रा पर आए हुए हैं जिनका आर्य समाजों में जहाँ तहाँ स्वागत हो रहा है। सभी वह मेरे द्वारा किये गये प्रचार की प्रशंसा करते हैं। दो व्यक्ति नौरो की सेर आए हुए हैं। वे भी जहाँ तहाँ मेरी कार्यों की प्रशंसा करते हैं। मॉरिशस वाले पुनः बुलाने का आग्रह कर रहे हैं। देखो कब जाना हो, अभी तो यहाँ इतना फैलाव हो गया है कि इसको छोड़कर कहीं [illegible] अत्यन्त कठिन है।

आज पत्रों की कहानी में अपने जिस पत्र का, इस वर्ष के आरंभ में लिखा है (५ जनवरी १९८०) पुनः पढ़ा जैसे सभी प्रश्नों का उत्तर दे चुका हूँ। आपने पत्रिका के बारे में पूछा है सो [illegible] में ही बन्द करनी पड़ गई थी। उसके लिए उपयुक्त व्यक्ति नहीं मिल सका अतः बन्द करनी पड़ी। आपने बेटी और अनल की पत्रिका आनन्दवाणी का प्रतिदिन मेरे पास बराबर आ रही है। अच्छी प्रगति पर है। मेरी प्रार्थना है कि दोनों को चिर आयु प्रदान करे और उत्तरोत्तर प्रगति हो।

आपने गणित के विषय में सूक्ष्म दृष्टि लेकर देखने की आवश्यकता है, निःसन्देह। पर मैं क्या करूँ मैं कामों में इतना [illegible] हूँ कि इधर उधर दृष्टि डाल ही नहीं सकता। फिर भी खोज तो रहता ही हूँ एक पुस्तक "प्राचीन भारत के वैज्ञानिक कर्णधार" (फाउण्डर्स आफ साइन्सेज इन इन्शेंट इण्डिया) का हिन्दी द्वारा डा० स्वामी सत्य प्रकाश जी। उस पुस्तक के [illegible] हैं उस में चतुर्थ अध्याय = गुरुत्वाकर्षण का [illegible] (गिनती) नवाँ अध्याय = मेधातिथि - अंकों को पहले पहल पराई तक पहुँचाने वाले दसवाँ अध्याय = [illegible] द्वारा बीजगणित का विश्लेषण [illegible] अध्याय = [illegible] - [illegible] कहो तो यह पुस्तक भी गोपाल के हाथ भिजवा दूँ। खेद नहीं है कि कोई व्यक्ति पुस्तकों का [illegible] जाना नहीं चाहता। आप मुझे यह भी लिखें आपके पास संस्कृत-हिन्दी संस्कृत-इंग्लिश - हिन्दी इंग्लिश कोष कौन कौन से हैं। आप कहते हैं कि मैं ऐसा क्या काम करूँ कि आपको सहयोग दूँ। मैंने ऊपर डा० [illegible] अग्रवाल के इंग्लिश पुस्तक का वर्णन किया है उसका यदि हिन्दी अनुवाद कर प्रकाशित हो जाए तो उपकार ही [illegible] है। हिन्दी जगत इस प्रकार की [illegible] से वंचित है। क्या आप यह भार उठा सकोगे यदि इस पर लो तो मैं प्रकाशन करूँ होगा.......

आप हो कि मॉरिशस गणित के सम्बन्ध में [illegible] जा रहे हो तो वेद में गणितविज्ञान [illegible] सामग्री होगी [illegible] डा० सत्य प्रकाश जी की जिस पुस्तक का वर्णन किया उसके [illegible] अध्याय में वेद ही अंकों के प्रथम [illegible] है ऋग्वेद के [illegible] अतः इसीलिए [illegible] क्योंकि है। विश्व के पुस्तकालय में ऋग्वेद सबसे प्रथम प्राचीन पुस्तक है अतः उसमें अंकों का उल्लेख मिल रहा है कि मेधातिथि [illegible] अंकों की [illegible] को १ से [illegible] तक [illegible] सम्भव है। उनकी इंग्लिश दो पुस्तकें [illegible] हैं जो [illegible] और [illegible] से सम्बद्ध है।

यह तो आपको ज्ञात ही है कि वैदिक लोग सृष्टि की अवधि चार अरब बत्तीस करोड़ वर्ष मानते और एक हजार चतुर्युगी और चौदह मन्वन्तर होते हैं। एक चतुर्युगी (सत्-त्रेता-द्वापर, कलि) में ४३,२०,००० (तैंतालीस लाख बीस हजार वर्ष होते हैं) एक कलियुग ४,३२००० वर्ष के है। आपको जानकर आश्चर्य होगा कि ऋग्वेद के अक्षरों की (ऋचाओं की नहीं) चार लाख बत्तीस हजार है। सत युग = ४ कलियुग; त्रेता = ३ कलियुग; द्वापर = २ कलियुग = इस प्रकार १ कलियुगों के बराबर एक चतुर्युगी ४३,२०,००० हुई इसी १००० से गुणा करने पर ४ अरब ३२ करोड़ वर्ष का एक कल्प होता है इसे सृष्टि कहते हैं यह ब्रह्मा का एक दिन और ऐसी ही प्रलय की अवधि १ रात्रि = ऐसे दिन रात वाले ३६५ दिनों का एक वर्ष और ऐसे १०० वर्षों की आयु ब्रह्मा की मानी जाती है। [illegible] (लोमश) [illegible] शरीर [illegible] १ [illegible] उखाड़ फेंक देते हैं और [illegible] कि पुनः ब्रह्मा की

Brought by Karuna 27/2/91

Telephone 567458 ओ३म्

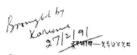

समर्पण शोध संस्थान

SAMARPANA SODHA SAMSTHANA

A Trust and an Institute dedicated to oriental research.

Ref. No. Arya Samaj, Karol Bagh, NEW DELHI. 110005 आर्य समाज, करोल बाग, नई दिल्ली ११०००५

संस्थान के उद्देश्य
शोध
TRUSTS OBJECTIVES
Research

★ [illegible]
★ Field of enquiry restricted to vedic lore, welcoming any Bhasical question demanding a study in depth.
★ [illegible]
★ Method: Traditional approach with an open mind and accept the knowledge gained to put into realistic practice.
★ [illegible]
★ Unresolved aspects arising during the course of research, are to be re-solved with comparative methods of modern science.

प्रकाशन
★ [illegible]

Publications
★ To publish unpublished studies in Indology. Re-print classics and masterpieces of historical science. Encourage publications of new works.

प्रिय पुत्र सतीश । सस्नेह आशीर्वाद

[illegible]

इस से अधिक क्या कर सकता है? तुम्हारा जीवन सफल है। आपको जानकर प्रसन्नता होगी कि अवध भारती का द्वितीय काण्ड भी तैयार हो गया है और मैं इसे २० दिन में [illegible] प्रेस में दे रहा हूँ। और [illegible] भी उसका
* विमोचन और [illegible] समारोह होगा।

३- मेरी चिन्ता का कारण यह भी था कि संस्थान में श्री [illegible] जी जो प्रकाशन कार्य कर रहे थे वह उसी दिन छोड़कर जा रहे थे। आप तो उन से भली भाँति परिचित ही हैं। उस दिन वह सभा में उपस्थित थे [illegible] नाराजगी और वह अपना एक संस्थान [illegible] पुस्तकें [illegible] रहे हैं। उन से कुछ बातों पर मतभेद था [illegible] पर [illegible]। उन्होंने अवध की [illegible] [illegible] जो [illegible] में दिया है [illegible]। [illegible] आपने द्वितीय काण्ड पर कार्य करने के लिए [illegible] की तलाश थी [illegible] में [illegible] एक व्यक्ति पर [illegible] मिल गए जिन्होंने अवध पर ही P.h.D किया है। उन्होंने कुल ४ महीने में सब कार्य पूर्ण कर दिया और [illegible] जी [illegible] के रहते [illegible] जी ने एक पैसा भी नहीं लिया मैंने सोचा है कि [illegible] के उद्‌घाटन समारोह पर [illegible] पुरस्कृत किया जाए।

४- रही चौथी बात कि इस प्रकार के साहित्य की मांग और [illegible] देखने वाले कितने लोग हैं, मूर्खों के लिये तो [illegible] साहित्य है ही नहीं पर जो विद्वानों, शोधकर्ताओं के काम की चीज है यदि उन्होंने कर दिया कि ऐसा आज तक देखने में नहीं आया तो हम सफल हुए। मुझे विश्वास है कि संस्थान के द्वारा [illegible] नहीं होगा। साहित्य के बारे में [illegible] [illegible] [illegible] हो उन [illegible] और [illegible] उत्तम यदि [illegible] हो तो [illegible] होगा।

५- पांचवां प्रश्न यह है कि आगे कौन? या आगे क्या? मैं मानता हूँ कि कोई तो व्यक्ति मिलेगा जो इस कार्य को संभाल ले। प्रिय सुरेश को और पुत्री कुसुम को अपने परिवार से, और प्रिय [illegible] जी को प्रिय [illegible] जी को [illegible] [illegible]। अब आप इस सत्य से तो परिचित ही हैं [illegible] कुसुम का जीवन [illegible] के लिये अर्पित है।

हाँ आपने अपने पहले पत्र में जो भारत से लौटते समय लिखा था और कुसुम के बारे में लिखा था कि वह अब आपकी छाया में रह कर आपकी [illegible] छाया बन जाए। [illegible] तो मैं नहीं [illegible] छाया में रहने वाला पौधा पनप नहीं पाता। [illegible] तो मैं भी हूँ परन्तु अभी वह परिपक्व नहीं हुई [illegible] [illegible] ही [illegible] शीघ्र ही कोई उपाय करूँगा।

६- [illegible] जो आपने १००० की राशि भेजी है और [illegible] है वह उत्तम है। यह राशि कम से कम एक लाख तक पहुँच जाए तो उत्तम है अधिक हो तो और उत्तम होगा। उन के पुत्र, पौत्र, प्रपौत्र, [illegible] पौत्रियां सभी सहयोग करें तो कुछ भी बात नहीं मैं भी प्रयत्न करूँगा। आज प्रिय मोहन, प्रिय [illegible] और प्रिय [illegible] आने वाले हैं। उन से मैं बात चलाऊँगा कि बाल [illegible] जी के नाम पर बाल-प्रकाशन [illegible] बनाकर बाल साहित्य तैयार कराया जाए जो बच्चों के लिये उपयोगी होगा। आज जब मैं पत्र लिख रहा था तो मोहन जी आए और उनके सामने आपका प्रस्ताव रखा और यह भी कहा कि आपका इसमें कितना भाग होगा। यदि सब मिलकर पच्चीस हजार प्रत्येक दे तो २५ में [illegible] और एक लाख हो जाएगा जिससे १ हजार प्रतिमास मिलेगा और बाल साहित्य तैयार हो जाएगा।

२

Telephone [illegible] ओ३म् दूरभाष—[illegible]

समर्पण शोध संस्थान

SAMARPANA SODHA SAMSTHANA

A Trust and an Institute dedicated to oriental research.

संस्थान के उद्देश्य

शोध

TRUSTS OBJECTIVES

Research

★ Field of enquiry restricted to vedic lore, welcoming any topical question demanding a study in depth

★ Method: Traditional approach with an open mind and accept the knowledge gained to put into realistic practice.

★ Unresolved aspects arising during the course of research, are to be resolved with comparative methods of modern science

प्रकाशन

Publications

★ To publish unpublished studies in Indology, the great classics and masterpieces of historical science. Encourage publications of new works

क० सं०
Ref. No.

[illegible] आर्य समाज, करोल बाग
[illegible] नई दिल्ली-११०००५

७ – अब आप भाष्य की चर्चा कर ही चुका हूँ इसके अतिरिक्त सामवेदभाष्य भी छप रहा है यह भाष्य भी अपने ढंग का अद्वितीय होगा इस पर आनुमानिक व्यय दो लाख आंका गया है। वेदों के छपवाने में सब से बड़ी कठिनाई स्वरों की है, सारी दिल्ली में एक ही प्रेस है जिसमें सामभाष्य छप रहा है और वह साल में ५२० पृष्ठ ही छापे हैं। आपको जानकर आश्चर्यमय हर्ष होगा कि [illegible] ने इस कठिनाई को समझा और कम्प्यूटर [illegible] प्रेस लगाने का निश्चय कर लिया उसने दो लाख का व्यय उठा कर प्रेस लगा दिया आज दिसम्बर में उसका प्रेस है जो वेद छाप रहा है। सामवेदभाष्य के उत्तरार्चिक का प्रथम पृष्ठ फोटो स्टेट कराकर भिजवा रहा हूँ इस में अभी और सुधार होगा जिसको पसन्द आएगा।

८ – इसके साथ कुछ श्री पं० [illegible] जी एम.ए. के दो ग्रन्थ [illegible] हिन्दी [illegible] छपवा रहा हूँ उसमें प्रथम पुस्तक वैदिक [illegible] है और दूसरी पुस्तक 'तीन अनादि तत्त्व' है। वैदिक [illegible] और योगेश्वर कृष्ण का [illegible] भी चल रहा है अब उत्तम कोटि का साहित्य निकलता ही रहेगा। [illegible] D.Litt. करने को लगा ही रहा है। मैं भी लेख कुछ न कुछ लिखने में लगा ही रहता हूँ। ईशोपनिषद् पर मैं विशेष लिखना चाहता हूँ।

९ – एक और विषय में जानकारी देना चाह रहा हूँ कि जब महर्षि दयानन्द के दिवंगत होने पर गुरुदत्त विद्यार्थी [illegible] ने इंग्लिश में वैदिक मैगज़ीन नामक पत्रिका निकलनी शुरू की थी उस समय के यूरोप और अमेरिका के बड़े बड़े व्यक्तियों के पास जाती थी रूस में लियो टाल्सटाय की निजी लाइब्रेरी में वैदिक मैगज़ीन की फाइलें आज यात्रियों को दर्शनार्थ रखी जाती हैं और उस पर लिखी गई टिप्पणियाँ [illegible] लिये आज भी दर्शकों को [illegible] करती हैं। गुरुकुल कांगड़ी में उसकी फाइलें सुरक्षित हैं उनका [illegible] अपनी लाइब्रेरी में रखवा रहा हूँ। कभी आपको [illegible] हो सकेगा।

१० – आपको यह जानकर अत्यन्त हर्ष होगा मुझे [illegible] आर्य समाज से निमंत्रण देने के लिए वहाँ से एक [illegible] आए और निश्चय कर गये हैं कि वहाँ के वेद सम्मेलन में आपने वेद पर बोलना है और [illegible] है। १५ जौलाई [illegible] अन्तिम [illegible] तक रहने का विचार है यदि और भी [illegible] रहा तो सोचूंगा।

Dedicated Oriental Research

(४)

११- गोडों के दर्द का सुनकर कुछ चिन्ता हुई आप क्या इलाज कर रहे हैं
मुझे तो नमक छोड़ने चिकनी चीजों के छोड़ने से बड़ा लाभ होता है
जब खाने लगता हूँ तो शुरू होने लगता है। आप दो महीने के लिए छोड़
कर देखें। आपने मेरे लिए जो गोडों पर बांधने के लिए भेजे हैं वह
गोडे को पूरी तरह नहीं कसते उसके किनारे फीते कम होने से ?
अधिक कहते हैं। आप गोडों का व्यायाम तो करते ही होंगे। अब
तो एक लिस्ट साइकल आती है उसको चलाना चलकर गोडों का व्यायाम
करता रहे तो लाभ होता है।

१२- प्रमोद की पत्नी अपने भाई के विवाह में गई हुई है उसको बेबी अनल
के समाचार मिल ही जाएंगे। सारे भारतवर्ष से आए युवकों का संघ
बेबी अनल के प्रभाव का फल था। श्री ... लोकसभा में
अखिल युवा चौपाल। सम्पूर्ण क्रान्ति अब नारा है, भावी इतिहास
हमारा है। १२ फरवरी से १६ फरवरी तक रहा मैं १२ फरवरी को
उद्घाटन समारोह में सम्मिलित हुआ था प्रधान मंत्री चन्द्रशेखर
जी ने उद्घाटन भाषण दिया था क्या है कुछ कह नहीं सकते क्यों
बेबी अनल से हम खुलकर विचार करने का विचार है।
शेष दिन तो मैं नहीं जा सका।

१३- आपका वैदिक गणित विषयक शोध क्या कुछ आगे
अथवा आगे कुछ मार्ग मिल रहा है या नहीं। मेरे पास जो
सामग्री थी वह आप तक पहुंचा दी थी। अब और
अधिक क्या पत्र को समाप्त करता हूँ।

भवदीय पिता
वेदानन्द सरस्वती
१८-२-९१

[illegible]
Sahibabad.
25th May 1996
8/6/96

प्रिय पुत्र सतीश,

सस्नेह आशीर्वाद।

मैं आज ही श्री आर्य नरेश द्वारा संस्थापित [illegible] साधना स्थली से लौटा तो अपनी डाक में आपका [illegible] 12/5/96 का लिखा हुआ पत्र प्राप्त हुआ। लगभग 10 दिनों के पश्चात फिर मुझे वापस वहाँ जाना पड़ेगा। सम्भवतः [illegible] मैंने आपको बताया होगा कि प्रतिवर्ष मई-जून महीनों में प्रशिक्षण शिविर का आयोजन होता है और वह मेरी ही अध्यक्षता में सम्पन्न होता है। मेरे साथ मेरी कुसुम और दिवाकर [illegible] प्रतिवर्ष जाते हैं। लगभग 25-30 व्यक्ति विभिन्न स्थानों से आकर प्रशिक्षण लेते हैं।

मेरी प्रशिक्षण शैली को लोग अत्यधिक पसन्द करते हैं। कोई कितना ही पढ़ा हो लेकिन मेरे प्रशिक्षण के बिना उनकी [illegible] नहीं होती। 20 वर्ष की आयु से लेकर 60 वर्ष तक के लोग जो बड़े व्यापारी, वकील, इंजीनियर होते हैं, बड़े उत्साह से भाग लेते हैं। कभी वह दृश्य भी देखने को मिले तो आनन्द होगा।

संस्थान के परिसर में डी. ए. वी. स्कूल सेक्टर [illegible] में है। आज सारे भारत वर्ष के डी. ए. वी. संस्थाओं के अध्यापक प्रिंसीपल एकत्रित हो और उस सम्मेलन का उद्घाटन भाषण मुझे देना था। प्रभु कृपा से वह भाषण अत्यन्त प्रभावशाली रहा। सम्मेलन में विचार हुआ कि डी. ए. वी. संस्थाओं के [illegible] तथा गुण का [illegible] किया जाए। इसके लिए प्रिंसीपल और अध्यापकों को धर्म शिक्षा, नैतिक शिक्षा प्रशिक्षण शिविर लगाकर योग्य किया जाए। इसके लिए मेरा नाम प्रस्तावित किया गया। मैं अभी जून की 24 तारीख से जुलाई की 4 तारीख तक इसी प्रशिक्षण देने के लिए पटना जा रहा हूँ। वहाँ पर पुत्री [illegible] मन्जु व अनिल जी से भेंट करूँगा। हो सके तो उन्हें पत्र लिख देना मेरे पास उनका पता नहीं है।

संस्थान ने अभी "वेदामृत" और "वेदों का यथार्थ स्वरूप" दो उत्कृष्ट ग्रन्थों का प्रकाशन किया है। वेदों का यथार्थ स्वरूप बम्बई के के. एम. मुंशी जी द्वारा संस्थापित "भारतीय विद्या भवन" से प्रकाशित वैदिक [illegible] का स्टीक [illegible] उत्तर है। वैदिक [illegible] ग्रन्थ

विश्वविद्यालयों कॉलेजों में पढ़ाई जाती है जिसे पढ़कर भारतीय व्यक्ति नास्तिक बन जाता है। अपनी संस्कृति एवं वेद के प्रति अश्रद्धा हो जाती है। उसका उत्तर देना आवश्यक था। इसके उत्तर में लिखी गई पुस्तक वेदों का यथार्थ स्वरूप पढ़ेंगे तो आपको वेद ज्ञान मिल जाएगा।

आपने अपने पत्र में पुरुष सूक्त का जिक्र किया है। नि:सन्देह वह शोध प्रबन्ध अपने आप में अद्वितीय है। हो सकता है कि कोई उससे उत्तम शोध कार्य कर दिखाये परन्तु अभी तक तो नहीं की है यह तो उस ग्रन्थ पर आई विद्वानों की सम्मति से ज्ञात होता है। मैं चाहता हूँ कि वेदों के २०, २५ सूक्तों पर उसी कोटि के कार्य हों परन्तु विद्वानों का अभाव है। पृथ्वी सूक्त को कन्या सूक्त पर कार्य करने को लगा रखा हुआ है देखो कब पूरा होता है।

आपने श्रीकृष्ण मूर्ति के कुछ कागज भेजे हैं उनमें और मेरे विचारों में समानता है उसके बारे में लिखा है। मेरा श्रीकृष्ण मूर्ति से क्या मुकाबला वह विश्व प्रसिद्ध व्यक्ति हैं और मैं भारत के एक कोने में भी नहीं जाना जाता फिर भी आपने मुझे उनके साथ जोड़ा है ईश्वर मुझे शक्ति दे कि मैं कुछ कर सकूँ। श्रीकृष्ण मूर्ति प्रत्येक भाषा पर अधिकार था और वह धारा प्रवाह इंग्लिश में बोल सकते थे मुझे तो संस्कृत हिन्दी पर भी अधिकार नहीं है। वह तो कुछ परमात्मा की देन है कि मेरा चिन्तन प्रत्येक व्यक्ति को मोहित कर लेता है। मेरा समय तो अब समाप्त हो रहा है अब तो आप की पीढ़ी का काम है कि वह वैसा करती है मैंने अपने सन्देश में अपनी अभिव्यक्ति की है।

अब विक्रम सम्वत २०४३ चल रहा है इस वर्ष को मैंने मनु वर्ष घोषित किया है अतः हर महीने मनु पर एक एक लेख लिख छपवा रहा हूँ। पूरा वर्ष अर्थात १२ महीने एक एक अंक निकालने का निश्चय है। यदि आपके यहाँ अथवा वहाँ के पुस्तकालयों में मनु पर कुछ कार्य हो तो मुझे सूचित करना। इन्साइक्लोपीडिया ब्रिटेनिका आदि पर मनु पर कुछ मैटर हो तो भिजवाना। अथवा जौलाई में जब आओ तो लेते आना।

ओ३म्

डी०ए०वी० कालेज प्रबन्धकर्त्री समिति, नई दिल्ली

के तत्त्वावधान में

अखिल भारतीय संगोष्ठी

विषय : "आर्य समाज का डी०ए०वी० में योगदान"

स्थान : डी०ए०वी० पब्लिक स्कूल, सैक्टर-2, टी०एच०ए०, राजेन्द्र नगर, साहिबाबाद, गाजियाबाद (उ०प्र०)

दिनांक : शनिवार 25-5-1996 प्रातः 10 बजे से 1 बजे

उद्घाटन : **स्वामी दीक्षानन्द जी सरस्वती**, अध्यक्ष, समर्पण शोध संस्थान, राजेन्द्र नगर, गाजियाबाद।

अध्यक्षता : **श्री ज्ञान प्रकाश चोपड़ा**, प्रधान डी०ए०वी० कालेज प्रबन्धकर्त्री समिति एवं आर्य प्रादेशिक प्रतिनिधि सभा।

विशिष्ट वक्ता :

श्री एम०एल० सेखड़ी, संगठन सचिव, डी०ए०वी० कालेज प्रबन्धकर्त्री समिति, नई दिल्ली।

श्री तिलकराज गुप्ता, सचिव, डी०ए०वी० कालेज प्रबन्धकर्त्री समिति।

श्री एम०एल० खन्ना, वरिष्ठ उप-प्रधान, डी०ए०वी० कालेज प्रबन्धकर्त्री समिति, नई दिल्ली।

श्री डॉ० सर्वदानन्द आर्य, कुलपति, चौधरी चरण सिंह, कृषि विश्वविद्यालय, हिसार।

श्री डॉ० वी० कुलवन्त, रीजनल डायरेक्टर, नॉर्थ बिहार। मैं इनके निमन्त्रण पर पटना जा रहा हूँ / 28 जून

श्रीमती चित्रा नाकरा, प्रिंसीपल, डी०ए०वी० पब्लिक स्कूल, विकासपुरी।

भारत भर के सभी डी०ए०वी० के प्राचार्यों से विनम्र प्रार्थना है कि इस संगोष्ठी में अपने सहयोगी अध्यापकों के साथ अवश्य सम्मिलित हों। गोष्ठी में सम्मिलित होने वाले सभी प्राचार्यों व अध्यापकों के आवास एवं भोजन आदि की व्यवस्था संगोष्ठी स्थल पर शुक्रवार 24-5-1996 रात्रि से लेकर 26-5-1996 की रात्रि तक उपलब्ध रहेगी। आपसे अनुरोध है कि अपने आने की पूर्व सूचना गोष्ठी के सह-संयोजक प्रिंसीपल श्री अशोक कुमार चावला को उक्त पते पर देने की कृपा करें। हमें पूर्ण विश्वास है कि आप अपने सहयोगियों के साथ इसमें अवश्य सम्मिलित होंगे।

रामनाथ सहगल	**बी०वी० गरखड़**	**अशोक कुमार चावला**
संयोजक	संगठन सचिव, (प० स्कूल) डी०ए०वी० कालेज प्रबन्धकर्त्री समिति, वरिष्ठ उप-प्रधान आ०प्रा०प्र० सभा	सह-संयोजक

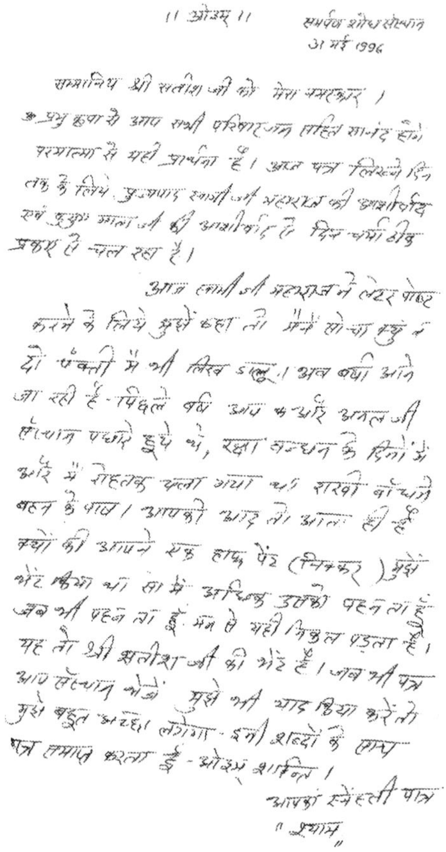

॥ ओउम् ॥ समर्पण शोध संस्थान
31 मई 1996

सम्माननीय श्री सतीश जी को मेरा नमस्कार।
प्रभु कृपा से आप सभी परिवारजन सहित सानंद होंगे परमात्मा से यही प्रार्थना है। आज पत्र लिखने के लिये पूज्यपाद स्वामी जी महाराज की आशीर्वाद एवं पूज्य माता जी की आशीर्वाद से दिनचर्या ठीक प्रकार से चल रहा है।

आज स्वामी जी महाराज ने लेटर पोस्ट करने के लिये मुझे कहा तो मैंने सोचा कुछ न दो पंक्ती मैं भी लिख डालूं। अब वर्षा आने जा रही है - पिछले वर्ष आप और अजल जी संस्थान पधारे हुये थे, रक्षा बन्धन के दिनों में और मैं रोहतक चला गया था शारदा [illegible] बहन के पास। आपकी याद तो आती ही है क्यों की आपने एक हाफ पेंट (निक्कर) मुझे भेंट किया था तो मैं अधिकतर उसको पहनता हूं अब भी पहनता हूं मन से यही निकल पड़ता है, यह तो श्री सतीश जी की भेंट है। जब भी पत्र आप संस्थान भेजें मुझे भी याद किया करें तो मुझे बहुत अच्छा लगेगा - इन्हीं शब्दों के साथ पत्र समाप्त करता हूं - ओउम् शान्ति।

आपका स्नेही पात्र
"श्याम"

Life is strange-how a small piece of gift and memory can make a long term impact on another person.

Mama Ji supported many persons, who come with a remoter reference some times, would start living with him and do little things for him. To the best of my memory he never said that a particular person cheated him.

Shyam was one of them. Amongst the chores he did was one to take dictation from Mama Ji for various letters and correspondence. The next letter is in his hand writing.

5/2/97
मुम्बई से
२५ जनवरी १९९७
इसके पश्चात् संस्थान में १

प्रिय पुत्र सतीश, आनन्दित रहो।

आशा है आप सपरिवार स्वस्थ एवं सानंद होंगे। आपका पत्र वायुयान,
रेलगाड़ी का सैर करता हुआ प्रिय राजन् के घर मुंबई में मिला। इसी प्रकार
कुछ दिन पहले प्रिय जोशी प्रिय अनिल यहीं इस घर में पधारे थे। उनसे आपको
यह पता लग गया होगा कि मैं आजकल मुम्बई में क्यों आया हुआ
हूँ। इन विशेष कारणों के अतिरिक्त एक कारण यह भी था कि दिल्ली
की सर्दी से बचकर मुंबई बैठकर काम कर लूंगा। विशेष कारण तो
जोशी से पता चल चुके होंगे। कुछ सन्देह इस लिये है कि आपके
पत्र में उसका ज़िक्र नहीं है। सबसे बड़ा कारण यह है कि मेरी
कुसुम ब्लड कैंसर जैसे भयंकर रोग से ग्रस्त हो गई है। दूसरा मेरी
दाहिनी आँख का आप्रेशन था वह आप्रेशन लगभग सवा साल
से आज कल, करते करते, टल रहा था इसी १८ जनवरी को
मेरी आँख का आप्रेशन सफलता पूर्वक सम्पन्न हो गया।
ईश्वर को शत् शत् धन्यवाद। जैसे मेरे आँखों का आप्रेशन
सवा वर्ष से टल रहा था, मैं समझता हूँ कि वैसे ही हम
लोगों की, मेरी कुसुम की अज्ञानता वश उसके रोग का
परिज्ञान भी टलता रहा, पाँच साल से किसी को इसकी
भनक भी नहीं थी. इस का भान तब हुआ कि जब पिछले
नवम्बर मास में प्रिय राजन् की बेटी की विवाह पर न आ सकी
बहुत चाहते हुये भी न आ सकी। तब जयपुर के भाई बहनों
को फिकर हुई और ईश्वर कृपा से भी, हम सब जयपुर पहुँच गये सब
प्रकार के टेस्ट करवाये अन्तत: यह रोग पकड़ में आया। यह कारण
था इसे बम्बई लाने का पुन: टाटा इन्स्टीट्यूशन में टेस्ट हुआ
और वहाँ के टेस्ट में भी वही परिणाम मिला। भारत में कई स्थानों
पर इसकी आयुर्वेदिक चिकित्सा होती है। इसी के आधार पर
दो महीने से आयुर्वेदिक चिकित्सा चल रही है। जिस सेकुद
लाभ है। वह भी अपना काम पूर्ववत् करती है, इसकी आत्म-
विश्वास और ईश्वर विश्वास बड़ा प्रबल है। उसका तो एक ही
मन्त्र है। अब सौंप दिया इस जीवन को सब भार तुम्हारे हाथों
में है जीत तुम्हारे हाथों में और हार तुम्हारे हाथों में।
परसों की ही बात है। —

कि उसे तीन दिन से बुखार (ज्वर) आ रहा था। प्रिय राजन् ने कहा कल तुम्हें डाक्टर को दिखना होगा। उसने कहा भाई साहब एक दिन रुक जाओ फिर ज्वर आया तो अवश्य ले जाना। रात्री को देखा गया ज्वर नहीं था फिर ले जाने का सवाल नहीं। इस प्रकार औषधि के साथ आत्म विश्वास से कोई चमत्कार हो जाये कुछ कहा नहीं जा सकता हम यही गाते हैं इस पार तुम्हारे हाथों में उस पार तुम्हारे हाथों में। प्रिय पुत्र इन दिनों मुम्बई रहते हुये मेरे कार्य की प्रगति दुगनी हो गई है। परन्तु कुछ न कुछ लिखते पढ़ते हैं। कुसुम के मन में भी अथर्व वेद के "केन" सूक्त पर रिसर्च करने पर तबियत मचल रही है देखो ईश्वर क्या करवाता है। सोचा है कि क्या भरोसा जिन्दगानी का

अभी १८ तारीख को मेरे आँखों का आप्रेशन सफल होगया। तब से पढ़ना लिखना बन्द कर रखा है। अपने ओर से डाक्टर ने कुछ बूंद देदी थी लेकिन बाहर के प्रोग्राम कब हम होने देते हैं। चार दिन पहले जोधपुर के मेयर ने FEX फैक्स द्वारा दश पन्नों का एक पत्र भेज दिया। जिसमें उन्होंने प्रार्थना कि की नगर निगम की ओर से आपके गुरु जी के शतपथ ब्राह्मण भाष्य पर एक संगोष्ठी होगी जिसके ग्यारह विषय हैं। इस में आपको आना होगा। जिसकी तारीखें ४.५.६ फरवरी हैं। परसों २५ तारीख को मैं दिल्ली के लिये प्रस्थान करूँगा। २६,२७.२८ रहकर २८ को सायं ५ बजे जयपुर के लिए चल दूंगा और एक रात्रि रुक कर जोधपुर पहुंच जाऊँगा। जहाँ जाकर मुझे यह सब प्रबन्ध करना होगा फिर इसी फरवरी महिने में २६,२७,२८ को उदयपुर में सत्यार्थ प्रकाश, शब्द, और राजर्षि मनु पर विशेष सम्मेलन होगा। यहीं बैठ कर महर्षि दयानंद स्वामी ने सत्यार्थ प्रकाश लिखा था। मार्च ७ से १४ तारीख तक मुझे अमृतसर जाना है। वहाँ की गर्ल्स कालेज की प्रिंसिपल श्रीमती [illegible] ने वहाँ के छात्रों एवं अध्यापकों को विशेषतया परिशिक्षण देने के लिये बुलाया है। प्रिय चौबीस मार्च होली पर अपने संस्थान का उत्सव मनायेंगे। आपने अपने पत्र में यह लिखा है कि संस्थान का यह स्थान लोगों की पहुँच से दूर है। इसलिये दिल्ली की ओर संस्थान बनाना चाहिये। [illegible] जी [illegible] भक्त निमन्त्रण भी देते हैं, और कहते हैं आपका सहयोग करेंगे। प्रिय सतीश आप ही बताओ, मैं इन सब परिस्थितियों में घिर गया हूँ। किस प्रकार किस आशा पर यह सब उधेड़ बुन करूँ। मेरे पीछे इन सब को कौन सम्भालेगा। ईश्वर

संभालने वाला संस्कृति और इंग्लिश का प्रधान विद्वान् होना चाहिये, विद्वान होने के साथ साथ मेरी स्तर की सुध-बुध होना भी आवश्यक है। ऐसा आदमी कहाँ मिलेगा, ब्रह्मर्षि सातलेकर जी के पश्चात् सब कार्य ठप हो गया। इसके लिए एक परम्परा की जरूरत है योजना का लिए होने चाहिये। परम्परा का तो यह हाल है जो हमने ऊपर वर्णित किया। प्रिय सुरेश को इसलिये संस्कृति विषय दिलवाकर एम॰ए॰ कराया जिसके लिए आप सहमत न थे परन्तु वह पँछि हाथों से निकल कर उड़ गया। पुत्री कुसुम ने भी अपनी बड़ी बहन श्यामा की बेटी शशि को गोद लिया और उसे अंग्रेजी में विशेष परिशिक्षण दिलवाया और उसने बड़ी योग्यता प्राप्त की यहां तक की पुत्री कुसुम से भी आगे बढ़ गई आजकल वह जयपुर में रहकर पी॰एच॰डी लिख रही है। यह कहानी तो अपनी घर की है। जिसकी आशा धूमिल हो रही है।

बाहर के व्यक्ति न रुचि लेते हैं, न उनकी योग्यता होती है। अब क्या कहानी लिखूँ, ईश्वर ही कोई रास्ता बतायेंगे इसी में आशा है। इस बार प्रिय सुरेश आने वाला पर ओह न हो सका। उसका एक पत्र कुसुम के नाम वह एक सहसा प्राप्त हुआ। पत्र को पढ़कर कुसुम को तसल्ली हुई। परिवार में सभी बच्चों को मेरा प्यार भरा नमस्कार कहना।

यह पत्र मैं अपने शिष्य श्याम से लिखवा रहा हूँ, कोई भूल हो तो सुधार लेना। और रूप की ओर से भी आपको नमस्ते।

[illegible]

ओ३म्

समर्पण शोध संस्थान

SAMARPANA SODHA SAMSTHANA

A Trust and an Institute dedicated to oriental research

Arya Samaj, Karol Bagh
NEW DELHI 110005

आर्य समाज, करोल बाग
नई दिल्ली ११०००५

क्र० सं०
Ref. No

संस्थान के उद्देश्य
शोध
TRUSTS OBJECTIVES
Research

प्रकाशन
Publications

1/7/95

प्रिय पुत्र सतीश,

सस्नेह आशीर्वाद,

आपका मलेशिया से लिखा हुआ 17 जून का पत्र 26 जून को संस्थान में मिला। पत्र पाकर हार्दिक प्रसन्नता हुई। प्रसन्नता इस लिये कि पुत्र ने पिता को चुनौती दी है और उस चुनौती का परिणाम पिता की परम्परा में संस्कृत एवं वैदिक प्रशिक्षण में आगे बढ़ना है। यदि आप इस प्रशिक्षण द्वारा मुझे हरा देंगे तो मैं अपना सौभाग्य मानूंगा। शास्त्र का कथन है कि सब जगह जीत की कामना करो, परन्तु पुत्र से हारने की कामना करो। "सर्वत्र जयमन्विच्छेत् पुत्रादिच्छेत् पराजयम्" यह संस्कृत सीखने की इच्छा कुछ विलम्ब से हुई।

मैं यत्र तत्र जिन शिविरों का आयोजन करता हूं उनमें तीन बातें रहती हैं- 1- संस्कृत 2- संस्कृति 3- स्वाध्याय। आपने मेरे भावों को इस प्रकार लिया है कि संस्कृत के साथ संस्कृति पर भी मनन करें। क्या पता कि मैं ही आपसे पढ़ने लगूं, यह बात इतिहास प्रसिद्ध है कि जब वाचस्पति मिश्र नामक बालक जब गुरु से पढ़ रहा था तब उसने अपने पिताजी को लिखा कि आजकल मैं अपने गुरुजी को पढ़ा रहा हूं। पिताजी इस पत्र को पढ़कर अति प्रसन्न हुआ और कहा कि देखो मेरा बेटा विद्वान् योग्य है कि गुरु को पढ़ा रहा है। आगे चलकर वही वाचस्पति मिश्र जब विद्यालय के आचार्य बने तब पुनः अपने पिता को पत्र लिखा कि आजकल मैं शिष्यों से पढ़ रहा हूं। वही क्या मेरे साथ घटित होगी कि, जब आप हम इकट्ठे बैठेंगे कि सम्भवतः मुझे कहना पड़े कि आजकल मैं पुत्र सतीश से पढ़ रहा हूं।

मैं 15 जुलाई को दिल्ली में लौट आऊंगा फिर संस्थान में आपके साथ मिल बैठूंगा। उस समय जो परस्पर चर्चा होगी उसी का नाम उपनिषद् होगा। क्या आप इस बात की स्वीकृति देंगे कि, इस पठन पाठन में क्या अन्य व्यक्ति भी सम्मिलित हो सकेंगे।

इस बार श्री आचार्य नरेश जी के उद्गीथ साधना स्थली, टोहर (हिमाचलप्रदेश) में 4 जून से 14 जून तक 10 दिन तक शिविर का आयोजन किया जो कि अत्यन्त सफल रहा। उनमें से कुछ व्यक्ति सम्भवतः आपके साथ बैठना चाहें।

सम्भवतः आपको यह ज्ञात होगा कि यहाँ अपने गुरु के नाम पर 'समर्पण शोध संस्थान' चला रहा हूं। वहां अपनी शिष्या कुसुमलता के नाम पर 'कुसुमलता आर्य प्रतिष्ठान' बनाकर उसके संचालन का बीड़ा उठा रहा हूं। 'समर्पण शोध संस्थान' के अन्तर्गत लगभग अब तक 40 पुस्तकें प्रकाशित कर चुका हूं और 'कुसुमलता आर्य प्रतिष्ठान' के अन्तर्गत लगभग इस वर्ष 20 छोटी बड़ी पुस्तकें निकालने का संकल्प है। सम्भवतः 17 ता० को 5 पुस्तकें देखने को मिल सकेंगी। आर्य प्रतिष्ठान के उद्देश्यों में यह उद्देश्य भी रखे हैं, कि जो छात्रा संस्कृत और वेद के लिए समर्पित हो उनको उच्च शिक्षा प्राप्त कराने के लिए छात्रवृत्ति देना, और दूसरे यह कि, जिन्होंने 'पुरुष सूक्त' की भाँति वेद विषय लेकर पी०एच०डी० किया है, उनके शोध प्रबंधों को प्रकाशित करवाना। तीसरे विधवा एवं असमर्थ कन्याओं के विवाह में योगदान करना।

आपको यह जानकर प्रसन्नता होगी कि डी.ए.वी मैनेजिंग कमेटी के प्रबन्धकर्त्ता सभा यह सोच रही है, कि डी.ए.वी के लेक्चरर, प्रोफेसर आदि को भी मेरे द्वारा धार्मिक, सैद्धान्तिक व नैतिक प्रशिक्षण दिलाया जाय। जहां तक डी०ए०वी पब्लिक स्कूलों में प्रशिक्षण देकर उन्हें तैयार करता हूं। अभी पिछले मास अम्बाला, चण्डीगढ़, सूरजपुर और जम्मू के स्कूलों में प्रशिक्षण देकर आया हूं। सितम्बर मास के आरम्भ में पुनः चण्डीगढ़ सेक्टर 7 में हो रहे शिविर में जाऊँगा और जुलाई मास के 6 ता० से 13 तक कटनी (मध्यप्रदेश) के स्कूल के छात्रों एवं अध्यापकों को प्रशिक्षण देने जा रहा हूं। वहां के रिजनल डायरेक्टर श्री वाचस्पति कुलवन्त मेरे और मेरे संस्थान से अतिशय जुड़े हुए हैं। उन्होंने ही जयपुर के पास हाईवे पर संस्थान के लिये भूमिदान देने का प्रस्ताव रखा है, जिसे मैंने अभी तक स्वीकार नहीं किया। वे इसी महीने के 21 व 22 ता० को संस्थान आये थे। मैंने उनके सामने प्रस्ताव रखा था, मैं अब वृद्ध हो चला हूं, इसलिये संस्थान के भविष्य के बारे में चिन्ता करनी चाहिये, जिससे इस विषय पर विचार करने के लिये एक सहयोगी सहानुभूति रखने वाले व्यक्तियों की बैठक 5 जुलाई को बुलाई है। उनसे सम्पर्क करके एवं पत्र व्यवहार करने के लिए श्री स्वामी चक्रपाणि जी को नियुक्त किया गया है। इसका परिणाम आप 17 ता० को सुन सकेंगे। मैं शरीर से अवश्य बूढ़ा हो गया हूं, परन्तु मन से जवान हूं। आप जैसे पुत्रों का सहयोग रहा तो यह संस्था विश्व स्तर की बन सकती है।

मैं मुम्बई प्रिय स्व० जानकी ज्ञानस्वरूप के पुत्री के न केवल विवाह में गया ही था, अपितु प्रिय राजन ने उनके ठहरने आदि का सारा प्रबंध करवा दिया था। यदि ये सहयोग न होता तो मुंबई जैसे शहर में बड़ी कठिनाई हो जाती। इसमें प्रिय राजन को बधाई पत्र देना चाहिये।

That is the way the letter ended-clearly it was dictated.

समर्पण शोध संस्थान

[illegible] साहिबाबाद (गाज़ियाबाद) उ. प्र. [illegible]

क्र. सं.: ....

तिथि [illegible]
6/12/99

संस्थान के उद्देश्य

शोध

* शोध का क्षेत्र: [illegible]
Field of enquiry restricted to vedic lore, welcoming any topical question demanding a study in depth.

* शोध-प्रणाली: [illegible]
Method: Traditional approach with an open mind and accept the knowledge gained to put in to realistic practice.

* [illegible]
Unresolved aspects: arising during the course of research, are to be resolved with comparative methods of modern science.

प्रकाशन

* [illegible]
Publications. To publish unpublished studies in indology. Re-print classics and masterpieces of historical science. Encourage publications of new works.

प्रिय पुत्र सतीश, सस्नेह आशीर्वाद।

आशा है सपरिवार आप स्वस्थ एवम् सानन्द होंगे।

आपका पत्र यथासमय मिल गया था। सब समाचार विदित हुए। प्रिय पुत्री बेबी और [illegible] कल सकुशल संस्थान पहुँच गए थे। बेबी को आपके लिए पत्र लिखते देख मुझे भी उत्साह हो आया। मेरा स्वास्थ्य ठीक नहीं है। पिछले [illegible] से मैं [illegible] के सहारे गाड़ी को खींच रहा हूँ। वैसे भी आयु का ८४ वाँ वर्ष आरम्भ हो चुका है। जीवन भर प्राणायामादि यौगिक क्रियाओं से बचता रहा हूँ। रात दिन स्वाध्याय, मनन, वेदों पर शोध-कार्य इत्यादि चलता रहा। श्रीमद् भगवद् गीता का पाठ तो नित्य होता रहा परन्तु उसके अनुरूप आचरण कभी नहीं किया। उसका फल तो भोगना ही होगा। परमात्मा यदि ६-८ साल का समय और दे दे तो अनुग्रह हो। जो काम बाकी रह गए हैं, उन्हें कर पाऊँगा।

आप यहाँ रहते हुए भी सदा चिन्तित रहते हैं कि हम मामा जी न रहेंगे तो उसके आगे संस्थान का क्या होगा। यह प्रश्न मेरे सामने भी सदैव बना रहता है। इसी के आधार पर मैंने पिछले दिनों एक मित्रों की सभा बुलाई और उनसे साग्रह निवेदन किया कि इस संस्थान को आप संभाल लें, इस पर उनकी जो प्रतिक्रिया हुई उसे आपके अवलोकनार्थ अविकल लिखकर भेज रहा हूँ इस पर विचार कीजिये। और अपने विचार से मुझे सूचित कीजिए और अब जब जौलाई में यहाँ आएँगे तो इस पर खुलकर विचार हो सकेगा। इस [illegible] समूह के प्रधान आप ही के साथ वाले [illegible] सतीश [illegible] हैं। इस विद्वत् समाज की ओर से लिखा हुआ पत्र अधोलिखित है :—

SAMARPANA SODHA SAMSTHANA, 4/42, Sector 5, Rajendra Nagar, Sahibabad (Ghaziabad) U.P. 201005 Ph. 91-623026
AN ORGANISATION PURELY DEDICATED TO ORIENTAL RESEARCH

श्रद्धेय स्वामी जी! सादर नमस्ते। प्रभु कृपा एवं आपके आशीर्वाद से सपरिवार ठीक हूँ। पिछले काफी दिनों से आर्ष शोध संस्थान की गतिविधियों में साथ सम्मिलित होने [illegible] की चर्चा आपसे होती रही है। जैसा कि मौखिक रूप से मैं आपकी जानकारी में ला चुका हूँ कि विभिन्न आर्ष संस्थाओं के कुछ समर्पणशील युवा स्नातक संयुक्त-रूप से वैदिक साहित्य पर महर्षि दयानन्द की दृष्टि से आधुनिक शोध-प्रविधियों के साथ शोध-कार्य करने के लिए उत्सुक हैं। मैं स्वयं भी इस स्नातक मण्डल का एक सदस्य हूँ।

मैंने आपसे प्रथम चर्चा में भी यही कहा था कि आप किसी एक व्यक्ति को समस्त अधिकार न सौंपकर एक समूह को संस्थान की व्यवस्था अथवा सञ्चालन का अधिकार दें। इस विषय में मैंने आपको इन स्नातकों से भी बातचीत का सुझाव दिया था। आपने यह उत्तरदायित्व मुझे सौंपा। अतः इन सभी मित्रों के मध्य मैंने आपसे हुई बातचीत को रखा। संस्थान के साथ संयुक्त होने की सभी स्नातकों की सहमति है। संस्थान के साथ संयुक्त होकर जो कार्य यह स्नातक समूह करना चाहता है आपके आदेशानुसार उसकी संक्षिप्त रूप-रेखा मैं आपको प्रेषित कर रहा हूँ —

हमारा उद्देश्य — वैदिक सिद्धान्तों का शिक्षण, प्रशिक्षण, अनुसन्धान, लेखन और प्रचार।

उद्देश्य की प्राप्ति हेतु प्रस्तावित कार्य

१. शोध-पत्रिका का प्रकाशन (सम्भवतः जो कि पूर्व में संस्थान से प्रकाशित भी होती रही है।
२. शोध-गोष्ठियों का आयोजन।
३. दयानन्दीय दृष्टि से सम्पन्न हुए वैदिक अनुसन्धान का सर्वेक्षण तथा शोध के सम्भावित विषयों/क्षेत्रों का पता लगाना। साथ ही विभिन्न विश्वविद्यालयों के शोध के इच्छुक छात्रों को इन विषयों में शोध-कार्य के लिए प्रेरित करना।
४. भारत के किसी विश्वविद्यालय से संस्थान के लिए ऐसी मान्यता प्राप्त करने का प्रयास करना जिससे कि संस्थान के अन्तर्गत शोध कर रहे अध्येता को भी शोध-प्रबन्ध प्रस्तुत करने पर सम्बद्ध विश्वविद्यालय पी० एच०डी० की उपाधि प्रदान करे।
५. पौरोहित्य प्रशिक्षण शिविर व वेद-विषयक कार्यशालाओं का आयोजन।
६. आर्य समाज के क्षेत्र में कार्यरत उपदेशकों के लिए पुनश्चर्या पाठ्यक्रमों का आयोजन।
७. दयानन्दीय दृष्टि से हो चुके वैदिक शोध (अप्रकाशित) के प्रकाशन की व्यवस्था।

समर्पण शोध संस्थान

४/४२, सै. ५, राजेन्द्र नगर, साहिबाबाद (गाजियाबाद) उ. प्र. २०१००५ ☎ ९१-६२३०२६

क्र. सं.: .... तिथि ....

संस्थान के उद्देश्य

शोध

* शोध का क्षेत्र: वेद अथवा वैदिक वाङ्मय सम्बन्धी कोई भी गम्भीर, आवश्यक प्रश्न, स्थल.
Field of enquiry restricted to vedic lore, welcoming any topical question demanding a study in depth.

* शोध-प्रणाली: प्राचीन आर्ष-प्रणाली का आग्रह-रहित स्वीकार एवं बुद्धि-संगत उपयोग
Method: Traditional approach with an open mind and accept the knowledge gained to put in to realistic practice.

* शोध के प्रसंग में उठ आये कुछ असमाहित स्थलों के समाधान के लिए अर्वाचीन तुलनात्मक अध्ययन के विधि एवं पाश्चात्य विज्ञान का भी यथावसर कृतज्ञतापूर्वक उपयोग
Unresolved aspects: arising during the course of research, are to be resolved with comparative methods of modern science.

प्रकाशन

* अप्रकाशित पुरातात्त्विक आर्ष-अनुसन्धानों के प्रकाशन के लिए, तथा प्रकाशित किन्तु सम्प्रति दुर्लभ प्राचीन ग्रन्थों के पुनः आधुनिक विज्ञानानुमोदित व्याख्याप्रकाशन के लिए व्यवस्था
Publications: To publish unpublished studies in indology. Re-print classics and masterpieces of historical science. Encourage publications of new works.

७. संस्थान से प्रकाशित ग्रन्थों के अन्तर्देशीय भाषाओं में अनुवाद [illegible] करना।

श्रद्धेय स्वामी जी! प्रस्तुत कार्य योजना नितान्त प्रारम्भिक है। आपके विचार जानने के पश्चात् हम लोग ही अन्य कार्यक्रम इस योजना का हिस्सा बनायेंगे। संस्थान में हो रहे कार्यों में इस बात का बराबर ध्यान रखा जायगा कि वह गतिविधियाँ व्यावहारिक रूप से आर्य समाज के प्रचार-प्रसार का भी हेतु बनें।

मैं इस समूह में सम्मिलित विद्वानों का नामोल्लेख भी आपसे करना चाहूँगा:

१. डॉ. सतीश प्रकाश (अमेरिका)
२. डॉ. सोम वेदालंकार
३. डॉ. सुरेन्द्र कुमार
४. डॉ. राजेन्द्र विद्यालंकार
५. डॉ. ब्रह्मदेव विद्यालंकार
६. डॉ. कृष्ण चन्द्र
७. डॉ. [illegible]
८. डॉ. प्रमोद कुमार
९. डॉ. नारायण मुखर्जी
१०. श्री दीपक कुमार (संयोजक)
११. श्री रामपाल
१२. श्री सुरेश गौतम

यह मण्डल संस्थान से संयुक्त होकर विविध गतिविधियाँ चलाने का प्रयास कर रहा है वह नितान्त संगठित कार्य होगा। इस

SAMARPANA SODHA SAMSTHANA, 4/42, Sector 5, Rajendra Nagar, Sahibabad (Ghaziabad) U.P. 201005 Ph. 91-623026
AN ORGANISATION PURELY DEDICATED TO ORIENTAL RESEARCH

मण्डल के अध्यक्ष कार्यों का वर्गीकरण करके तदनुसार सदस्यों को वितरित करेंगे। अध्यक्ष की अनुपस्थिति में उपाध्यक्ष कार्यों का वर्गीकरण करेंगे।

श्रद्धेय स्वामी जी! मैं आपको केवल अपनी कार्ययोजना प्रेषित कर रहा हूँ। यह स्नातक मण्डल किस रूप में या किन अधिकारों के साथ संस्थान से जुड़े यह आपको तय करना है अथवा इस विषय में हम बैठकर किसी निष्कर्ष पर पहुँच जाएंगे। संस्थान की व्यवस्था जैसी आप चाहेंगे वह हमें स्वीकार्य होगी।

आशा है आप उपरिलिखित पत्र से सन्तुष्ट होंगे। इस पत्र के उपरान्त विद्वानों की एक बैठक संस्थान में हुई जिस पर मैंने अब तक का हुआ कार्य और भविष्य में होने वाले कार्य पर प्रकाश डाला और अपेक्षा निवेदन किया कि आगे के सभी कार्य इसी पद्धति और शैली से हों, मैं ऐसा चाहता हूँ। स०शो० संस्थान रजिस्टर्ड संस्था है। उसके कुछ सदस्य हैं उनमें इन नए विद्वानों को भी सदस्य बना दिया जाएगा। उन्हें सदस्य बनाने के निमित्त हम एक बैठक १३ जून को बुला रहे हैं। उसके पश्चात् वह अपना कार्य आरम्भ कर देंगे। समर्पण शोध संस्थान का पुस्तकालय जिसमें लगभग १० हजार पुस्तकें हैं उन्हें समर्पित कर दिया जाएगा। शोध-संस्थान की प्रकाशित पुस्तकें जिनका मूल्य १० लाख है वह भी उन्हें समर्पित कर देंगे। और नकद २० लाख रुपया जो बैंक में सुरक्षित रहेगा उसके ब्याज से ही वह काम चलाएंगे। मूलधन को वह touch नहीं करेंगे। आशा है आप इससे सहमत होंगे। आपके आने पर इन विद्वानों से मिला सकूँगा।

आपको ज्ञात ही है पुत्री कुमकुम के निधन पर मैंने उसके नाम पर एक प्रतिष्ठान की स्थापना की है। उसके आधीन भी लगभग २० पुस्तकें छाप रहा हूँ। इस प्रतिष्ठान को विदुषी महिलाओं को समर्पित करने का विचार है। उसमें बेबी को भी ले लेना चाहता हूँ। आशा है आप सहमत होंगे। जब जनवरी में आप देहली आएंगे तब इस विषय पर खुलकर बातें करूँगा। और अधिक क्या! श्री०डॉ० सतीश प्रकाश जी अमेरिका वालों का पता 85-31 148 Street Briarwood N.Y. 11435 —

भवदीय पिता
वेदानन्द

समर्पण शोध संस्थान

क्र. सं.: ……………

Method: Traditional approach with an open mind and accept the knowledge gained to put as to realistic practice.

Unresolved aspects: arising during the course of research, are to be resolved with comparative methods of modern science.

Publications: To publish unpublished studies in indology. Re-print classics and masterpieces of historical science. Encourage publications of new works.

प्रिय पुत्र … जी, सप्रेम आशीर्वाद,

आशा है आप सपरिवार स्वस्थ एवं सानन्द होंगे। और …

[illegible]

SAMARPANA SODHA SAMSTHANA, 4/42, Sector 5, Rajendra Nagar, Sahibabad (Ghaziabad) U.P. 201005 Ph. 91-683086
AN ORGANISATION PURELY DEDICATED TO ORIENTAL RESEARCH

आप जैसे ही भारत आएँ तो कहीं बंगाल न जाकर सीधे मेरे पास आएँ। एक सप्ताह का समय मैंने आपके लिए सुरक्षित रखा है। २४ जुलाई से २६ जुलाई तक मैं चण्डीगढ़ के डी०ए०वी० वीमेन कालेज के शिविर में व्यस्त रहूँगा। इसलिए १७ से २२ तक का समय आपके लिए सुरक्षित रखा है। और अधिक क्या, मेरा पुनः-पुनः आशीर्वाद।

[illegible]

स्वामी [illegible]जी,

यही विशेष पत्र है जो मैं स्वयं आपके हाथ में थमा दूंगा अमरीका प्रस्थान से पहले। दिल्ली और [illegible] के बीच के [illegible] के 3 पन्ने मैं ने कम से कम दो बार पढ़े जो [illegible] विस्मरणीय है। मेरे [illegible] की उसके बाद (23/7) से लेकर 5 अगस्त तक (आपकी [illegible] और ऐन्टीबायोटिक के मुताबिक बाद के आगे, अन्त का सारा ब्यौरा मैंने मुझे सुनाया। कुछ मेरी उत्सुकता भी थी और कुछ आनन्द जी की उन घटनाओं और व्यक्तियों के बारे में जो सुनी और समझनी चाहता।

कहते हैं जब किसी महान व्यक्ति का 'अन्त' का समय आता है तो एक भूकम्प का आगमन है जो आसपास के लोगों को चेतावनी दे देता है वह क्यों? इसलिये कि जब [illegible] और धन पर कब्जा करने की बातें और षड्यन्त्र होते हैं। यही कुछ [illegible] हुआ है।

② मुझे यह जानकर हैरानगी, दुःख और पीड़ा हुई कि किसी [illegible] ऐसे सज्जन थे आपके इस ऐन्टीबायोटिक के इलाज के विरुद्ध थे। क्या इसलिये कि जो [illegible] करने में उन्होंने आपके नुकसान [illegible] या [illegible] उनकी मृत्यु के बाद भी [illegible]? आखिर कोई लिखत पढ़त तो उन [illegible] ही है नहीं। [और जो आपके इलाज के मुकाबले के लिये केवल [illegible] हजार [illegible]]

दुःख तो और भी इस बात का था कि इन सभी में एक MBBS डा भी है जिसको आपने ही डायरी में दाखिले से लेकर [illegible] पर [illegible] भी 10-12 दिन के लिये था। जबकि उसे पता था कि आपको एक दिन का दौरा हस्पताल में 21/7 को पड़ चुका था तभी तो आपको 21/7 को अस्पताल ले जाना नहीं लिया। और दूसरा दौरा 23/7 को पड़ा, तभी तो [illegible] 24/7 की बजाय 27/7 को हुआ। [illegible] आपको बरेली के प्राकृतिक चिकित्सालय में ले जाने की बात करता रहा तो कोई औचित्य भी! [illegible] उसको अनुभव तो क्या, लिहाज भी नहीं।

③ यही कुछ [illegible] के साथ हुआ था। उनकी बिमारी का 1955 में पता चला था [illegible] बैठे आदि के रोगों के प्राकृतिक इलाज [illegible] करती रही। अन्त में अस्पताल [illegible] ले जाना तो [illegible] था। [illegible] उनकी [illegible] और [illegible] अखबार में पढ़ा कि [illegible] कालोनी मिली है तो, मैं [illegible] कि उनके [illegible] होते हैं।

(4) और यह एक बड़ा कारण है कि चाहे जितने अधिक प्रतिभाशाली और मेहनती व्यक्ति हो चाहे कितने अधिक कमाई वाला, [illegible] एक परिवार ने आर्थिक पक्ष फिसलने नहीं देना। कोई और कारण लिखे जाते स्वामी जी ने 40 वर्ष तक किताबें और [illegible] उन्होंने भी व्यक्ति को करोड़ 24 घण्टे के बताया है, [illegible] के मिलावट पैसा। मुझे इस बात का दुःख नहीं है कि आप मुझे नहीं समझ सके। यह/ये आपकी [illegible] का सीमित [illegible]। मैंने अमन जी से पूछा, क्या मामा जी ने मेरे एक 5 पेज के पत्र का जिक्र नहीं किया जो मैंने ... यहाँ से (6 पेज) को लिखा था? न आपने मुझे उसका जवाब लिखा, न मामी जी [illegible] गाजियाबाद था। पर अमन जी ने कहा कि "मुझे समझायें"। पर उस पत्र का उन्होंने कोई जिक्र नहीं किया मुझसे भी।

विनम्र सादर: [illegible]

(5) अब आपको क्या लिख रहे हैं, अतीत 10-15 वर्ष [illegible] लिखते हैं। मामा जी, आपके जैसे स्वाभिमानी व मेहनती, सीधे व सच्चे [illegible], व्यवहार के साथ आपका मन किसी व्यक्ति, समाज के प्रति कटुता भी सकता है या कष्ट दिया जा सकता है, या किसी के विपरीत गलत [illegible] कह दी है। तो कुछ व्यक्तियों के लिये आप सही अर्थों में धृतराष्ट्र हैं। धृतराष्ट्र केवल महाभारत का ही एक पात्र नहीं है। हमेशा हर युग में [illegible] एक [illegible] इसलिये कि हर दो व्यक्तियों के लिये बन जाए, वहीं धृतराष्ट्र पैदा हो जाता। इसके कारणों तो [illegible] पता है क्या होता है।

पर मेरा आर्थिक सम्बन्ध इसी तरह बैंक में रहेगा और पिछले 25 वर्षों से निरन्तर चलता आ रहा है। मैं एक चोटी पर हूँ जहाँ [illegible] दोनों बच्चों को देखने को मुझे गर्व और आनन्द है। पर मेरी चाहत कुछ भी नहीं है। जीवन मेरे लिये [illegible] का नाम है। यही मेरे [illegible] का धर्म और कर्म है, कि कहीं भी कोई [illegible] बनाये।

हे [illegible] भगवान की [illegible] को [illegible] के लिये रहना है। ~~[illegible]~~ उनकी [illegible] के लिये मेरी शुभ कामनाएं सम्मिलित हैं।

आपका पुत्र सतीश
6 बजे

दूरभाष :४६,२३०२६ ओ३म् Ph.: 623026

समर्पण शोध संस्थान

४/४२ सै० ५ राजेन्द्र नगर, साहिबाबाद (गाजियाबाद) उ० प्र० २०१००५

SAMARPANA SODHA SANSTHANA

4/42, Sector 5, Rajendra Nagar, Sahibabad, (Ghaziabad) U.P. 201005

क्रम सं०.............. तिथि ...

11/3/02

प्रिय सतीश! सस्नेह आशीर्वाद

अभी-२ आपका भावनात्मक पत्र मिला, तत्काल ही मैं पत्रोत्तर लिखाने में संलग्न हो गया, पहली पंक्ति में आपने लिखा है, अब आप ही रह गये हैं जिनको मैं हिन्दी में पत्र लिखकर हिन्दी को ताजा कर लेता हूँ। नहीं नहीं आप हिन्दी को ही ताजा नहीं करते, अपितु अपनी राष्ट्रीयता को ताजा करते हैं। इस प्रकार मैं भाग्यशाली व्यक्ति हूँ जो आपकी राष्ट्रीयता को जगाता रहता हूँ। राष्ट्रीयता की चार शक्तियां आधार हैं १. भूमि, २. जनता, ३. भाषा, ४. संस्कृति, जब ये चारों एक हो जाते हैं तब राष्ट्र बनता है अन्यथा राज्य रहता है, एक मात्र भूमि पर किसी का शासन होना राज्य है परन्तु किसी भी राज्य में उपरिलिखित चारों तत्व अखण्ड रूप से चलें तो वह राष्ट्र होता है, ऋग्वेद में स्वयं भाषा बोलती है "अहं राष्ट्री संगमनी वसूनाम् । अहं चिकितुषी प्रथमा यज्ञियानाम्" मैं देशवासियों को जोड़ने वाली कड़ी हूँ और परस्पर मिलन कराने में सहायक हूँ। हम आप में कितनी ही दूरी हो लेकिन भाषा एक कड़ी है जो हमें जोड़ रही है सर इकबाल ने हिन्द के तराने में यह वाक्य लिखा था "गुरबत में हों अगर हम रहता है दिल वतन में समझो हमें वहीं तुम, दिल हो जहां हमारा" तराने के पहले शब्द को परिवर्तन करके कहा जा सकता है "दूरी भी हो भला ही रहता है दिल वतन में समझो हमें वहीं तुम दिल हो जहां हमारा" यह आपकी राष्ट्रीयता है जो प्रतिवर्ष आपको भारत खेंच कर लाती है इसके लिये आपको मुबारकबाद देता हूँ।

Dedicated Oriental Research

* Field of enquiry restricted to vedic lore, welcoming any topical question demanding a study in depth.

* Method: Traditional approach with an open mind and accept the knowledge gained to put into realistic practice.

* Unsolved aspects arising during the course of research, are to be resolved with comparative methods of modern science.

प्रकाशन

Publications

* To publish unpublished studies in indology. Reprint classics and masterpieces of historical science. Encourage publications of new works.

आपने लिखा है कि बेवी वापिस आ गयी है, इसका अभिप्राय यह है कि अनल अभी भारत में ही है पिछले वर्ष अक्टूबर मास में मैं एक परिवार में मेहमान बना रहा था तो मेरी आंखें चकित हो गयी कि जब मैंने जन समूह में बेवी और अनल को देखा, तदोपरान्त उनके साथ वार्तालाप हुआ अनल जी ने अपनी भावना को व्यक्त करते हुए कहा था, कि आप भारतीय भाषा और संस्कृति के बारे में सरलतम पद्धति तैयार करें जिससे कि मैं अमेरिका में सांस्कृतिक संदेश पहुंचा सकूं. लौटते समय मैं आपसे मिलूंगा और वह सब विचार लेकर जाऊंगा आप तो जानते ही हैं कि मैं संस्कृत एवं संस्कृति के प्रचार के लिये सरलतम पद्धति अपनाता हूँ उनके लिये भी वह पद्धति निर्माण कर रखी है मैं तो प्यासे चातक भांति एक टक निहारता रहा कि वे कब आयेंगे कि जब मैं इन्हें देखकर अपनी प्यास बुझाऊंगा और इन्हें सांस्कृतिक जल पिलाकर इनकी प्यास बुझाऊंगा आपके पत्र से ज्ञात होता है कि वापिस बेवी ही गयी है अनल नहीं तो कुछ संतोष है यदि दोनों ही बिना मिले गये हैं तो मुझे अवश्य खेद होगा। सम्भवतः यह आपको पता न हो कि जब अनल जी अमेरिका जा रहे थे उनकी विदाई के उपलक्ष्य में श्री योगेश मुंजाल के घर पर विदाई भोज किया तो मैंने कहा कि आपको यज्ञोपवीत पहनना होगा उन्होंने बड़ा उत्साह दिखाया और सहर्ष यज्ञोपवीत पहना इस प्रकार हमको जोड़ने वाली संस्कृति नामक कड़ी बन गयी यह भी राष्ट्रीयता की पहचान है यजुर्वेद में ऋषि ने लिखा "सा प्रथमा संस्कृति विश्ववारा" वह प्रथम सामर्थ्य वाली पहली संस्कृति है जो विश्व के लिये वरणीय है. अर्थात् सार्वभौम संस्कृति है क्या ही अच्छा हो
* कि आप और वे मिलकर संस्कृत - संस्कृति - राष्ट्र का निर्माण करें और इसके प्रचार में जुट जायें।

अगली पंक्तियों में आपने लिखा है कि आपने आर्य समाज और वेद के प्रचार में ही ख्याति प्राप्त की है आप जब नये स्थानों और लोगों से मिलकर जो संतोष होता है वह मैं समझ सकता हूँ जिसका कि मैं भी स्वयं शिकार हूँ यह बात सत्य है विदुरनीति में लिखा है "संसार में दो व्यक्ति अत्यन्त
* दुर्लभ है एक वक्ता और दूसरे श्रोता" "वक्ता श्रोता च दुर्लभः"

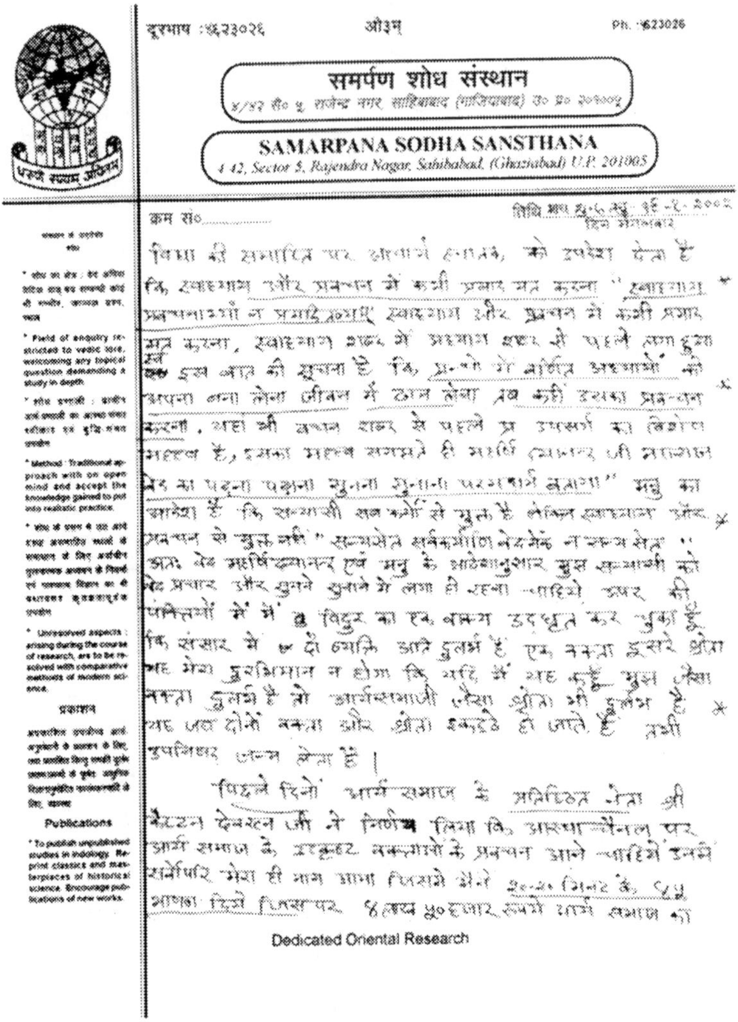

दूरभाष : ६२३०२६ ओ३म् Ph. : 623026

समर्पण शोध संस्थान

४/४२ सैक्टर ५, राजेन्द्र नगर, साहिबाबाद (गाजियाबाद) उ० प्र० २०१००५

SAMARPANA SODHA SANSTHANA

4/42, Sector 5, Rajendra Nagar, Sahibabad, (Ghaziabad) U.P. 201005

क्रम सं०.......... तिथि ... १६-२-२००२ दिन मंगलवार

शिक्षा की समाप्ति पर आचार्य स्नातक को उपदेश देता है कि, स्वाध्याय और प्रवचन में कभी प्रमाद मत करना "स्वाध्याय प्रवचनाभ्यां न प्रमदितव्यम्" स्वाध्याय और प्रवचन में कभी प्रमाद मत करना, स्वाध्याय शब्द में अध्याय शब्द से पहले लगा हुआ स्व इस बात की सूचना है कि, ग्रन्थों में वर्णित अध्यायों को अपना बना लेना जीवन में ढाल लेना तब कहीं इसका प्रवचन करना, यहां भी वचन शब्द से पहले प्र उपसर्ग का विशेष महत्व है, इसका महत्व समझते ही महर्षि दयानन्द जी महाराज वेद का पढ़ना पढ़ाना सुनना सुनाना परमधर्म बताया" मनु का आदेश है कि संन्यासी सब कर्मों से मुक्त है लेकिन स्वाध्याय और प्रवचन से मुक्त नहीं " संन्यसेत् सर्वकर्माणि वेदमेकं न संन्यसेत् " अतः वेद महर्षि दयानन्द एवं मनु के आदेशानुसार मुझ संन्यासी को वेद प्रचार और सुनने सुनाने में लगा ही रहना चाहिये ऊपर की पंक्तियों में मैं विदुर का एक वाक्य उद्धृत कर चुका हूँ कि संसार में ये दो व्यक्ति अति दुर्लभ हैं एक वक्ता दूसरे श्रोता यह मेरा दुरभिमान न होगा कि यदि मैं यह कहूँ मुझ जैसा वक्ता दुर्लभ है तो आर्यसमाजी जैसा श्रोता भी दुर्लभ है यह जब दोनों वक्ता और श्रोता इकट्ठे हो जाते हैं तभी उपनिषद् जन्म लेता है।

पिछले दिनों आर्य समाज के प्रतिष्ठित नेता श्री कैप्टन देवरत्न जी ने निर्णय लिया कि आस्था चैनल पर आर्य समाज के उत्कृष्ट वक्ताओं के प्रवचन आने चाहियें उनमें सर्वोपरि मेरा ही नाम आया जिसमें मैंने २०-२० मिनट के ८४ भाषण दिये जिस पर ४ लाख ५० हजार रुपये आर्य समाज को

प्रकाशन

Publications

Dedicated Oriental Research

अर्थ ले गया, बीस मिनट के प्रवचन का दस हजार
रुपया वक्ता की ओर से आस्था चैनल वालों को देना
पड़ता है जिससे वे डेढ़ सौ देशों में संदेश पहुंचाते हैं
पूर्णतः स्वस्थ न होने पर भी मुझे यह कार्य करना पड़ा
संध्या और हवन प्रक्रिया का कार्यक्रम प्रति सप्ताह आस्था
चैनल वालों की ओर से प्रसारित किया जाता है हर
शनिवार को लगभग ५½ संध्या पाठ होता है और रविवार
को ४ ½ बजे प्रातः दैनिक अग्निहोत्र का प्रदर्शन भी होता
है यह सब वेदमिशन के लिये एक संन्यासी का कर्तव्य है।

प्रिय विनोद ने दूरभाष पर आपको जिस यज्ञ का वर्णन
किया वह अपने आप में अपूर्व था वह यज्ञ इन्दौर प्रदेशान्तर्गत मऊ
ग्राम में हुआ वह मात्र गायत्री मन्त्र द्वारा ही आहुति देने का था
जिसमें लगभग प्रातः सायं दस हजार व्यक्तियों की उपस्थिति रहती
थी प्रातः आठ बजे से लेकर रात्रि के दस बजे तक गायत्री महायज्ञ
के लिये बनी हुई यज्ञशाला की पुरुष और स्त्रियों के द्वारा परिक्रमा
निरन्तर चलती रहती थी इसी प्रकार हैदराबाद में गायत्री महायज्ञ
का आयोजन किया गया जिसको सनातन धर्मी लोगों ने जिसमें
अग्रवाल जाति के लोग और जैन लोगों ने बढ़-चढ़कर भाग लिया वह
भी एक अपूर्व यज्ञ था उसकी उपलब्धि यही थी कि जो पौराणिक
सनातनी भाई आर्यसमाज से घृणा करते थे और जो जैन सम्प्रदाय
वेद और मन्त्रों के न मानने के कारण नास्तिक माने जाते थे उन्होंने
अपूर्व योगदान दिया और यह कहा कि हम आर्य समाज को घृणा की
दृष्टि से देखते रहे परन्तु श्री स्वामी दीक्षानंद जी ने जो इसका रूप
उपस्थित किया है वह हमारे चमत्कार बन गया और इसकी इन्होंने
भूरि-२ प्रशंसा की।

पिछले वर्ष प्रिय सुरेश जब भारत आया था तो उसने
आग्रहपूर्वक पर अपने किये शोध प्रबन्ध को प्रकाशित करने का आग्रह
किया इसके लिये वह १ लाख धनराशि भी दे गया, आजकल मैं उसे
देखने में लगा हूँ उसका सम्पादन कर रहा हूँ उसको पढ़ने से मुझे
लगा कि इसने भी अच्छा कार्य किया है इन सब बातों को सोचकर
मैं अपने को भाग्यशाली मानता हूँ और प्रायः कहता हूँ कि जीवन
मे मैं जितना सफल हूँ शायद ही कोई व्यक्ति होगा परिवार के और
परिवार से भिन्न जिन भी व्यक्तियों से मेरा सम्पर्क हुआ है वे

A book on 10 fundamental differences between
Arya Samaj & Sanatanis from a layman to intellectual point of view

दूरभाष : ६२३०२६ ओ३म् Ph. : 623026

समर्पण शोध संस्थान

४/४२ सै० ५, राजेन्द्र नगर, साहिबाबाद (गाजियाबाद) उ० प्र० २०१००५

SAMARPANA SODHA SANSTHANA

4 42, Sector 5, Rajendra Nagar, Sahibabad, (Ghaziabad) U.P. 201005

* Field of enquiry restricted to vedic lore, welcoming any topical question demanding a study in depth.

* Method : Traditional approach with an open mind and accept the knowledge gained to put into realistic practice.

* Unresolved aspects : arising during the course of research, are to be resolved with comparative methods of modern science.

प्रकाशन

Publications

* To publish unpublished studies in indology. Reprint classics and masterpieces of historical science. Encourage publications of new works.

क्रम सं०..........

तिथि आज सु० ६ तदनु १९।११।२००२ (मंगलवार)

सभी मानते हैं कि यदि स्वामी दीक्षानंद का सम्पर्क हमें न मिला होता तो न जाने हम कहां भटकते होते जिसको देखो वह वेद, आर्यसमाज और दयानन्द के मिशन में लगा हुआ है प्रिय रमेश आर्य समाज कालका जी का मन्त्री है पुत्री सुमित्रा और प्रिय रामगोपाल दोनों ही आर्य समाज नारायणा के प्रधान और मन्त्री रहे हैं प्रिय रमेश (गुड्डू) ने पटेल नगर की शाखा आर्य समाज में जो विद्यालय चला रखा है वो ऐसा लगता है कि वह गुरुकुल ही चला रहा है इसमें [illegible] और मुस्लिम बच्चे भी संध्या और अग्निहोत्र के मंत्र जानते हैं अभी फरवरी मास की १२ तारीख को महर्षि दयानन्द जन्मोत्सव मनाया जिसमें सभी बच्चों ने भाग लिया जहां महर्षि दयानन्द के कुछ कार्यों का मंच पर अभिनय करवाया वहां वीर हकीकत राय के बलिदान का भी अभिनय मंच पर उपस्थित किया जयपुर में प्रिय राजेश (बब्बू) आर्य समाज की सेवा में बराबर लगा रहता है सत्संगों में इसी के गीत गूंजते हैं अपनी स्वर्गीया बहिन कुसुमलता के नाम पर एक संगीतात्मक कैसेट तैयार किया है जो बड़ा लोकप्रिय है आप भी अपने ढंग से भारतीय संस्कृति को फैलाने में रुचि लेते हैं यह क्या कम बात है। इसी बसन्त पर्व पर १६ और १८ तारीख को प्रिय सुनील रवि ने परिवार के सब सदस्यों को आमन्त्रित किया उसने [illegible] में अपनी रिहायश के लिये नया भवन बनाया है जिसका प्रवेश मेरे द्वारा सम्पादित हुआ १६ और १८ को सामवेद ब्राह्मण पारायण यज्ञ के साथ २ गृह प्रवेश यज्ञ भी सम्पन्न हुआ उसने अपने घर में एक यज्ञशाला भी बनाई है इसी धुन में वह कार्यमुक्त होकर

Dedicated Oriental Research

वेद का स्वाध्याय व आर्यसमाज के कार्य में लगेगा इन्दौर में विनोद तो आर्यसमाज के कार्य में अहर्निश लगा ही रहता है।

मेरे इन्दौर आगमन के समय तो आप गुजराल साहब के घर मिलने ही आये थे मैं उनके गृह पर उसके पश्चात उनके बड़े भाई के पुत्र के गृह पर एवं उनके बहन के गृह पर कुल मिलाकर १२ महीने आराम पूर्वक रहा मेरा ~~[illegible]~~ मस्तिष्क और वाक् शक्ति निरन्तर कार्य करती रही इन घरों में प्रतिदिन दैनिक अग्निहोत्र होता ही रहता है उसके साथ मेरे प्रवचन भी होते रहे मेरी सेवा के लिए गुरुकुल वेद विद्यालय से ब्रह्मचारी आते रहे जहां वह सेवा करते थे वहां मैं उन्हें वैदिक विचार धारा देता रहता और कुछ आवश्यक लेख भी लिखवाता रहा। विहार के विजय झा का प्रेस पास होने से पुस्तकें भी प्रकाशित करवाता रहा इस समय में लगभग दस पुस्तकें प्रकाशित करवा ~~[illegible]~~ चुका हूं दो पुस्तकें तो लगभग पूर्ण कुसुम की पुष्प सूक्त की भांति बड़ी हैं बाकी कुछ छोटी हैं बीच में एक छोटी सी घटना हो गयी सित० मास की २३ तारीख को मैं कार में बैठा जा रहा था कि रोड ब्रेकर पर गाड़ी उछली और मेरी कमर में जर्क आ गया जो कि अभी तक दर्द बना हुआ है धीरे-२ ठीक हो रहा है १५% रह गया है 85% दूर हो गया लिखने पढ़ने का कार्य बराबर चल रहा है अब तो यही विचार है कि जो भी विचार मस्तिष्क में आते हैं उन्हें लेखबद्ध कर दूं।

आपको सम्भवतः ज्ञात न होगा कि मैंने अपनी अवस्था को देखकर यह विचार किया कि इस संस्थान को एक ट्रस्ट बनाकर इसे समर्पित कर दिया जाय अतः सितम्बर 2001 की पहली तिथि को मैंने सम्पूर्ण संस्थान समर्पित कर दिया जिसके ~~[illegible]~~ मन्त्री पद पर डॉ० देवरत्न जी मुम्बई प्रधान पद पर श्री बृजमोहन जी गुजराल, कोषाध्यक्ष पद पर श्री महात्मा आनन्द स्वामी जी के पौत्र प्रथम सुरी जी श्रीयुत वाचस्पति कुलवन्त श्री विश्वनाथ जी (उपप्रधान डी० ए० वी०) सुपुत्र राजपाल एण्ड सन्स के मालिक श्री जयदेव जी इत्यादि इसमें जयदेव जी के साले श्री स्वामी सत्यम् जी भी विशेष व्यक्ति हैं आज मुदने के

Only [illegible] – [illegible]

Wonderful presentation from the [illegible] in thought content.

दूरभाष : ६२३०२६ ओ३म् Ph. : 623026

समर्पण शोध संस्थान

४/४२ सै० ५, राजेन्द्र नगर, साहिबाबाद (गाजियाबाद) उ० प्र० २०१००५

SAMARPANA SODHA SANSTHANA

4/42, Sector 5, Rajendra Nagar, Sahibabad, (Ghaziabad) U.P. 201005

6

क्रम सं०.............. तिथि..............

बाद कौन देखने आयेगा कि मेरे पीछे क्या हो रहा है अपने सामने ही जो देख लेना अच्छा होगा कि यह ट्रस्ट क्या काम करता है।

ट्रस्ट ने तत्काल यह निर्णय लिया है यहां के उप-देशक विद्यालय खोला जाय जो कि मुम्बई के उपदेशक विद्यालय की शाखा हो उसकी नियमावली भी तैयार करली गयी है कुछ छात्रों के नाम भी आ गये हैं विद्यालय की रूप रेखा मेरे मस्तिष्क में है वह कब मूर्तरूप लेता है यह भविष्य के गर्भ में है।

आप जानते ही हैं कि मेरी रुचि वेद के अनुसन्धान में है मेरे अपना पुत्री कुसुम के अधूरे छूटे हुए शोध कार्यों को आगे बढ़ाना मैं अहर्निश इस प्रयत्न में रहता हूं कोई योग्य व्यक्ति मिले कि जिससे मैं इन कार्यों को करवा सकूं अभी चार दिन पहले डा० पुत्री कुसुम लता के डीलिट की उपाधि के लिए किये जा रहे अथर्ववेद के वेन सूक्त के कार्य को मुरादाबाद के निकट कन्या गुरुकुल की स्नातिका छात्रा को सौंपा है मुझे लगता है कि वह कुसुम की भांति इस पर शोध कार्य करके संस्थान के भविष्य को उज्ज्वल करेगी मेरे पास पुस्तकालय की भांति १४ स्थलों पर शोध कराने का मैटर विद्यमान है आप जब वैदिक गणित पर कुछ विचार विमर्श कर रहे थे तो मैं मन ही मन बड़ी प्रसन्नता अनुभव कर रहा था अकस्मात वह कार्य बीच में ही रुक गया।

* Field of enquiry restricted to vedic lore, welcoming any topical question demanding a study in depth.

* Method : Traditional approach with an open mind and accept the knowledge gained to put into realistic practice.

* Unresolved aspects : arising during the course of research, are to be resolved with comparative methods of modern science.

प्रकाशन

Publications

* To publish unpublished studies in indology. Reprint classics and masterpieces of historical science. Encourage publications of new works.

Dedicated Oriental Research

आपने अपने पत्र के साथ आंग्ल भाषा का एक लेख भेजा है जिसे पढ़कर अपने विचार स्पष्ट(?) व्यक्त करने को कहा है खेद है कि मेरा इंग्लिश का ज्ञान न के बराबर है यहां रह रहे एक बन्धु को वह पत्र दिखाया भी, लेकिन उनकी समझ में भी नहीं आया अतः इस पत्र में इसका उत्तर देना सम्भव नहीं समझने पर ही लिखूंगा।

आपने अपने पत्र के अन्त में कुछ बातें पिछली दोहराई हैं कुछ बातें स्मरणीय हैं और कुछ बातें विस्मरणीय हैं पिछले वर्ष आपका एक दिन का मिलन अविस्मरणीय रहेगा

वही दिन तो था कि जिस दिन अनाल(?) जी और आपके [illegible] छद्म वेश से मुक्ति दिलाने के लिये [illegible] आलय में भर्ती कराया गया। शेष पारिवारिक व्यक्तियों से सम्बद्ध बातों पर मैं अधिक ध्यान नहीं देता हर अच्छी बात को आशीर्वाद देता हूँ और शेष बातों स्मरण नहीं करता अन्त में आपने मेरे कार्यों की इस ईसाई मिशनरियों से तुलना की है जिसपर मैं गम्भीरता से विचार कर रहा हूँ। मैं उस संस्कृति का उपासक हूँ जो सार्वभौम संस्कृति है जो कि एक मात्र विश्व शान्ति की वाहिका है जिसके लिये सर इकबाल ने लिखा था — "यूनान मिस्र रोमा सब मिट गये जहां से बाकी अभी मगर है नामो निशां हमारा, कुछ बात है कि हस्ती मिटती नहीं हमारी सदियों रहा है दुश्मन दौरे जमां हमारा" दूसरे प्रसिद्ध शायर ने लिखा था "वो दीने हजाजी का बेबाक बेड़ा निशां जिसका अक्साए आलम में पहुंचा न जेहूं में अटका न कुल्जम में अटका किए वे सिपर जिसने सातों समुन्दर वो डूबा दहाने में गंगा के आकर" ये इस्लामी शायर इस संस्कृति की दाद दे रहे हैं कि मैं उस संस्कृति का संदेश वाहक हूँ लोग पूछते हैं कि वो कौन सी हस्ती है जो मिटती नहीं वह एक मात्र वेद की हस्ती है जिसकी गूंज स्व० श्रीमती इन्दिरा गांधी यू एनो में ऋग्वेद का अन्तिम सूक्त पढ़ कर गयी थी "संगच्छध्वं संवदध्वं सं वो मनांसि जानताम्" मैं सत्य का ऋत का [illegible] का सद् का स्वाहा का सत्य का संदेश वाहक हूँ आपको इस वाक्य पर विचार करना होगा मेरे इस को स्वामी सत्य प्रकाश जी ने समझा था और कहा था कि स्वामी दीक्षानन्द अपनी परम्परा का अन्तिम व्याख्याकार है शायद कोई आगे पैदा हो जाय ईश्वर शरण(?)

[illegible]

[illegible] दीक्षानन्द सरस्वती

दूरभाष : ४६२३०२६ ओ३म् Ph. 4623026

समर्पण शोध संस्थान

४/४२ सै० ५, राजेन्द्र नगर, साहिबाबाद (गाजियाबाद) उ० प्र० २०१००५

SAMARPANA SODHA SANSTHANA

4/42, Sector 5, Rajendra Nagar, Sahibabad, (Ghaziabad) U.P. 201005

* Field of enquiry restricted to vedic lore, welcoming any topical question demanding a study in depth.

* Method : Traditional approach with an open mind and accept the knowledge gained to put into realistic practice.

* Unresolved aspects arising during the course of research, are to be resolved with comparative methods of modern science.

Publications

* To publish unpublished studies in indology. Reprint classics and masterpieces of historical science. Encourage publications of new works.

क्रम सं०.......... तिथि 16/6/2002
6/7/2002

प्रिय पुत्र सतीश !

सस्नेह आशीर्वाद !

कल सायंकाल 15 जून को आपके द्वारा 5 जून का लिखा हुआ पत्र पन्द्रह जून को मिला। आज 16 जून के मध्याह्न साढ़े तीन बजे पत्रोत्तर लिखने बैठा हूँ।

सर्वप्रथम आपको सूचित करते हुए हर्ष होगा कि मैं 28 जुलाई से 8 अगस्त तक आश्रम में ही रहूँगा। उसमें से जितना हिस्सा आप लेना चाहें ले सकते हैं। मैंने अपनी डायरी में आपके नाम को ये तिथियां अंकित कर दी हैं आप निश्चिन्त रहें।

आपको सूचित करते हुए आश्चर्यजनक हर्ष होगा कि मैंने एक सितम्बर दो हजार दो को सम्पूर्ण संस्थान श्री कैप्टन देवरत्न प्रधान सार्वदेशिक सभा को समर्पित कर दिया है। उन्होंने भी धार्मिक एवं सांस्कृतिक उत्थान हेतु सुयोग्य व्यक्तियों का एक ट्रस्ट बनाकर कार्य आरम्भ करने का निश्चय किया है। मुम्बई के समीप करजत (महाराष्ट्र) में एक अन्तर्राष्ट्रीय अनुसन्धान केन्द्र "विश्व वैदिक विहार" नाम से संस्था की स्थापना की है उसी की शाखा के रूप में Dedicated Oriental Research समर्पण शोध संस्थान कार्य करेगा। मुम्बई की इस संस्था के पास लगभग एक करोड़ रुपया राशि है,

दूरभाष : ६२३०२६ ओ३म् Ph.: 623026

समर्पण शोध संस्थान

४/४२ सै० ५, राजेन्द्र नगर, साहिबाबाद (गाजियाबाद) उ० प्र० २०१००५

SAMARPANA SODHA SANSTHANA

4/42, Sector 5, Rajendra Nagar, Sahibabad, (Ghaziabad) U.P. 201005

२

* Field of enquiry restricted to vedic lore, welcoming any topical question demanding a study in depth.

* Method : Traditional approach with an open mind and accept the knowledge gained to put into realistic practice.

* Unresolved aspects : arising during the course of research, are to be resolved with comparative methods of modern science.

Publications

* To publish unpublished studies in indology. Reprint classics and masterpieces of historical science. Encourage publications of new works.

क्रम सं०........ तिथि १६ - 6 - २००२

२

जिसकी सहायता से दोनों संस्थायें चलेंगी। लाहौर में जिस विद्यालय में मैंने शिक्षा ग्रहण की थी उसका नाम उपदेशक विद्यालय था। मैंने भी उसी की शाखा आपके घर के निकट उपदेशक विद्यालय के नाम से खोली थी जिसमें श्री जयदेव जी आदि ब्रह्मचारी अध्ययन करते थे वही विद्यालय अब यहाँ खोला जा रहा है। जिसमें दश छात्रों से अधिक न लिये जायेंगे। जिनके निवास, भोजन, भविष्य-निधि, शिक्षा सबका प्रबन्ध संस्थान की ओर से होगा। उसकी नियमावली छप चुकी है और देश के उच्च-कोटि के विद्वानों के पास भेज दी गयी है। पाठ्यक्रम में अभीष्ट परिवर्तन एवं परिवर्धन जो भी करना होगा वह सब किया जायगा। आपके आने पर विस्तार से आपको सब सूचित कर दिया जायगा।

यह तो सर्वविदित है कि जिसका जन्म हुआ है उसकी मृत्यु भी अवश्यम्भावी है। आँखें मूँद जाने के पश्चात किसने देखा कि मेरे उत्तराधिकारियों ने कार्य को आगे बढ़ाया है अथवा घटाया है। कम से कम मुझे तो आँखों से देखने का अवसर मिलेगा कि

Dedicated Oriental Research

मेरे पीछे शोध का कार्य एवं प्रकाशन का कार्य किस प्रकार प्रगति पर है।

संस्कार विधि में महर्षि दयानन्द ने संन्यासी के लिये लिखा है कि वह हर समय मृत्यु को याद रखे। "गृहीत इव केशेषु-मृत्युना धर्ममाचरेत्" अर्थात् मृत्यु ने केशों से प्राणी को पकड़ा हुआ है इसलिये व्यक्ति धर्म का आचरण करे। यह (यह) संसार मर्त्य कहलाता है और वह (वह) संसार अमृत कहलाता है इसीलिये हिन्दुओं में एक रिवाज है अन्त्येष्टि संस्कार से पहले मृत व्यक्ति का मुण्डन कर दिया जाता है जिससे कि मृत्यु को पकड़ने का साधन मिल ही न सके यह कल्पना अच्छी है। परन्तु आश्चर्य की बात है कि जब किसी मनुष्य का जन्म होता है वह मां की कोख से सिर के बल आता है। मानो मृत्यु ने केशों से पकड़कर अपने राज्य में बुला ~~लिया~~ लाती है। अस्तु। मैंने तो बालों को सुरक्षित रखा हुआ है जिससे कि मृत्यु को लाने और ले जाने में असुविधा न हो। यह तो अवश्यम्भावी है कि मेरा जब शरीरान्त हो जायगा, तो मेरे पीछे रहने वाले मेरे सिर को जरूर मूंडेंगे। लेकिन मैं मुक्ति में जाने का विचार नहीं रखता हूँ पुनः संसार में आऊँगा और अपने छूटे हुए कार्यों को फिर शुरू करूँगा। अपने गुरुजनों के शब्दों में लिख रहा हूँ "बार-बार नर जीवन पाऊँ। बार-बार बलिदान-चढ़ाऊँ। ब्रह्म तो भी मुझसे रूठे तेरा, जाये नहीं भुलाया॥"

दूरभाष : ६२३०२६ ओ३म् Ph. : 623026 ४

समर्पण शोध संस्थान

४/४२ सैo ५, राजेन्द्र नगर, साहिबाबाद (गाजियाबाद) उo प्रo २०१००५

SAMARPANA SODHA SANSTHANA

4 42, Sector 5, Rajendra Nagar, Sahibabad, (Ghaziabad) U.P. 201005

* Field of enquiry restricted to vedic lore, welcoming any topical question demanding a study in depth.

* Method : Traditional approach with an open mind and accept the knowledge gained to put into realistic practice.

* Unresolved aspects : arising during the course of research, are to be resolved with comparative methods of modern science.

Publications

* To publish unpublished studies in indology. Reprint classics and masterpieces of historical science. Encourage publications of new works.

क्रम सं०............ तिथि............

अपने अपने पत्र में राष्ट्रीयता के चार तत्वों के अतिरिक्त धर्म को महत्व दिया है। धर्म अति व्यापक तत्व है उसको समझना आसान नहीं। भगवान् व्यास ने महाभारत में धारणात्मक शक्ति को धर्म कहा है। वह श्लोक इस प्रकार है :—

"धारणाद्धर्म मित्याहु धर्मो धारयते प्रजा: ।
य: स्यात्धारण संयुक्त: स धर्म इति निश्चय: ॥"

जिस तत्व की यह योग्यता (quality) है कि वह धारणात्मक शक्ति है व्यक्ति, समाज, परिवार, राष्ट्र को बैलेंस करता है वह निश्चित धर्म है। आप जानते ही हैं बैलगाड़ी से लेकर वायुयान तक जब कभी घुमाव पर आते हैं तब उन्हें थोड़ा दाएं अथवा बाएं थोड़ा सा झुकना पड़ता है। यदि यात्री यह हठ करे कि मैं अपने यान को सीधा रखूँगा तो निश्चय ही वह मृत्यु को निमन्त्रण दे रहा होगा। वेद में लिखा है कि "पृथ्वी धर्म पर ठहरी हुई है"। वैज्ञानिकों का कथन है कि "सूर्य और पृथ्वी के मध्य जो गुरुत्वाकर्षण है उसी पर पृथ्वी ठहरी हुई है।"

Dedicated Oriental Research

वेदों में न केवल सूर्य और पृथ्वी के सम्बन्ध को धर्म माना है अपितु
गृहस्थ आश्रम में प्रवेशार्थी पति को सूर्य और पत्नी को पृथ्वी
मानकर उस सम्बन्ध को अटूट माना है तलाक की कोई गुंजाइश
नहीं। पति कहता है – "द्यौरहं पृथ्वी त्वं तावेव विवहावहै –
सह रेतो दधावहै"; एवं "पत्नी त्वमसि धर्मणा अहं गृहपतिस्तव"।

महाभारत युद्ध में श्री कृष्ण सारथि थे वह किस
घुमाव पर कहाँ झुकना है जानते थे, कहाँ नहीं झुकना है
वह सब जानते थे। उनका लक्ष्य विजय था। विजय ही धर्म है। लक्ष्य?
आप जानते हैं युद्धभूमि में महारथी कर्ण का रथ का पहिया दलदल
में धँस गया। श्री कृष्ण अर्जुन से कहते हैं यही समय है
कर्ण को मारो। अर्जुन कहता है यह अधर्म है। हम और
आप क्या फैसला करें कि धर्म क्या है? भगवान व्यास ने
श्री कृष्ण के इस समस्त आचरण को योग कहा है इसीलिये
वह योगेश्वर नाम से प्रसिद्ध हुए। गीता के अन्तिम श्लोक
में सञ्जय पुकार उठा – "यत्र योगेश्वरः कृष्णो यत्र पार्थो धनुर्धरः।
तत्र श्रीर्विजयो भूतिर्ध्रुवा नीतिर्मतिर्मम॥"

पत्र लम्बा हो रहा है अतः इसको यहीं रोककर आपके
अवकाश के दिनों में बात करेंगे। ~~मित्र~~

पिछले वर्ष जब सुरेश भारत आया था तब वह
~~अप~~ अग्नि देवता विषयक प्रबन्ध को छापने का आग्रह
करते हुए एक लाख रुपया दे गया था। मैं उसे छाप
रहा हूँ। मेरी भी वही कठिनाई है जो किसी धार्मिक
व्यक्ति के सामने आती है। उसमें पर्याप्त सुधार करना
पड़ रहा है और ग्रन्थ का ग्यारहवाँ अध्याय तो उसमें नहीं
है। यदि सम्भव हो और आप उसे फोन कर सकें तो सूचित कर
दें। मैं भी उसे पत्र लिखने का प्रयत्न करूँगा। [illegible]
[illegible]

COMMENTATORS & ANALYSTS EXTRAORDINAIRE

Twelve years ago, I started writing **Reflections,** a reincarnation of my life-long passion of writing letters. The big difference was that that my reflective writings went public-from one to many, as I started sharing them with friends and relatives. And, from there, it went to their friends and relatives, and so on. Years ago, a student of mine created a blog, but seldom had I posted anything. I don't have a website either. It is all emails in a bcc-electronically old-fashioned mode.

I have several mailing lists and I am used to this inefficient mode of communication. I have Facebook and Twitter accounts too, but they too have remained unused. That is my approach to communication. Naturally, some of my readers write back and give comments. At times, a small dialog takes place. It has added clarity, expanded the topic, and sharpened my own thoughts.

For a number of reasons, not all the comments and commentators are included in the book-only those comments which are concise and strong. In reflective style of writings, inclusion of comments adds a new flavor. Initially, I never saved the comments. Also, sometimes, no comments were received. That is why the space following some **Reflections** is blank.

It is not merely a time to thank them, but also share a piece of immortality that this book may bring! When I look at the credentials of these persons I am myself awed and wowed. These comments have come out of their incredible rich backgrounds. I don't think this list can be easily matched. Here are the names in some order:

Raju **Abraham**: Known for six years. English professor-has taught in Baroda/India, Sana/Yemen, and presently in Oman with University of Nizwa, where I was a visiting professor for one semester, Spring-2009.

Anand R. Bhatia, aged 70+, is a retired professor of business from California State University, San Bernardino. We have known each other for over 30 years mainly for our common ideas and values, though we grew up extremes cities-he, in Mumbai and me, in Bathinda. Anand is a very good story writer, but this flair is sacrificed for the time being for his love for real estate investments. I often tease him about marketing his voice and laughter, which are very deep and full.

Sushil K. Bhatnagar, age 73, is my first cousin who is having a nice legal practice in Delhi after retiring from the Central Bureau of Investigation-India's counterpart of the FBI of the US. His blood ties with Swami Mama Ji are the same as mine. As a matter of fact, his wife was recommended to him by Mama Ji when he was hosted by Sushil's would-be-father-in-law-in 1962. We finished high school and college in the same years. We both enjoyed writing letters to each other so much that if they were all piled up, the stack could go 18" high.

Avnish Bhatnagar: My son, age 45, works at Google. His comments are fewer, but deep.

Bhanu Joshi, age 70+, has been acquainted with me for 30+ years. He has PhD in chemistry and is retired recently as a chemist. He started the Center of the Divine Associates of Yogeshwar in Las Vegas, and ran it for 20 years before getting disenchanted by the successor of its founder, Late Pandurang Shastri. For years, he performed all Vedic ceremonies and ***sanskars*** for the Hindu community of Las Vegas.

Girish Khosla, aged 66, is a man who has achieved far more and variety of successes than a person with PhD or MBA would do. He continues to learn from new people and situations all the time. They are his books, indeed. For the last five years, he has been living the life of a ***vanprasthi***. (detached from his family, but not aloof) Since coming to the US, 25 years ago, he has founded the Arya Samaj of North America, an Arya Samaj ***mandir*** in Detroit area, a unique multi-lingual monthly magazine, the ***Navrang Times***, and multi-million$ institution, Gandhi dham for the 2001-Gujarat earthquake orphans.

With his selfless attitude and spirits, on the top of pleasant disposition, Girish is trusted by people of all shades-both in India and the US. His son, Bhuvnesh cooperates with him in all ventures. That gives Girish a break and confidence that his legacy is on sound footing. Girish is also carrying the Arya Samaj legacy of great Acharya Ram Dev, his maternal grandfather, who intimately knew Acharya Krishna/Swami Deekshanand. Lately, Girish has been spending six months in India and six in the US.

BhuDev Sharma 80+: Known since 1990, math professor-taught in India, Trinidad and several universities in the US, now back in India. He organized World Association of Vedic Studies and its biennial conferences in India and the USA. He is an able educational administrator. For several years, he also published the ***VISHWA VIVEK***, the first Hindi monthly magazine in the US.

Rahul Bhatnagar: Distantly related-physician by training in India. He has an interesting job of medical director of drug safety with a pharmaceutical company; very astute commentator and analyst of nearly all my ***Reflections***. He can refine an issue to a state that becomes undistinguishable from the one started with.

Gopal Dass: Retired cardiologist, settled in Las Vegas-has interesting hobbies-known for seven years.

Satyam **Moorty**: Emeritus English professor, Southern Utah University, Cedar City-known since 1978.

RS **Nigam**: Retired Professor of Commerce and Director of Delhi School of Economics-known for 25+ years.

Rene Riendero: Life explorer and realtor. Wrote a book on her experiences of visiting India. It did encourage me to become a writer.

Harpreet Singh: A rare combination of computer science, finance, active spirituality, and creative writing-always exploring and stretching his limits. He is 39 years old and known for 15 years-initially through his parents.

Shankar and Sangeetha Venkatagiri is a couple in their 40s, who left their fulltime US jobs 12 years ago and went back to India. I got to know them through my son. Shankar works for IIM, Banglore and Sangeetha in social work. They are fully adjusted in India with two kids-one is adopted.

Steve Wunderink: known for 15 years as a fellow toastmaster. He and his wife are pastors of a church that they started six years ago. He writes regular columns, blogs and post videos in social media-has written three books. He and I live in the same housing development.

Subhash Sood: Physician by training in India, UK and USA, however, studied other systems of medicine too. He never practiced for profit-eccentric to a certain degree. However, he was deeply drawn into by Scientology-established the first center in Ambala Cantt/India and translated several scientology books from English into Hindi. He suddenly died of a stroke in 2007 at the age of 73-in a 100-year old, now a dilapidated mansion in which he was born, as the only son of a well-known physician. He was my most avid reader and friend for over 25 years.

E. **Sooriamurthy**: Retired physics professor Madurai University, India-known since 1968-during our common PhD days at Indiana University, Bloomington. His son, Raja, computer science professor at Carnegie Mellon is an avid reader of my ***Reflections*** too. The second father-son duo fan of my ***Reflections***!